Inflectional Identity

OXFORD STUDIES IN THEORETICAL LINGUISTICS

GENERAL EDITORS: David Adger, *Queen Mary, University of London*; Hagit Borer, *University of Southern California.*

ADVISORY EDITORS: Stephen Anderson, *Yale University*; Daniel Büring, *University of California, Los Angeles*; Nomi Erteschik-Shir, *Ben-Gurion University*; Donka Farkas, *University of California, Santa Cruz*; Angelika Kratzer, *University of Massachusetts, Amherst*; Andrew Nevins, *Harvard University*; Christopher Potts, *University of Massachusetts, Amherst*; Barry Schein, *University of Southern California*; Peter Svenonius, *University of Tromsø*; Moira Yip, *University College London.*

For a complete list of titles published and in preparation for the series, see pp. 367.

Inflectional Identity

Edited by

ASAF BACHRACH AND ANDREW NEVINS

OXFORD
UNIVERSITY PRESS

OXFORD
UNIVERSITY PRESS

Great Clarendon Street, Oxford OX2 6DP

Oxford University Press is a department of the University of Oxford.
It furthers the University's objective of excellence in research, scholarship,
and education by publishing worldwide in

Oxford New York

Auckland Cape Town Dar es Salaam Hong Kong Karachi
Kuala Lumpur Madrid Melbourne Mexico City Nairobi
New Delhi Shanghai Taipei Toronto

With offices in

Argentina Austria Brazil Chile Czech Republic France Greece
Guatemala Hungary Italy Japan Poland Portugal Singapore
South Korea Switzerland Thailand Turkey Ukraine Vietnam

Oxford is a registered trade mark of Oxford University Press
in the UK and in certain other countries

Published in the United States
by Oxford University Press Inc., New York

British Library Cataloguing in Publication Data
Data available

Library of Congress Cataloging in Publication Data
Data available

Typeset by SPI Publisher Services, Pondicherry, India
Printed in Great Britain
on acid-free paper by
Biddles Ltd., King's Lynn, Norfolk

ISBN 978–0–19–921964–3 (Pbk.)
ISBN 978–0–19–921925–4 (Hbk.)

1 3 5 7 9 10 8 6 4 2

Contents

General Preface

The theoretical focus of this series is on the interfaces between subcomponents of the human grammatical system and the closely related area of the interfaces between the different subdisciplines of linguistics. The notion of "interface" has become central in grammatical theory (for instance, in Chomsky's recent Minimalist Program) and in linguistic practice: work on the interfaces between syntax and semantics, syntax and morphology, phonology and phonetics, etc. has led to a deeper understanding of particular linguistic phenomena and of the architecture of the linguistic component of the mind/brain.

The series covers interfaces between core components of grammar, including syntax/morphology, syntax/semantics, syntax/phonology, syntax/pragmatics, morphology/phonology, phonology/phonetics, phonetics/speech processing, semantics/pragmatics, intonation/discourse structure as well as issues in the way that the systems of grammar involving these interface areas are acquired and deployed in use (including language acquisition, language dysfunction, and language processing). It demonstrates, we hope, that proper understandings of particular linguistic phenomena, languages, language groups, or inter-language variations all require reference to interfaces.

The series is open to work by linguists of all theoretical persuasions and schools of thought. A main requirement is that authors should write so as to be understood by colleagues in related subfields of linguistics and by scholars in cognate disciplines.

This volume is a counterpart to volume eight of the series (on paradigm uniformity) and focusses on morphology as an interface between syntax and phonology. The thrust of the book is to argue against output-dependent approaches to paradigm structure, and to propose a new understanding which depends on featural organization and the operations on representations. The editors have brought together a cohesive collection of papers arguing that identify effects in inflectional morphology can be understood as the outcome of interactions between learnability heuristics, syntactic feature organization and the associative structure of the lexicon.

David Adger
Hagit Borer

The Contributors

ADAM ALBRIGHT received his BA in linguistics from Cornell University in 1996 and his Ph.D. in linguistics from UCLA in 2002. He was a Faculty Fellow at UC Santa Cruz from 2002–2004, and is currently an Assistant Professor at MIT. His research interests include phonology, morphology, and learnability, with an emphasis on using computational modeling to investigate issues in phonological theory.

ARTEMIS ALEXIADOU's research has concentrated on theoretical and comparative syntax, with special interest in the interfaces between syntax and morphology and syntax and the lexicon. Her books include *Adverb Placement* (Benjamins 1997), *Functional Structure in Nominals* (Benjamins 2001), *Noun Phrase in the Generative Perspective* (co-authored with Liliane Haegeman and Melita Stavrou, Mouton de Gruyter 2007) and *The Unaccusativity Puzzle* (co-edited with Elena Anagnostopouplou and Martin Everaert, OUP 2004). She is currently working on various projects, including the form and interpretation of nominals, adjectival modification, verbal alternations and the role of non-active morphology.

ASAF BACHRACH is a doctoral student at the Department of Linguistics and Philosophy at MIT. His research focuses on morphosyntax and neurolinguistics. His theoretical work centers on the representation and consequences of identity in a cyclic model of grammar. His brain research, using non-invasive imaging techniques as well as the study of impaired populations, investigates the neural correlates of syntactic complexity and on-line parsing and lexical access.

JOHN FREDERICK BAILYN's research has been focused on theoretical linguistics and its applications to the Slavic languages, especially Russian and Serbo-Croatian, since his 1995 Cornell dissertation, *A Configurational Approach to "Free" Word Order in Russian*. His interests focus on the status of word order variation in natural language, and on related issues of scope and binding. He is also fascinated by Slavic morphophonology, micro-variation in syntax, and the interaction of syntactic movement and binding. Outside of linguistic theory he is interested in musical cognition, animal psychology, international and interdisciplinary education, and alternative and underground cultural movements, especially in music. He is on the linguistics faculty at Stony Brook University.

ANDREA CALABRESE studied at the University of Padova, at the Scuola Normale Superiore of Pisa and at the Massachusetts Institute of Technology where he obtained his Ph.D. in Linguistics in 1988. From 1989 to 1997 he taught at Harvard University and since 1997 he has been teaching at the University of Connecticut. He also has a visiting teaching position at the University of Siena. His main interests are phonology, morphology and historical linguistics. He published more than 50 articles in books and journals such as *Linguistic Inquiry, The Linguistic Review, Studies in Language, Brain and Language, Journal of Neuro-Linguistics,* and *Rivista di Linguistica.* His recent book, *Markedness and Economy in a Derivational Model of Phonology* (Mouton de Gruyter, 2005), proposes a theory integrating phonological rules and repairs triggered by markedness constraints into a derivational model of phonology. In the past few years, he has also been working on a book in which he investigates the historical phonology of the Indo-European languages in the light of recent developments in phonological theory.

JONATHAN DAVID BOBALJIK's theoretical research has focused on morphology and syntax, and his descriptive work has mainly concentrated on Itelmen, an indigenous language of the Kamchatka peninsula, Russia, where he has conducted fieldwork since 1993. Recent publications include "Itelmen Reduplication: Edge-In Association and Lexical Stratification" (*Journal of Linguistics,* 2006), "The Domain of Agreement" (*Natural Language and Linguistic Theory,* 2005, with Susi Wurmbrand), and "Where's Phi? Agreement as a Post-Syntactic Operation" (forthcoming in *Phi Theory,* OUP).

MORRIS HALLE's research has focused on phonology and related areas. Among his publications are *The Sound Pattern of English* (1968), co-authored with Noam Chomsky, "Stress and Accent in Indo-European" (*Language* 73 (1997)), "Distributed Morphology" (*MIT Working Papers in Linguistics* 30 (1997)) and *From Memory to Speech and Back: Papers on Phonetics and Phonology* 1954 to 2002 (Mouton de Gruyter, Berlin 2002). Halle retired in 1996 as Institute Professor at MIT but has continued his research. *The Meter of a Poem* (co-author Nigel Fabb) is in the final stages of preparation and should appear in 2008.

ALEC MARANTZ's research concerns the theory of morphology and architecture of grammar. With David Embick, he has recently completed a project exploring the consequences of blocking phenomena for the theory of grammar (*Linguistic Inquiry,* 2008). Using magnetoencephalographic (MEG) measurements, he is currently exploiting the results of the theory of Distributed Morphology to uncover the brain mechanisms underlying language comprehension.

GEREON MÜLLER's main research interest is grammatical theory, with a special focus on syntax and morphology. An underlying assumption that guides his research is that the rules and constraints that are at the heart of syntactic and morphological systems of individual languages are both conceptually simple and highly abstract. He is currently working on a derivational theory of the morphology/syntax interface that adheres to this tenet by reconciling aspects of the minimalist program and optimality theory. His major publications are concerned with displacement processes, including wh-movement, scrambling, verb-second, and remnant movement; as in his books *A-Bar Syntax* (Berlin 1995) and *Incomplete Category Fronting* (Dordrecht 1998); repair phenomena, as in *Elemente der optimalitaetstheoretischen Syntax* (Tübingen 2000);

argument encoding types; and syncretism in inflectional morphology as in *Subanalysis of Argument Encoding in Distributed Morphology*, which he co-edited with Jochen Trommer (Leipzig 2006).

ANDREW NEVINS received his PhD in linguistics from MIT in 2004 and currently teaches linguistics at Harvard University. He is a researcher in formal morphology and phonology and has published articles contributing to the study of Hindi, Basque, Slovenian, Turkish, and Brazilian Portuguese. Recent publications have appeared in *Linguistic Inquiry* and *Natural Language and Linguistic Theory*.

PETER SVENONIUS (Ph.D. UC Santa Cruz) is a professor and senior researcher at CASTL, Norway's center of excellence in theoretical linguistics, in Tromsø, Norway. Among other topics, he has worked on predication, on Scandinavian microcomparative syntax, and on the syntax of expressions of location and directed motion cross-linguistically.

JOCHEN TROMMER's research explores theoretical aspects of the interfaces between morphology, phonology, and syntax using both derivational and constraint-based approaches. His thesis, *Distributed Optimality*, fuses central ideas from Distributed Morphology and Optimality Theory. Among his recent publications are "Hierarchy-based Competition and Emergence of Two-Argument Agreement in Dumi", *Linguistics*, 2006, and "Case Suffixes, Postpositions, and the Phonological Word in Hungarian", *Linguistics*, 2007. His current research focuses on a radically minimalist reconception of morphological Spellout ("Core Morphology") and the strictly concatenative analysis of non-concatenative morphology.

DONCA STERIADE's recent research deals with the interfaces between phonetics-phonology and phonology-morphology. Recent publications include *Phonetically Based Phonology*, co-edited with Bruce Hayes and Robert Kirchner (Blackwell 2004), "The Phonology of Perceptibility Effects: The P-Map and its Consequences for Constraint Organization", in *On the Nature of the Word* edited by Sharon Inkelas and Kristin Hanson (MIT Press 2004), "Contrast" in the *Cambridge Handbook of Phonology*, edited by Paul de Lacy (CUP 2007), and "Knowledge of Similarity and Narrow Lexical Override" in P. Novak and C. Yoquelet (eds.) BLS 29.

Abbreviations

1	first person
2	second person
3	third person
Abl	ablative
Acc	accusative
Adj	adjective
Aux	auxiliary
Com	comitative
CP	complementizer phrase
Dat	dative
Dim	diminutive
DM	Distributed Morphology
DO	direct object
DP	determiner phrase
Du	dual
Erg	ergative
Ess	essive
Fem	feminine
Gen	genitive
Ill	illative
Inf	infinitive
Inst	instrumental
IO	input-output
IO	indirect object
IPA	International Phonetic Alphabet
LF	logical form
Loc	locative
LPM	Lexical Phonology and Morphology
Masc	masculine
MS	morphological structure
Neut	neuter
Nom	nominative

NP   noun phrase
Obl   oblique
OO   output-output
OP   optimal paradigms
OT   Optimality Theory
Perf   perfect
PF   phonetic form
Pl   plural
PP   prepositional phrase
Sg   singular
SPE   *The Sound Pattern of English*
TP   tense phrase
UG   universal grammar
UR   underlying representation
VI   vocabulary item
Voc   vocative
VP   verb phrase

1

Introduction: Approaching inflectional identity

ASAF BACHRACH AND ANDREW NEVINS

1.1 Overview

The topic of this volume is inflectional identity. We group together under the term *inflectional* the morphological markers that participate in a "paradigmatically-related" alternation to express case, person, number, gender, or class distinctions. *Identity* covers and classifies a range of identity and similarity relations among the phonological form of these items. We refer, informally, to any *n*-way classification of verbal or nominal inflection as a paradigm, where the two (or more) dimensions could be tense and agreement (on verbs) or conjugation class and case (on nouns).[1] The primary focus of study here will be on inflectional rather than derivational morphology (e.g., nominalization of verbs or the formation of the superlative form of an adjective), as one of the key puzzles is identity-of-form among items that have no clear derivational history with respect to each other.

The overarching themes that emerge in the study of inflectional identity include questions of whether a set of inflectionally-related forms (e.g., all of the case endings within a certain declension class of nouns, or all of the singular stems for a certain conjugation class of verbs) share a common "base" from which identity of form can be understood to emerge, and questions of the division of labor between representational and derivational theories of the phonological form of closed-class morphemes.

Effects of the force of identity–in form and in patterning of phonological behavior of inflectional items–have been implicated in grammatical study for quite some time. While historical linguistics has made repeated appeal to such forces (analogy, leveling, functional analogy; see Paul 1880, for example), this

---

[1] See Williams (1981; 1994); Wunderlich (1996); Carstairs (1987); Stump (2001) for models in which paradigms and their organization play a central role.

kind of teleological reasoning was not easy to capture in SPE-style generative phonology (e.g., Chomsky and Halle 1968) because such models function in terms of rules with inputs and outputs applying to underlying and interme-diate representations with no formal mechanism for talking about the result or the target, i.e., the structural descriptions of rules cannot look ahead, and must refer to input but not to what will be accomplished by output.

Authors such as Kenstowicz and Kisseberth (1977) and others have long noticed the appeal of teleological reasoning in the explanation of certain phonological patterns. One such case, discussed by Kenstowicz and Kisseberth (p. 153), is a morpheme structure constraint in the Nilotic language Alur. In this language CVC roots can have either two alveolar stops (e.g., tado, tato) or two interdental stops (e.g., ðeθo or θeðo) but not a mixture (e.g., *θedo or teðo). Setting up a rule that assimilates the place of the first stop to the sec-ond or vice-versa would impose directionality and asymmetric dependency, neither of which is motivated by the data. By contrast, a simple condition, or constraint (e.g., *[α anterior] V [−α anterior]) on the output offers a more concise and intuitive characterization of the generalization.

This work in the 1970s prepared the stage for the rise of output-based constraints, paradigm-level constraints, and eventually Optimality Theory. The OT formalism makes the expression of teleological explanation very easy. In addition, constraints can make reference to pairs or sets of derivationally-unrelated surface forms, unlike derivational rules. Thus, rather naturally this framework also brought about the attempt to capture paradigmatic regularity forces as the result of constraints on the form of paradigm members, often directionally imposed by a subset of forms in the paradigm (McCarthy 2005; Kenstowicz 1996; Steriade 1999; Downing et al. 2005).

Interestingly, however, Kenstowicz and Kisseberth also invoke, in the same era, another important issue for any attempt to capitalize on paradigmatic regularity as a form of explanation, namely the fact that the notion of para-digm itself often lacks an explicit definition and is often applied to a particular analysis in an intuitive or case-specific fashion. One of the important areas of research to which we hope this volume contributes is laying out formal demarcations of the sets of forms in which paradigmatic identity effects are predicted to apply.

In what follows, we will touch on a number of contemporary approaches to paradigm structure that have shaped linguistic theorizing since the emer-gence of generative phonology, i.e., the era beginning with the publication of Chomsky and Halle (1968) and continuing until today. A number of different answers have been put forward regarding the mechanisms underlying para-digmatic relations. While we will not attempt here to provide a comprehensive survey of the field, we aim to highlight key aspects of approaches to inflectional identity. After illustrating what we believe to be two of the central issues in the study of inflectional identity, we turn to a discussion of the individual chapters of this volume within the context of a number of individual case studies chosen from the literature.

1.2 The identification of base of identity and scope of identity effects

In this section, we introduce two important general questions that should be pursued in explaining identity effects through the notion of paradigm. The first is the *asymmetry* question: why do inflectional identity effects go from some members in the paradigm towards others, and not vice versa? The second is the *inclusion* question: what is the set of relevant forms that learners put together into the set of inflectionally-related elements? These are two things a theory of paradigms should provide. In what follows we illustrate these two core questions with brief case studies.

1.2.1 *The asymmetry question*

When identity effects pull one morphological form *A* towards an unexpected phonological shape in order to look more like *B*, one question that logically arises is, why didn't *A* pull *B* towards it instead? As a case study, consider, for example, the factors governing Spanish diminutive allomorphy, as discussed in Kenstowicz (2005).[2] As a rough approximation, Spanish has two diminutive suffixes, *-it-* and *-cit-*, which are chosen allomorphically: *-cit-* follows nouns ending in a sonorant consonant, while *-it-* occurs elsewhere. Thus, the word *corona* 'crown (f.)' has the diminutive *coronita*, while the word *ratón* 'mouse (m.)' has the diminutive *ratoncito*. Now consider the word *ratona* 'mouse (f.)'. By the phonological conditions stated above, we expect the diminutive to be *ratonita*, in a manner entirely parallel to *coronita*. Nonetheless, it is *ratoncita*.

(1.1)   a.   corona   coronita   'crown (fem.)'
        b.   ratona   ratoncita,*ratonita   'mouse (fem.)'
        c.   ratón   ratoncito   'mouse (masc.)'

Kenstowicz's explanation is that the masculine and feminine forms of 'mouse' compose a paradigm, and thus *ratoncito* exerts pressure for identity on *ratoncita*. The immediate question arises about the directionality of this identity-yielding effect. Why couldn't things go the other way, i.e., why

---

[2] Earlier studies include Jaeggli (1980), Crowhurst (1992), Harris (1994), and Aguero-Bautista (1998).

couldn't the otherwise well-formed *ratonita* exert pressure on the masculine, yielding **ratonito*?[3] We dub this the *asymmetry* question.

In this particular case, an insight to the question might be found in an exploration of independent evidence from the theory of morphological markedness. It has often been observed that the behavior of the two genders masculine and feminine in Romance languages (and perhaps more generally) is not of equal status. In particular, masculine gender is more frequent in the lexicon in terms of types (there are more masculine roots than feminine), is represented more often in corpora in terms of token frequency, and is chosen as the default gender for adoption of new nouns. In addition, in languages with more complex case systems, one finds fewer overtly-marked case distinctions (i.e., more syncretism) for the feminine gender than for the masculine. All of these diagnostics point towards an unequal behavior of masculine and feminine genders in which masculine is less marked, i.e., more of the default or less "costly" than the feminine gender within this formal binary opposition (Greenberg 1966).

Returning to the Spanish diminutives case, we might understand the asymmetry, where the masculine exerts influence on the form of the feminine, as the result of a more widespread directionality. As masculine gender is unmarked in Spanish (e.g., Harris 1991), the asymmetry effect here may reflect a more general principle: unmarked forms affect marked forms, and not vice versa. Thus, the asymmetry question can in principle be resolved by explicitly identifying an asymmetric base of derivation, with the important desideratum being a general theory for identifying the base, presumably from independently deducible factors.

1.2.2 *The inclusion question*

In the common process in which a set of morphologically-related forms contains A,B,C,D,E,F, and only A,B,C,D participate in an identity effect, another question that arises is why E,F are not included in the identity effect. Consider, as an example, the phenomenon of Brazilian Portuguese (BP) stem readjustment in the plural, as discussed by Ferreira (2004). BP has a morphophonological rule that converts the liquid [l] into the vowel

---

[3] This example is expository in nature, and it would divert from the discussion in the text to provide an alternative analysis here. Briefly, a source of the difference between *coronita* and *ratoncita* lies in the fact that the former is inherently specified as an *-a* Class noun, while the latter only becomes part of the *-a* class by virtue of being the feminine counterpart of an animate noun (thus subject to Harris's (1991) "cloning rule"). If diminutive allomorph selection occurs before "gender cloning," then it will apply to the stems *corona* and *ratón*, yielding *coron(a)+ita* and *raton+cit*. Gendered cloning of animate nouns follows, yielding *ratoncito* and *ratoncita*. The "identity" effect would thus not be an asymmetric relation between masculine and feminine but rather would be between the gender-unspecified root and its suffixed variants.

[i] before the plural suffix -*s*,[4] yielding alternations such as *jornal/jornais* ("newspaper" sg./pl.). The diminutive -*zinh(o)*- is added to such stems (with similar phonological conditions as Spanish, above), yielding the diminutive *jornalzinho* (notice that the [l]-to-[i] rule does not apply before [z]). Surprisingly, however, the plural diminutive is *jornaizinhos*, the result of the fact that the liquid-to-[i] rule has "overapplied" with no phonological environment to trigger it.[5]

(1.2)   singular   plural
    a.   jornal   jornais   'newspaper'
    b.   jornalzinho   jornaizinhos diminutive
    c.   jornalzão   jornalzões   augmentative

Overapplication occurs when a phonological process that is attested in a specific context in the language has applied in a case which did not contain the relevant context. In many cases, the context has been "destroyed" by another phonological or morphological process. In other cases, overapplication might occur in one member of the paradigm, due to the influence of other members of the same paradigm. Underapplication describes the inverse situation, where a phonological process fails to apply in a certain case that does exhibit the required context.

Ferreira's explanation for the overapplication of stem-readjustment in *jornaizinhos* is that the nondiminutive plural and the diminutive plural constitute a paradigm, and an identity effect demands identical stem realization in both forms. What remains mysterious is the fact that in the plural augmentative, *jornalzões*, this identity effect is not in force. Why should the noun and its diminutive form a paradigm to the exclusion of the augmentative? We henceforth refer to this issue as the *inclusion* question.

In this particular case, an insight to the question might be found in an exploration of independent evidence from the morphology of gender: namely, while the diminutive never changes the gender of its stem, the augmentative can change the gender of the stem (e.g., *o mulherzão*, 'the-masc. woman-aug.masc.'). This independent difference may provide the basis for a solution, explores by Ferreira, namely that the augmentative, unlike the diminutive, becomes the "head of the word" (in the sense of Di Sciullo and Williams

---

[4] That this is morphologically-conditioned can be witnessed by the fact that it does not apply root-internally, e.g., *pulsar* 'to pulse'.

[5] Earlier studies include Menuzzi (1993) and Lee (1999). Bachrach and Wagner (2006) note that these overapplication effects apply in compound formation as well and propose that -*zinho*, the diminutive, is a case of compounding, not affixation, and thus subject to regular compound phonology. An analysis along those lines does not encounter the problem in the text if -*zao*, the augmentative, does not constitute a case of compounding.

1987 or contemporary implementations of the notion). Thus, one way of delimiting the scope of an identity effect might be relativizing the subset of participating forms to those that share the same headed substructure, as determined by formal notions of headship such as control of gender specification.

In addition, there may be metrics of inclusion that are more semantically-based. The idea that semantic relatedness might have an effect on morphological structure receives independent (though indirect) support through work by Baayen and colleagues (cf. Bertram, Baayen, and Schreuder 2000) on morphological family size. Bertram et al. discovered that the family size of a Dutch word (the number of other distinct forms in the language containing the same base, e.g., *work, works, worked, clockwork, workman, woodwork, worker, homework*) speeds up the reaction time (RT) in a lexical decision task on any single word containing this base. This general finding was replicated in five of six experiments for inflectional and derivational suffixes but did not hold for the deadjectival suffix *-heid* '-ness'. For this suffix, no significant correlation was observed between family size and RT. However, once the authors removed semantically opaque family members, the corrected family size did correlate with reaction time. This set of results suggests that morphological co-activation (a diagnostic of relatedness) is sensitive to semantic relatedness in a way that might ultimately tie "head of a word" to a more semantically-based set of diagnostics.

1.2.3 *Paths towards predictive theories of bases and subparadigms*

In the examples above, we provided two possible solutions for the case studies at hand. In the case of the asymmetry question, we appealed to markedness. But is the asymmetry question always resolved by the principle in which the basis for inflectional identity is the *unmarked form*? (In fact, Albright's chapter on Yiddish in this volume, to which we return in Section 1.5, suggests a plural-to-singular identity effect which would contradict this principle). This is a question that demands further exploration. For example, do overapplying identity effects always go from third person to first, which would be expected on the basis of unmarkedness? This remains to be seen.

In the case of the inclusion question, we appealed to headedness and headship as an explanation for the fact that some affixed forms are included in a paradigm while others are not. But is a family of inflectionally-identical forms always determined by sharing a common head? This question becomes particularly thorny when one looks at the verbal domain, where identity effects arise for certain verbs in certain tenses. The fact that this only happens for verbs of certain conjugation classes makes it look like the verb is the determining head of the word, but, on the other hand, the fact that it is tense-conditioned (and moreover contemporary syntactic theory takes inflection/tense to be the most prominent head of a word) suggests that this issue again demands more attention. For example, are all English compounds which share a right-hand head-of-the-word (e.g., *blockhead, blackhead, redhead*) thought of as constituting a paradigm? The work of Bertram, Baayen, and Schreuder (2000) would answer in the affirmative, based on diagnostics of facilitated reaction time, but it remains an open question whether all related forms that can exert facilitation in lexical decision will be subject to the force of phonological identity effects.

The asymmetry question and the inclusion question illustrate the need for a rigorous formalization of the principles governing the formation of the paradigms and "mini-paradigms" used in invoking identity effects. Many researchers continue to argue for the introduction of powerful inter-derivational output-based constraints which are predicated over paradigms, without direct attention to these questions.

The chapters in this book can be read both as a critical evaluation of recent transderivational analyses but also as examples of attempts to pave the way for an integrative approach to what yields identity-based effects and their directionality among particular paradigm members and not others. By concentrating closely on the morphological analysis of the forms at hand, many of these questions become illuminated. Throughout this introduction, we will situate the contributions of the chapters in this volume, exemplifying many of the issues with critical discussion of the empirical terrain of inflectional identity recently explored through a paradigmatic lens.

1.3 Paradigm-based explanations, their pitfalls, and alternatives

The first three chapters in the volume present a critical look at paradigm-based explanations. In second chapter, Jonathan Bobaljik examines the Optimal Paradigms framework, proposed by McCarthy (2005), and discusses cases of a syntactic difference between the category of nouns and verbs as a way of explaining phonological effects. Syntactic categories are invoked as an explanatory force in identity effects and raise many important foundational and implementational issues that arise when one pursues this intuitively very plausible line of explanation in serious depth. The third chapter, by Morris Halle and Alec Marantz, examines the "No Blur" principle of paradigm structure, proposed by Cameron-Faulkner and Carstairs-McCarthy (2000), and raises a case study from Polish that addresses the question of "inclusion" with regard to which dimensions of paradigm organization should be within the scope of statements about syncretism. The fourth chapter, by Peter Svenonius, shows that an apparent paradigm effect in Sámi stems is better understood through a more principled look at phonological structure.

As a first point in the discussion, we will consider recent models of paradigm-based identity effects. The Optimal Paradigms framework, introduced by McCarthy (2005), is an attempt to explain phonological patterns in certain categories (e.g., noun vs. verb) as the result of the affixal environments in which those words occur rather than as the result of their syntactic category. It is thus an attempt to derive a pattern of inflection from phonotactics of the language rather than what appears otherwise to be the influence of morphological category on phonological shapes. To give a concrete example (one which is not explored by McCarthy but a plausible candidate for an OP-type analysis), consider the difference in stress in English noun-verb pairs such as *récord* (n.) vs. *recórd* (v.). The traditional explanation for this contrast is that verbs with a heavy second syllable have final stress, while many disyllabic nouns with prefixes or pseudoprefixes have initial stress (Hayes 1981, 313 ff, e.g., *cónvent, íncome, ádage*). The difference is thus characterized as the result of category-specific stress templates. However, the question arises, why couldn't it be the other way around? In other words, why couldn't nouns have the final stress pattern and verbs have the initial stress pattern?

The Optimal Paradigms line of explanation allows the possibility of considering these effects in the context of affixation. While the majority of overt *verbal* suffixes include a vowel, e.g., *-ed, -ing*, the most frequent suffix to nouns does not contain a vowel: *-s*. The noun *récord*, in its affixed plural form *récords*, still retains a penultimate stress pattern. However, the verb *recórd*, with its past and progressive forms *recórded* and *recórding*, now shows penultimate, rather than final stress. The general tendency then is for affixation to yield a penultimate stress pattern for these forms:

(1.3) Verbs with Stem-Final Stress, Nouns with Stem-Initial Stress:
        noun forms   récord, récords   2 out of 2 penultimate
        verb forms   recórd, recórding, recórded   2 out of 3 penultimate

Consider now the hypothetical *recórd (n.) vs. *récord (v.). The progressive and past forms, *récording and *récorded, would show a highly marked pattern of initial stress on a light syllable followed by two unstressed heavy syllables.

(1.4) Hypothetical: Nouns with Stem-Final Stress, Verbs with Stem-Initial Stress:

| noun forms | recórd, recórds | 0 out of 2 penultimate |
| verb forms | récord, récording, récorded | 1 out of 3 penultimate |

Comparing (1.3) with (1.4), the Stem-Final pattern stress in verbs clearly emerges as preferable overall when one considers the set of affixed forms. The Optimal Paradigms consideration of the affixed forms (the entire "paradigm" of verbal forms) thus yields insight into why the pressure for penultimate stress in the affixed forms might be leading to the final-stress pattern in bare verbal forms. In fact, the OP claim would be that stem-final stress in the verb *record* is the result of a sacrifice in order to accommodate penultimate stress in the affixed forms; in a sense, "overapplication" of stem-final stress even in an unexpected place.

OP requires the use of "second order" constraints, in which the input and output of an optimization tableau is not a single input form mapped to its output form but an entire paradigm of input forms mapped to an entire paradigm of output forms. It is straightforward to point out that analogical "extension" effects, in which a phonological alternation is extended to a verb in which it did not exist before, would require third-order constraints. Constraints which demand identity of alternation patterns *between* paradigms require entire sets of the paradigms from different verb types (i.e., constraints over sets of sets of output forms) as the input and output to the tableaux. The current logic of OP always yields what analogical theorists call "leveling": a phonological pattern overapplies in places it should not, driven by paradigmatic considerations, and enforces identity among related forms. However, leveling effects are important in their own right as an identity effect that illustrates reanalysis of the base(s) of derivation.

To see this issue in context, consider European Portuguese (EP), which exhibits an analogical extension effect in the vowel height of third conjugation (*-ir*) verbs. EP has two relevant phonological processes: Prosodic Lowering, which lowers mid-vowels e, o to ɛ, ɔ under main stress, and Morphological Raising, which raises mid-vowels e, o to i, u in the present tense first person singular and in the present subjunctive.[6] Verbs whose final stem vowels are mid-vowels are eligible for both processes, yielding alternations such as [dormír, dúrmu, dɔrməs] in (1.5a.):

---

[6] See Harris (1974), Quicoli (1990), Wetzels (1995), and Mascarenhas et al. (2005) for much more detailed discussion of the facts.

(1.5)   infinitive   2sg   1sg
   a.   dormír   dɔ́rməs   dúrmu   'sleep'
   b.   escovár   escɔ́vəs   escóvu   'brush'
   c.   puńír   púnəs   púnu   'punish'
   d.   fuʒír   fɔ́ʒəs   fúʒu   'flee'

Verbs whose final stem vowels are mid-vowels but are not in the third conjugation, however, are not subject to Morphological Raising: (cf (1.5b.)). Third conjugation verbs with a high stem vowel are (vacuously) subject to Morphological Raising but not to Prosodic Lowering (1.5c.).

However, the alternation between a low mid-vowel in the 2sg and a high vowel in the 1sg has been extended to some verbs whose underlying stem vowel is etymologically a high vowel, such as *fugír* 'flee' (1.5d.), yielding "exceptional" alternations of the form "infinitive [u], 2sg [ɔ]". The OP model, and indeed any model that has whole paradigms entering as candidates to a computation aiming to minimize alternations and maximize faithfulness among members of a related paradigm, is at a loss to explain the "importation" of nonfaithful alternations into a paradigm.[7] Cases of leveling and analogy are thus perhaps better understood as reanalysis of the underlying form providing the derivational base for inflectionally-related members. When the underlying form is reanalyzed in favor of a neutralized variant of the related outputs, leveling occurs; when it is reanalyzed in favor of a more abstract variant of the related outputs, extension occurs. In other words, many cases of both identity-creating and identity-destroying changes in the form of a paradigm are perhaps best understood in terms of a change in an underlying form rather than a negotiation among the surface forms.

Returning to the asymmetry question, Jonathan Bobaljik's chapter in this volume delves into a number of issues related to OP implementations of leveling. McCarthy's OP paper proposed that noun-verb asymmetries in the morpheme structure constraints of Classical Arabic arise as an epiphenomenon of synchronic constraints that evaluate entire inflectional paradigms, enforcing maximal uniformity within the paradigm, at the cost of forcing overapplication of phonological processes in very specific environments. As discussed in the *récord/recórd* example above, the idea is that apparent phonological sensitivity to morphosyntactic category (N/V) is a result of accidental, emergent properties of the classes of inflectional affixes with which nouns and verbs may combine.

---

[7] See Maiden (1991) for a discussion of height alternations within a theory of their potential functions in Romance morphology.

A question that arises here is why stems undergo optimization to accommodate affixes and not vice versa. Perhaps an appeal to open vs. closed class item may be one way to make the cut in general. However, Bobaljik concludes that there is no good answer in the case of Arabic as to why it is affixes that determine the form of stems and not vice versa, since Arabic stems are the result of a fixed set of closed-class non-concatenative templates, which could logically just as easily force phonological accommodation in the other direction. Through a case study of Itelmen noun/verb differences in epenthesis (nouns alternate but verbs do not, retaining schwa even when phonologically "unnecessary" in some forms), Bobaljik advocates a cyclicity-based explanation for the difference between nouns and verbs: the hypothesis is that the morphosyntactic structure of these categories interfaces with phonological process such as syllabification according to possibly different dynamic timing. This opens a potentially fruitful research strategy, as it leads one to ask questions about syntactic differences in word formation between nouns and verbs,[8] and whether the cycle of syntactic transfer to the phonology coincides with the cycle of transfer to semantic interpretation.

In their chapter in this volume, Halle and Marantz critically explore further issues involved in employing reference to paradigm structure in explanations of inflectional identity effects. They discuss Carstairs-McCarthy's NoBLUR constraint on paradigms (Carstairs-McCarthy 1994), which states that "In every morphological category, at most one affix may appear in more than one stem class." In other words, suppose there are four conjugation classes in a given language. In the expression of, say, the nominative, there can be patterns of the forms in Systems 1, 2, and 3 below, but not System 4 where there are two separate affixes, a and b, used in more than one class.

(1.6)		class I	class II	class III	class IV
	System 1:	a	a	b	c
	System 2:	a	b	c	d
	System 3:	a	b	c	c
	*System 4:	a	a	b	b

In effect, No Blur requires that no more than one marker can fail to identify inflection class unambiguously, but in System 4, both a and b fail to identify a class unambiguously. Noyer (1994) suggests that there is a violation of No Blur

---

[8] It is not however altogether clear that cyclicity alone can explain phonological asymmetries in nouns and verbs. In the Portuguese verbal system, all mid vowels (i.e., e, o) become [−ATR] under primary stress (i.e., ɛ, ɔ). This does not happen in the nominal system, however. One could posit a different cycle of vowel lowering for verbs than nouns, but it is not obvious that the invocation of cycles adds anything to the category difference.

within the English past tense and participle endings for classes of irregular verbs, which can be viewed as conjugation classes. Verbs of the type *played* are Class I, verbs of the type *dwelt* are Class II, verbs of the type *put* are Class III, verbs of the type *beat, beaten* are Class IV, and verbs of the type *showed, shown* are Class V:

(1.7) I   II   III   IV   V
    -d   -t   -Ø   -Ø   -d   +past
    -d   -t   -Ø   -n   -n   +past, +participle

The past tense has more than one marker appearing in multiple places. Noyer notes that Class V is in fact gradually becoming leveled out to *have showed* in many dialects of English, and suggests more generally that No Blur is a learnability bias but not a grammatical constraint, and moreover that this learnability bias can be overcome in cases of small numbers of class/category combinations.

Cameron-Faulkner and Carstairs-McCarthy (2000) consider seven conjugation classes of Polish nouns, which show an apparent violation of No Blur in the dative. In the dative, the suffixes *-owi* and *-u* occur in more than one class. Cameron-Faulkner and Carstairs-McCarthy (2000) note that an apparent solution to this problem is to redefine the classes using "superclasses" so that the dative *-u* of classes 3 and 4 is the exponent of only one class (a move that is in spirit not unlike the class-feature decomposition of Alexiadou and Müller's and Trommer's chapters in this volume). However, Halle and Marantz point out that this misses the fact that *-u* is the "elsewhere item" throughout the paradigm, appearing in the locative of classes 2, 4, 5, and 7, the vocative of classes 2 and 7, and the genitive of classes 6 and 7. No Blur is a constraint on identity that is formulated to only look at "horizontal" rows (e.g., across conjugation classes) of paradigms but misses the fact that elsewhere items appear in "vertical" (e.g., across cases) syncretisms as well. Müller (2006) points out that the Icelandic nominal declension also exhibits a good deal of transparadigmatic syncretism (unexpressible via No Blur, which is formulated only for single categories), and suggests that the correct upper bound restriction on "paradigm economy" (i.e., on the number of distinct signals/markers within a set of inflectionally-related forms) comes when there is one maximally underspecified marker per domain.

In reanalyzing the Polish declension, Halle and Marantz propose an alternative employing *impoverishment* (Bonet 1991; Noyer 1992; Halle 1997), a restrictive form of feature changing (in which there is only feature deletion) prior to morphological realization. Deletion of case features in the appropriate categories will render the resultant feature bundle compatible only with the elsewhere item. This essentially leads to two sources of syncretism: underspecification for class (e.g., -*owi* is for all datives) or impoverishment of case features (yielding -*u*, the default for the entire paradigm) in the relevant set of stems. This account provides an explanation for cases where No Blur is violated, attributing the two blurring affixes to two distinct grammatical mechanisms, neither of which directly refer to paradigm structure. The existence of transparadigmatic identity effects poses, in this case, an instance of the inclusion question which is answered not by referring to paradigms but to sets of features and potentially underspecified markers that express them.

Many of the identity effects we have discussed involve phonological effects which are unexpected from the point of view of regular phonological computation based on the locally derived morphological structure of the form in question. Svenonius's chapter in this volume presents a detailed and enlightening discussion of the morphophonologically complex consonant gradation in Northern Sámi. Consonant gradation has a phonological origin but is currently a morphologically-driven process, used to mark different cases in the nominal domain and different tenses in the verbal one. The author discusses the difficulty in determining the base form in such alternations, highlighting a common issue in the analysis of paradigms.

In the Sámi nominal domain, even and uneven syllable stems pattern differently with respect to consonant gradation. In fact, whenever one class presents a strong form, the other class will present a weak form, and vice versa. Such a situation might suggest the effect of a paradigmatic constraint. However, Svenonius demonstrates that a purely derivational account can account for the pattern without appeal to paradigms. Moreover, this account is flexible enough to accommodate exceptions to the pattern alluded to above, a fact that might be difficult to handle in a paradigmatic approach.

1.4 Sources of identity effects: Shared morphological features

The next section of this volume is composed of proposals exploring particular perspectives on the *inclusion* question raised at the outset. The chapters by Artemis Alexiadou and Gereon Müller, Andrea Calabrese, and by Jochen Trommer, answer the question of what is included in a set of relevant

inflectionally-identical forms, by examining the morphosyntactic basis of featural identity, in the Jakobsonian tradition of decomposition.

Decomposition (or "subanalysis" as it is sometimes called) is an approach
to morphological structure that adopts the principle that shared signals reflect
shared structure. Decompositional analyses of syncretism appeal to shared
structure either at the level of subtrees of hierarchically organized morphosyntactic nodes, or at the level of morphosyntactic features on these nodes. At the
level of shared featural identity, for example, the identitical suffixes for the dual
and the plural in the indefinite noun paradigm of Sámi (Vinka 2001) reflect
a shared feature within the subparts of the categories "dual" and "plural",
namely the shared value of a feature: [−singular].

To appreciate the role of shared substructural identity, one can consider a
case study involving the distribution of the allomorph -*t*- and its accompa-
nying suppletive stems in Latin, and their subsequent loss in proto-Romance.
In pre-classical Latin, a number of suffixes contained an initial -*t*- (probably
reflecting an older morphological structure), including -*turus* (future active
participial), -*tor* (agentive nominalizer), -*tio* (eventive nominalizer), -*tum*
(supine), and -*tus* (past participle).

In stems ending in a coronal, a phonologically transparent process modified
the final stem consonant and suffix initial consonant (e.g., *vid* + *tus* → *viit-tus*
→ *viissus* → *visus* 'seen'). In Classical Latin these processes became opaque
and stem alternations such as *vid/vis* 'see' were treated as stem allomorphs
on a par with "genuine" allomorphs as in *jub/jus* 'order'. Following Aronoff
(1994), we assume that as a consequence, the -*t* initial suffixes were reanalyzed
as V-initial and the suffixal -*t* became part of a stem allomorph (cf. Aronoff
1994 on the *t*-stem).

The use of this *t*-stem allomorph (sometimes also reanalyzed with an -*s*-
instead of -*t*-) in Latin, also called the perfect passive participle, became rather
heterogenous. Thus, the verb *premere* "press" used the participial allomorph
in *pressus* (past participle), *pressu:rus* (future active), and *ex-pressor* "agentive
noun". Learners of Classical Latin were confronted with a peculiar empirical generalization: a number of seemingly unrelated V-initial suffixes were
all associated with the *t*-stem allomorph. The question is how speakers of
Classical Latin represented this generalization in their grammars. Aronoff
postulates an affix specific rule that determines which stem would surface.
This solution does not assume any morphosyntactic relation among the environments where the *t*-stem surfaces. As a result, this solution is not compatible
with the principle invoked above that phonological identity reflects syntactic
identity.

Embick (2000), attempting to preserve this principle proposes that these seemingly disparate sets of "deverbal" categories all share the stem allomorph *press-* because they share a common syntactic structure: a subtree of Aspect-*v*-Root that does not combine with Tense. Infinitive forms involve combination with Tense, and no syntactically projected aspectual head and as a result, take *prem-*. The remaining forms take *pres-*. Perfect passive participial forms are characterized by lack of head movement of Aspect to Tense, thus resulting in analytic forms (e.g., *ama:tus sum* 'loved.participle auxiliary-1sg.'). Future forms do not involve a Tense node but rather encode future by a modal head. Finally, deverbal agentives do not involve a Tense node. Most importantly, Embick shows that "deponent verbs", active verbs that have an analytic perfect (compare *ama:vi:* 'I have loved' with *hortatus sum* 'I have exhorted') are also the result of failure of Aspect to raise to Tense.

The distribution of Latin *t*-stems, then, signals a shared identity: presence of Aspect and lack of Tense within the morphological word of the root verb. However, in Romance languages, the distribution of *t*-stems became dramatically reduced. The primary reason was that many of the *t*-inducing suffixes dropped out of the language. Only two relevant suffixes remained, the past participle *-(t)us* and the agentive *-(t)or*. In addition, gradual loss of the synthetic perfect forms and of the deponent/nondeponent difference would have led to a situation in which the distribution of the *t*-stems was no longer so clean. At this point, a predictive question arises: would learners of Romance languages preserve the distribution of the Latin stems? The decompositional perspective expects learners of Romance to be biased against what became an unnatural *t*-class and to prefer a distribution of stem allomorphs that reflects a morphosyntactically natural class. This prediction is not shared by the affix specific rule perspective.

Steriade (2002) observes that in two Romance descendents of Latin, the (now reduced) unnatural *-t-* class has been clearly discarded. In Romanian and French the *t*-stem is only used for the perfective past participle. The agentive, which is not perfective, takes the unmarked stem. Italian, a more conservative Romance language, appears at first to falsify the prediction of "shared form, shared structural identity", since the *t*-stem still seems to be used as a base of the agentive. Following Tucker (2000), Steriade argues that despite surface appearance, Italian does not make use of the *t*-stem in the agentive derivation. If Steriade is correct then Italian presents a particularly interesting case. While in contemporary Italian the surface facts support the Latin original rule, learners ignore these data in favor of a less arbitrary rule: one which makes sense from the point of view of featural identity at the morphological level.

Tucker (2000) discusses the fact that in contemporary Italian, many agentive formations (e.g., *lavoratore*) are ambiguous between a derivation from the past participle + agentive *-ore* and a derivation from the infinitive + agentive *-tore* (1.8a.b.).

(1.8)		infinitive	past participle	agentive	
	a.	lavora-re	lavorat-o	lavoratore	'work'
	b.	acquisi-re	acquisit-o	acquisitore	'acquire'
	c.	fonde-re	fus-o	fonditore	'melt'
	d.	invade-re	invas-o	invasore	'invade'

Thus, *lavoratore* is ambiguous between a derivation as *lavora+tore*, built on the infinitive, or as *lavorat+ore*, built on the past participle. However, other agentives are clearly built on the infinitive (1.8c.) or the past participle (1.8d.). Tucker conducted elicitation and acceptability experiments, revealing that speakers of contemporary Italian overwhelmingly prefer the infinitive as the base for novel agentives, despite the apparent positive evidence provided to the contrary.

Steriade provides further evidence that at least as early as 12th-century Italian, new agentive forms were no longer constructed on the basis of the perfect stem. This is evidenced by the fact that verbs which had innovative perfect forms in Italian, such as (1.9), built their agentives on the infinitive and not on the perfect. In other words, Italian agentive formation came to respect the shared substructure generalization, in which agentives do not share features or structure with the perfect but rather with the infinitive:

(1.9)	Latin perfect	victus	collectus
	Italian restructured perfect	vinto	colto
	Italian infinitive	vincere	cogliere
	Italian agentive	vincitore	coglitore
		*vintore	*coltore
		'conquer'	'harvest'

This discovery, coupled with Tucker's results above, strongly suggests that extant Italian agentives containing a perfect *t*-stem are best understood as lexical borrowings from Latin[9] and not the products of synchronic morphological operations. It seems that the Italian learners, just like their Romanian and French counterparts, simply "refused" to learn the featurally unnatural dependency between the agentive and the past participle. The difference

---

[9] One must assume that these borrowed agentives are treated as noncompositional by speakers of contemporary Italian.

between Italian and the other two Romance languages is that Italian contains many "borrowed" agentives and that in Italian the agentive suffix has been reanalyzed as *t*-initial, while remaining V-initial in the other two languages.

The case above is an illustration of restructuring of the grammar (in particular, the conditions for shared allomorph selection) in favor of shared structural identity, with an example from the interaction of derivational and inflectional morphology with Tense and Aspect subtrees. We take this case to be an illustration of an important type of answer to the inclusion question for inflectional morphology more generally: learners disprefer accidental homophony and will seek an underlying grammatical motivation as the basis for a shared phonological form. The three chapters in this section pursue this idea within the realm of the morphological features underlying inflectional morphology.

The contributors to this section propose that learners treat surface forms as related phonologically when they are related morphologically at the level of identity of morphological features underlying case and conjugation class. Treating categories such as conjugation class and case as not atomic but rather composed of binary features, allows for the expression of two types of processes: *grouping* (i.e., why, say, conjugation classes X and Y should behave together) and *opposition* (i.e., why, say, conjugation classes A and Z are distributed in a polar organization). The contributors to this section also argue that features may be ordered along specific dimensions, i.e., hierarchically organized within a feature structure or characterized by sets of implicational relations among feature values.

Trommer's chapter in this volume tackles the question of Amharic verb classes, which are traditionally grouped into macro-classes A, B, and C. He shows that these can be decomposed into more primitive features such as "gemination in the perfective" and "vowel quality X after root-consonant 2." This feature-based decomposition (which groups classes A and B with respect to a certain feature) enables an explanation of syncretism in certain morphological environments. Class A verbs look like Class B verbs in the so-called *as*-derivation due to the basic DM mechanism of feature deletion ("impoverishment"), which renders Class A featurally identical to B in terms of morphophonological conjugation features, and hence phonologically similar as a result. Trommer captures implicational relations among these features by using the tools of feature geometry, which allow autosegmental delinking to delete not only a single feature but also all of its constituent dependents. The importance of having a hierarchical representation of features thus comes from the fact that features which are deleted together in the same environment do not consitute random subsets of the universe of features but rather follow implicational trends in their patterning.

Alexiadou and Müller, in their chapter in this volume, also pursue a featural decomposition of conjugation classes and focus on the empirical phenomenon of transparadigmatic syncretism. They also pursue a decomposition of the morphological exponents of abstract case[10] (e.g., the morphological categories "ACC" etc.) into more fine-grained binary features in the general tradition of Bierwisch (1967). Finally, they adopt a hierarchy of features so that, when multiple possible underspecified affixes could be considered to realize a morphosyntactic exponent, not only the number of features, but also *which* features are specified (e.g., specification for number is more important than specification for case) is a consideration governing affix choice. The paper contains three detailed case studies, in Russian, Greek, and German. Importantly, Alexiadou and Müller situate the role of class features such as conjugation class in the syntax, as syntactic probes seeking specification for phi-features. This allows for a novel treatment of "indeclinable" nouns and a rethinking of why fusional inflection might exist in the first place.

In discussing specific values of certain features, Calabrese makes central use of markedness to derive patterns of syncretism. An important issue within the study of markedness is how and where markedness information is encoded. Calabrese, in his work on phonological markedness (Calabrese 1988 et seq.) and his chapter in the present volume, represents markedness through *filters*, which constitute grammatical statements of markedness (indeed, this filter-based notion of markedness has been taken up by Optimality Theory in the form of declarative constraints).

The nature, origin, and representation of markedness remain important open questions in morphological theory, and other perspectives exist. A different view of the representation of markedness is in terms of "amount of structure" and this is the view taken in underspecification-based proposals such as Avery and Rice (1989) in feature-geometric phonology and by Harley and Ritter (2002) in morphology. In these models, markedness can be directly read off the representation by the number of nodes that are explicitly present. A third, functionalist perspective on the representation of markedness is that it is "grounded" in the interface that ultimately exchanges representations with the module of interest. Hayes et al. (2004) represents an attempt to derive all

---

[10] For compelling recent arguments that morphological case is distinct from abstract case (which is assigned syntactically), see Legate (2007).

phonological markedness from phonetic difficulty (broadly speaking). Similarly, one might pursue within morphology the notion that morphosyntactic markedness may be grounded in conceptual difficulty (e.g., that the cognitive representation of pluralities is inherently more complex than singularities).[11] This possibility has not been widely explored within the theory of morphological markedness. A final possibility is that morphological markedness, as typologically revealed, may be a property of the nature of acquisition mechanisms and the filters of diachrony but not an inherent part of the computational system of language: this is the view endorsed by Hale and Reiss (2000) and Blevins (2004) for phonology and by Hawkins (2004) for syntax, though, to our knowledge, it has not been explicitly proposed as a factor in discussions of morphological markedness. However, one possible analog is usage-based or "Zipfian" markedness, i.e., the idea that markedness is a grammaticalization of usage frequencies over time. The notion of markedness as an inverse reflection of text frequency has been espoused by Greenberg (1966) and more recently Haspelmath (2006), though Greenberg noted it to be problematic particularly for person, since narratives inherently vary on their frequency of use of first and second person as opposed to third, despite the universal markedness of the former over the latter.

Calabrese's analysis of case system patterns in terms of featural decomposition combined with explicit feature co-occurrence restrictions allows a treatment of syncretisms in terms of morphological markedness. In the study of markedness within linguistic theory, there are important distinctions that govern where marked features may be avoided, neutralized (syncretism), or deleted (impoverishment). A crucial distinction made by Calabrese is between context-free vs. context-sensitive markedness. Thus, context-free markedness may ban/disprefer the value of a particular feature (e.g., [+location], shared by locative, ablative, and instrumental cases) everywhere within the grammar, while context-sensitive markedness may ban a feature value only within the context of others (e.g., [−location] is deleted when it co-occurs with [+peripheral] and second declension features).

The contributors to this section emphasize the organization of features in hierarchical and/or implicational relations among feature values. This representational perspective examplifies a possible answer to the inclusion characterizing which sets of features will be likely to form natural classes for identity effects.

---

[11] See Feigenson and Carey (2005) for a recent study of the prelinguistic represetation of plurality.

1.5 Sources of identity effects: Asymmetric dependence on a base

The third section includes two very different approaches to singling out a base of derivation, crucial under the rubric of the asymmetry question proposed above. The chapter by John Bailyn and Andrew Nevins includes a proposal that Russian nouns are based not on any single output form but rather on an abstract stem of derivation formed by a nominal root followed by a theme vowel. This move simplifies the otherwise puzzling derivation of the genitive plural. The chapter by Adam Albright includes a proposal that learners single out a base of derivation (a "kennform" in the sense of Wurzel (1989)), which is the information-theoretically most informative surface form, and use this as the basis for inflectional identity. The chapter by Donca Steriade provides a case study in the relation between the paradigmatic structure of the nominal case system and denominal derivational morphology. Elaborating on Albright's proposal, Steriade proposes that speakers make use of privileged members of the derived lexicon, "kennforms" in Wurzel (1989), and have access to potentially multiple bases from which identity effects derive.

Much recent literature has emphasized the output-oriented aspect of morphophonological computation (although this issue is independent of how much constraint interaction plays a role in the theory of grammar). In an output-oriented view, paradigms represent an "egalitarian" collection of output forms. This stands in contrast to a view of paradigms in which what binds all forms together is sharing a common base of derivation. In their attempt to explain a change in progress in Japanese, Ito and Mester (2004) employ this egalitarian property of paradigm organization, through a combination of allomorphic identity and anti-homophony as both globally computed over the verbal paradigm.

Ranuki is a process of *ra*-deletion, a spreading grammatical change in contemporary colloquial Japanese. Standard Japanese verbs can be divided into V-final and C-final verbs, e.g., *tabe* ('eat') and *tob* ('fly'). Suffixal endings show allomorphic distribution depending on whether the verb stem is V-final or C-final, as shown below:

(1.10)

		V-final	*C-final*
a.	present negative	V-nai	C-anai
b.	plain present	V-ru	C-u
c.	inchoative	V-joo	C-oo
d.	conditional	V-reba	C-eba
e.	causative	V-sase	C-ase
f.	passive	V-rare	C-are
g.	imperative	V-ro	C-e
h.	potential	V-rare- (V-re, colloq.)	C-e

Ranuki takes place in the potential form of the verb ((h.) above) so that standard *tabe-rare* surfaces instead as *tabe-re*. Ito and Mester (2004) propose to analyze this change as the promotion of an anti-homophony constraint (requiring paradigm contrast) that evaluates entire paradigms via pairwise comparison of the outputs of different cells in the paradigm. Thus, the constraint PARCONTRAST is violated by every phonologically identical (homophonous) pair.

As can be seen above, the potential and passive slots of V-final verbs are identical: both are *tabe-rare*. While in standard Japanese, PARCONTRAST is ranked lower than input-output faithfulness, the claim is that, in the colloquial grammar, PARCONTRAST has been promoted and leads to truncation of the suffix from *-rare* to *-re*.

In answering the "asymmetry" question posed earlier in this introduction, and in answering the question of why truncation is chosen to satisfy PAR-CONTRAST (as opposed to other phonological changes) to render the V-final potential *-(ra)re* different from the passive *-rare*, Ito and Mester propose a set of ALLOCORR constraints which enforce correspondence between allomorphs of the same morpheme.

The basic intuition behind this new constraint is that two allomorphs are 'better' the more similar they are. It is plain to see that in standard Japanese, the allomorphs *rare~e* for the V-final and C-final potential form are by far the worst pair with respect to ALLOCORR. By replacing the potential V-form *rare* with *re*, the Ranuki innovation of colloquial Japanese not only fixes the homophony violation with the passive but also reduces the distance between the V-final and C-final potential allomorphs (*re~e*). No other relevant phonological change would have resulted in a more optimal pair. Nor would have Ranuki in the passive resulted in fewer violations of ALLOCORR (*-re* would not be more similar to the existing C-final passive allomorph *-are* than the full form *-rare*, assuming that deletion and insertion are equal on this count). The asymmetry question is thus answered by inspecting the existing C-final allomorphs: the potential's C-final allomorph (*-e*) is the one that would best match a proposed modification of its corresponding V-form.

The inclusion question, however, is left open in Ito and Mester's paper. Note that the C-final allomorph for the potential remains identical to the C-final allomorph for the imperative. Why is Ranuki the only contrast-enforcing repair that occurs? Replacing C-final *-e* in the imperative with *-o* would both avoid a violation of this condition and would decrease the violation of ALLOCORR, as *-o* is more similar to the V-final imperative allomorph *-ro*. However, such a change does not occur.

In their evaluation of the constraint ALLOCORR, Ito and Mester argue for a view of the C-final vs. V-final allomorphs as a case of allomorph selection.

The traditional view is that in most cases (apart from the imperative and the potential) the relation between the two forms of each morpheme is purely phonological, involving deletion (e.g., Kuroda 1965 and McCawley 1968). However, this is not the case in the potential, where in standard Japanese there is genuine allomorphy between -*rare* and -*(r)e*. An alternative analysis of the change between standard Japanese and colloquial Japanese, then, would be loss of the -*rare* suffix for the potential; the rest is due to operation of the truncation rule at a morphophonological boundary (/tob-re/ → [tob-e]). Loss of this suffix (and an extension of the -*r*/ Ø alternation) results in the *re*~*e* pattern. This explanation would preserve the phonologically-based insight regarding the majority of the paradigm and avoid the asymmetry or inclusion questions, as there is no reference to homophony avoidance in the grammar itself.[12]

In fact, one might consider the consequences of modifying an output-oriented constraint explanation to paradigmatic effects; instead of negotation of anti-homophony across verb types and allomorphy correspondence within verb types at the same time, one could consider the broader consequences of assuming a single, distinguished base of derivation (as suggested above, where C-final and V-final forms in Japanese are derived from a single underlying form and Ranuki involves reanalysis of the underlying form).

The chapter by Albright in this volume represents an answer to the asymmetry question by postulating that the "most informative" member of a paradigm is the one to exert asymmetric force of identity effects. As most Optimality Theoretic implementations of output-output faithfulness focus on asymmetric effects in derivational morphology, Albright's contribution is an interesting application of the output-based model to inflectional morphology. It is important to point out that the model is one in which the base of inflectional identity has two properties: it is based on a surface form[13] and it is based on a single form. Albright considers the loss of final devoicing in nouns in Yiddish, explaining this as the result of the fact that learners took the plural form as the base of derivation. Thus, in reanalyzing the underlying

---

[12] There are various reasons that the allomorph -*rare* may have dropped out of the language. It could be that learners prefer to have all allomorphs derived by phonological rule and thus prefer to maintain a single -*re*, with a deletion applying. It also may be the case that the motivation for the loss of potential -*rare* lies in a learning algorithm which aims to avoid homophony in acquiring vocabulary items. Note however that in such an alternative analysis of Ranuki, the grammar itself would not enforce anti-homophony among affixes, nor would it include measurements of the similarity of allomorphs.

[13] Recalling the European Portuguese discussion, a surface form literally means the form that shows vowel reduction; that is, if the infinitive were chosen as the most informative form, Albright would assume that learners do not undo vowel reduction in the infinitive to construct an underlying representation with a nonreduced vowel.

form for the paradigm on the basis of the plural and requiring an asymmetric base, the voiced obstruent came to surface in the singular as well. In support of this, Albright also shows that idiosyncratic properties of the plural such as vowel length were imported to the singular as well. Crucial in this explanation, then, was the fact that Yiddish learners chose to organize inflectionally-related forms around a distinguished member, computed from a surface form (the plural), and through a single form alone. We will put aside the first hypothesis here for the present discussion, and pursue the learning consequences of adopting a base of inflection, abstract or otherwise, from a single form with a case at hand.

The idea that speakers cannot "cobble together" an underlying representation from multiple sources of information–or perhaps, to put it less strongly, that there is an increasing cost for each additional surface form that must be integrated in order to deduce an underlying form–is challenging to integrate with some cases in which analogical leveling and extension might occur. Consider again the case of analogical lowering in European Portuguese (EP), discussed above (cf. (1.5)).

(1.11) a. fugir [fuʒír] 'to flee'
        b. fuju [fúʒu] 'I flee'
        c. foges [fóʒəs] 'You flee'
        d. cf. fuga [fúga] 'fugue, flight' (noun)

Learning (1.11) requires extracting two kinds of information: height of the stem vowel, and conjugation class; however, these are not jointly found in one surface form. Given that neutralization to [u] occurs in the infinitive and 1sg of [−low] -*ir* verbs, one would expect the 2sg to become the UR, as it is least neutralized and hence most informative. Therefore, once the pattern in (1.11) develops in the language (due to extension), one would think that the UR would be the 2sg. However, if the base of derivation (or underlying form) were indeed /fɔg/, we would expect that the deverbal noun would become **fóga* as well, and perhaps that the orthography of the infinitive would restructure. The fact is that the [ɔ] in the 2sg form is unpredictable, and hence should become the source of a new underlying representation leading to restructuring of the infinitive (or the stem more generally) as **fog-ir*, counter to fact. Conversely, as there is no plausible rule elsewhere in EP which would take an underlying /u/ to [o] in the 2sg (or the 3sg or 3pl where this also happens), we are at an impasse with the single-base-of-derivation hypothesis. It seems that there must be two distinct bases: fug for the infinitive and related noun and fɔg for the 2sg. (Either of these could be the base for the 1sg, as this could result from independently attested vowel harmony raising [o] to [u] in 1sg). Renalysis of the 2sg as fɔg came from paying attention to the 2sg as a base, as it is an environment in which stress falls on the stem and neutralizing vowel harmony does not apply, and hence is most phonologically informative in general. However, the infinitive is also most informative in terms of conjugation class information, as it has unambiguously third conjugation ending. Albright's notion of a most informative base for underlying-form construction in a set of inflectional items thus raises important further questions for tradeoffs between maintaining phonological or morphological information.

The puzzle to the "single kennform" approach posed by the Portuguese data might be resolved in the architecture proposed in Donca Steriade's chapter, in her discussion of Romanian nominal morphophonology. Steriade focuses her discussion on a set of stems (e.g., K-stems) that end in a class of consonants subject to velar palatalization in the plural when followed by high front vowel declension endings (e.g., kolak, kolatʃ-i 'bagel sg., pl.'). However, these vowel endings are not present in all noun classes (e.g., fok, fok-uri 'fire sg., pl.'). Steriade demonstrates that, in denominal formations, palatalization only happens if it happened in the plural form (iŋ-kolatʃ-i 'to roll up'), either failing to happen or choosing another allomorph otherwise (in-fok-a 'to fire up'). This behavior is somewhat similar to what happens with English fricative-final nouns and irregular voicing in the plural and in the denominal, e.g., *shelf, shelves, to shelve*, where the plural and the denominal verb share a stem allomorph, although in Romanian the phenomenon is much more systematic and occurs for a variety of phonological processes, interacting in interesting ways with singular tantum nouns and proper names (which lack plurals altogether and hence cannot undergo palatalization in derived forms). Steriade develops an architecture where the computation of derivational phonology is inflection-dependent on a privileged set of derived surface forms. She suggests that one reason that in Romanian the plural is a privileged base-of-identity is due to the fact that it provides indispensable information about a noun's declension type, thus advancing further the possibility, raised above, that "informativeness" of what is chosen as an underlying form or as one of many split-bases involves morphological as well as phonological information.

The chapter by Bailyn and Nevins in this volume represents a different answer to the asymmetry question. They demonstrate that, counter to initial appearances, it is not an output form that is determining the identity effects but rather a more abstract, pre-derivational stem for affixation. Given that paradigmatic constraints are additions to the grammar, one wants to make sure that there is no alternative explanation for the phenomenon that does not call for "extra machinery", as discussed above with reference to the Ranuki example. Bailyn and Nevins take up the analysis of the Russian genitive plural. In traditional descriptions, this case stands out as the only plural case which exhibits gender-sensitive allomorphy. Moreover, the actual surface form of the plural genitive seems to correlate with the form of the nominative singular in what might be described as an anti-homophony relation. The authors propose a reanalysis of the case morphology in Russian that eliminates the need to refer to gender in the genitive plural and which demonstrates that the apparent relation between the nominative singular and the genitive plural are mere reflections of cyclic morphology (once one properly parses the nominal stem form). The new analysis provides a novel perspective on other puzzles in Russian such as paucal morphology.

1.6 Conclusions

The chapters in this collection thus implicate many key determinants of inflectional identity. The first is the learner's most basic tendency to avoid accidental homophony. The second is the role of subatomic identity at the level of abstract binary features. The third is the role of asymmetric bases that generate the stem for inflectional forms. Inflectional morphology lies at a nexus of many grammatical interfaces: phonological well-formedness, the reflex of syntactic agreement and concord operations, and, most crucially, the interface with the lexicon, an inherently associative data structure which attempts to optimize for access and storage. The patterns of inflectional identity constitute a rich and varied set of natural language phenomena without any single underlying cause. To paraphrase J. L. Borges, it is surely a labyrinth, but it is a labyrinth devised by human minds and a labyrinth destined to be deciphered by human minds.

References

Aguero-Bautista, Calixto (1998) 'Cyclic and identity effects in Spanish diminutives and augmentatives', Generals paper, MIT.

Aronoff, Mark (1994) *Morphology by Itself: Stems and Inflectional Classes*. Cambridge, MA: MIT Press.

Avery, Peter, and Keren Rice (1989) 'Segment structure and coronal underspecification'. *Phonology* 6: 179–200.

Bachrach, Asaf, and Michael Wagner (2006) 'Syntactically-driven cyclicity vs. output-output correspondence: The case of Adjunction in diminutive morphology', in *Penn Linguistics Colloquium Special Session on Distributed Morphology*.

Bertram, Raymond, Harald Baayen, and Robert Schreuder (2000) 'Effects of family size for complex words'. *Journal of Memory and Language* 42: 390–405.

Bierwisch, Manfred (1967) Syntacfic features in morphology: general problems of so-called pronominal inflection in German. In *To honour Roman Jakobson* The Hague: Mouton. 239–70.

Blevins, Juliette (2004) *Evolutionary Phonology*. Cambridge: Cambridge University Press.

Bonet, Eulalia (1991) Morphology after syntax: Pronominal clitics in Romance. Doctoral dissertation, MIT.

Calabrese, Andrea (1988) Towards a theory of phonological alphabets. Doctoral Dissertation, MIT.

Cameron-Faulkner, Thea, and Andrew Carstairs-McCarthy (2000) 'Stem alternants as morphological signata: Evidence from Blur avoidance in Polish'. *Natural Language and Linguistic Theory* 18: 813–35.

Carstairs, Andrew (1987) *Allomorphy in Inflexion*. London: Croom Helm.

Carstairs-McCarthy, Andrew (1994) 'Inflection classes, gender and the Principle of Contrast'. *Language* 70: 737–88.

Chomsky, Noam, and Morris Halle (1968) *The Sound Pattern of English*. New York: Harper and Row.

Crowhurst, Megan (1992) 'Diminutives and augmentatives in Mexican Spanish: A prosodic analysis'. *Phonology* 9: 221–53.

Di Sciullo, Anna Maria, and Edwin Williams (1987) *On the Definition of Word*. Cambridge, MA: MIT Press.

Downing, Laura, T. Alan Hall, and Renate Raffelsiefen (2005) *Paradigms in Phonology Theory*. Oxford: Oxford University Press.

Embick, David (2000) 'Features, syntax, and categories in the Latin perfect'. *Linguistic Inquiry* 31.2: 185–230.

Feigenson, Lisa, and Susan Carey (2005) 'On the limits of infants' quantification of small object arrays'. *Cognition* 97.3: 295–313.

Ferreira, Marcelo (2004) 'Diminutives in Brazilian Portuguese and output-output correspondence', presented at the 34th Linguistic Symposium of the Romance Languages, Salt Lake City, UT.

Greenberg, Joseph (1966) *Language Universals, with Special Reference to Feature Hierarchies*. Janua Linguarum, Series Minor, 59, The Hague: Mouton.

Hale, Mark, and Charles Reiss (2000) 'Substance abuse and dysfunctionalism: Current trends in phonology'. *Linguistic Inquiry* 31: 157–69.

Halle, Morris (1997) 'Impoverishment and fission', *PF: Papers at the Interface, MITWPL* 425–50.

Harley, Heidi, and Elizabeth Ritter (2002) 'Person and number in pronouns: A feature-geometric analysis'. *Language* 78.3: 482–526.

Harris, James W. (1974) 'Evidence from Portuguese for the "Elsewhere Condition" in phonology'. *Linguistic Inquiry* 5: 61–80.

—— (1991) 'The exponence of gender in Spanish'. *Linguistic Inquiry* 22: 27–62.

—— (1994) 'The OCP, Prosodic Morphology and Sonoran Spanish diminutives: A reply to Crowhurst'. *Phonology* 11: 179–90.

Haspelmath, Martin (2006) 'Against markedness (and what to replace it with)'. *Journal of Linguistics* 42.1: 25–70.

Hawkins, John A. (2004) *Efficiency and Complexity in Grammars*. Oxford: Oxford University Press.

Hayes, Bruce (1981) A metrical theory of stress rules. Doctoral dissertation, MIT.

—— Robert Kirchner, and Donca Steriade (2004) *Phonetically-Based Phonology*. Cambridge: Cambridge University Press.

Ito, Junko, and Armin Mester (2004) 'Morphological contrast and merger: *Ranuki* in Japanese'. *Journal of Japanese Linguistics* 20: 1–18.

Jaeggli, Osvaldo (1980) 'Spanish diminutives', in F. H. Nuessel, Jr (ed.), *Contemporary Studies in Romance Languages*, Indiana University Linguistics Club, pp. 142–58.

Kenstowicz, Michael (1996) 'Base identity and uniform exponence: Alternatives to cyclicity', in *Current Trends in Phonology: Models and Methods*, University of Salford Publications, pp. 363–93.

—— (2005) 'Paradigmatic uniformity and contrast', in *Paradigms in Phonological Theory*. Oxford: Oxford University Press, pp. 145–69.

—— and Charles Kisseberth (1977) *Topics in Generative Phonology*. New York: Academic Press.

Kuroda, Shige-Yuki (1965) Generative grammatical studies in the Japanese language. Doctoral dissertation, MIT.

Lee, Seung-Hwa (1999) 'Sobre a formação do diminutivo do português brasiliero'. *Revista de estudos da linguagem* 8.

Legate, Julie (2007) 'Morphological and abstract case'. *Linguistic Inquiry*.

Maiden, Martin (1991) *Interactive Morphology: Metaphony in Italian*. London: Routledge.

Mascarenhas, Salvador, Andrew Nevins, and Ashtamurty Killimangalam (2005) 'Exceptions as reanalysis in Portuguese vowel height alternations', presented at the Association for Portuguese Linguistics, Porto, Portugal.

McCarthy, John (2005) 'Optimal Paradigms', in *Paradigms in Phonology Theory*, Oxford: Oxford University Press, pp. 170–210.

McCawley, James D. (1968) *The Phonological Component of a Grammar of Japanese*. The Hague: Mouton.

Menuzzi, Sergio (1993) 'On the prosody of the diminutive alternation *-inho/-zinho* in Brazilian Portuguese', Ms., HIL/Leiden.

Müller, Gereon (2006) 'Notes on Paradigm Economy', in Gereon Müller and Jochen Trommer (eds.), *Linguistische Arbeits Berichte 84: Subanalysis of Argument Encoding in Distributed Morphology*. Institut für Linguistik, Universität Leipzig, pp. 161–95.

Noyer, Rolf (1992) Features, positions and affixes in autonomous morphological structure. Doctoral dissertation, MIT.

—— (1994) 'Paradigm structure constraints and lexical generative capacity', in *The Proceedings of NELS 24*. Amherst, MA: GLSA, pp. 427–41.

Paul, Hermann (1880) *Prinzipien der Sprachgeschichte*. Halle: Max Niemeyer.

Quicoli, Carlos (1990) 'Harmony, lowering, and nasalization in Brazilian Portuguese'. *Lingua* 80: 295–331.

Steriade, Donca (1999) 'Lexical conservatism in French adjectival liaison', in *Formal Perspectives in Romance Linguistics*. John Benjamins, 243–70.

—— (2002) 'Well-formedness conditions vs. lexical generalizations: The morphophonology of Romance agentives', paper presented at NELS 33, Cambridge, MA.

Stump, Gregory (2001) *Inflectional Morphology: A Theory of Paradigm Structure*. Cambridge: Cambridge University Press.

Tucker, Emily (2000) Multiple allomorphs in the formation of the Italian agentive. MA thesis, UCLA.

Vinka, Mikael (2001) 'Impoverishment as feature deletion: Dual and plural agreement in Sámi'. *Lund University Working Papers in Linguistics* 48: 183–91.

Wetzels, Leo (1995) 'Mid-vowel alternations in the Brazilian Portuguese verb'. *Phonology* 12: 281–304.

Williams, Edwin (1981) 'On the notions "lexically related" and "head of a word"'. *Linguistic Inquiry* 12.2: 245–74.

—— (1994) 'Remarks on lexical knowledge'. *Lingua* 92: 7–34.

Wunderlich, Dieter (1996) 'Minimalist morphology: The role of paradigms', in G. Booij and J. van Marle (eds.), *Yearbook of Morphology 1995*. Dordrecht: Kluwer, pp. 93–114.

Wurzel, Wolfgang (1989) *Inflectional Morphology and Naturalness*. Dordrecht: Kluwer.

2

Paradigms (Optimal and otherwise): A case for skepticism

JONATHAN DAVID BOBALJIK*

This chapter aims to contribute to the debate on the status of inflectional paradigms in grammatical theory, with special reference to the theory of Optimal Paradigms (OP, McCarthy, 2005), a particular version of Paradigm Uniformity. OP proposes that certain systematic phonological differences between nouns and verbs should be analyzed as arising from contingent facts about the individual affixes making up the nominal and verbal inflectional paradigms. I argue here that the Arabic data presented in OP does not support the OP model (as against, for example, cyclic alternatives) and that consideration of similar phenomena in Itelmen, a language with richer inflectional paradigms, suggests that it is morphosyntactic category, and not paradigm properties, that determines phonological behavior.

2.1 Introduction

The broad research question in which the following remarks are situated asks: Does grammar ever (need to) make direct reference to the structure or arrangement of information in a paradigm? In other words, do paradigms, as structures in anything like their traditional sense, play a role in (synchronic) grammatical analysis beyond being simply a convenient descriptive device for tabulating various facts? These questions are in turn connected to the issue of locality in grammar–the degree to which the system must consider

* For discussion of the material presented here and related ideas I am particularly grateful to John Alderete, Seth Cable, Michael Kenstowicz, Alec Marantz, John McCarthy, Glyne Piggott, Susi Wurmbrand, a reviewer for this volume, audience members at Rutgers University and at the MIT Paradigms Workshop, and course participants at the 2005 LSA Summer Institute. Portions of the research reported here have been supported by grants from FCAR (2002-NC-75019) and SSHRC (410-2002-0581). I am especially grateful to the members of the Itelmen community who have shared their language with me.

alternative derivations/representations in evaluating the well-formedness of a given derivation or expression. In previous work, I have attempted to articulate a skeptical position regarding the status of paradigms as domains for the operation of synchronic grammar, addressing arguments from syncretism (Bobaljik 2002b) and from morphosyntactic generalizations involving agreement and verb movement (Bobaljik 2003). In this chapter, I extend this perspective to another aspect of morphophonological relations among words, specifically the type of paradigm-internal identity effect exemplified in the Optimal Paradigms (OP) model of McCarthy (2005) (see also Cable 2004).

In OP, McCarthy proposes that noun-verb asymmetries in morpheme structure constraints in Classical Arabic are epiphenomenal and certain phonological differences in the syllabification of nouns and verbs are the result of accidental, emergent properties of the classes of inflectional affixes with which nouns and verbs may combine. The specific analysis that McCarthy presents is claimed to be crucially dependent on the traditional notion of an inflectional paradigm. Constraints on the syllabification of one inflected form exert a synchronic influence on the syllabification of other forms in the paradigm (but not beyond). Put differently, in evaluating the well-formedness of a given word, the grammar must consider not only the pieces of that word and how they are combined but must also evaluate the phonological well-formedness of other, related words, specifically all and only the other inflected forms that share a stem–the traditional paradigm. McCarthy's proposals thus have the right form to constitute an argument that the paradigm is "a real object, and not the epiphenomenal product of various rules" (Williams 1994: 22).

In section 2.2, I argue that McCarthy's work fails to make the case for the necessity of a paradigm-based analysis on the Arabic data he presents. I argue that key asymmetries that underpin the analysis appear to be inaccurately stated and that reference to a base even within inflected forms both underlies a potential alternative (2.3.2.1) and is independently necessary under McCarthy's own account (2.3.2.2) (see also Albright 2002). In section 2.4, I turn away from the narrow discussion of the analysis of Arabic and to a discussion of one leading idea behind OP, namely the proposal that phonological differences between classes of stems may be the by-product of contingent properties of the affixes making up the paradigms in which those stems participate. Arabic, I contend, is a poor language to make this point, since its inflectional paradigms are extremely uniform, and thus the contribution of the morphosyntactic category (noun or verb) is hard to tease apart from the contribution of the affixes. I therefore offer a detailed discussion of syllabification contrasts in Itelmen, where the issues are similar (noun-verb asymmetries in cluster tolerance at juncture) but where the phonological asymmetries track morphosyntactic category and not the kind of accidental properties of individual paradigms that OP would expect. While the issue cannot be resolved from two languages alone, the considerations below, I submit, should at the least raise questions about the viability of the leading idea that OP expresses. Specifically, I contend that skepticism regarding the role of paradigms in the analysis of these facts, in the sense of OP or otherwise, is warranted.

2.2 OP and morphological relatedness

2.2.1 *Locality and derivational history*

It has long been recognized that morphological structure and relatedness play a role in phonology. A typical example, given by McCarthy, is the difference in syllabification in the English pair *lightning* (two syllables) and *lightening* (three syllables). If it is assumed that both derive from the same segmental input, then one of these should be the optimal syllabification, the other not. For example, if the parse *light.ning* is taken to be the optimal syllabification, why should the trisyllabic parse, with syllabic *n*, be possible, let alone obligatory, for the gerund *lightening*?

A derivational approach to this question would build on the observation that *lightening* is derived from the verb *lighten*. In the verbal form, the parse of *n* as syllabic is required, and this syllabification is inherited by the derived form. By contrast, since *lightning* is not (synchronically) derived from *lighten*, there is no influence from the verb and the optimal surface syllabification is chosen. In this sketch of an account, morphological relatedness effects reflect the derivational history of a word. Phonological similarity among morphologically-related words is the product of the inheritance of prior structure. This is, of course, the familiar notion of the phonological *cycle* (Chomsky and Halle 1968). This view is asymmetric and privileges the notion "derived from". Phonological constraints on the base form may influence the derived form but not the other way around. The same asymmetry is recast in monostratal OT as *Base Priority* within *Trans-Derivational Correspondence Theory* (TCT, Benua 2000). The cycle and Base Priority can be seen as expressing an idea that I will refer to as the *Local Determination Hypothesis* (LDH), given in (2.1).[1]

---

[1] The phrasing of (2.1) glosses over the treatment of non-additive derivation, such as truncation. Benua discusses examples of English nickname formation (for some varieties) where the derived form contains only a subset of the base, a key example being the English (varietal) nickname *L[æ]r*, derived from *L[æ]rry*, preserving the vowel from the base even though such a vowel is otherwise prohibited in

(2.1) *Local Determination Hypothesis*

To predict the surface form of a word, it is sufficient to know:

- the constituent pieces of that word.
- their morphological arrangement/hierarchical structure = derivational history.
- the phonology of the language.

In putting forward the OP proposal, McCarthy contends that the LDH is false. Specifically, while McCarthy accepts the asymmetry inherent in the notion "derived from" for understanding identity effects in derivational morphology, he claims that "[i]nflectional paradigms are different from derivational hierarchies; in paradigms, all members are co-equal in their potential to influence the surface phonology of other members of the paradigm" (OP: 174). In other words, a central thesis of OP is that the surface form of a word is not locally determinable in the sense of (2.1). In addition to the information listed there, the following is necessary.

(2.2) The phonological characteristics of the other members of that word's paradigm.

Put differently, in order to predict the phonological form of some combination Stem+Affix$_1$, it is necessary to know the phonological forms of the set of words {Stem+Affix$_2$, ... Stem+Affix$_n$} where Affix$_2$, ... Affix$_n$ are the other inflectional affixes that the stem could have combined with. It is this proposal that requires the notion of paradigm in synchronic grammar.

2.2.2 *OP–the proposal and the evidence*

McCarthy's primary evidence for OP comes from morpheme structure constraints in Classical Arabic, specifically restrictions on the templates of verb and noun stems. The basic workings of the theory can be illustrated with one of the examples McCarthy considers, namely restrictions at the right edge of the stem (other examples will be discussed below). Here, one finds an asymmetry between nouns and verbs. Although there are some 15 templates (conjugations) for verbal stems (OP: 178), these templates all share the property that they end in CVC]. No verbal stem template ends in CV:C] or CVCC]. Noun stems, on the other hand, are not subject to this restriction. Although there are significantly fewer noun stem templates than verb stem templates (OP: 209), noun stem templates are more diverse at the right edge and may freely end in CVC], CV:C] or CVCC]. OP is a proposal to derive this difference from

---

a monosyllabic, *r*-final word. The key aspect of the LDH is the asymmetry, hence (2.1) could be readily rephrased.

an independent difference between nouns and verbs, namely the inventories of inflectional suffixes with which noun and verb stems combine. Nominal inflectional suffixes are all vowel-initial. By contrast, the inflectional suffixes with which verbs combine are drawn from a mixed array of V-initial and C-initial morphemes.

The theory that links these observations is the following. OP constraints are a species of output-output faithfulness constraints that place a premium on a stem keeping a constant shape throughout its inflectional paradigm. OP constraints take entire inflectional paradigms as inputs and incur violations whenever the stem shows an alternation.[2] OP will be satisfied by those stem shapes that are able to freely combine with all relevant affixes. For verbs, which must combine with both V- and C-initial suffixes, this restricts possible stems to those ending in CVC], whereas nouns need only combine with V-initial suffixes and thus are freer in their stem shapes.

To see this theory at work, consider a hypothetical Arabic verb stem ending in CV:C], /faʕaːl/, with a long vowel in the second syllable. Given independently motivated constraints of Arabic phonology, such a stem could surface faithfully before a vowel-initial suffix (such as masculine singular-*a*), yielding *faʕaːl-a*. However, before a consonant-initial suffix (such as second person feminine singular *-ti*), the result of simple concatenation would be **faʕaːl-ti*. This form has a super-heavy medial syllable, something that is categorically disallowed by Arabic phonology. Various alternative candidates would be possible, such as *faʕal-ti*, with vowel-shortening in the closed syllable, and some such candidate should emerge as optimal. Yet whatever "repair" is chosen to avoid the super-heavy medial syllable, that repair will introduce an alternation into the surface form of the stem in the paradigm: *faʕaːl* ~ *faʕal*. And it is precisely such alternations that a highly ranked OP faithfulness constraint proscribes. Parallel considerations apply to stems ending in CVCC], which would also yield an unsyllabifiable sequence at juncture with C-initial suffixes. Because verbal inflection contains C-initial suffixes, only stems ending in CVC] may surface uniformly throughout the

---

[2] Note that under McCarthy's proposal, OP effects are limited to the inflectional paradigm, understood in its traditional sense, i.e., the set of realizations of a single lexeme for the various morphosyntactic features it may bear. This limitation to paradigms distinguishes McCarthy's proposal from other output-output faithfulness proposals such as *Uniform Exponence* (Kenstowicz 1997), *Anti-Allomorphy* (Burzio 1996), and *Lexical Conservatism* (Steriade 1998), some of which also use the term "paradigm uniformity". For these latter authors, like McCarthy, morphological relatedness effects are not confined to the relation "derived from" but unlike McCarthy are also not confined to the paradigm in its traditional sense. For Steriade, for example, relatedness effects extend to "a set of words sharing a morpheme ... or a set of phrases sharing a word" (Steriade 2000). The restriction to something like the inflectional paradigm is crucial to McCarthy's analysis (see section 2.3.2.2 below for discussion), and as my narrow interests concern the nature of paradigms, I will not discuss the other proposals here.

paradigm. And thus only such stems are permitted. For nouns, by contrast, all inflectional suffixes are V-initial; the final C of the stems is thus always syllabifiable as an onset, and the issue of medial super-heavy syllables does not arise. Stem shapes ending in CV:C] and CVCC] are possible alongside CVC].

There is in fact one further step in the theory, which McCarthy dubs the logic of *Stampean occultation*. The synchronic grammar as just sketched does not in fact exclude verb stems ending in underlying CV:C] or CVCC]. What the grammar forces is, in effect, under- or overapplication of the repair. For example, highly-ranked constraints of Arabic phonology force shortening in closed syllables; thus underlying /faʕa:l/ must surface as *faʕal-* before a C-initial suffix *(faʕal-ti)*. OP then "transmits" this shortened form throughout the paradigm; underlying /faʕa:l/ must also surface as *faʕal-* before V-initial suffixes *(faʕal-a)*, the motivation for shortening here not lying within this particular form but rather in the need to be consistent throughout the paradigm. The result is complete neutralization: underlying /faʕa:l/ (or /faʕl/) would always surface as *faʕal-*, and the surface forms would be indistinguishable from those of underlying /faʕal/. Thus, McCarthy suggests that since the child could never distinguish underlying CVC] stems from underlying CV:C] or CVCC], there would be no motivation to set up distinct lexical representations, and only one of these stem shapes will thus be usable. The logic of occultation is not relevant in the next section, but I will come back to it again in section 2.3.2.2, suggesting that the argument is incomplete in an important way.

To summarize, the apparent success of OP in explaining the noun-verb asymmetry in stem template inventories constitutes the primary argument against the LDH in (2.1), and in favor of the richer set of assumptions incorporating (2.2). The key piece of the argument is the claim of directionality, namely that the phonological influence runs *from* inflected forms *to* the stems contained in them and is thus not statable via the "derived from" relationship. The form **faʕa:l-a* is excluded as an inflected form of a verb, not because anything is locally wrong with that form but because that form implies a stem shape /faʕa:l/ and that stem shape is not combinable with certain other affixes. A further set of considerations (touched on below) leads McCarthy to propose (as noted above) that the deviations from "derived from" influences lie solely within the domain of the inflectional paradigm. This further step constitutes the argument in favor of paradigms. In the next sections, I address these in turn, showing that the key evidence for directionality, and for paradigms, are not established in the OP work.

2.3 Stems, bases, and morphemes

2.3.1 *Directionality: Open and closed*

The logic of OP uses contingent phonological properties of inflectional morphemes as a class to predict the properties of stem shape templates. Because there are C-initial verbal inflectional suffixes, verbal stems may not end in CV:C] or CVCC]. Of course, for this analysis to work the shapes of the inflectional affixes must be known first, and McCarthy states that these must simply be stipulated. Relevant discussion is in footnote 13 of his work, where the question is attributed to Linda Lombardi. I repeat the note here.

> This analysis, then, uses the form of the inflectional morphemes to predict properties of the stem templates. Why should the explanation go this way? That is, why stipulate the form of the inflectional morphemes and then use that to explain the stem templates, instead of stipulating the stem templates and using them to explain the inflectional morphemes? The inflectional morphemes are a closed class and they must be listed in any case, but the stems are an open class. The grammar, then, is responsible for explaining which stem shapes are and are not permitted, but it is not responsible for explaining why the handful of noun inflections are all vowel-initial—this is just an accident. (OP: 184, n. 13)

This paragraph goes directly to the heart of the argument for directionality. The key argument for OP is that the Arabic examples are not base-prioritizing but that the shape of a stem is constrained by properties of the range of affixes which may be added to it. The central argument would be obviated if the stem templates were stipulated, and the influence runs outwards, from stems to affixes, consistent with base priority. As stated in the passage above, McCarthy's argument for the direction of influence from inflected forms to stems relies on an asymmetry in open versus closed classes. I contend, though, that this argument is flawed and that the key asymmetry is not there. Specifically, the morphemes over which the structural constraints in question are stated (the stems) form no more of an open class than the inflectional morphemes they combine with. McCarthy's error in the quote above lies in not distinguishing the stems from the constituent morphemes that make up the stems.

A classic insight of autosegmental phonology regarding root and pattern morphology (McCarthy 1981; 1985), now standard textbook fare, recognizes that the stems are morphologically complex objects consisting of at least three distinct morphemes: a root (three consonants in the basic case), a vocalic melody (expressing aspect and voice), and a stem template (CVC pattern). Crucially, under this analysis, the template itself is a distinct morpheme. While the roots form an open class, the stem-forming morphemes (the templates) do not; they consist of a closed class of morphemes and, in fact, a rather small class (15 for the verbs and 7 for the nouns, OP: 209).

This idea is partially illustrated here. The table in (2.3) gives a sampling of stem forms, with the model root *k-t-b*, showing how, in addition to the root consonants, the vowels, and prefixes, the arrangement of consonants itself is a minimal unit of sound:meaning correspondence, i.e., a morpheme. In this case, the "meaning" is the *binyan* or conjugation, indicated by roman numerals in the table, where different conjugations are associated with different meanings such as causative and reciprocal, as indicated.[3] For example, the pattern CVCCVC marks the second conjugation (causative), independent of the choice of root consonant, vocalic melody, and prefixes.

(2.3)		PERFECTIVE		IMPERFECTIVE	
		ACTIVE	PASSIVE	ACTIVE	PASSIVE
I		katab	kutib	aktub	uktab
II (Causative)		kattab	kuttib	ukattib	ukattab
III (Reciprocal)		kaatab	kuutib	ukaatib	ukaatab
IV (Causative)		ʔaktab	ʔuktib	ʔaktib	ʔaktab

The schema in (2.4) illustrates the association of the various morphemes to construct example stems.

(2.4)   k   t   b   'write'   k   t   b   'write'
        | | | | /\ |
        C V C V C   'present'/conj 1   C V C C VC   'cause to X'/conj 2
          \ / | |
           a   'active'   u   i   'passive'

Thus, even laying aside the vocalism, an inflected verb has at least three morphemes: the root, the conjugation (template), and the inflectional affixes, as in (2.5), where μ stands for "morpheme", and linear order is abstracted away from.[4]

---

[3] The table is taken from a larger table in McCarthy (1981: 385), with approximate meanings from McCarthy (1993: 16). John McCarthy (personal communication 2004) points out that the association of templates with meaning is a property of the verbal system but not of the nominal system. Thus, nominal templates, qua morphemes, would appear to have a role similar to the theme vowels of Indo-European languages, marking membership in a particular inflectional class. This does not bear on the point made in the text, though, so long as these are formally treated as morphemes distinct from the root. See also the next footnote.

[4] In later treatments, such as McCarthy (1993) and Ussishkin (2000), it is proposed that there is only a single template for the verbs (CVCVC) and that all other stem shapes are derived by affixation to this template. If anything, this strengthens the remarks made here. Restrictions on stem shape are

(2.5) $[\ [\ [\ \mu_1 \ ] \ \mu_2 \ ] \ \mu_3 \ ]$
          $[\ [\ [\ \text{ROOT} \ ] \ \text{CONJ} \ ] \ \text{INFLECTION} \ ]$

Thus, when McCarthy talks about "stem shape" he is really talking about the shape of a particular morpheme, μ_2, the morpheme that combines with a root to yield a stem (perhaps something like the "little" v and n morphemes of Marantz 2001; see also Arad 2003 for a treatment of Hebrew root and pattern morphology in these terms). It is the roots that constitute an open class, while the class of stem-formatives (whether seen as templates or affixes) is not only closed but rather small, as noted already. The key asymmetry between open and closed classes that McCarthy appeals to is thus not there. At best, there are two closed classes of affixes, those at μ_2 and μ_3 in (2.5). Even if it were granted that the members of one class should be stipulated and constraints on the other thereby learned (I will challenge this below), McCarthy's argument does not answer Lombardi's question, and thus does not establish the necessity of inwards-running influence.[5] The work does not provide evidence for one of its key conclusions–namely, the view that the form of the stem is dependent upon the variety of inflectional affixes that stem might combine with, i.e., (2.2).

2.3.2 *On bases*

McCarthy appears to have another reason in mind, in addition to that just cited, for rejecting a base-prioritizing approach to the Arabic morpheme structure constraints. Specifically, he notes the inapplicability of Benua's TCT/Base Priority model to these cases on the following grounds.

TCT is not applicable to inflectional paradigms because it is an asymmetric, base-prioritizing theory ... In TCT, the base is the first step in the recursive evaluation. The derived form, which is the next step in the recursive evaluation, is obtained from the

morpheme structure constraints holding over a small class of morphemes that are added to roots, not the roots themselves. Also relevant here is a body of psycholinguistic evidence for the independent morphemic status of templates; see for example Boudelaa and Marslen-Wilson (2004; 2005), brought to my attention by Alec Marantz.

[5] Elsewhere in the work, McCarthy suggests that "OP supports the minimalist goals of Generalized Template Theory (GTT), which seeks to eliminate templates and similar stipulations from linguistic theory, replacing them with independently motivated constraints" (OP: 171). This might be construed as an argument that the templates should be derived, and the identity of the (inflectional) affixes stipulated. At best, OP purports to derive the "template of templates" from independent constraints (i.e., the grammar sets bounds on possible templates), but OP does not derive the identity of individual templates and thus does not in any way obviate the need to state those templates as the individual morphemes (either as templates, or as affixes to a basic template, as in the references cited in the previous footnote), expressing conjugation classes and meanings such as "causative" as noted above. While some aspects (such as the ban on final clusters) may be explained within the system, OP does not eliminate templates as such, and the shape of individual pairings of sound (template) and meaning (conjugation class etc.) must still be learned on an item-by-item basis.

base by applying a morphological operation, such as affixation. Inflectional paradigms have no base in this sense...(OP: 172)

In the Arabic cases that McCarthy presents, inflected forms are obtained from an identifiable morphological unit (the stem) by applying a morphological operation, namely affixation. So why is the stem not the base of inflection (see also Albright 2002, this volume)? As I understand it, the implicit reason that Base Priority is rejected for inflection is that Base Priority is held to be only applicable when the base is an independently occurring word (see Kenstowicz 1997; Cable 2004; and section 2.4.2.2 below for criticism). Thus, derivation (as opposed to inflection) is derivational, proceeding in a sequential fashion and establishing outputs that OO faithfulness constraints may refer to. But inflection is not. Phonology does not evaluate inflected forms in this step-wise fashion. Thus, the stem does not correspond to the output of an evaluation, and cannot be the target of a base-prioritizing OO faithfulness constraint. Put differently, intermediate stages of a derivation that do not happen to be expressible as words in their own right have no tangible status and cannot serve as the target of correspondence constraints.

The assumption that inflectional paradigms have no base could provide a theory-internal motivation for rejecting a base-prioritizing (i.e., cyclic) analysis of the Arabic facts, thus perhaps deflecting the criticism of the previous section. I believe there is good reason, though, to challenge the assumption that inflectional paradigms have no base in the relevant sense. On my reading, McCarthy in fact must assume, internal to the OP approach, that Arabic verbs do have a base in precisely the sense that is needed for Base-Priority, a view that is supported by relatively simple considerations from other languages. The considerations that lead to this view also point to a flaw in the appeal to Stampean occultation as mentioned above. I treat these in turn, with reference to the OP paper, and return to the general issue of bases again in section 2.4.2.

2.3.2.1 *Arabic bases*   In order to discuss the issue of bases, we must introduce another set of noun-verb template shape asymmetries discussed by McCarthy, this time at the left edge of the stem. Here, the nouns are more restricted than the verbs: noun stem templates may not begin with a cluster, while verb stem templates may. This difference is related (under OP) to the fact that there are CV-inflectional prefixes for verbs (which allow a cluster-initial consonant to be syllabified as a coda), but there are no inflectional prefixes for nouns.

What is important for present concerns is an exception to these restrictions, noted (without discussion) by McCarthy. Specifically, the ban on stem-initial clusters in nouns does not hold of nominalized verbs (OP: 188). These may have [CCV-initial stems. McCarthy shows that OP-faithfulness, combined with the inventory of nominal inflection in the language, should render such stems unusable, all else being equal. Hence, there must be some aspect of the grammar which allows the noun stem to inherit a property of the verb stem across the category-changing derivational morphology.

Within McCarthy's assumptions, there appears to be only one candidate for the force that has this effect, namely Base Priority, adopted by McCarthy elsewhere in the work for morphological relatedness effects in derivation (OP: 174). The implicit logic is relatively clear–initial [CCV is permitted in verb stems by virtue of the inventory of verbal inflection (via the logic of OP). Base Priority overrides the general restrictions on nouns that ban [CCV stems by allowing deverbal nouns to inherit phonological characteristics of their verbal base. The problem, though, is that this requires that the verb *stem* (i.e., devoid of inflectional morphology and not constituting a legitimate output in its own right) serve as a base for the computation of Base Priority.

From a derivational perspective, this should be unsurprising. Derivation often runs on stems, even in highly inflecting languages where the stems may not surface as independent words. German strong verbs provide a simple illustration. Verbs like *sprechen* 'to speak' (strong verbs with mid vowels) have the basic inflectional paradigm in (2.6). Note that the stem is *sprech-*, with the mid vowel *e*; this must be the underlying form in order to predict the other forms, such as the high vowel *i* in the second and third persons singular (and the imperative).[6]

(2.6) German   *sprech-en* 'speak-INFIN'
also *be-sprech-en* 'discuss', *(sich) ver-sprech-en* 'misspeak', etc.

	PRESENT		PAST		PARTICIPLE
	SG	PL	SG	PL	
1PSN	sprech-e	sprech-en	sprach	sprach-en	ge-sproch-en
2PSN	sprich-st	sprech-t	sprach-st	sprach-t	
3PSN	sprich-t	sprech-en	sprach	sprach-en	
Imperative:		sprich			

Although the stem is readily identifiable as *sprech-*, this stem does not form a word on its own. For strong verbs of this sort, exactly those members of the inflectional paradigm that have-Ø affixes, namely the 3sg/1sg simple past and the imperative, undergo obligatory stem vowel changes.

---

[6] Not all aspects of the vowel quality in the past and participle forms are predictable from the vowel quality of the stem alone, though there are a variety of sub-regularities. For evidence (compelling in my view) that the infinitive/present stem is the basic form, from which the others are derived, see Wiese (2004; 2005).

Despite the fact that the verb stem never surfaces as a word on its own, it is this stem which forms the base for derivation, as shown in (2.7).

(2.7)   [[Be-sprech]-ung]   'meeting, discussion' (nominalization -*ung*)
        [[Ver-sprech]-er]   'slip of tongue' (nominalization -*er*)

The same point can be made with compounding. Thus *essen* 'to eat' and *treffen* 'to meet' conjugate like *sprechen* in all relevant respects. Like *sprechen*, the stem never surfaces as a word in its own right, yet it is the stem that is the basis for compound formation, as shown in (2.8).

(2.8)   Ess-lokal   'eating-place'   *ess   Imperative *iss*,   Past *ass*.
        Treff-punkt   'meeting-point'   *treff   Imperative *triff*,   Past *traff*.

If identity effects in derivation are the result of Base Priority enforcing identity to a base, then it would seem we must conclude that the verb stem is an accessible base in whatever sense is relevant. If correspondence theory necessarily relies on actual outputs (i.e. words) for the running of Base Priority, then such an approach should not be able to enforce identity effects in deverbal derivation in languages like Arabic and German. Although one may avoid an appeal to Base Priority in the analysis of German (simple IO faithfulness may suffice), for Arabic, Base Priority is crucial, since it is only Base Priority that allows the deverbal nouns to escape an otherwise general ban applying to noun templates.

Thus, it seems that within McCarthy's own data, there is indeed a base in the verb in precisely the sense necessary for Base Priority to apply in deverbal derivation, shielding the deverbal nouns from constraints that apply to other noun stems. Yet if there is a base for the verb, then it cannot be the absence of a base alone that triggers OP effects.

2.3.2.2 *Bases and Stampean occultation*   At this point, I would like to return briefly to the logic of Stampean occultation (see section 2.2.2). Here, too, I suggest that faithfulness to a base must play an important role in verbal paradigms, despite McCarthy's claim to the contrary. Recall that the logic of Stampean occultation runs, in essence, as follows.

The prohibition of CV:C] (and CVCC]) verbal stem templates is not a matter of synchronic phonology as such. Rather, a CV:C] stem would be forced to undergo vowel shortening before C-initial suffixes. A highly ranked OP constraint enforces uniformity of stem shape throughout the paradigm and thus forces overapplication of this shortening. This overapplication yields absolute neutralization with CVC] stems throughout the entire paradigm. The grammar alone does not exclude CV:C] stems but, never being distinguishable from CVC] stems, they would be unusable. As McCarthy puts it:

Though the underlying form *fa ʕa:l* is in principle possible . . . , learners will never be motivated to set it up as an actual lexical item because it is hidden or 'occulted' by the actually occurring *fa ʕal*, with which it always neutralizes. (OP: 181)

Recall, though, that OP restricts comparison to the members of an inflectional paradigm. Thus, neutralization forced by OP will not be sufficient to ensure true absolute neutralization but only neutralization within the paradigm. The logic of OP dictates that *fa ʕa:l* and *fa ʕal* neutralize throughout the inflectional paradigm but the distinction could emerge in the context of derivational morphology. It seems that such a situation should not be excluded in principle. Consider, for example, the English verbs *dam* (to block a river) and *damn* (to condemn to hell). The two are identical throughout the meager inflectional paradigm of English: [dæm], [dæmiŋ], etc., (note that the present participle is not *dam*[n]*ing*), yet a difference emerges in derivational contexts; compare "a *dammable* river" [m] versus "a *damnable* wizard" [mn] (possible, if stilted), also *damnation* [mn], etc. Assuming this example can be shown to generalize, it shows that absolute neutralization in inflectional paradigms is alone not sufficient to trigger occultation. Derivational morphology may reveal underlying differences that are neutralized throughout a paradigm. In theory, then, the argument in OP is incomplete. It should be possible for verbs to have underlying CV:C] and CVCC] final templates, where the underlying difference from a CVC] template is revealed only in nominalizations. In order for Stampean occultation to apply, McCarthy must assume that the uniformity of the stem shape throughout the paradigm is faithfully transmitted into derived forms as well. Once again, the only engine in OP that can achieve this is Base Priority but that engine requires that the verb have an identifiable base, in the relevant sense.

2.3.3 *Section summary*

To summarize the discussion of directionality, I have presented evidence that McCarthy's two arguments against local determination are at best incomplete. In particular, the work does not, if I am right, provide crucial evidence that it is the inventory of inflectional affixes that determines the shape of the stem template-forming morphemes, as opposed to the other way around. The argument from open and closed classes relied on taking the stem to be a basic morphological unit, rather than recognizing that stem-forming templates are morphemes in their own right. In addition, I have argued that inflectional paradigms must have a base in whatever sense is relevant to Base Priority, within the logic of the system. Hence the general argument that Base Priority (i.e., cyclicity) cannot be used to explain morphological relatedness effects in inflection appears to rest on a questionable premise. For the reasons stated above, I conclude that the crucial ingredients of an argument that any relation beyond "derived from" is necessary are not established in the OP work. In the next section, I leave the specifics of that work and turn to considerations at a more general level.[7]

2.4 Itelmen and the source of noun-verb asymmetries

A major aspect of OP, brought out nicely in the discussion in Cable (2004), is the idea that phonological differences among nouns and verbs should not be described by allowing the phonology to make reference to these categories but instead should be derived from contingent facts about nouns and verbs and their associated inflectional morphology.[8] We have just seen above how the theory is supposed to apply to Classical Arabic. Under McCarthy's treatment, accidental properties of the different classes of inflectional morphemes effect restrictions on the stems with which they combine. The explanatory work is being done by paradigm membership. Any appeal to the categories noun and verb is relevant only indirectly, inasmuch as it determines such paradigm membership.

This conception of the grammar should lead us to expect that when inflectional class and morphosyntactic category diverge, OP effects should track paradigm membership and not morphosyntactic category. We might call this the *thesis of category-neutral phonology* (TCNP). The real interest in OP will lie in testing the TCNP not against Arabic (which has remarkably uniform paradigms) but instead against languages where the relevant phonological

[7] In Bobaljik (2002a), I suggested that the core Arabic facts may be accounted for under the stipulation that syllabification in verbs proceeds cyclically, where syllabification in nouns is non-cyclic. Such an account may describe the differences, in particular, in enforcing more stringent syllabification requirements on verb stems. As McCarthy notes (OP: 199) this account essentially stipulates the noun-verb difference in the grammar, whereas, he contends, OP deduces it. The discussion above shows that this is only partly correct. All approaches considered have some stipulated difference between nouns and verbs, from which the remaining observed differences follow. The question is whether the OP approach is the right kind of stipulation—arbitrary properties of classes of morphemes. I will argue in the next sections that this is not obviously the right kind of stipulation and that the categorical distinction is empirically a better one. Positing that verbs are syllabified cyclically and that nouns are not has the added benefit that it will provide for a uniform analysis of the Arabic facts and those from Itelmen to be presented below. Why might this be the case? One speculation, capitalizing on recent ideas in syntax, is that the cyclic nature of verbal derivation arises because inflected verbs are multiphasal (in terms suggested by Chomsky 2001) while nouns are not. It is not clear that this will work, but as a research strategy it seems to me to be a coherent alternative direction to pursue (cf. Barragan and Newell 2003 on Cupeño).

[8] As a reviewer points out, defending the TCNP in general would appear to be a fairly significant undertaking in light of a large array of descriptive differences among categories in many languages, such as differences in stress assignment. See Smith (2001) for a survey.

differences among paradigms cross-cut the morphosyntactic categories. For example, imagine a language like Arabic but in which feminine nouns had a consonant-initial inflectional suffix or in which intransitive verbs (but not transitives) had only vowel-initial inflection. The expectations should be clear: feminine nouns should be restricted to CVC] stem templates, while intransitive verbs should not. I will argue in the remaining sections that Itelmen shows the right kinds of idiosyncratic vagaries among paradigms but that, nevertheless, the phonology neatly tracks the noun-verb divide rather than the contingent properties that the OP intuition would lead us to expect.

In other words, between the two cases considered here (Arabic and Itelmen), OP effects are attested only where they are indistinguishable from category-sensitivity (Arabic). Of course, it will most likely be possible to describe the data in a manner consistent with the TCNP, for example by appeal to various ancillary assumptions and additional constraints, (see Cable 2004 for a detailed analysis of the Itelmen facts from an OP perspective). However, I maintain that Itelmen shows exactly the kind of divergence between contingent properties of paradigm inventories and category membership that should be the best case for an argument for OP but that, nevertheless, the best predictor of syllabification is category–not paradigm–membership.

2.4.1 *Itelmen syllabification*

In order to make the argument just noted, it will be necessary to provide some background on Itelmen phonology. The discussion here is based on Bobaljik (1998), to which the reader is referred for additional detail.

Itelmen (also Itel'men, Kamchadal) is a Chukotko-Kamchatkan language now spoken only by some 30 or so people on the Okhotsk coast of Russia's Kamchatka peninsula. One remarkable property of the language is its striking tolerance of large consonant clusters. Some examples of initial, medial, and final clusters of up to five or six consonants are given in (2.9).[9]

---

[9] The Itelmen data is mostly taken from my own field notes, supplemented with examples from Volodin (1976). For additional discussion of Itelmen syllabification, with special reference to its implications for Government Phonology, see Tarasenkova (2006). Special transcription conventions include the following: s,z are (I believe) apical, post-alveolar, non-retroflex fricatives, which should therefore be written with an underdot (omitted for typographic reasons); ñ represents a glottalized nasal (sometimes written as ʔn–whatever its phonetic manifestation turns out to be, it behaves phonologically as a single segment and not as a sequence of glottal stop plus *n*; the historical source appears to be *n+t#*); a superscript *w* at the beginning of a word indicates that the whole word is pronounced with pursed lips–a proper characterization of this process awaits further work. Note also that I have suppressed an automatic gemination of single consonants in post-tonic position in the representations. (I am not convinced that all speakers follow this but it is immaterial to present concerns.) Finally, the reader is cautioned that some aspects of vowel quality in unstressed syllables are not always easy to pin down with certainty (stress is initial except that inflectional prefixes are not counted).

(2.9) čkpəč   'spoon'   tɸsčŋin   'You are carrying it.'
       kɬqzuknen̓   'they were'   mskčen̓   'I will make them.'
       sitɬxpk'eɬ   'with embers'   k'ənsɬxč   'Boil it!'

Although consonant clusters may be of arbitrary length, certain consonants are barred from medial position in a cluster. Namely, the [+sonorant] consonants {m, n, ŋ, r, l, z} must be adjacent to a vowel. This yields schwa epenthesis in the environment described in (2.10), as detected by schwa-zero alternations.[10]

(2.10) $\emptyset \rightarrow \vartheta \begin{Bmatrix} C \\ \# \end{Bmatrix}$ ___[+sonorant] $\begin{Bmatrix} C \\ \# \end{Bmatrix}$

Some relevant examples of sonority-driven alternations are given in (2.11).

(2.11) a. ɬxəm   ~   ɬxm-en̓   'sable' sg, pl
        b. spəl   ~   spl-ank   'wind' direct, locative[11]
        c. ʷtχəz-xʔal   ~   ʷtχz-enk   'road' ablative, locative

Interestingly, there is a sharp phonological contrast between nouns and verbs with respect to sonority-driven epenthesis: verb stems do not alternate. Specifically, all verb stems that have a schwa in the environment described by (2.10) preserve that schwa even when epenthesis is not necessary. This is illustrated by the pairs in (2.12), which are representative of all sonorant-final verb stems.

(2.12) a. t-zəl-čen   1SG-give-1SG>3SG   'I gave it.'
        b. zəl-en   give-2SG>3SG   'You gave it.'   *zlen
        c. t-ɬəm-čen̓   1SG-kill-1SG>3PL   'I killed them.'
        d. q-ɬəm-in   2IMP-kill-2>3SG   'Kill it!'   *qɬmin
        e. spəl-qzu-in   windy-ASP-3SG   'It was windy.'
        f. spəl-in   windy-3SG   'It was windy.'   *spl-in

In (2.12a.), epenthesis is necessary to shield the /l/ in the verb stem /zl/ from occurring illicitly in cluster-medial position. In (2.12b.), however, the environment for epenthesis is not met on the surface; though locally unmotivated,

---

[10] As Itelmen lacks voiced stops (except in loan words), it is not clear whether the relevant feature is sonority or voicing. The segment z is listed as a sonorant on the basis of its behavior as described in the text; importantly, the voiceless counterpart is not. Note that {β, j} also do not occur cluster medially, but I have not found sonority-driven alternations that would indicate that they participate in the rule in (2.10). So far as I can tell, nothing in the present discussion hinges on the correct formulation of the rule, so long as it adequately characterizes the range of schwa-zero alternations. Note in addition that there are exceptions at the left edge of the word, i.e., in the stressed syllable (see Bobaljik 1998).

[11] This particular form is also attested (with variation) as *spal-ank*; this is not true for most other alternating forms, especially not the plurals.

epenthesis is obligatory, a case of overapplication. The other pairs make the same point.[12]

In Bobaljik (1998), I argued that the N-V asymmetries in syllabification should be accounted for in cyclic terms. Syllabification (and hence epenthesis) proceeds cyclically in verbs, starting with the root, whereas nouns are syllabified only once at the end of the derivation. Since a stem-final consonant will (by definition) not be followed by a vowel on the first cycle, (verb) roots like /zl/ and /ɬm/ will undergo epenthesis before any suffixes are added. In nouns, by contrast, suffixes are added before syllabification is computed.

A key part of the argument for cyclicity in verbs comes from opacity effects regarding the present tense suffix. The present tense suffix has four surface allomorphs: -s, -z, -əs, and -əz. The alternation in voicing is determined uniquely by the following segment but the schwa-zero alternation is determined solely by the preceding segment, as follows directly from cyclic application of (2.10). Examples illustrating the relevant environments are given in (2.13).

(2.13) a. t-tχ̣ zu-s-kičen
           1SG-stand-PRES-1SG
           'I am standing'

        b. ɬeru-z-in
           gripe-PRES-3SG
           'she gripes'

        c. ɬ-qzu-z-in
           be-ASP-PRES-3SG
           'she is'

        d. t'-il-əs-kičen
           1SG-drink-PRES-1SG
           'I am drinking'

        e. il-əz-in
           drink-PRES-3SG
           'he drinks'

        f. spəl-əz-in
           windy-PRES-3SG
           'It is windy'

The cyclic derivations in (2.14) show how each of the four allomorphs of the present tense suffix arises. The important derivations are those of (2.13d.) and (2.13e.). The environment in (2.13e.) is similar to that found with verb stems (and to the derivation of *lightening* discussed in section 2.2). The V-initial suffix should bleed epenthesis; the correct result is obtained by having epenthesis apply before the agreement suffix is added. Similarly, a cyclic derivation explains epenthesis in (2.13d.) which is obligatory on cycle 2, even though the environment is later destroyed by the devoicing rule applying on the next cycle.[13]

---

[12] Treating the schwa as part of the verb root underlyingly would not change the nature of the problem, which would then be stated as a morpheme-structure constraint: noun roots can, but verb roots cannot, end in CR] where R is any [+sonorant] consonant.

[13] The examples in the right column of (2.9) show that cluster-medial /s/ is tolerated; that is, /s/ does not count as a sonorant for the purposes of (2.10).

(2.14)	V__C (2.13a.)	V__V (2.13b.)	C__C (2.13d.)	C__V (2.13e.)	
	[tχzu]	[ɬeru]	[il]	[il]	Cy1 Root
	[tχzu] + z	[ɬeru] + z	[il] + z	[il] + z	Cy2 Present Tense
	—	—	[il ə z]	[il ə z]	Epenth
	[tχzu z] + ki...	[ɬeru z] + in	[ilɔ z] + ki...	[ilə z] + in	Cy3 Agr
	[tχzu s] + ki	—	[ilə s] ki...	—	Devoicing
	t-tχzu-s-kičen	ɬeru-z-in	t'-il-əs-kičen il-əz-in		OUTPUT

This completes the sketch of the basic Itelmen syllabification pattern from a cyclic perspective. The account relies on a stipulated difference between nouns and verbs, namely that the rule in (2.10) applies cyclically in verbs, but post-cyclically in nouns. As Cable (2004) observes, the Itelmen facts look ripe for investigation from an OP perspective: on the one hand, the OP philosophy rejects such stipulated differences between morphosyntactic categories, on the other, the putatively cyclic effects are very much of a kind with the syllabification patterns investigated by McCarthy, at least as far as verb roots are concerned. The optimal syllabification in the more restrictive environment (before C-initial suffixes) is carried over throughout the paradigm, even where it is not forced on the surface, yielding overapplication of epenthesis. In the next section, I will present what I take to be the guiding intuition of an OP approach to the Itelmen facts, as exemplified by the careful analysis in Cable (2004), and set out three reasons that I am sceptical of this intuition.

2.4.2 *Cable 2004*

Part of the OP research strategy is to derive noun-verb asymmetries in phonology from contingent facts about the inflectional morphemes they combine with, i.e., properties of the paradigms. Itelmen verb roots look like a good target for an OP analysis, extending the epenthesis that is obligatory before C-initial suffixes into the same roots before V-initial suffixes. Unlike Arabic, however, in Itelmen there are V-initial and C-initial suffixes in both nominal and verbal inflectional paradigms. How, then, can OP account not only for the behavior of verbs but also for the noun-verb asymmetry?

Cable (2004) provides an intriguing suggestion, building on the notion of base discussed in section 2.3.2 above. As noted there, OP is embedded within a monostratal framework in which correspondences can be evaluated between input and output, and among outputs, but not among intermediate stages of a derivation, where those are not independently occurring words. In Itelmen, as in many languages, verbs are bound morphemes and the verb stem cannot surface as a word in its own right. By contrast, noun stems often do surface in their bare form; this is the most common singular, non-oblique form.

Cable capitalizes on this difference between nouns and verbs by proposing a subtle change to McCarthy's conception of where OP applies. While McCarthy argues that inflectional paradigms have no base, and hence that base-sensitive correspondence constraints cannot apply (see quote in section 2.3.2), Cable suggests instead that the noun stem in Itelmen does count as a base, and that OP applies only to those word classes that lack an independently occurring free base. In keeping with the general OP philosophy, under Cable's approach, it is not inflection versus derivation that is the dimension of variation but rather the contingent property of whether or not there is a discrete base, as an independently available output, to which OO constraints can apply.

The deft move that makes this succeed descriptively is that having a base will bleed OP constraints, even if the base-identity constraints are themselves ranked too low to have any effect. Thus there is a constant ranking across categories: OP > syllabification > BaseIdent. Verbs lack a base, hence OP will be relevant and trigger overapplication of epenthesis, but for nouns the independent base makes OP irrelevant, while at the same time the ranking of BaseIdent under whatever constraints effect syllabification ensures that each form of the noun receives its locally optimal syllabification. The result is alternations in nouns but none in verbs.

I will proceed now to three arguments from Itelmen, each of which suggests that the N-V asymmetries are about the categories "noun" and "verb" and not about contingent properties of individual lexical items and their associated paradigms.

2.4.2.1 *Category-neutral roots*   In Itelmen, some roots have a double life, occurring with the same meaning as both verbs and nouns. One such root is *spl* 'wind' (2.15a. b.), which we have already seen above. However, most verbal roots do not occur as nouns without additional derivational morphology (if at all). Thus, simple nouns corresponding to the stems in (2.15c. d.) are unattested.

(2.15)   a.   spəl-   verb: 'be windy' (of weather) cf. (2.12)
         b.   spəl   noun: 'wind' cf. (2.11)
         c.   zəl-   verb: 'give'
         d.   ɬəm-   verb: 'kill'
         e.   *zəl, ɬəm   unattested as nouns

Occurrence as a free root or not is exactly the independent characteristic which determines whether or not OP applies. Nouns are exempted from the uniformity effect of OP because their root counts as a base. Yet it turns out that the few relevant verbs whose root also counts as a base are not thereby exempted from the OP-driven overapplication of epenthesis. The contingent fact "my root can surface as a word" has no bearing on the phonological behavior of a verb root. Overapplication occurs in the verb root /spl-/ even though that root does have a corresponding base occurring as an independent word. If anything, the OP research strategy (with Cable's modification to accommodate Itelmen), should lead us to expect the opposite.

2.4.2.2 *Baseless nouns*   The opposite problem occurs as well. While it is in general the case that nouns and verbs differ along the dimension of having a corresponding free base, just as some verbs have a root that does occur as an independent word, there are also nouns that lack a base. As far as can be determined, these nouns behave phonologically like nouns, and not like verbs. That is, they show syllabification-driven alternations in stem form rather than maintaining a uniform stem throughout their paradigms.

In the preceding discussion, I noted that most nouns bear no overt morphology in the singular, non-oblique form. However, there is a sizeable number of nouns that require a singular suffix that is lost in the plural (Volodin 1976; Bobaljik 2006). These nouns thus lack an identifiable base in the sense of occurring as an independent word. Examples of four classes of nouns taking singular suffixes are given in (2.16).

(2.16)		UR	Sg	Pl	gloss
	-m	/txtu/	txtu-m	txtu-ń	'dugout canoe'
		/atno/	atno-m	atno-ń	'village' (also 'home')
	-n	/kəmlo/	kəmlo-n	kəmlo-ń	'grandchild'
		/reβla/	reβla-n	reβla-ń	'falcon'
	-ŋ	/qtχa/	qtχa-ŋ	qtχi-ń	'leg'
		/iʔleβeno/	iʔleβeno-ŋ	iʔleβeno-ń	'boat pole'
	-č	/p'e/	p'e-č	p'e-ń	'child, son'
		/xk'i/	xk'i-č	xk'i-ń	'hand'

Another class of nouns showing this behavior is the reduplicative nouns (see Bobaljik 2006). Such nouns show reduplication in the singular but no reduplication in the plural. As a result, the base of such nouns never occurs as a free word. The reduplicating nouns themselves fall into two classes; of particular interest here are the ones in (2.17a.) which show a schwa-zero alternation in the root.

(2.17) a. alternating bases:[14]

Singular	Plural	
kəp-kəp	kpə-ń	'tooth'
k'uɸ-k'uɸ	k'ɸə-ń	'claw'
ʷčeɬx-ʷčeɬx	ʷčɬx ə-ń	'cowberry'

  b. non-alternating bases:

Singular	Plural	
silq-silq	silq-ań	'meat with berries'
ŋəl-ŋəl	ŋəʔl	'roe, caviar'
tam-tam	tam-eń	'growth, tumor'

The nouns in (2.17a.) are baseless, like verbs. Under a TCNP approach, the absence of a base should trigger OP effects, thus uniformity of syllabification throughout the paradigm. However, the nouns in (2.17a.) fail to pattern with verbs, patterning instead like other nouns, showing schwa-zero alternations.

As it happens, the relevant consideration for these nouns is not the sonority driven epenthesis discussed above but rather a minimality-driven epenthesis requiring that all words have at least one vowel (including schwa). Minimality-driven epenthesis is needed independently of reduplication, as shown in (2.18).[15]

(2.18) a. ʷqəsχ ~ ʷqsχ-ɐń/ʷqsχ-aj   'dog' sg, pl, pejorative
        b. čkəp ~ čkp-əń   'fungus' sg, pl

The fact that minimality, rather than sonority, is at issue in the reduplication patterns opens a possible avenue of account within OP. Nevertheless, the data constitute another example in which differences in word class membership (whether or not there happens to be a free base) turn out to be irrelevant for predicting phonological behavior, while the basic N-V asymmetry remains.

2.4.2.3 *Transitive-intransitive differences*   At this point, let us return to the verbal domain. Itelmen has a fairly rich system of inflectional morphology.

---

[14] I believe that what I transcribe as [u] in the singular is the realization of ə before [ɸ]; likewise [e] is the effect of palatalization induced by /ɬ/ = [ɬʲ].

[15] While there is some overlap in the application of these rules, they cannot be entirely collapsed. For example, minimality is insufficient to drive epenthesis in (2.11c.), where sonority would not drive epenthesis in (2.18)–the clusters broken up in those examples do occur medially when minimality is not at issue, cf. (2.9). Note also that minimality-driven epenthesis overapplies, occurring in both base and reduplicant, as is readily apparent in (2.17a.). Outside of reduplication, however, minimality-driven epenthesis is truly a last-resort operation, occurring only if no other morphological or syntactic process brings a vowel into the word. There is certainly no requirement that every root or stem have a vowel on the surface.

Nevertheless, certain quirks emerge. Among these is a distinction between the inventories of morphemes available for transitive and intransitive verbs. This distinction turns out to be quite germane to the present discussion.

Consider again the derivations used to illustrate opacity in (2.13d.) and (2.13e.). The full, cyclic derivations are given here.

(2.19)   a. _V   b. _C[−voice]

    il   il   Root ('drink')

    [il] z   [il] z   Cycle 1—Tense

    [il] əz   [il] əz   Epenthesis (Devoicing N/A)

    [iləz] in [iləz] kičen   Cycle 2—Agreement

    ——   ilə s kičen   Devoicing (Epenthesis N/A)

    iləzin   t'iləskičen   Output

These derivations illustrate opacity since the environment for epenthesis before the present tense suffix is not met on the surface. In (2.19a.) the agreement suffix is V-initial, and _zV is not an environment for epenthesis, while in (2.19b.) the agreement suffix is voiceless, triggering devoicing of the present tense suffix (and we know independently that /s/ is not among the class of consonants requiring epenthesis).

Now, to this point, we have been looking at the distinctions between verbal and nominal inflectional paradigms. In fact, under OP, there should be no a priori expectation that these are the right groupings of morphemes to examine. Rather, the phonological behavior of a given verb stem should be a product of that verb's "paradigm," i.e., the set of affixes that that verb stem may combine with, even where these are a subset of the affixes in the language. It so happens that for intransitive verbs all the affixes that may occur after the present tense morpheme will fall into one of the two classes in (2.19). (The regular transitive paradigm, by contrast, has affixes that begin with a voiced consonant, such as the 3>3 suffix -nen, as in sk-əz-nen [make-PRES-3>3SG] 'he is making it.') For the intransitive verbs, then, the entire paradigm is opaque. No member of the paradigm of any intransitive verb should ever require epenthesis before the present tense affix, and thus there is no occurring surface form that can serve as the basis for overapplication.[16]

By OP, this difference between transitive and intransitive verbs is exactly the kind of difference that should be relevant and which should yield different phonological behaviour between these classes. Yet the syllabification patterns

---

[16] As far as I can tell, this argument can only be constructed for the present tense marker, since the devoicing does not apply to the other stem-final sonorants, such as -l, -m. This makes it technically possible, though ad hoc, to divorce the analysis of the syllabification of the present tense morpheme from the other syllabification patterns in the system.

are the same for both classes. The divide in Itelmen is between verbs and nouns, not among paradigms with and without (surface) environments for epenthesis.

2.4.3 *Section summary*

The considerations from Itelmen just discussed do not provide a knock-down argument against OP. It is possible to describe the Itelmen facts in a manner consistent with OP (as Cable does, for example, by adducing a sympathy-theoretic account for the present tense syllabification that is distinct from the other aspects of Itelmen verbal syllabification). What emerges though is a conspiracy. A variety of extra measures are invoked, precisely to accommodate a deviance from the expectations of OP. There is a basic asymmetry in Itelmen syllabification between nouns and verbs (possibly the same asymmetry as stipulated for Arabic, see fn. 7), but under Cable's account this asymmetry emerges as the result of a variety of unrelated properties. The clearest way to appreciate this aspect of the analysis is to consider a variety of "Itelmen primes", that is languages which are just like Itelmen but minus one of the various extra considerations that Cable proposes. Indeed, the research program of reducing noun-verb asymmetries to contingent properties of the pieces of inflection would suggest that these Itelmen primes should be the unmarked case. On this program, it is the phonological shape of the paradigm members that is supposed to be relevant; if transitive and intransitive suffixes differ in a phonologically relevant way, then the transitive/intransitive dimension should be one which the syllabification patterns track.

I submit that no good examples of such an effect have yet been discovered.[17] In Classical Arabic, it happens that paradigm membership and lexical category coincide. Where the two diverge, as in Itelmen, the most straightforward generalization refers to lexical category. I suspect that the Itelmen case, rather than the expectations of TCNP and OP, constitutes the general case. Of course, the making or breaking of such a contention will not turn on the specific analysis of Arabic or Itelmen but rather on a broader cross-linguistic survey of phonological systems. My money is on morphosyntactic categories and against the TCNP.

---

[17] While the discussion of Arabic and Itelmen is limited to syllabification, Glyne Piggott (personal communication, 2005) notes that OP-induced overapplication should be expected for all kinds of phonological properties of stems that can be affected by the affixes they combine with. Thus, under OP reasoning, one might expect to find a noun-verb asymmetry where all verb stems are nasalized, because some verbal inflectional affixes are nasal, or where all stative verb stems bear a low tone, since some inflections limited to stative verbs have a dominant low tone. This opens the realm of possible examples of OP effects quite wide; time will tell if any convincing examples do emerge.

2.5 Conclusion

OP and Cable's extension provide intriguing analyses of a variety of phonological systems. My primary interest in examining the OP system lies in the question of whether it motivates direct appeal to paradigms as the domain of synchronic grammatical computation. Certainly, OP is formulated in these terms, hence, if the analysis it provides is compelling (as against conceivable, paradigm-free alternatives), then this would constitute evidence for paradigms. I do not claim here to have shown that OP is untenable. However, I hope to have raised some significant questions regarding certain core assumptions, and in particular, to have shown that the key question of direction of influence among morphologically related words has not been sufficiently established. In addition, I have drawn out what I see to be one of the key theses that would bear on the feasibility of OP as a general proposal, namely the TCNP. For the one language that I have examined in detail that had the potential to tease out the differences between class-membership and paradigm influences (namely Itelmen), the available data come down suggestively against the TCNP (and hence against OP). Ultimately, the question is empirical and should hinge not on the analysis of one or two languages but on a larger survey. My (admittedly Itelmenocentric) hunch is this: such a survey will reveal that lexical category is a recurring predictor of distinct phonological behavior, whereas the contingent properties of paradigms are not. I would be unsurprised if clever analytic minds will be able to "save" a technical analysis incorporating OP over this range of data, but I will be surprised if OP turns out to be the norm wherever category and paradigm membership diverge (as they do in Itelmen). Why might this be so? The answer, I contend, is the LDH in (2.1): the computation of grammatical well-formedness is local. To predict the surface form of a word, it is sufficient to know the constituent pieces of that word, their hierarchical arrangement, and the general phonology of the language. Reference to other members of that word's paradigm is neither needed nor possible.

References

Albright, Adam (2002) The identification of bases in morphological paradigms. Ph.D. dissertation, UCLA.

—— This volume. 'Inflectional paradigms have bases, too'.

Arad, Maya (2003) 'Locality constraints on the interpretation of roots: The case of Hebrew denominal verbs'. *Natural Language and Linguistic Theory* 21.4, 737–78.

Barragan, Luis and Heather Newell (2003) 'Cupeño morphology is inherently stressful', in *Proceedings of WECOL*.

Benua, Laura (2000) *Phonological Relations Between Words.* New York: Garland.

Bobaljik, Jonathan David (1998) 'Mostly predictable: Cyclicity and the distribution of schwa in Itelmen', in Vida Samiian (ed.), *Santa Cruz, CA Proceedings of,* CSU, Fresno, 14: 28.

—— (2002a) 'Paradigmaticity without paradigms', paper presented at Rutgers University, March 2002.

—— (2002b) 'Syncretism without paradigms: Remarks on Williams 1981, 1994', in Geert Booij and Jaap van Marle (eds.), *Yearbook of Morphology 2001.* Dordrecht: Kluwer, pp. 53–85.

—— (2003) 'Realizing Germanic inflection: Why morphology does not drive syntax'. *Journal of Comparative Germanic Linguistics* 6.2–3: 129–67.

—— (2006) 'Itelmen reduplication: Edge-in association and lexical stratification'. *Journal of Linguistics* 42: 1–23.

Boudelaa, Sami, and William D. Marslen-Wilson (2004) 'Abstract morphemes and lexical representation: the CV-skeleton in Arabic'. *Cognition* 92: 272–303.

—— —— (2005) 'Discontinuous morphology in time: Incremental masked priming in Arabic'. *Language and Cognitive Processes* 20.1–2: 207–60.

Burzio, Luigi (1996) 'Surface constraints versus underlying representation', in Jacques Durand and Bernard Laks (eds.), *Current Trends in Phonology: Models and Methods.* European Studies Research Institute, University of Salford Publications, Salford, pp. 97–122.

Cable, Seth (2004) 'Phonological noun-verb dissimilarities in Optimal Paradigms', paper presented at Workshop on (Non)-identity Within a Paradigm, MIT.

Chomsky, Noam (2001) 'Derivation by phase', in Michael Kenstowicz (ed.), *Ken Hale: A Life in Language.* Cambridge, MA: MIT Press, pp. 1–52.

—— and Morris Halle (1968) *The Sound Pattern of English.* New York: Harper & Row.

Kenstowicz, Michael (1997) 'Base-identity and uniform exponence: Alternatives to cyclicity', in J. Durand and B. Laks (eds.), *Current trends in Phonology: Models and Methods.* University of Salford, Salford, pp. 363–94.

Marantz, Alec (2001) 'Words', Unpublished manuscript, MIT, Cambridge, MA.

McCarthy, John J. (1981) 'A prosodic theory of nonconcatenative morphology'. *Linguistic Inquiry* 12.3: 373–418.

—— (1985) *Formal Problems in Semitic Phonology and Morphology.* New York: Garland.

—— (1993) 'Template form in Prosodic Morphology', in Laurel Smith Stvan, Stephen Ryberg, Mari Broman Olsen, Talke Macfarland, Linda DiDesidero, Anne Bertram, and Larin Adams (eds.), *FLSM III: Papers From the Third Annual Formal Linguistics Society of Mid America Conference.* Bloomington, IN: Indiana Linguistics Club, pp. 187–218.

—— (2005) 'Optimal Paradigms', in Laura Downing, Tracy Alan Hall, and Renate Raffeleisen (eds.), *Paradigms in Phonological Theory.* Oxford: Oxford University Press, pp. 170–210.

Smith, Jennifer L. (2001) 'Lexical category and phonological contrast', in Robert Kirchner, Joe Pater, and Wolf Wikely (eds.), *Papers in Experimental and Theoretical Linguistics 6: Workshop on the Lexicon in Phonetics and Phonology*. Edmonton, AB: University of Alberta, pp. 61–72.

Steriade, Donca (1998) 'Lexical conservatism and the notion base of affixation', paper presented at the LSA meeting, New York, and Current Trends in Phonology II, Royamount. Available at http://www.linguistics.ucla.edu/people/steriade/papers/LexicalConservatism.pdf.

—— (2000) 'Paradigm uniformity and the phonetics-phonology boundary', in Janet Pierrehumbert and Michael Broe (eds). *Papers in Laboratory Phonology 6*. Cambridge: Cambridge University Press, pp. 313–35.

Tarasenkova, Oksana (2006) 'A Government Phonology account of complex clusters in Itelmen', Unpublished manuscript, University of Connecticut at Storrs.

Ussishkin, Adam (2000) The emergence of fixed prosody. Ph.D. dissertation, University of California at Santa Cruz.

Volodin, Aleksandr P. (1976) *Itel'menskij jazyk [The Itelmen Language]*. Leningrad: Nauka.

Wiese, Bernd (2004) 'Unterspezifizierte Stammparadigmen: Zur Systematik des Verbablauts im Gegenwartsdeutschen', Unpublished manuscript, IDS, Mannheim.

—— (2005) 'Form and function of verb ablaut in contemporary standard German', in Robin Sackmann (ed.), *Studies in Integrational Linguistics*. Amsterdam: John Benjamins.

Williams, Edwin (1994) 'Remarks on lexical knowledge'. *Lingua* 92: 7–34.

3

Clarifying "Blur": Paradigms, defaults, and inflectional classes

MORRIS HALLE AND ALEC MARANTZ

3.1 Structure of paradigms or organization of inflectional classes

Despite the emphasis placed on paradigms in many recent papers on morphology and phonology, we believe that linguists are, for the most part, using "paradigm" as a convenient cover term for a variety of distinct morphological issues. For example, much discussion within OT of "paradigm uniformity" uses "paradigm" to point to issues of allomorphy between "related" forms of a stem or root that do not crucially rely on paradigms in any demonstrable sense. These discussions employ paradigms to provide a set of forms that might be related via output-output constraints. Similarly, recent proposals enforcing anti-homophony between paradigm cells hinge not on paradigm structure per se but rather on claims about output-output correspondence relations between forms.

Here we review another claim that paradigms play a role in the theory of morphology: Andrew Carstairs-McCarthy's work (1994) on what he calls the "No Blur Principle". Through an examination of Carstairs-McCarthy's analysis of Polish (Cameron-Faulkner and Carstairs-McCarthy 2000), we demonstrate that "No Blur" is a claim directly about the organization of inflectional classes of stems, not about paradigms in the usual sense from the literature. We argue that even if "No Blur" were supported as a principle, it would provide no evidence for the reintroduction of paradigms as a functional concept within morphological theory. However, we also demonstrate that "No Blur" is in certain ways inconsistent with Carstairs-McCarthy's (hereafter C-M's) general theory of morphology. In particular, to give "No Blur" empirical force, C-M must assume (i) that a given stem may belong to only one inflectional class, i.e., that inflectional classes neither are organized into a hierarchy of classes and subclasses nor cross-classify the set of stems, and (ii) that paradigms may not include accidentally homophonous affixes. But C-M's own analysis of Polish effectively violates the first assumption and his treatment of syncretism within paradigms violates the second. We demonstrate that the driving force behind C-M's analyses is really just the standard working assumptions of morphologists: avoid accidental homophony and maximize generalizations. With these principles, we are led to accounts of syncretism that effectively de-Blur paradigms in the relevant cases. Thus, when the empirical situation is examined, No Blur adds nothing to the auxiliary principles that would be necessary in any case.

3.2 Blurring, contrast, and the information content of affixes

C-M (1994) assumes that a fundamental principle governing all language learning is Eve Clark's Principle of Contrast that "[e]very two forms contrast in meaning" (737). He notes (ibid.) that "[i]f the principle is at all close to being correct, exact synonyms should be nonexistent or rare ... Yet when we focus on inflectional affixes rather than complete word forms, exact synonymy is apparently widespread ... Even in English ... we can identify three distinct suffixal realizations for the past participle form of the verb (*-(e)n*, *-(e)d*, and *-t*) and various nonsuffixal realizations (vowel change as in *sang* ... and more radical stem allomorphy ...). So inflectional morphology seems hard to reconcile with the Principle of Contrast ... " Nevertheless, C-M sets out to show that there is a "way of reconciling the principle with the inflectional facts."

In a spirit similar to that behind pedagogical grammars, C-M assumes that the data about inflections of a language are stored by speakers in the form of paradigms, and hence, in acquiring language, speakers acquire a set of paradigms. He defines the notion of paradigm relevant for purposes of his discussion as:

Paradigm$_1$: the set of combinations of morphosyntactic properties or features (or the set of "cells") realized by inflected forms of words (or lexemes) in a given word-class (or major category or lexeme-class) in a given language. (739)

That is, the units under discussion are the complexes of grammatical features whose phonetic exponents are the different affixes. On this view, the cells of a paradigm are derivative notions, defined in terms of "morphosyntactic properties".

As C-M notes, this view of paradigms and the Principle of Contrast appears to give rise to an obvious objection. For example, the three affixes of the English participle *-(e)n*, *-(e)d*, and *-t* are "in competition" in the sense that "they realize exactly the same morphosyntactic properties and ... the contexts in which they occur (i.e., the lexemes to which they attach) are not distinguish-able in any nonarbitrary fashion (e.g., phonologically or semantically)." This set of competing affixes and innumerable similar competing affix sets familiar to morphologists "thus constitute clear prima facie evidence that the Principle of Contrast does not apply to inflectional morphology" (740).

C-M observes that it is possible to construe competing affixes as obeying the Principle of Contrast "inasmuch as they contrast in respect of the inflection classes with which they are associated" (740). In other words, English -*en* is not just an exponent of the past participle, but rather the exponent of the past participle for the class of verbs *take, break, choose, drive, prove*, and about 50 others, whereas -*t* is the exponent of past participle for the class: *burn, learn, buy, mean, keep*, and about 35 others, etc. The recognition of inflectional classes of verbs does not render the different affixes appropriate for each class distinct semantically, as long as meaning is construed in the normal fashion. But since C-M does not want these semantically identical suffixes to constitute counter-evidence to Clark's Principle, he amends Clark's Principle as requiring phonetically distinct forms to contrast not in meaning but rather in "information content", where "'information content' should be understood as embracing not just extralinguistic meaning, such as plural-ity or pastness, but also interlinguistic information such as gender or stem shape" (741).

C-M is fully aware of the obvious objection to this move, which is that "[i]t renders inflection class diversity consistent with the Principle of Contrast only at the expense of trivializing the principle entirely" (741). He proposes to avoid this consequence by "saying that a given affix can have a given inflection class as part of its information content only if that affix is uniquely associated with that inflection class."

Any two affixes which are each restricted to one inflection class will differ in infor-mation content . . . their coexistence is therefore consistent with the [Principle of Con-trast]. But if we find two or more affixes each of which appears in more than one inflection class then they will not differ in information content . . . and their coexistence will be inconsistent with the principle . . . Within any set of competing classes, each affixal realization for every cell must be either (a) peculiar to one class, or (b) the only realization for that cell which is shared by more than one class [the class default in case (b)]. (742)

This stipulation about affixes–completely internal to C-M's theory of morphology–is codified as the No Blur Principle:

Within any set of competing inflectional affixal realizations for the paradigmatic cell, no more than one can fail to identify inflection class unambiguously. (742)

In evaluating the No Blur principle, one must keep in mind the procedure C-M uses for creating and displaying paradigms of noun and verb inflections. For nouns, for example, a full set of nouns from a language is first divided according to classifications that make a difference in the grammar; so, for example, a given stem might be of a particular gender, where gender triggers agreement and is thus relevant beyond the allomorphy of inflections. Within each class identified by this criterion, a two-dimensional matrix can be drawn, the rows of the matrix corresponding to sets of morphosyntactic features, such as case and number, expressed by inflection. For each class of nouns, a collection of allomorphs for particular sets of case and number features, e.g., nominative plural, dative singular, further divides the nouns into columns of inflectional classes, identified solely by the allomorphs the nouns take for combinations of case and number features (see the example in (3.6) below). Nouns belong to the same inflectional class–the same column–if they take exactly the same set of affixes for expressing the various combinations of case and number that are overtly realized in the language. On this view, inflectional classes emerge as columns in paradigms of forms. Inflectional classes become more interesting when there are implicational relations among the allomorphs for sets of words, e.g., if "takes -a in the dative singular" implies "takes -e in the locative singular".

This understanding of inflection class provides the backdrop for explaining what kinds of paradigms are supposed to be ruled out by No Blur. Two such organizations of inflectional classes are relevant here, one in which inflectional subclasses appear to nest within inflectional classes and one in which inflectional classes cross-classify a set of words. Both of these are prima facie violations of No Blur. The imaginary paradigm in (3.1) illustrates the first case disallowed by No Blur; the subparadigm of Polish nouns in (3.2) illustrates the second. In (3.1) the allomorphs of the dative suffix classify nouns into two groups, "takes -a in the dative" and "takes -b in the dative" while the allomorphs of the locative classify nouns into four groups, "takes {-c, -d, -e, or -f} in the locative". Within each of the classes determined by the dative allomorphs, there are two subclasses determined by the locative allomorphs. Since, in this paradigm, the dative suffixes fail to identify their inflectional classes unambiguously (they appear in two classes each), the subclass case violates No Blur.

(3.1)

Class	1	2	3	4
Dative	a	a	b	b
Locative	c	d	e	f

The second type of paradigm that violates No Blur, one in which inflectional classes cross-classify words, is shown in (3.2)–a subpart of the Polish paradigm in (3.6) that we will examine in the central portion of this chapter. Here there are two classes of nouns identified by the allomorphs of the dative suffix, "takes -owi in the dative" and "takes -u in the dative". In addition, there are two classes identified by the allomorphs of the locative suffix, "takes -e in the locative" and "takes -u in the locative". These classes identified by the dative and locative suffixes are apparently independent, so they cross-classify the Polish nouns. That is, being of the "takes -owi in the dative" class does not predict which class a noun will be in with respect to the locative and vice versa. Since dative and locative suffixes do not unambiguously identify the class (column) of a Polish noun, the paradigm in (3.2) is Blurred, in violation of No Blur.

(3.2)

Class	1	2	3	4
Dative	-owi	-owi	-u	-u
Locative	-e	-u	-e	-u

To provide No Blur with empirical teeth, C-M needs two additional assumptions: one that prevents a stem from appearing in more than one inflectional class and one that disallows accidental homophony between affixes. We show below that C-M effectively violates the first assumption in his treatment of the "information content" of a stem, where information content is the notion that links No Blur to the Principle of Contrast. In addition, in offering no account of syncretism between rows of a paradigm, C-M effectively violates the assumption preventing accidental homophony as well. If C-M allowed stems to belong to more than one inflectional class, we could redraw the paradigm in (3.1) as in (3.3). Now each of the locative suffixes uniquely identifies a class, indicated by the capital letters at the top of each column, while each of the dative suffixes uniquely identifies the numerical class at the top of each column.

(3.3)

Class	1, C	1, D	2, E	2, F
Dative	a	a	b	b
Locative	c	d	e	f

Note that under C-M's approach to paradigmatic organization, the affixes themselves organize the stems into classes–columns–and the labels on the columns are not significant. Thus re-labeling the classes in (3.1) as in (3.3) would not change the fact that the paradigm is Blurred in the technical sense. However, when C-M relates No Blur to the Principle of Contrast, he gives content to the label of the inflectional class–the informational content of a class-identifying affix involves the class as an entity that can be referred to. Once classes are features with "information content", one needs to ask whether stems may or may not belong to more than one class, since they may in fact be both, e.g., class 1 and also masculine.

In a similar manner to the transformation of (3.1) into (3.3), the paradigm in (3.2) would be effectively de-Blurred as in (3.4), where the dative allomorphs determine the numerical classes, 1 or 2, and the locative allomorphs the letter classes, A or B.

(3.4)

Class	1, A	1, B	2, A	2, B
Dative	-owi	-owi	-u	-u
Locative	-e	-u	-e	-u

Again, the labeling of the columns reveals how the affixes cross-classify the sets of stems here. As long as class membership is "information content", class labels are meaningful within the grammatical system and the labeling in (3.4) provides an analysis consistent with No Blur. An additional principle would be required to rule out this sort of analysis in which stems belong to more than one inflectional class.

If unique affixes could be homophonous, then we could de-Blur the paradigm in (3.1) as in (3.5), recognizing two distinct dative suffixes that happen to both be pronounced "a" (the "b" suffix would then be the default dative suffix as allowed under No Blur). Now the two dative suffixes pronounced "a" each uniquely identify an inflectional class (1 and 2).

(3.5)

Class	1	2	3	4
Dative	a_1	a_2	b	b
Locative	c	d	e	f

3.3 Blurring in the Polish nominal declension

A tour of the Polish masculine singular noun paradigms discussed in Cameron-Faulkner and Carstairs-McCarthy 2000 (hereafter C-F/C-M) demonstrates how these additional assumptions against homophony and against belonging to more than one class are necessary to give force to No Blur (we reproduce the transcription of the Polish data from the cited article).

(3.6)

Class	1	2a	2b	3	4
Nom	profesor+	Polak+	koń+	pies+	pan+
Gen	profesor+a	Polak+a	koni+a	ps+a	pan+a
Dat	profesor+owi	Polak+owi	koni+owi	ps+u	pan+u
Inst	profesor+em	Polaki+em	koni+em	ps+em	pan+em
Loc	profesorz+e	Polak+u	koni+u	psi+e	pan+u
Voc	profesorz+e	Polak+u	koni+u	psi+e	pani+e

Class	5	6	7
Nom	kupiec+	dwór+	kraj+
Gen	kupc+a	dwor+u	kraj+u
Dat	kupc+owi	dwor+owi	kraj+owi
Inst	kupc+em	dwor+em	kraj+em
Loc	kupc+u	dworz+e	kraj+u
Voc	kupcz+e	dworz+e	kraj+u

(3.7)   Summary of affixes

Class	1	2	3	4	5	6	7
Nom/Acc	–	–	–	–	–	–	–
Gen/Acc	a	a	a	a	a	u	u
Dat	owi	owi	u	u	owi	owi	owi
Inst	em	em	em	em	em	em	em
Loc	e	u	e	u	u	e	u
Voc	e	u	e	e	e	e	u

The nouns represented by the examples in (3.6) are masculine lexemes from what are known as the *o*-stems in traditional grammars of Polish. Not all masculine nouns fall into these inflectional patterns; for example, a subclass of masculine nouns share endings with the feminine *a*-stems in the singular. The endings in (3.6) are shared by neuter nouns, except that neuter nouns take the ending -*o* in both the accusative and nominative. This syncretism reflects a more general feature of the Slavic languages where the accusative has the same exponent as the nominative, if the noun is inanimate, and the same exponent as the genitive, if the noun is animate. (See Gunkel 2003 for a recent account of the Polish noun paradigms.)

Note that the stem allomorph before the locative and vocative -*e* suffixes is always distinct from the stem allomorph in the nominative, genitive, dative, and instrumental. While the shift in stem-final consonant from the Gen/Dat/Instr stem to the stem used before -*e* has traditionally been treated as the result of the phonological process of palatalization, and while the final consonant before the -*e* is "functionally palatal" within the phonology of

Polish, the palatalization rule that yields the -*e* stem from the base stem is not phonetically transparent.

As C-F/C-M point out, the paradigm as shown in (3.6) violates No Blur in a number of places. Consider just the Dat row of the paradigm. Since both -*owi* and -*u* occur in more than one noun class, both fail to identify their inflectional class unambiguously. No Blur allows one such "default" affix per cell (row) but it specifically prohibits more than one; all other affixes in a cell must "identify inflection class unambiguously". Since neither -*owi* nor -*u* is a "class identifier", the distribution of affixes in the dative cell of (3.6) is contrary to No Blur. A formally identical violation of No Blur is found in the genitive.

As explained above, to generate an apparent violation of No Blur, C-F/C-M require two additional assumptions. The first is the constraint that inflectional class features cannot cross-classify stems, with each stem potentially belonging to more than one class. A striking feature of the classes (1–7) in (3.6) is that they seem to be organized around the distribution of the -*u* allomorphs of the various case suffixes. Suppose we assigned class features to the nouns in (3.6) according to the appearance of -*u*, so class A has -*u* in the Gen, class B -*u* in the Dat, class C -*u* in the Loc, and class D -*u* in the Voc. All the nouns in (3.6) would belong to the superclass Z, i.e., the traditional *o*-stem class that determines all the non -*u* allomorphs of the case/number affixes. The 7 classes in (3.6) would now be identified by the following features:

(3.8)

Class	1	2	3	4	5	6	7
Features	Z	Z, C, D	Z, B	Z, B, C	Z, C	Z, A	Z, A, C, D

The "information content" of the Loc -*u* would be [masc, sing, Loc, Z, C], of the Gen -*u*, [masc, sing, Gen, Z, A], and so forth. Technically, in a framework like Distributed Morphology, the affixes themselves would realize the case and number features on a terminal node from the syntax; the gender and inflectional class features would be contextual and would refer to features of the stem to which the case/number node has been attached. So, for example, -*u* would realize the features [Dat, sing] in the environment of [Z, B] (gender is irrelevant here but relevant as a contextual feature for the realization of the Nom suffix on class Z (*o*-stem) nouns).

On this analysis, the Principle of Contrast is obeyed: each affix has unique information content. Each -*u* affix in any row of the paradigm in (3.6) is a "class identifier", although the class features cross-classify the nouns (the non -*u* affix in each row would be the default for class Z stems). Therefore, -*u* in the Loc row identifies class C, -*u* in the Gen row class B, and so forth.

As explained above however, a crucial assumption of C-M's work on paradigms is that inflectional class structure is "flat", i.e., that inflectional class features do not cross-classify stems. The classes emerge as columns in paradigms organized on the basis of the distribution of allomorphs, without considering classes as possible features of stems; classes derived in such a manner will not "nest" or cross-classify stems. On such a view, a noun can't be both class Z and class A, for example. However, in order to relate No Blur to the Principle of Contrast, C-M equates the "information content" of class features with the information content of features like "masculine" and "singular" and "dative case". This moves inflectional classes from being epiphenomenal by-products of paradigm organization into being something to which the grammar may refer. In C-M's analysis–and in anyone's analysis–affixes must have information content that involves the conjunction of such features as [dative and singular]. If affixes are associated with conjunctions of features with "information content", and inflectional classes are information content, then inflectional class features may be conjoined with the information content of affixes and the information associated with stems. Inflectional class features may thus cross-classify stems. But if inflectional classes can cross-classify stems, No Blur becomes empirically vacuous; it can always be satisfied as we have done in (3.8), by allowing each affix to define an inflectional class.

C-M clearly believes that inflectional classes are special; although a stem may have many different features (gender, form, animacy, etc.) that could serve as contextual triggers of affixal allomorphy, each stem must belong to only a single inflectional class, where such classes are defined solely in terms of their effect on allomorphy. Each of the other feature types–gender, form, and animacy, for example–have implications beyond allomorphy (syntactic agreement, phonology, and semantics respectively). Inflectional classes are defined only by allomorphy and only trigger allomorphy.

Once No Blur is recognized to depend on a stipulation about inflectional classes, it loses any connection to the Principle of Contrast or any other independently motivated principle or consideration. Call this stipulation the "Single Inflectional Class Principle". We do not need both No Blur and the Single Inflectional Class Principle; the former depends on the latter, and the latter by itself would cover the empirical ground C-M attributes to No Blur. A Single Inflectional Class Principle is directly related to the account of inflectional allomorphy but only derivatively related to paradigms. The empirical force of No Blur, then, does not rely on paradigms or paradigm structure.

As explained above, the second assumption necessary to provide empirical teeth to No Blur is that there is no accidental homophony in a row (cell) of a paradigm. If each -u in the Dat row of the paradigms, for example, were a distinct affix, homophonous with the other -*u*, there would be no Blur in the Dat row–each -*u* would be a class identifier.

However, as just discussed, for No Blur to be related to the Principle of Contrast, inflectional class must be treated on a par with case and number under the notion of "information content." Thus there should be no difference, in principle, between the vertical (case) and horizontal (class) dimensions in the paradigm in (3.6)–both dimensions represent differences in information content. But if the vertical and horizontal dimensions are equivalent, and we cannot have homophony in the horizontal dimension (in a row), we should not have homophony in the vertical dimension either. However, C-F/C-M claim that there are multiple homophonous -*u*'s in the vertical dimension: a Gen -*u*, a Dat -*u*, a Loc -*u*, and a Voc -*u*. In fact, for C-F/C-M the Gen -*u* and Dat -*u* are distinct class identifiers that identify different classes. If homophonous affixes, -*u* and -*u*, can express Gen and Dat respectively, why can't homophonous -*u* and -*u*, express class A and class B respectively?

In sum, C-F/C-M require two major assumptions to give No Blur empirical content: stems may belong only to a single inflectional class and there may be no accidental homophony in a paradigm. The first assumption already covers the empirical ground of No Blur but is not in any way related to the Principle of Contrast or to paradigm structure. The second assumption is massively violated by C-F/C-M in their own analysis of Polish.

Recall that the paradigm in (3.6) appears to violate No Blur. Of course C-F/C-M do not explicitly conclude that (3.6) satisfies No Blur because No Blur is empirically vacuous. Rather, according to C-F/C-M, the appearance of Blur in (3.6) is a misperception. Instead of being categorized into the seven classes shown in (3.6), Polish (masculine singular *o*-stem) nouns can be re-categorized into the three classes in (3.9).

(3.9)	Class	1/2/5	3/4	6/7
	Nom	-	-	-
	Gen	a	a	u
	Dat	owi	u	owi
	Inst	em	em	em
	Loc	u ~ e	u ~ e	u ~ e
	Voc	u ~ e	u ~ e	u ~ e

There is an error in table (3.9) from C-F/C-M (2000). As can be seen from (3.6), the vocative affix for classes 3/4 is -*e*, not -*u*~*e* (-*u* alternating with -*e*) as in (3.1). As we show below, this seemingly minor oversight has serious consequences. In (3.9) as given, it looks as if the choice of Loc and Voc suffixes is completely independent of the organization of the stems into the three inflectional classes (columns). C-F/C-M claim that the choice of -*e* in the Loc or Voc is in fact independently determined by consideration of the available stem allomorphs for a noun (see below) and independent from inflectional class. To the extent that choice of -*e* correlates with other affix allomorphy and thus falls into the inflectional class system, C-F/C-M's analysis is undermined.

Putting aside the Loc and Voc exponents for the moment, it is obvious that in (3.9) in the Gen, -*u* is the class identifier as it figures with nouns of one class only, whereas -*a*, which figures with two classes, is the class default. By the same reasoning, in the Dat, -*u* is the class identifier, whereas -*owi* is the class default.

While the recategorization of affixes in (3.9) thus satisfies No Blur and, according to C-F/C-M, therefore also Clark's Principle of Contrast, this is done at the cost of treating the Gen -*u* quite differently from the -*u* of the Dat. The fact central to the Polish nominal paradigm (3.6), that -*u* is the default suffix for the entire paradigm, is totally lost sight of in C-F/C-M's analysis. As remarked above, on their analysis this is a case of accidental homophony (which is not allowed to avoid No Blur on the horizontal dimension). Karl Verner noted in 1876, (101) "linguistics cannot totally rule out accident, but accidents en masse like here ... it cannot and must not countenance." The fact that the No Blur Principle forces us to countenance such instances of accidental homophony en masse suggests that there is something fundamentally wrong with the principle.

In fact, as we now show, C-F/C-M's proposed analysis of Polish fails on their own terms. As displayed in (3.6), -*u* is found in the Loc with stems of classes 2, 4, 5, and 7, whereas -*e* occurs with stems of classes 1, 3, and 6. These same suffixes figure also in the vocative, but here -*u* appears in classes 2 and 7 and -*e* appears elsewhere. Since in both Loc and Voc neither affix is a class identifier, this distribution of affixes violates No Blur. In order to account for this affix distribution without Blur, C-F/C-M introduce a subclassification of stems into those that do and those that do not have "majority and minority alternants." As is clear from (3.6), the form of the stem taking Loc or Voc -*e* is always distinct from the form used in other cases. The -*e* stem involves a final consonant change that is the result of the phonological process of palatalization. C-F/C-M suppose that choice of -*e* is connected with the existence of the palatalized stem alternant rather than with declension class; that is, in a sense the marked palatalized stem chooses the -*e* allomorph rather than the -*e* allomorph triggering palatalization. They remark that "[w]here -*e* occurs, the stem alternant that accompanies it is a minority alternant peculiar ... to the vocative and possibly also the locative. On the other hand, where -*u* occurs, its stem alternant is the same as the one generally found elsewhere in the ... paradigm" (823). Choice of -*e* vs. -*u* for Loc and Voc, then, is not a matter of declension class. Rather, across the classes in the paradigm in (3.6), -*e* will attach for Voc or Loc if there exists a "minority stem alternant" for that case for that stem, with -*u* attaching elsewhere. The suffix -*e* thus differs "in information content" from -*u*, where information content, as noted above, specifically includes stem shape. The distribution of -*e* vs. -*u* in the Loc and Voc, therefore, is predictable within a declension class and these affixes no longer violate No Blur.

From the description above, it may be difficult to unpack all the information that C-F/C-M are attributing to Polish stems or to see the way the information interrelates. First, one must know for each stem whether or not it has a minority stem alternant for the Voc and for the Loc. The existence of a minority stem form for the Voc does not entail the existence of a minority stem form for the Loc, as seen in classes 4 and 5 in (3.6). C-F/C-M point out that this knowledge about stem alternants requires a comparison with other forms of a noun, since the minority stem alternant does not simply end in a palatal consonant–it must contrast with a non-palatal stem form elsewhere in the paradigm. Traditionally this alternation in stem form for the cases expressed by -*e* has been explained by referring to the rule of Polish phonology that spreads the feature [−back] from -*e* to the immediately preceding consonant (for discussion see Gussmann 1980; Rubach 1984; Czaykowska-Higgins 1988; and Szpyra 1995). This in turn triggers several other phonological rules which account for the fact that before the -*e* affix noun stems end with "palatal-type" consonants, contrasting with the form of the stems before other suffixes.

Second on the C-F/C-M account, in addition to assigning the features [+/−minority stem alternant Loc] and [+/−minority stem alternant Voc] to each noun, we must further stipulate that Loc -*e* attaches to stems that have a minority stem alternant in the Loc, whereas Voc -*e* attaches to stems that have a minority stem alternant in the Voc. Finally, both Loc and Voc -*e* must also actually choose the minority stem alternant. This third stipulation does not follow from the second on an account like C-F/C-M's, since generalizations about minority stem alternants are independent of actually choosing such alternants; for example, Dat -*u* will only attach to stems with a Voc minority stem alternant, although the Dat -*u* does not choose this alternant.

It is at this point that the error in table (3.9) becomes critical. C-F/C-M's analysis crucially depends on the forms of the Voc and Loc being independent of the three inflectional classes in (3.3)–it is only on this assumption that they may claim that the choice between -*e* and -*u* in the Loc and Voc does not involve inflectional class and cannot Blur the paradigm. The intuition is that one will learn whether a stem has a minority alternant in the Loc and/or Voc by hearing these forms–they are not productively generable from the majority alternant by a phonological rule triggered by the -*e* suffix. The distribution of the -*u* allomorph of the Voc and Loc suffixes is thus not connected to the distribution of -*u* elsewhere in the paradigm, which is governed by inflectional class.

However, note from the paradigm in (3.6) that the allomorphy of the Voc suffix–the choice of -*u* or -*e*–is not independent of the distribution of -*u* elsewhere in the paradigm: the presence of -*u* in the dative, with a majority stem alternant, predicts the Voc in -*e* with the minority stem alternant (this is not shown in (3.9), reproduced from C-F/C-M (2000)). One must be able to predict from the existence of a single stem (the majority stem) with -*u* in the Dat that a minority stem will exist for the Voc, and presumably one must also be able to predict the "minority stem" form of the Voc stem with the -*e* suffix from the "majority" stem form. Since the distribution of -*u* (vs. -*e*) in the Voc is in fact connected with the inflectional class system that accounts for the distribution of -*u* elsewhere in the paradigm, the Voc allomorphy is a matter of inflectional class and should Blur the paradigm. The C-F/C-M analysis fails to draw the connection between inflectional class, "is in class 3/4 in (3.9)", and the form property, "has a minority stem alternant in the Voc". It is also not clear whether the C-M system should allow implicational generalizations that go from inflectional class to "intrinsic" features of stems like phonological form (i.e., features with implications beyond inflectional allomorphy). While the No Blur paradigm might be comfortable with (default) statements relating, e.g., gender to inflectional class (Polish masculine nouns fall into the *o*-stem class by default), it should probably not allow implications from inflectional classes to gender or form, such as, "class 3/4 implies minority stem alternant in the Voc". Allowing implications of this sort treats inflectional class on a par with other features and not simply as the consequence of paradigmatic organization. If inflectional class features could participate in such implications equally with, e.g., gender, it would be a mystery why they would obey the Single Inflectional Class principle. As explained above, since a stem can be class 3/4 and masculine, it should be able to carry both a class A and also a class B feature, were class features like other features.

3.4 Syncretism, impoverishment, and a Distributed Morphology analysis

We conclude this chapter by sketching an alternative account of the Polish facts which successfully captures the generalizations that C-F/C-M note, as well as the syncretism across cases that they fail to acknowledge. This account treats all the nouns in (3.6) as belonging to the same declension class, the *o*-stems, and it is not necessary that these nouns only be masculine (as most of (3.6) is the same for neuter nouns of the same declension), nor that all masculine nouns fall into this class (as they do not in Polish). The alternative account is based on the theory of Distributed Morphology, DM (e.g., Halle and Marantz 1993; Halle 1997).

In DM it would be assumed that each case ending of the Polish declension is composed of a set of morphological features, including case and number features. In the PF branch of the grammar, Vocabulary Items (VIs) are inserted into the terminal nodes bearing case and number features and thereby realize these features. The Vocabulary Items are underspecified with respect to the morphosyntactic feature bundles that they may realize. All Vocabulary Items compete for insertion into any given node; the most highly specified item whose features do not conflict with the features at the node wins the competition and is inserted (the familiar "elsewhere" condition). The Case VIs for the Polish nouns under discussion are given in (3.10). We assume that a full analysis of Polish would decompose the cases into case features that cross-classify the cases according to syntactic generalizations and in accordance with patterns of syncretism across Polish nominal paradigms. For present purposes, we provide just a cover label for each case. This leads to an accidental homophony between Loc and Voc -*e*, which calls out for a feature system in which the decomposition of both Loc and Voc would include some feature X that -*e* could mention.

(3.10) a. [Nom] ←→ Null   (more probably the vowel "yer" familiar
                                                    from the analysis of Slavic languages)
     b. [Gen] ←→ /a/
     c. [Dat] ←→ /owi/
     d. [Inst] ←→ /em/[1]
     e. [Loc]
              } ←→ /e/
     f. [Voc]
     g. [ ] ←→ /u/   (default)

Since, with the exception of the default VI, listed last, the items in (3.10) each have a single specified case feature and cover all the Polish cases under discussion, there will never be occasion to select the default -*u*. We know,

---

[1] Unlike the other suffix beginning with /e/, the Inst ending does not cause palatalization of the stem-final consonant. For some discussion, see Halle and Nevins in press.

however, that the default in (3.10) figures in various cases. Given the way competition among affixes drives the insertion of VIs, we can implement formally the insertion of the default exponent *-u* by "impoverishment," i.e., by deleting the case features in morphemes when they attach to stems of a particular class. Since the distribution of the default *-u* is not completely predictable from the phonological form of the stems in this declension, we need to mark the stems that trigger impoverishment of the various case features by a diacritic (disregarding here any subregularities leading to generalizations about the distribution of these diacritics across stems). If a stem impoverishes the case feature X, we give it the feature $[-X]$. With that notation, the relevant impoverishment rules are listed in (3.11). When a stem deletes the case feature on the case/number suffix, the default in (3.10) will be the only VI eligible for insertion.

(3.11) i.   Gen $\rightarrow$ ø / $[-$Gen$]$ + _____
        ii.   Dat $\rightarrow$ ø / $[-$Dat$]$ + _____
        iii. Loc $\rightarrow$ ø / $[-$Loc$]$ + _____
        iv.   Voc $\rightarrow$ ø / $[-$Voc$]$ + _____

If the four impoverishment features, $[-$Gen$]$, $[-$Dat$]$, $[-$Loc$]$, and $[-$Voc$]$, are all independent, a stem could have none of the features, all of the features, one of the features, or any combination of two or three of the features. If the features cross-classified the stems in this way, there would be 12 subclasses in (3.6), not the 7 shown, thus not all possible combinations of impoverishment features are exemplified. The classes in (3.6) are defined by the sets of impoverishment features shown in (3.12). The reader may note that (3.12) is effectively identical with (3.8)–the impoverishment features serve to describe the distribution of the default *-u* across the subclasses of Polish stems from this particular declension class (the *o*-stems).

(3.12) 1. null
       2. $[-$Loc, $-$Voc$]$
       3. $-$Dat
       4. $[-$Dat, $-$Loc$]$
       5. $-$Loc
       6. $-$Gen
       7. $[-$Gen, $-$Loc, $-$Voc$]$

The restrictions on the distribution of impoverishment features suggests that the Polish *o*-class obeys the following implicational generalizations among its features:

(3.13) a. *[−Gen, −Dat]   No noun impoverishes both Gen and Dat
        b. *[−Dat, −Voc]   No noun impoverishes both Dat and Voc
        c. −Voc → −Loc   Nouns that impoverish Voc impoverish
                                 also Loc
        d. [−Gen, −Loc]   Nouns that impoverish Gen and Loc
            → −Voc   impoverish also Voc
        (in addition to these generalizations, neither Nom nor Instr nor Acc
        impoverish)

Note that these generalizations express knowledge about syncretism across cases. So, for example, speakers that hear a form with -*u* in the vocative can predict from (3.13.c) that the noun will also take -*u* in the locative. For present purposes, the most important generalization is the one that prohibits impoverishment in both the dative and the vocative in the same stems, (3.13b.). This means that a speaker hearing -*u* in the dative will predict -*e* in the vocative for the same stem, since the -*u* in the dative implies [−Dat] and (3.13b.) prohibits a stem from carrying both [−Dat] and the [−Voc] feature that would trigger -*u* in the vocative. As indicated above, this generalization means that, contra C-F/C-M, the distribution of -*e* vs. -*u* in the vocative is connected with the distribution of -*u* in other cases, and thus -*e*∼-*u* in the vocative does Blur the declension classes in a Carstairs-McCarthy-style paradigm.

Our analysis of Polish consists of the following pieces: (i) a set of six case endings for the Polish nouns in this inflectional class in (3.11), (ii) a set of four impoverishment rules that account for the syncretic distribution of the default -*u* in (3.12), (iii) a set of four generalizations about the distribution of the impoverishment rules that further restrict the distribution of -*u* in (3.13), and (iv) the literature on Polish phonology that explains the palatalization processes triggered by the Loc/Voc -*e* suffix. We have shown that the combination of (iii) and (iv) is superior to C-F/C-M's account of stem allomorphs and affixes in the Loc and Voc cases, most obviously because it connects these Loc/Voc facts to the distribution of the default -*u* throughout the paradigm (as we pointed out, C-F/C-M require in addition a double stipulation that -*e* attaches to stems that have a minority stem alternant and also chooses to attach to this alternant). Our analysis also accomplishes what C-F/C-M totally overlook: an account of syncretism along the vertical dimension of a paradigm. However, as explained above, in order to give No Blur empirical content, C-F/C-M must assume a principle avoiding "accidental homophony" in both the vertical and horizontal dimensions of a paradigm. Thus the fact that they allow homophonous -*u*'s in the vertical dimension while disallowing homophonous -*u*'s in the horizontal dimension undermines their analysis.

3.5 Inflectional classes and features

We conclude by re-examining what "No Blur" really claims about paradigms. As C-M points out, if we disallow accidentally homophonous affixes and we disallow the assignment of stems to multiple inflectional classes, then a Blurring affix will be one which covers two or more classes of stems, when another affix occurs in the same row of the paradigm as the "default" for that row. Formally, then, Blurring shows up as the necessity to include a disjunction of features in the information content of an affix–this affix attaches to {class A, class B} (the curly brackets, as usual for rule notations, indicate a collapsing of two different environments with the exception of the material in the brackets, and thus a lack of a generalization that might unify the bracketed material). For example, in (3.6), if *-owi* is treated as the default Dat marker, *-u* would be marked as attaching to class 3 or class 4 stems. This kind of disjunction shows that some generalization about syncretism is being missed; why does a single affix cover these two classes? (what do the classes have in common such that the affix should attach to both of them?) That is, No Blur doesn't rely on paradigms in any crucial sense; it is simply a statement about trying to maximize generalizations (avoid disjunctions) in morphological analysis.

Clearly Carstairs-McCarthy is right in emphasizing that principles of language acquisition ultimately should explain facts about the distribution of forms across the paradigms generated by the inflectional features of a language. In particular, we have no real idea about how a child assigns features to Vocabulary Items or separates stems into declensional classes. Until we have a better specific understanding of what the child brings to language acquisition (other than the principles of Distributed Morphology), we can do no better than endorse the traditional assumptions that the child seeks to minimize homophony and maximize generalizations. As explained in detail above, Carstairs-McCarthy fails to demonstrate that further principles are required. He needs these traditional assumptions in any case, and they fully cover the relevant examples without recourse to additional principles such as "No Blur".

We are still left with the question of whether the principles of grammar include a prohibition against stems belonging to more than one "arbitrary" inflectional class. Note that our own DM analysis of Polish connects the subclasses of the *o*-stems to impoverishment rules deleting case features prior to Vocabulary Insertion. We do not know whether impoverishment-triggering features would have the same status as arbitrary inflectional class features in Carstairs-McCarthy's view and thus whether our analysis violates the kind of Single Inflectional Class principle that he seems to require. Consider the class of Polish masculine nouns that behave like *a*-stems (i.e., like most feminines) in the singular but like *o*-stems in the plural; this behavior does not seem remarkable from a cross-linguistic perspective and it does involve individual stems belonging to more than one inflectional class. Thus we do not hold out much hope that a principle prohibiting membership in multiple inflectional classes will survive detailed analyses of inflectional morphology cross-linguistically, but we do not wish to draw any general conclusions about the principle from the small body of Polish data examined here.

References

Cameron-Faulkner, Thea, and Andrew Carstairs-McCarthy (2000) 'Stem alternants as morphological signata: Evidence from Blur avoidance in Polish'. *Natural Language and Linguistic Theory*: 813–35.

Carstairs-McCarthy, Andrew (1994) 'Inflection classes, gender and the Principle of Contrast'. *Language* 70: 737–88.

Czaykowska-Higgins, Ewa (1988) Investigations into Polish morphology and phonology. Ph.D. thesis, MIT.

Gunkel, Lutz (2003) 'Syncretism and case underspecification in Polish noun paradigms', in *Generative Linguistics in Poland: Morphosyntactic Investigations*. Instytut Podstaw Infomatyki, Warszawa, 49–62.

Gussmann, Edmund (1980) *Studies in Abstract Phonology*. Cambridge, MA: MIT Press.

Halle, Morris (1997) 'Distributed Morphology: Impoverishment and fission'. *MIT Working Papers in Linguistics* 30, pp. 425–49.

—— and Alec Marantz (1993) 'Distributed Morphology and the pieces of inflection', in K. Hale and J. Keyser (eds.), *The View from Building 20*. Cambridge, MA: MIT Press, pp. 111–76.

—— and Andrew Nevins. 'Rule application in phonology', paper presented at the CUNY Symposium on Phonology: Representations and Architectures, 2004. To appear in Charles Cairns and Eric Raimy (eds.), *Contemporary Views on Architecture and Representations in Phonological Theory*.

Rubach, Jerzy (1984) *Cyclic and Lexical Phonology: The Structure of Polish*. Dordrecht: Foris.

Szpyra, Jolanta (1995) *Three Tiers of Polish and English Phonology*. Lublin: Wydawnictwo Uniwersytetu Marii Curie-Sklodowskiej.

Verner, Karl (1876) 'Eine Ausname der ersten Lautverschiebung'. *Zeitschrift für vergleichende Sprachforschung* 23: 97–130.

4

Paradigm generation and Northern Sámi stems

PETER SVENONIUS*

4.1 Introduction

Northern Sámi, a Finno-Ugric language spoken mainly in Northern Norway, Sweden, and Finland, has a system of consonant gradation which affects consonants at the center of a prosodic foot: the coda of the stressed syllable and the onset of the following syllable (stress is word-initial). Consonant gradation is illustrated in (4.1) for two typical nouns (angle brackets signal that the example is given in the standard orthography; unreferenced examples are generally from Nickel 1990).[1]

(4.1) ⟨*viessu*⟩ 'house', ⟨*čiehka*⟩ 'corner'

	Singular	Plural	Singular	Plural
Nom	⟨viessu⟩	⟨viesut⟩	⟨čiehka⟩	⟨čiegat⟩
Acc	⟨viesu⟩	⟨viesuid⟩	⟨čiega⟩	⟨čiegaid⟩
Ill	⟨vissui⟩	⟨viesuide⟩	⟨čihkii⟩	⟨čiegaide⟩

* Many thanks to Berit Anne Bals, Marit Julien, Patrik Bye, and the participants in the MIT workshop on Paradigms for helpful discussion. Donca Steriade provided particularly stimulating feedback on the presentation, Berit Anne Bals was very patient with all my many questions during the write-up, and Patrik Bye's detailed comments on the first draft were especially valuable. Thanks also to the two anonymous reviewers for Oxford for their remarks, which have been useful in rethinking the introduction and conclusion.

[1] The data in this chapter represent the Kautokeino (Guovdageaidnu) dialect (see Sammallahti 1998, Bals et al. 2005 for further information about the phonological details). Phonemic and phonetic representations, when used, are based on the conventions presented in Bals et al. (2005), using the following non-IPA symbols (adopted from the standard orthography):

Here:	š	č	ž	c	z
IPA:	ʃ	tʃ	dʒ	ts	dz

Overlong geminates are written C:C. Other symbols correspond more or less to their usual IPA values, in phonetic and phonemic representations marked with square brackets and slashes.

Abbreviations used here Nom[inative], Acc[usative], Ill[ative], Loc[ative], Com[itative], Ess[ive]. Some works on Northern Sámi grammar recognize a genitive but it is always identical to the accusative.

Loc	⟨viesus⟩	⟨viesuin⟩	⟨čiegas⟩	⟨čiegain⟩
Com	⟨viesuin⟩	⟨viesuiguin⟩	⟨čiegain⟩	⟨čiegaiguin⟩
Ess	⟨viessun⟩		⟨čiehkan⟩	

Observe the pattern of geminate versus non-geminate *s* in the root of the first example, and the corresponding pattern of *g* alternating with *hk* in the second. The long (two segment, CC) examples appear in cells in the paradigm that call for Strong Grade, while the short (C) examples are Weak Grade. Specifically, Strong Grade is found in the nominative singular, the illative singular, and the essive.

A different distribution of Strong and Weak Grade is seen in (4.2).

(4.2)   ⟨*gielu*⟩ 'bloodclot', ⟨*vuoluš*⟩ 'that which is underneath'

	Singular	Plural	Singular	Plural
Nom	⟨gielu⟩	⟨gillomat⟩	⟨vuoluš⟩	⟨vullošat⟩
Acc	⟨gilloma⟩	⟨gillomiid⟩	⟨vulloša⟩	⟨vullošiid⟩
Ill	⟨gillomii⟩	⟨gillomiidda⟩	⟨vullošii⟩	⟨vullošiidda⟩
Loc	⟨gillomis⟩	⟨gillomiin⟩	⟨vullošis⟩	⟨vullošiin⟩
Com	⟨gillomiin⟩	⟨gillomiiguin⟩	⟨vullošiin⟩	⟨vullošiiguin⟩
Ess	⟨gielun⟩		⟨vuolušin⟩	

Here, the nominative singular and the essive are *not* in the Strong Grade, rather the other forms are (the illative singular is Strong in both (4.1) and (4.2)). Another example of this pattern is shown in (4.3), where ⟨hcc⟩ and ⟨lg⟩ are Strong Grade centers, and ⟨z⟩ as well as (counterintuitively) ⟨lgg⟩ are Weak.

(4.3)   ⟨*boazu*⟩ 'reindeer', ⟨*bálggis*⟩ 'path'

	Singular	Plural	Singular	Plural
Nom	⟨boazu⟩	⟨bohccot⟩	⟨bálggis⟩	⟨bálgát⟩
Acc	⟨bohcco⟩	⟨bohccuid⟩	⟨bálgá⟩	⟨bálgáid⟩
Ill	⟨bohccui⟩	⟨bohccuide⟩	⟨bálgái⟩	⟨bálgáide⟩
Loc	⟨bohccos⟩	⟨bohccuin⟩	⟨bálgás⟩	⟨bálgáin⟩
Com	⟨bohccuin⟩	⟨bohccuiguin⟩	⟨bálgáin⟩	⟨bálgáiguin⟩
Ess	⟨boazun⟩		⟨bálggisin⟩	

Similar alternations can be observed in the adjectival and verbal paradigms. There are also nouns which do not show any alternation, like those in (4.4) (⟨á⟩ = /aa/).

(4.4)   ⟨*gahpir*⟩ 'cap' ⟨*ákšu*⟩ 'axe'

	Singular	Plural	Singular	Plural
Nom	⟨gahpir⟩	⟨gahpirat⟩	⟨ákšu⟩	⟨ákšut⟩

Acc	⟨gahpira⟩	⟨gahpiriid⟩	⟨ákšu⟩	⟨ákšuid⟩
Ill	⟨gahpirii⟩	⟨gahpiriidda⟩	⟨ákšui⟩	⟨ákšuide⟩
Loc	⟨gahpiris⟩	⟨gahpiriin⟩	⟨ákšus⟩	⟨ákšuin⟩
Com	⟨gahpiriin⟩	⟨gahpiriiguin⟩	⟨ákšuin⟩	⟨ákšuiguin⟩
Ess	⟨gahpirin⟩		⟨ákšun⟩	

There are two different aspects to the complexity of the system: one is the paradigmatic distribution of the Strong and Weak forms, which is historically but not synchronically phonologically conditioned, and the other is the complexity of the phonological relationship between the Strong and Weak forms. In this chapter, I present an analysis which is based on a phonologically somewhat abstract element (an infixal timing slot which is responsible for the Strong Grade) interacting with a simple concatenative morphology and declension class features. Once these devices are accepted, then a fairly simple analysis emerges.[2]

Historically, a process of lengthening applied to consonants immediately following a stressed foot nucleus, if the following syllable was open (Sammallahti 1998; Bye 2001). Thus the alternation between nominative and accusative would have looked something like the following, for a few common stem shapes, given an accusative suffix -*m*.[3]

(4.5)

Root	**Nominative**	**Accusative**	
CVCV	CVC.CV	CV.CV-m	
*viesu	*vies.su	*vie.sum	(cf. (4.1))
CVCVC	CV.CVC	CVC.CV.C-em	
*gielum	*gie.lum	*giel.lu.mem	(cf. (4.2))
*poazoj	*poa.zoj	*poaz.zo.jem	(cf. (4.3))
CVCVCV	CVC.CV.CV	CVC.CV.CV-m	
*kapera	*kap.pe.ra	*kap.pe.ram	(cf. (4.4))

After various phonological changes, including the loss of many word-final consonants including the accusative -*m* suffix, obscured the phonological basis for the alternations, they became morphologized. I propose that this be represented in terms of sets of stem-forming suffixes, some of which have as a component a floating autosegment. This floating autosegment, which I represent as μ, adds a timing slot or mora to the coda of the first stressed syllable to its left—in other words it is infixal. I annotate its infixal character by

---

[2] Diphthong simplification can also been seen at work in the paradigms above. I believe this to be fully regular and phonologically conditioned but will not discuss it in this chapter.

[3] These starred examples are oversimplified approximations of historical reconstructions for illustrative purposes; for careful reconstructions see Sammallahti (1998).

superscripting μ and attaching an arcing line to it, thus: $\text{-}^{\mu\frown}$; when this is attached to a root, for example of form CVCV, it can be represented as in (4.6a.), exemplified for *viessu* "house" in (4.6b.).

(4.6) a. CV́CV-$^{\mu\frown}$ → CV$^{\mu}$CV
       b. viesu-$^{\mu\frown}$ → vie$^{\mu}$su → viessu

The table in (4.7) shows the synchronic derivation of some of the nouns displayed in the examples above; various phonological details will be discussed below. The symbol $\sqrt{}$ stands for the root.

(4.7)

Root	Nominative	Accusative	
Class 1 (E)	$\sqrt{}$-$^{\mu\frown}$	$\sqrt{}$-a	
viesu- 'house'	⟨viessu⟩	⟨viesu⟩	(cf. (4.1))
Class 2 (O)	$\sqrt{}$-	$\sqrt{}$-$^{\mu\frown}$a	
gielum- 'bloodclot'	⟨gielu⟩	⟨gilloma⟩	(cf. (4.2))
Class 3 (C)	$\sqrt{}$-u	$\sqrt{}$-$^{\mu\mu\frown}$o	
boazu- 'reindeer'	⟨boazu⟩	⟨bohcco⟩	(cf. (4.3))
Class 4 (NA)	$\sqrt{}$-	$\sqrt{}$-a	
gahpir- 'cap'	⟨gahpir⟩	⟨gahpira⟩	(cf. (4.4))

Historically, something like the CVCV pattern in (4.5) gave rise to Class 1 in (4.7), which I call E below (for Even number of syllables). Something like the CVCVC pattern gave rise to Classes 2 (O for Odd number of syllables) and 3 (C for Contracted), while the CVCVCV pattern gave rise to Class 4 (NA for Non-Alternating).

Synchronically, class membership must be learned along with a root (though there are some phonological clues), and is necessary in order to derive the right pattern of Strong and Weak Grade. A paradigm is entirely determined by a set of two or three stem-forming suffixes like the ones displayed in (4.7). For instance, the locative and comitative case forms are always built from the same stem as the accusative, and the essive is always built from the same stem as the nominative singular (the illative behaves differently in different classes).

This analysis makes clear predictions which can be tested. It predicts, for example, that the locus of the consonant mutation characteristic of Strong Grade must bear a certain phonological relationship to the position of the suffix triggering it. Since syntax narrowly constrains the ordering of affixes (see for example Julien 1996; 2002), predictions are made even when the affix contains no other phonological material than $^{\mu\frown}$.

For example, consider the pattern of consonant mutation in the E Class noun *muitalus* 'story', illustrated in (4.8).

(4.8) ⟨*muitalus*⟩ 'story'

	Singular	Plural
Nom	⟨muitalus⟩	⟨muitalusat⟩
Acc	⟨muitalusa⟩	⟨muitalusaid⟩
Ill	⟨muitalussii⟩	⟨muitalusaide⟩
Loc	⟨muitalusas⟩	⟨muitalusain⟩
Com	⟨muitalusain⟩	⟨muitalusaiguin⟩
Ess	⟨muitalussan⟩	

The E pattern shows Strong Grade in the nominative singular, the illative singular, and the essive. The third syllable here bears secondary stress. Thus, $^{\mu\frown}$ is predicted to target the root-final *s*. Since there is no length contrast in consonants word-finally, this is imperceptible in the nominative singular but visible in the illative and essive.

Derivational suffixes, which on independent grounds are expected to attach more closely to the root than a case suffix, can change the class membership of a root. For example, the derivational suffix -*s* illustrated in (4.9) derives O Class nouns, as can be seen by comparing the E pattern of the underived noun *suorbma* 'finger' on the left to the O pattern of the derived noun *suorpmas* 'ring' on the right.

(4.9) ⟨*suorbma*⟩ 'finger', ⟨*suorpmas*⟩ 'finger ring'

	Singular	Plural	Singular	Plural
Nom	⟨suorbma⟩	⟨suorpmat⟩	⟨suorpmas⟩	⟨suorbmasat⟩
Acc	⟨suorpma⟩	⟨suorpmaid⟩	⟨suorbmasa⟩	⟨suorbmasiid⟩
Ill	⟨surbmii⟩	⟨suorpmaide⟩	⟨suorbmasii⟩	⟨suorbmasiidda⟩
Loc	⟨suorpmas⟩	⟨suorpmain⟩	⟨suorbmasis⟩	⟨suorbmasiin⟩
Com	⟨suorpmain⟩	⟨suorpmaiguin⟩	⟨suorbmasiin⟩	⟨suorbmasiiguin⟩
Ess	⟨suorbman⟩		⟨suorpmasin⟩	

In fact, derivational suffixes can themselves undergo consonant gradation, if they fall within the phonologically defined position where μ must be affixed. For example, the suffix -*huoč*, illustrated in (4.10); the *č* in the suffix exhibits consonant gradation.

(4.10) ⟨*bárdni*⟩ 'boy', ⟨*bártnehuoš*⟩ 'poor boy'

	Singular	Plural	Singular	Plural
Nom	⟨bárdni⟩	⟨bártnit⟩	⟨bártnehuoš⟩	⟨bártnehuoččat⟩
Acc	⟨bártni⟩	⟨bártniid⟩	⟨bártnehuočča⟩	⟨bártnehuoččaid⟩
Ill	⟨bárdnái⟩	⟨bártniide⟩	⟨bártnehužžii⟩	⟨bártnehuoččaide⟩
Loc	⟨bártnis⟩	⟨bártniin⟩	⟨bártnehuoččas⟩	⟨bártnehuoččain⟩
Com	⟨bártniin⟩	⟨bártniiguin⟩	⟨bártnehuoččain⟩	⟨bártnehuoččaiguin⟩
Ess	⟨bárdnin⟩		⟨bártnehuožžan⟩	

In the derived form, the autosegment μ attaches to the final *č* of the suffix, as seen in the illative singular and essive forms (word-finally the segment surfaces only as a *š*). The root is too far from the stem-forming suffixes and does not undergo consonant gradation, surfacing in the Weak Grade, as shown.

In the next section, I motivate the assumption that the Strong Grade is essentially derived from the Weak Grade.

4.2 The nature of the alternation

The previous section exhibited many different manifestations of the Strong–Weak Grade alternation, including the following, presented here with orthographic representations side by side with broad phonemic representations.

(4.11)	Strong		Weak		
	⟨ss⟩	[ss]	⟨s⟩	[s]	(cf. (4.1))
	⟨hk⟩	[hk]	⟨g⟩	[g]	(cf. (4.1))
	⟨ll⟩	[ll]	⟨l⟩	[l]	(cf. (4.2))
	⟨hcc⟩	[hhc]	⟨z⟩	[z]	(cf. (4.3))
	⟨lg⟩	[ləg]	⟨lgg⟩	[lgg]	(cf. (4.3))
	⟨rbm⟩	[rəʔm]	⟨rpm⟩	[rʔm]	(cf. (4.9))
	⟨rdn⟩	[rəʔn]	⟨rtn⟩	[rʔn]	(cf. (4.10))
	⟨žž⟩	[dč]	⟨čč⟩	[tč]	(cf. (4.10))

Nickel (1990: 27–30) lists 147 such Strong–Weak pairs, organized into various groupings. Superficially, the alternations seem heterogeneous but I suggest that consonant gradation can be modeled in every case as the result of a timing slot, which I have represented above as μ, being added to the consonant center. μ is essentially a phonological segment in the language, like *h* or *ʔ*, but surfaces with different values depending on its phonological environment (this does not rule out the possibility that μ is underlyingly the same as *ʔ* or *h*). Various phonological rules apply to the combination of μ plus a consonant or sequence of consonants to derive the surface output.

4.2.1 *Productivity*

The system of consonant gradation is highly productive and is applied to new coinages and loans in the language. In general, new words are assigned to the E class; for instance, the examples in (4.12) show pairs in which the nominative singular (the first of each pair) is Strong Grade and the accusative singular is Weak Grade. I give Norwegian cognates though the words might have been borrowed from Swedish or some other language.

(4.12) a. ⟨porseliidna⟩ ∼ ⟨porseliinna⟩ (cf. Nor. *porselen*, 'porcelain')
   b. ⟨parlameanta⟩ ∼ ⟨parlameantta⟩ (cf. Nor. *parlament*, 'parliament')
   c. ⟨diftoŋga⟩ ∼ ⟨diftoŋgga⟩ (cf. Nor. *diftong*, 'diphthong')

Certain suffixes (as noted in the Introduction) are associated with the O class, and this may lead to new words being O class; the following examples illustrate this, as the nominative singular (the first one) is Weak Grade and the accusative singular Strong Grade.

(4.13) a. ⟨politihkar⟩ ∼ ⟨politihkkara⟩ (cf. Nor. *politiker*, 'politician')
   b. ⟨mekanihkar⟩ ∼ ⟨mekanihkkara⟩ (cf. Nor. *mekaniker*, 'mechanic')
   c. ⟨teknihkar⟩ ∼ ⟨teknihkkara⟩ (cf. Nor. *tekniker*, 'technician')

Whether the original word more closely resembles the Weak or Strong Grade varies.[4] For example, a cognate to *charm* (Nor. *sjarm*, [šarm]) has recently been borrowed, and alternates between Strong [*šarəʔma*] (nominative) and Weak [*šarʔma*] (accusative); judging from the phonological dissimilarity of the Strong form to the Norwegian, it seems that the word was introduced into Sámi as a Weak form.[5] On the other hand, words including *ks* and *kt* and *kst* clusters (among others) in their centers may tend to be borrowed as Strong, since there are Strong centers with those clusters in Northern Sámi but not Weak ones. For instance, the word *doctor* (Norwegian *doktor*) has entered the language as Strong *doaktaara*, Weak *doavttiir* (the Northern Sámi word is class O so the Weak form is nominative singular and the Strong form is accusative singular).

 The same $k \sim v$ alternation is seen in the minimal pair in (4.14). Norwegian *lefse*, a thin potato-meal tortilla, has been borrowed as Weak *leavssa* in the accusative, alternating with Strong *leaksa* in the nominative; but 'text' (Nor. *tekst*) has been borrowed as Strong, alternating with a form with *v*.

(4.14) a. ⟨leaksa⟩ ∼ ⟨leavssa⟩ (cf. Nor. *lefse*, 'potato tortilla')
   b. ⟨teaksta⟩ ∼ ⟨teavstta⟩ (cf. Nor. *tekst*, 'text')

New words are also sometimes assigned to the NA class. This may happen if a consonant center is not gradable or if the word is somehow inconsistent with

---

[4] Special thanks to Berit Anne Bals for discussion on this point.
[5] If the donor word had been used as a Strong Grade form, then the alternation would presumably be between *šarʔma* and **šarma*.

Northern Sámi patterns. I know of no recent loan words entering Class C but Class C nouns can be derived.[6]

Because of the productivity of consonant gradation, root alternants cannot simply be listed. Part of competence in Northern Sámi is the presence of a system that predicts the Weak from the Strong form, or the Strong from the Weak form, or both from some underlying representation. Bals (2002) has shown that children learn to correctly use the consonant gradation process before the age of three (in fact, the phonologically simplest alternation–gemination–is already being correctly used by the age of two).

4.2.2 *The direction of the alternation*

I have argued that part of the linguistic competence of a Northern Sámi speaker is knowing how to create an alternating Strong–Weak pair; the simplest statement of this knowledge will be as a rule applying to an underlying form. This leads us to the question of which form is the underlying one, a question that turns out to be surprisingly difficult to answer. I briefly discuss the complications, then turn to the solution.

A possible clue regarding the direction of the alternation is the morphological markedness of the forms themselves. For example, since the Strong Grade is used in the nominative singular of class E nouns and for the infinitive and third person singular present of bisyllabic verbs, it might be thought that Strong Grade is the unmarked form. However, Weak Grade is also used for some extremely frequent forms, including the syncretized accusative/genitive in the class E nominal paradigm, and the first person singular present and second person singular present in the verbal paradigm; so both Strong and Weak Grade appear in forms which are high in frequency and low in markedness.

Another kind of attempt to establish the directionality of an alternation is to examine its acquisition. The forms that children acquire first might be taken as unmarked, and their overgeneralizations might reveal what kinds of rules they are postulating. Here the data reported in Bals (2002) gives a complex picture. For many C–CC alternations, children appear to prefer C over CC, that is, they use the Weak Grade. However, for several CC–C:C alternations, they prefer C:C over CC, that is, they prefer the Strong Grade. There seem to be overgeneralizations in both directions. Furthermore, the phonological processes which obscure or even reverse the length contrasts

---

[6] The *Sámi giellatekno* database (giellatekno.uit.no), which is fairly comprehensive, lists about 1,800 O-class nouns, over 2,000 words of the NA class, and about 400 C-class nouns. The E class is much larger. Thanks to Trond Trosterud, Linda Wiechetek, and Eugenia Romanova for assistance in extracting these figures from the electronic dictionary.

(a few of which were illustrated above) are being acquired at the same time as the morphological process. Thus, while the examination of the acquisition process may eventually determine which form is to be treated as basic, the data currently available do not settle the matter.

A more useful indication might come from non-alternating forms. If the process is a shortening process, then any form which entered the lexicon as underlying short would remain short, never lengthening morphologically; so if the process is a shortening process then there should be a set of non-alternating short words. There is a set of non-alternating words with C centers but I suggested above that they have been assigned to Class NA. There are also a few non-alternating words with C:C centers but these could also be in the NA class. Alternatively, they could be the result of a regular phonological rule applying to lengthen certain underlying geminates. The upshot is that the vast majority of words in Northern Sámi regularly undergo consonant gradation, and there are not enough kinds of neutralizations to settle the matter.

An example discussed in Bals et al. (2005) is the alternation between /nn/ and /n/ in Strong [*meannu*] Weak [*meanu*] 'disposition', and between /ʔn/ and /n/ in Strong [*deaʔnu*] Weak [*deanu*] 'large river'. This would seem to favor an account in terms of shortening, if no underlying distinction between the two short forms could be found. But Bals et al. (2005) point out that all four examples in their database of Strong non-glottalized geminate nasals are in words with an initial nasal (like *meannu*), and no words with glottalized nasals begin with a nasal (cf. *deaʔnu*). Thus a systematic lengthening process can be stated even here. Bals et al. (2005) also note that some speakers have alternations in recent loans which involve geminate and overlong nasals without pre-stopping (e.g., [*seam:maa*]~[*seammaa*] 'same'). On the analysis here, this represents an underlying Weak /mm/, lengthened in the Strong Grade; but on an alternative account which proposed derivation of Weak forms from Strong ones, it would be unclear why shortening could not also apply to a geminate nasal (e.g., /mm/) to produce a singleton nasal. Thus at least this one example points in the direction of lengthening over shortening.

Since consonant gradation is morphologized, and it is far more common for morphology to be essentially additive, I will assume that consonant gradation involves the addition of material to a basic form. This means that the accusative form of E nouns (and, for example, the infinitive form of bisyllabic verbs) is taken to be basic, or closer to the basic form. If the basic form has a single C center, then a morphological process of Strengthening makes it CC, and if a basic form is CC, then Strengthening makes it C:C. This has the appealing result that the three-way length contrast need not be represented underlyingly; non-alternating C:C roots can be analyzed as underlyingly CC, undergoing a phonological lengthening process in their Weak Grade form. If so, all C:C forms can be derived.

Another reason to assume lengthening over shortening is that the extra segment has predictable phonological properties. That is, the Strong Grade usually (or even always) has a segment which can be analyzed as relatively underspecified, its features predictable from the other segments present. It is not clear whether a shortening rule could be stated that would make the right predictions.

Specifically (as already outlined in the Introduction), I will assume that the consonant gradation process is the addition of a timing slot (or two, in the case of the C class) to the coda of a stressed syllable. In the nominal domain, I associate it with a set of stem-forming suffixes; they attach to the right edge of the word, and consonant gradation affects the closest stressed syllable to the left. In the verbal domain, I associate consonant gradation with agreement suffixes. Again, the process affects the closest suitable consonant center. I also show that many derivational suffixes include the segment that leads to consonant gradation.

4.3 The phonological manifestations of Strong and Weak Grade

The simplest examples of consonant gradation involve an alternation between geminate and simple consonants, as illustrated in (4.1) and (4.2) in the Introduction. The morphological paradigms have been illustrated in detail, so henceforth I generally only give two forms, usually the nominative singular and the accusative singular, to illustrate the Strong and Weak Grade. Since the phonology is now in focus, I switch to a phonemic transcription, signaled by slashes, occasionally supplemented by a broad phonetic transcription in square brackets.

4.3.1 *Alternations where Strong is one segment longer than Weak*
Gemination is the manifestation of Strong Grade for all singleton fricatives and non-nasal sonorants.

(4.15)   a.   /guollii/ 'fish' nominative, Strong, CC
         b.   /guolii/ 'fish' accusative, Weak, C

Northern Sámi has a three-way length contrast in consonants, so that alternations like that in (4.16) are also found.

(4.16)   a.   /gol:li/ 'gold' nominative, Strong, C:C
         b.   /gollii/ 'gold' accusative, Weak, CC

The extra-long consonant center in (4.16a.) is the manifestation of the Strong Grade, alternating with a Weak Grade geminate in (4.16b.). Thus it is important to keep in mind that C, CC, and C:C are phonological descriptions, while Strong and Weak Grade are morphological notions.

The general pattern is the one already illustrated in (4.15)–(4.16):

(4.17) a. Strong Grade CC — Weak Grade C
        b. Strong Grade C:C — Weak Grade CC

I argued above that consonant gradation is essentially additive and that the Weak Grade is closer to the underlying representation. The Strong Grade is the surface realization of the underlying form plus one extra timing slot in the coda, which is added morphologically, in a fashion to be detailed below.

The simplest pattern is illustrated in (4.18) for a few selected consonant centers; for fuller inventories see Sammallahti (1998), Bye (2001), or Bals et al. (2005).

(4.18) Fricatives and Sonorants

	Short			Long		
Underlying	l	s	f	ll	ss	ff
Weak Grade	l	s	f	ll	ss	ff
Strong Grade	ll	ss	ff	l:l	s:s	f:f

In such examples, it can easily be seen how the Strong Grade can be derived from the underlying form by the addition of a timing slot or mora. However, consonant gradation is not always a simple matter of consonant length. For certain stops, it involves pre-aspiration, as illustrated in (4.19) for the CC—C alternation and in (4.20) for the C:C—CC alternation.

(4.19) a. /neahpii/ 'nephew' nominative, Strong, CC
        b. /neapii/ [neabi] 'nephew' accusative, Weak, C

(4.20) a. /lahhtii/ 'floor' nominative, Strong, C:C
        b. /lahtii/ 'floor' accusative, Weak, CC

The pattern in (4.19) also involves voicing and frication in the case of /t/, e.g., in *[goahtii]–[goaðii]*, a word for a kind of hut. The general pattern is outlined in (4.21).

(4.21) Stops and Affricates, and Pre-aspirated Stops and Affricates

	Short			Long		
Underlying	p	t	c	hp	ht	hc
Weak Grade	b	ð	z	hp	ht	hc
Strong Grade	hp	ht	hc	hhp	hht	hhc

There are also alternations involving pre-stopped nasals. I depict these with a glottal stop, following Bals et al. (2005), though it could also be represented as a homorganic stop as in Sammallahti (1998: 51) (e.g., /gopmii/ rather than /goʔmii/); there may be a dialectal difference along these lines.

(4.22) a. /joʔɲa/ 'lingonberry' nominative, Strong, CC
     b. /joɲa/ 'lingonberry' accusative, Weak, C

(4.23) a. /goʔʔmii/ [gomʔmii] 'ghost' nominative, Strong, C:C
     b. /goʔmii/ 'ghost' accusative, Weak, CC

The pre-stopped nasal series can be represented as in (4.24), assuming that pre-stopping is completely predictable from the morphological contexts of the Strong and Weak Grade.

(4.24) Pre-stopped nasals

	Short			Long		
Underlying	m	n	ɲ	ʔm	ʔn	ʔɲ
Weak Grade	m	n	ɲ	ʔm	ʔn	ʔɲ
Strong Grade	ʔm	ʔn	ʔɲ	mʔm	nʔn	ɲʔɲ

These tables are far from exhaustive; Northern Sámi has a rich inventory of consonants and I am only providing a tiny representative sample of the full range of alternations.

4.3.2 *Alternations where Strong is two segments longer than Weak*

There are two main kinds of examples where the Strong is two segments longer than the Weak Grade. First, there are cases like /jahhkii/, 'year', or /vivːvaa/, 'son-in-law', given here in (4.25)–(4.26).

(4.25) a. /jahhkii/ 'year' nominative, Strong, C:C
     b. /jagii/ 'year' accusative, Weak, C

(4.26) a. /vivːvaa/ 'son-in-law' nominative, Strong, C:C
     b. /vivaa/ 'son-in-law' accusative, Weak, C

Sammallahti (1998: 49) proposes a rule which he calls Primary Lengthening, which lengthens a geminate consonant (or a cluster starting with *h*) following a short vowel and preceding a long one. On the analysis here, the underlying center in /jahhkii/ is a /k/, and consonant gradation lengthens that /k/ to /hk/, which satisfies the conditions for Primary Lengthening. Thus the center of the Strong form in (4.25) is phonologically changed from CC to C:C and similarly for /vivaa/ in (4.26).

The second situation in which a C ~ C:C alternation arises is in a certain class of nouns known as "contracted" nouns and illustrated by /*boazu*/ 'reindeer' in (4.3) above. The essential part of the pattern is shown in (4.27)–(4.28). Here I place accusative above nominative in order to maintain a consistent order of Strong and Weak forms.

(4.27) a. /bohhco/ 'reindeer' accusative, Strong, C:C
       b. /boacuu/ [boazu] 'reindeer' nominative, Weak, C

(4.28) a. /sul:lo/ 'island' accusative, Strong, C:C
       b. /suoluu/ 'island' nominative, Weak, C

Here, the structural conditions for primary lengthening are not met and the overlong consonant center must be derived morphologically. This has been hinted at in (4.7) in the Introduction above: there is a stem suffix in this class of noun (the C class) which adds not one but two timing slots. This will be discussed further in section 4.4.

4.3.3 *Alternations where Strong is the same length as Weak*

For certain consonant centers, both Strong and Weak forms are approximately the same length, but the Strong form is voiced while the Weak form is voiceless, e.g., as illustrated in (4.29).

(4.29) a. /ruž:žuu/ [rud:čuu] 'ravine' nominative, Strong, C:C
       b. /ruč:čuu/ [rut:čuu] 'ravine' accusative, Weak, C:C

(4.30) a. /gieddii/ 'meadow' nominative, Strong, CC
       b. /giettii/ 'meadow' accusative, Weak, CC

Both examples in (4.29) are overlong due to secondary lengthening Sammallahti (1998: 49), while both are simply geminate in (4.30). Bye (2001) analyzes such forms as underlyingly clusters of a voiced and a voiceless stop (or affricate). In the Weak Grade, the voiced stop assimilates and the cluster surfaces as a geminate. In the Strong Grade, a timing slot is added to the coda of the stressed syllable and this preserves the voicing in the voiced segment. See Bye (2001) for details of the phonological rules at work.

It seems that a similar surface neutralizing effect takes place in certain /s/-initial clusters. There are many apparently non-alternating forms like *beaska*, a word for a reindeer-skin tunic, repeated here in (4.31) (represented here as neither phonemic nor phonetic, for the moment).

(4.31) a. "beaska" 'tunic' nominative, Strong
       b. "beaska" 'tunic' accusative, Weak

There is no perceptible difference here in consonant length and thus there is a contrast with forms like that in (4.32).

(4.32) a. /muosskii/ 'isthmus' nominative, Strong, C:C
       b. /muoskii/ 'isthmus' accusative, Weak, CC

However, for many speakers, there is a difference in the quality of the diphthong in (4.31) (this was brought to my attention by Berit-Anne Bals). Descriptively, it is as if the stress peaks earlier in the nominative form than in the accusative; this might be analyzed in terms of the diphthong being shortened by the following C:C center (cf. Sammallahti 1998: 40). This suggests that there is in fact a consonant gradation alternation which is obscured by some phonological or phonetic process, as implied by (4.33) (adapting conventions from Sammallahti 1998: 40 to mark the diphthong in the Strong Grade as short).

(4.33) a. /beasska/ [bĕăska] 'tunic' nominative, Strong, C:C
       b. /beaska/ [beaska] 'tunic' accusative, Weak, CC

This would be a case where the underlying phonemic difference is very nearly phonetically neutralized. I will not attempt a more formal statement of the rule affecting (4.31) but not (4.32).[7]

4.3.4 *Alternations where the Weak is longer than the Strong*

I turn to a situation in which the Weak Grade is phonetically longer than the Strong Grade, illustrated with *nieida* in (4.34).

(4.34) a. [nieida] 'daughter' nominative, Strong
       b. [nieitta] 'daughter' accusative, Weak

(4.35) a. [jaaurii] 'lake' nominative, Strong
       b. [jaaurrii] 'lake' accusative, Weak

The usual effect of consonant gradation is to lengthen the coda of the stressed syllable. But the coda in each of these clusters is underlyingly a glide, which shows no length contrast pre-consonantally. Furthermore, the lengthening of consonants after glides is phonologically systematic in the language.

---

[7] It may be predictable on the basis of vowel quality. Bals et al. (2005) give the following words as failing to undergo consonant gradation, like *beaska*: *meastu, feasta, leastu, faasmi, maaski, goaski*; all have /a/ before the /sC/ cluster. Like *muosskii* are words with some other vowel before the cluster, for example (in the Weak Grade): *giista, biistu, duuski, luosti, luosku, šuušmi, luuspi, oostu*, and *oosku*; but Bals et al. (2005) also list three alternating words with /a/ before an /s/-initial cluster: *baaste, laasta,* and *aaski*.

Therefore, following Bye (2001), I assume that stops lengthen phonologically after short glides while long glides surface as vowels. This is roughly suggested by the representations below, representing the labial glide as /v/.

(4.36)　a.　/niejjta/ [nieida] 'daughter' nominative, Strong
　　　　　b.　/niejtta/ [nieitta] 'daughter' accusative, Weak

(4.37)　a.　/jaavvrii/ [jaaurii] 'lake' nominative, Strong
　　　　　b.　/jaavrrii/ [jaaurrii] 'lake' accusative, Weak

This pattern is systematic for what I analyze as glide-initial clusters (following Bye 2001), a few examples of which are illustrated in (4.38).

(4.38)　Glide-initial clusters

Underlying	jv	jst	jt	vr	vg	vs
Weak Grade	ivv	isst	itt	urr	ukk	fss
Strong Grade	iv	ist	id	ur	ug	ks

4.3.5　*Other alternations*

A rather exotic-looking alternation (already exemplified in (4.14) in section 4.2 above) is one between *k* as the initial member of a cluster and *v* (variously surfacing as *f*, usually before an obstruent, or *u*, usually before /s/ and /š/).[8]

(4.39)　a.　/gaaktii/ 'jacket' nominative, Strong
　　　　　b.　/gaavtii/ [gaaftii] 'jacket' accusative, Weak

(4.40)　a.　/raksa/ 'diaper' nominative, Strong
　　　　　b.　/raavssa/ [raaussa] 'diaper' accusative, Weak

The lengthening of the fricative in the Weak Grade in (4.40) is a case of Bye's (2001) Coda Maximization. Certain other details of the phonological alternation remain unclear, for example how the Strong–Weak alternation manifests itself in an alternation between *k* and *v*. This is perhaps the most challenging example to motivate in terms of the addition of a timing slot to derive the Strong Grade.

One final example I will point out is the one in which a schwa appears in the Strong Grade, seen in (4.41). Since ⟨bálggis⟩, 'path' is a member of the C class of nouns in which the nominative is Weak Grade, I place accusative over nominative in (4.41).

---

[8]　Bals et al. (2005) suggest rather that these can be understood in terms of an alternation between *k* and *u*, if the consonant following *u* in (4.39) is pre-aspirated and the sequence *uh* is realized as *u*, which sounds like *f*.

(4.41) a. /baallkaa/ [baaləgaa] 'path' accusative, Strong
        b. /baalkkiis/ [baalggiis] 'path' nominative, Weak

(4.42) a. /maarrfii/ [maarəfi] 'sausage' nominative, Strong
        b. /maarffii/ [maarffi] 'sausage' accusative, Weak

This pattern is systematic for heterorganic clusters starting with /r/ and /l/ and /ð/. Homorganic clusters do not surface with schwa, as illustrated in (4.43).

(4.43) a. /alltuu/ [alduu] 'female reindeer' nominative, Strong
        b. /alttuu/ [aldduu] 'female reindeer' accusative, Weak

The Weak members of all three of the above pairs show the effects of a rule Bye (2001: 124) calls Coda Maximization, which lengthens the second member of a sonorant-initial consonant cluster.

As usual, I assume that the Strong Grade adds a timing slot to the stressed syllable, which ends with /r/ or /l/ here. In (4.43), this has the expected effect, namely lengthening the /l/. The realization of the extra timing slot as a schwa just in case the liquid-initial cluster is heterorganic must be due to another phonological rule.

There remain many more phonological details concerning the derivation of surface forms from underlying root forms plus the addition of a timing slot. I first presented the simplest ones in 4.3.1–4.3.2 (gemination of liquids and fricatives, addition of pre-aspiration to stops and affricates, addition of pre-glottalization to nasals), in which something essentially consonantal is added. I then moved in 4.3.3–4.3.4 to alternations which are less transparent but still relatively phonologically tractable (the voicing alternation, the glide-initial clusters). Finally, in 4.3.5 I presented the ones which are least natural-looking from this perspective ($k \sim v$, insertion of schwa), for which phonological rules have to be posited.

There are many more complicated phonological rules at work in Northern Sámi but I will not attempt to elucidate them here (the works I have cited go much further than I could in this space towards a phonologically responsible account). I have mainly tried to outline the idea that the Strong Grade systematically represents (the phonetic manifestation of) the addition of a timing slot to the stressed syllable. This is important because it reduces a great deal of the apparent morphological complexity of the Northern Sámi paradigm to phonology. I hope to have at least made plausible the claim that the phonological effects of consonant gradation can be unified under an analysis in which something is added morphologically in the Strong Grade, with various phonological interpretations.

I turn in section 4.4 to various ways in which Strong Grade emerges in the morphological system and show that they are cleanly captured by assuming that μ is a part of certain suffixes, both derivational and inflectional. These facts would not be equally easily captured if Strong and Weak Grade were assumed to be properties of words, or of stems, or of roots.

4.4 The nominal paradigm

Here I detail the analysis which I briefly outlined in (4.7) in the Introduction. Recall the paradigm with no consonant gradation from (4.4), repeated below in (4.44) with hyphens to indicate the case and number suffixes.

(4.44)   ⟨gahpir⟩ 'cap', ⟨ákšu⟩ 'axe'

	Singular	Plural	Singular	Plural
Nom	⟨gahpir⟩	⟨gahpir-at⟩	⟨ákšu⟩	⟨ákšu-t⟩
Acc	⟨gahpir-a⟩	⟨gahpir-ii-d⟩	⟨ákšu⟩	⟨ákšu-i-d⟩
Ill	⟨gahpir-ii⟩	⟨gahpir-ii-dda⟩	⟨ákšu-i⟩	⟨ákšu-i-de⟩
Loc	⟨gahpir-is⟩	⟨gahpir-ii-n⟩	⟨ákšu-s⟩	⟨ákšu-i-n⟩
Com	⟨gahpir-iin⟩	⟨gahpir-ii-guin⟩	⟨ákšu-in⟩	⟨ákšu-i-guin⟩
Ess	⟨gahpir-in⟩		⟨ákšu-n⟩	

This I called the NA paradigm, as there is No Alternation of consonant gradation. As indicated, a plural suffix can be isolated in all non-nominative cases, with allomorphs -*ii* after consonants and -*i* after vowels.

The singular case suffixes can be analyzed as having allomorphs which follow consonants and allomorphs which follow vowels; I abbreviate that below by putting the extra post-consonantal vowel in parentheses (the *a* before the nominative plural is inserted by regular epenthesis and so is not indicated). The non-nominative plural case suffixes follow the plural morpheme, which is vocalic, and so have only a post-vocalic allomorph. There is no essive plural.

(4.45)

	Singular	Plural
Nom	-	-t
Acc	-(a)	-d
Ill	-(i)j	-de, -da
Loc	-(i)s	-n
Com	-(i)jn	-kujn
Ess	-(i)n	

These suffixes can be used for all the different classes of nominals, with their many different forms of consonant gradation, if a few simple rules of stem formation are adopted.[9] The first important observation to make is that, throughout all the different classes of nouns, the essive form always has the same Grade as the nominative singular. Thus they are formed from the same stem. Since the nominative singular is the most basic case, arguably caseless (Bittner and Hale 1996), and the essive is used mainly as a predicative case, I assume this is a semantically-grounded fact.

Consider the class which Sammallahti (1998) calls imparisyllabic because, historically, the key forms have an odd number of syllables; this is the class that I called O, for Odd, in the Introduction. A full paradigm was presented in (4.2); here the (Strong) accusative singular and (Weak) nominative singular represent the paradigm.

(4.46) a. /gilloma/ 'bloodclot' accusative, Strong
        b. /gieluu/ 'bloodclot' nominative Weak

(4.47) a. /vulloša/ 'thing underneath' accusative, Strong
        b. /vuoluš/ 'thing underneath' nominative, Weak

The nominative in each case is identical to the stem for the essive in -*n*; stripping off the accusative -*a* gives the stem to which all the other case suffixes in (4.45) are attached. The formation of the two stems can be assumed to involve suffixation of a categorial nominal suffix to a category-less root, as proposed by Marantz (2007). One suffix is chosen in a nominative singular or essive context; call this the "absolutive" suffix. It is null for class O. Another suffix is chosen for all other cases. Call this the "basic" suffix. For class O, it consists only of the infixal timing slot, -$^\mu$⌒, whose effects were discussed in some detail in section 4.3.[10]

The nouns in (4.46) and (4.47) also show other differences between their absolutive and basic stems. In this they are typical of class O nouns. Another pair is given in (4.48)–(4.49).

(4.48) a. /bea?naga/ 'dog' accusative, Strong
        b. /beana/ 'dog' nominative, Weak

(4.49) a. /oahhpaasa/ 'guide' accusative, Strong
        b. /oahpis/ 'guide' nominative, Weak

In both (4.46) and (4.48), the final consonant in the basic stem is absent from the absolutive. Northern Sámi allows only a very small class of consonants to

[9] The illative plural makes an additional distinction: -*ide* after consonant-final stems, and -*idda* after vowel-final stems.

[10] As before, I abstract away from the alternation in the diphthong (assume that the diphthong simplifies preceding a center vowel).

remain word-finally; O-class stems which end in other consonants (usually *g* or *m*) lose them at the right edge of the absolute stem by a regular phonological deletion rule.[11]

In (4.47) and (4.49), the final consonant is *s* or *š*, which are among the consonants which are permitted word-finally. Thus nothing exceptional needs to be said about that. In addition, there is a vowel before that consonant which changes from the absolutive to the basic stem. Such alternations are limited to certain suffix shapes, and therefore I assume that the stem-forming suffixes include the vowel in question. For example, the root *oahp-* combines with the suffix -$^{\mu\frown}$*aas* to form a basic stem or with the suffix -*is* to form an absolutive stem.

The third class to be dealt with here is the Contracted class, henceforth C, historically a class which had consonant-final stems, illustrated in (4.3) in the Introduction, the crucial forms of which are given here in (4.50)–(4.51).

(4.50) a. /bohhco/ 'reindeer' accusative, Strong
        b. /boacuu/ 'reindeer' nominative, Weak

(4.51) a. /baallkaa/ 'path' accusative, Strong
        b. /baalkkiis/ 'path' nominative, Weak

The main difference between the O class and the C class is that in the C class, the Strong Grade is always overlong, C:C, regardless of whether the Weak Grade is short or long. This can be perfectly captured if the basic stem-forming suffix contains two instances of μ; two timing slots attached to a short consonant center will create an overlong one and, since a syllable cannot be longer than overlong, two timing slots attached to a long consonant center will simply have the same effect, overlength. In (4.51), there is an absolutive suffix -$^{\mu\frown}$*iis*.

Common in the C class is the *o* ~ *u* alternation seen in (4.50), identical to the alternation in the O class examples in (4.46) and (4.47), and suggesting a more regular rule unifying the absolutive stem suffixes of the two classes, perhaps a floating [+high] feature. The case and number suffixes are identical to those in the NA paradigm.

---

[11] Of the approximately 1,800 O-class nouns in the *Sámi giellatekno* database, about 400 end in *g* like (4.48), 95 end in *m* like (4.46), and a handful end in other consonants which are necessarily deleted word-finally. The others end in those consonants which are permitted word-finally, namely *s* like (4.49) (about 900), *r* like (4.13) (about 200), *l* (about 80), *š* like (4.47) (under 60), or *t* (2). The distribution of *n* is complicated, with 24 examples being deleted word-finally and 17 examples surfacing word-finally (plus 14 examples which are surface realizations of underlying *m*). As with the figures mentioned in fn. 6, these numbers include compounds and thus represent smaller numbers of distinct stems.

The last class is the most important one in terms of productivity and sheer number of members, probably over ten thousand. I present it last of the four classes because in one way it is the most complex. In the E class, three different stem types must be distinguished, as seen in (4.1) in the Introduction. Crucial forms for key examples are given here.

(4.52) a. /viessuu/ 'house' nominative, Strong
        b. /viesuu/ 'house' accusative, Weak
        c. /viissuj/ 'house' illative, Strong

(4.53) a. /basste/ 'spoon' nominative, Strong
        b. /baste/ 'spoon' accusative, Weak
        c. /basstii/ 'spoon' illative, Strong

(4.54) a. /čiehka/ 'corner' nominative, Strong
        b. /čiega/ 'corner' accusative, Weak
        c. /čiihkii/ 'corner' illative, Strong

(4.55) a. /goahtii/ 'hut' nominative, Strong
        b. /goaðii/ 'hut' accusative, Weak
        c. /goahtaaj/ 'hut' illative, Strong

As with the O and C classes, there is consonant gradation in a stem-forming affix but, unlike the the O and C classes, μ is in the absolutive suffix and absent from the basic suffix. This derives the pattern of consonant gradation seen in the nominative and accusative forms (recall that the essive is based on the absolutive, and the comitative and locative are based on the basic form, as are the plurals).

The illative, however, cannot be simply based on the basic form as it was in the other classes. In the E class, it always has the same Strong Grade as the absolutive-based forms. However, the illative also has some peculiarities. For one thing, the *a*, which is otherwise part of the stem in nouns like *čiehka*, is changed to *i* in the illative, as is the *e* in *basste*, and the *ii* that appears on all stem forms in *goahtii* changes to *aa* in the illative (these changes apply only to the singular forms). Thus, rather than trying to derive the E-class illative singular from the absolutive stem, I suggest that the E class has three stem-forming suffixes. I call the third "dative"; it is only selected for E class nouns in the context of illative singular features. I assume that it is a categorial nominal head, in complementary distribution with the heads that derive absolutive and basic stems.

4.5 Derivation

The way I have employed the autosegmental μ, it is not connected to any particular meaning; it is like a phonemic segment in the language in that it turns up as a phonological part of various morphemes. If it were a part of a root, its effects would never be seen, since no process deletes it; it would simply be realized as an unvarying consonantal segment in a coda. Its importance to the nominal inflectional system has already been seen. Here I show that it can also be part of a derivational morpheme, verifying the claim made in the Introduction. The discussion is based largely on data and descriptive observations presented in Nickel's (1990) Chapter 12.

4.5.1 *Derivation without* μ

First, there are derivational morphemes which do not have any μ associated with them. For example, the suffix *-u* can be added to a verb root to derive an abstract nominal; it attaches to verb roots, replacing the thematic vowel and deriving regular nouns of the E class. As with all E nouns, the derived nominal gets Strong Grade in the nominative singular, illative singular, and the essive.

(4.56) bal-a- *v.* 'fear' (infinitive /*ballaht*/)
      a. /balluu/ *n.* 'fear' nominative, Strong
      b. /baluu/ *n.* 'fear' accusative, Weak

Similarly, the suffix *-uus* can be added to a verb root to derive a noun of the O class, which undergoes regular consonant gradation in all forms except the nominative singular and the essive, as expected.

(4.57) jug-a- *v.* 'drink' (infinitive /*juhkaht*/)
      a. /juguus/ *n.* 'drink' nominative, Weak
      b. /juhkosa/ *n.* 'drink' accusative, Strong

Derivational suffixes can also derive nouns of class NA, which do not undergo any consonant gradation. One such suffix is deverbal *-n*, which gives a kind of habitual agentive, "one who habitually V's".

(4.58) soađ-a- 'combat, make war' (infinitive /*soahtaht*/)
      a. /soađan/ *n.* 'combatant, one who fights' nominative
      b. /soađana/ *n.* 'combatant, one who fights' accusative

4.5.2 *Consonant gradation in suffixes*

I have suggested that μ when it is part of a suffix attaches to the coda of the nearest stressed syllable, viewed from its point of attachment at the right edge of a word. This means that if a derivational suffix is large enough, μ-bearing affixes attaching to it will induce consonant gradation in the suffix, not in the root. This can be seen with various derivational suffixes, for example the instrument nominalizer *-aaldak*.

(4.59)   sihk-uu- *v.* 'wipe' (infinitive /sihhkuuht/)
   a.   /sihkaaldat/ *n.* 'cloth for wiping' nominative
   b.   /sihkaaldaga/ *n.* 'cloth for wiping' accusative
   c.   /sihkaaldaahkii/ *n.* 'cloth for wiping' illative

The underlying /k/ of the suffix surfaces as /g/ in the Weak Grade form seen in the accusative. In the Strong Grade, it is pre-aspirated by μ to form /hk/; but this is not a licit word-final cluster in Northern Sámi, so the nominative surfaces with a final /t/. The expected Strong Grade form surfaces where it is followed by a vowel, for example the illative singular form in (4.59c).

4.5.3 *Derivation with* μ

There are also derivational suffixes which include μ as part of their lexical entry. One important one is the "Aktio" suffix -$^{\mu \frown}m$ (the suffixal part surfaces as -*n* when word-final). It derives Class NA nouns from verb roots.

(4.60)   čaal-ii- *v.* 'write' (infinitive /čaalliiht/)
   a. /čaalliin/ *n.* 'writing' nominative
   b. /čaalliima/ *n.* 'writing' accusative

Another one is deverbal -$^{\mu \frown}iluuš$, which derives E nouns denoting undergoers.

(4.61)   soj-a- *v.* 'yield' (infinitive /sočč̌aht/)
   a.   /sožžiluuš/ *n.* 'something that yields easily' nominative
   b.   /sožžiluuša/ *n.* 'something that yields easily' accusative
   c.   /sožžiluuššii/ *n.* 'something that yields easily' illative

Two important facts can be noted about the nominal forms in (4.61). One is that the verbal root appears in its C:C form, as if the nominalization were added to the infinitive stem rather than to the root. This means that two μ's can be added to a single root. The effect is productive and gives rise to three-way C—CC—C:C contrasts, for example *sojaan—socče—sožžiluuš* 'I yield, it/he/she yields, sth that yields', or *caagaan—caahke—cahhkiiluuš* 'I smolder, it/he/she smolders, sth that catches fire easily'.

The other thing to notice is that just as already seen in (4.59), the consonant gradation induced by stem suffixes occurs not in the root but in the suffix, because the infixal μ seeks the first stressed coda to the left of its point of attachment. In the nominative singular, the consonant gradation is undone by the fact that the affected coda is word-final; thus it surfaces short. But the effects of gradation can be seen by examining the illative singular form in (4.61c).

The structure can be represented as a cyclic derivation of suffixation and infix alignment.

(4.62) Derivation of illative *sožžiluuššii*, 'something which yields easily, pushover'

Root:	soj-
Verbal Stem Affix:	soj-$^{\mu\frown}$
Infix Aligned:	so$^{\mu}$j-
Derivational Suffix:	so$^{\mu}$j-$^{\mu\frown}$iluuš
Infix Aligned:	so$^{\mu\mu}$j-iluuš
Dative Stem Suffix:	so$^{\mu\mu}$j-iluuš-$^{\mu\frown}$
Infix Aligned:	so$^{\mu\mu}$j-iluu$^{\mu}$š
Illative Case Suffix:	so$^{\mu\mu}$j-iluuš-$^{\mu\frown}$ij
Surface realization:	sožžiluuššii

I know of no empirical evidence bearing on the order of operations, apart from the obvious linear order of the suffixes. Thus the construction could also be represented as below.

(4.63) A representation of illative *sožžiluuššii*

soj -$^{\mu\frown}$ -$^{\mu\frown}$iluuš -$^{\mu\frown}$ -ij
yield -*v* -UNDRGO -DAT -ILL
sožžiluuššii

4.6 μ in the verbal paradigms

There are several morphemes with the property μ in the verbal paradigm as well. With verbs, it is less clear that class distinctions are needed but allomorphy is clearly sensitive to syllable count or stress. The difference between even-syllabled and odd-syllabled stems is important, and odd-syllabled verbs generally do not show consonant gradation in the root at all. I will refer to verbs whose prosodic structure makes them pattern with simple disyllables as the ES verbs, for Even-Syllabled, and to the others as OS, for Odd-Syllabled.

4.6.1 *Inflectional suffixes*

First, there are agreement affixes which have the infixal component. In the most common paradigm, the first and second person singular are in the Weak

Grade, while the third person singular is in the Strong Grade, as are all the
dual and plural forms in the present tense.

(4.64) ES verb, present tense: *boahtit* 'come'

PERSON	Singular	Dual	Plural
1	/boaðaan/	/boohte/	/boahtiih/
2	/boaðaaht/	/boahtibeahhtii/	/boahtibehteht/
3	/boahtaa/	/boahtiba/	/boohteht/

In the past tense, the pattern is nearly the reverse, with the first and second
person being in the Strong Grade and all the other forms being Weak, except
the third person plural.

(4.65) ES verb, past tense: *boahtit* 'come'

PERSON	Singular	Dual	Plural
1	/boohten/	/booðijme/	/booðiimeht/
2	/boohteht/	/booðijde/	/booðiideht/
3	/booðii/	/booðijka/	/boohte/

Since the suffixes are also largely distinct in the different tenses, and given the
hypothesis tendered here that the language has an infixal $^{\mu\frown}$ segment which
exists as a part of certain morphemes, it is a simple matter to identify which
agreement suffixes bear $^{\mu\frown}$ and which do not; in the present tense, the third
singular, the dual, and the plural do, and in the past tense, the first singular,
the second singular, and the third plural do.

The pattern of reversal, where the forms which are Strong in the present are
Weak in the past, has historical origins just as was seen for the nominal paradigm in the Introduction. Roughly, something like (4.66) must have occurred
(for a more careful reconstruction see Sammallahti 1998, Appendix F).

(4.66) Rough historical reconstruction for *boahtit* 'come'

	First person	Third person
PRESENT	*poa.te-em	*poat.te
PAST	*poat.te-.j-em	*poa.te-j

Just as with the nouns, the consonant center is strengthened before an open
syllable. This happened in the third person past and in the first person present.

On the analysis presented here, the association in the modern language
of Strong Grade with first person singular in the past tense is completely
independent of what happens to the first person singular in the present.

4.6.2 *Derivational suffixes*

Derivational suffixes that create verbs can also carry μ, as expected, for example the transitivizer -$^{\mu\frown}d$, which attaches to unaccusatives to form transitive
verbs (Julien to appear).

(4.67)   vuojuu- *v.* 'sink' (unaccusative) (infinitive */vuoččuuht/*)

    a.   /vuoččuudiiht/ *v.* 'sink' (transitive) infinitive

    b.   /vuoččuudaan/ *v.* 'sink' (transitive) first person singular present

Because the output of -*ᵘ⌒d* suffixation is a three-syllabled or OS verb, there is no consonant gradation in the first person singular, as shown.

If a derivational suffix is large enough, then consonant gradation will occur in the suffix, just as was seen above for nouns, for example, the inadvertent causativizer *-haaht*, which attaches to transitive and unergative verbs.

(4.68)   čieruu- *v.* 'cry' (infinitive */čierruuht/*)

    a.   /čieruhaahhtiht/ *v.* 'inadvertently make cry' infinitive

    b.   /čieruhaahtaan/ *v.* 'inadvertently make cry' first person singular present

As can be seen, the suffixed form has four syllables and is a regular verb of the ES paradigm. Hence, the suffixal part of the causative, /haaht/, appears in the Strong Grade in the infinitive (the pre-aspiration lengthening from /ht/ to /hht/) and in the Weak Grade in the first person singular.

In fact, a suffix can cause a non-alternating OS verb to become ES by adding a single syllable. When it becomes ES, it shows consonant gradation effects. For example *-ast* is called a "diminutive" suffix, and when added to a verb it gives an attenuative sense or a sense of something done in haste (it also replaces the stem vowel of OS stems).

(4.69)   mujtalii- *v.* 'tell' (infinitive */mujtaliiht/*)

    a.   /mujtalasstiht/ 'tell a little, tell in haste' infinitive

    b.   /mujtalastaan/ 'tell a little, tell in haste' first person singular present

Because consonant gradation is triggered by a suffix, it is the third syllable of the infinitive which receives a lengthened coda, not the first, just as was seen in the nominal paradigms.

4.6.3 *Inflectional suffixes on top of inflectional suffixes*

The richness of the inflectional system of Northern Sámi provides a sight not seen in the nominal system, namely that of an inflectional suffix showing consonant gradation. Hitherto we have only seen roots and derivational suffixes affected by consonant gradation, but here we see that even inflectional suffixes undergo it. In order to see the effect it is first necessary to present the OS conjugation paradigm.

As mentioned above, there is a separate series of agreement suffixes for OS verbs, i.e., those with three-syllabled stems. None of these agreement suffixes bear μ, so there is no consonant gradation in the OS paradigm. However, certain mood suffixes, namely the Potential and the Conditional, have the effect of causing a stem to change class, so that an ES verb with a Potential or Conditional suffix takes OS agreement, and an OS verb with a Potential or Conditional suffix takes ES agreement.

(4.70)   Comparison of an OS verb (/*mujhtaliiht*/ 'tell') and an ES verb in the Potential mood (/*gullaaht*/ 'hear')

AGR	OS Indicative	ES Potential
1 sg	/mujhtaalan/	/gulaačan/
2 sg	/mujhtaalaht/	/gulaačaht/
3 sg	/mujhtaala/	/gulaača/
1 du	/mujhtaaleʔne/	/gulaačeʔne/
2 du	/mujhtaaleahhpii/	/gulaačeahhpii/
3 du	/mujhtaaleabaa/	/gulaačeabaa/
1 pl	/mujhtaaliiht/	/gulaačiiht/
2 pl	/mujhtaalehpeht/	/gulaačehpeht/
3 pl	/mujhtaaliiht/	/gulaačiiht/

The potential morpheme for ES stems, as seen above, is -*č*; for OS stems, it is *eačč*; attached to an OS stem, it induces the ES agreement paradigm, as can be seen below. The ES agreement paradigm was already presented above but is repeated here for convenience.

(4.71)   Comparison of an ES verb (/*gullaaht*/ 'hear') and an OS verb in the Potential mood (/*mujhtaaliiht*/ 'tell')

AGR	ES Indicative	OS Potential
1 sg	/gulaan/	/mujhtaaleaččaan/
2 sg	/gulaaht/	/mujhtaaleaččaaht/
3 sg	/gullaa/	/mujhtaaleažžaa/
1 du	/gulle/	/mujhtaaležže/
2 du	/gullabeahhtii/	/mujhtaaleažžaabeahhtii/
3 du	/gullaabaa/	/mujhtaaleažžaabaa/
1 pl	/gullaaht/	/mujhtaaleažžaaht/
2 pl	/gullaabehteht/	/mujhtaaleažžaabehteht/
3 pl	/gulleht/	/mujhtaaležžeht/

The important point to note here is that the third person singular, the dual, and the plural all show Strong Grade forms. Since I have coupled the consonant gradation to the suffixes themselves, rather than to cells in a paradigm, exactly the right result is achieved: the suffixes which trigger Strong Grade forms in the simple ES present indicative do the same thing in the OS potential but, since they are removed from the root by a morpheme that constitutes a (secondarily) stressed syllable, the consonant gradation effect is seen only on the Potential suffix.

The fact that consonant gradation affects roots, derivational suffixes, and even inflectional suffixes shows its phonological nature: if it is in the right phonological environment, it occurs. The fact that its distribution is absolutely constrained by inflectional and derivational categories shows its morphological nature; it is never triggered simply by a phonological environment.

4.7 Conclusion

I have shown that Northern Sámi makes extensive use of a phonologically sophisticated system of consonant gradation. I have only illustrated a few of the many dozens of phonological alternations and only sketched a representative sample of the morphological contexts in which they occur. Still, I hope to have given the reader an impression of the intricacy of the surface pattern.

I have argued that these patterns of consonant gradation can be understood as a simple expression of a relatively well-understood kind of morphological system, one in which affixes, which are pairings of syntactico-semantic function and phonological content, are concatenated. I have tried to keep mechanisms to a minimum, in search of a kind of minimalist morphology.

The devices necessary in this account include the following. First, there must be a phonological segment in the language (μ) which has a range of surface manifestations depending on its phonological environment (e.g., /l/ before /l/, /h/ before /t/, etc.). This segment must also have a particular prosodic property which causes it to infix (this property could either be a phonological or a morphological property). Also on this account, some morphemes must have distinct synonymous allomorphs; for example there can be a stem-forming suffix with μ as a component and one without it. Allomorphy can be sensitive to phonology (a suffix can be sensitive to whether the last foot in the stem has two syllables or not, for example), or it can be sensitive to class features (roots can be divided into classes on grounds that are not transparently semantic nor phonological, and a suffix can be specified to attach only to a root of a given class).

All of these assumptions, I think, are fairly well motivated by phenomena documented in other languages. One consequence of the analysis is that some phonological rules must be fairly "unnatural"; for example, a phonological rule must be able to yield the $k \sim v$ alternation in examples like *leaksa* ~ *leavssa* mentioned in section 4.2.

The unnatural phonological rules cannot be replaced with sets of allomorphs. To see why, consider an attempt to do so which is not very different from the analysis suggested here. Suppose that instead of a stem-forming suffix with μ, there is a different stem-forming suffix including an infixal /k/ which attaches to roots like the one in *leavssa*. Then the $k \sim v$ alternation could be separated from the other alternations in order to avoid positing phonologically unnatural rules. The problem is the generality of the alternation: it is productive and fully general; it is induced by every stem-forming suffix, agreement suffix, and derivational suffix that induces Strong Grade anywhere. Each one of those suffixes would have to have two allomorphs, one for changing v to k and another for other alternations. The generality of the process strongly suggests unifying consonant gradation in the way I have done by making the substance of the alternations a matter of phonology and the distribution of the Grades a matter of morphology.

References

Bals, Berit Anne (2002) The acquisition of grade alternation in the Kautokeino dialect. Master's thesis, University of Tromsø.

Bals, Berit Anne, David Odden, and Curt Rice (2005) 'Topics in North Saami phonology', Ms., University of Tromsø and Ohio State University; available at www.ling.ohio-state.edu/~odden/Saami.pdf.

Bittner, Maria, and Ken Hale (1996) 'The structural determination of case and agreement'. *Linguistic Inquiry* 27: 1–68.

Bye, Patrik (2001) Virtual phonology: Rule sandwiching and multiple opacity in North Saami. Ph.D. thesis, University of Tromsø.

Julien, Marit (1996) *Syntactic Word Formation in Northern Sámi*. Oslo: Novus.

—— (2002) *Syntactic Heads and Word Formation*. New York: Oxford University Press.

—— (to appear) 'Roots and verbs in North Saami', in Diane Nelson, Ida Toivonen, and Bill Palmer (eds.), *Saami Linguistics, Current Issues in Linguistic Theory* 288. Amsterdam: John Benjamins.

Marantz, Alec (2007) 'Phases and words', in Sook-hee Choe (ed.), *Phases in the Theory of Grammar*. Seoul: Dong-in, pp. 196–226.

Nickel, Klaus Peter (1990) *Samisk Grammatikk*. Oslo: Universitetsforlaget.

Sammallahti, Pekka (1998) *The Saami Languages: An Introduction*. Kárásjohka: Davvi Girji OS.

5

Class features as probes

ARTEMIS ALEXIADOU AND GEREON MÜLLER*

In this chapter, we address (i) the form and (ii) the function of inflection class features in a minimalist grammar. The empirical evidence comes from noun inflection systems involving fusional markers in German, Greek, and Russian. As for (i), we argue (based on instances of transparadigmatic syncretism) that class features are not privative; rather, class information must be decomposed into more abstract, binary features. Concerning (ii), we propose that class features qualify as the very device that brings about fusional inflection: They are uninterpretable in syntax and act as probes on stems, with matching inflection markers as goals, and thus trigger morphological Agree operations that merge stem and inflection marker before syntax is reached.

5.1 Introduction

This chapter investigates the form and the function of inflection class features in a minimalist grammar; more specifically, we address the status of noun class features in three languages with fusional noun inflection systems, namely, Russian, Greek, and German.

As for the form of class features, we will argue that they are not to be viewed as privative features like [class I], [class II], etc. (as is standardly assumed), but as more abstract, binary features like $[\pm\alpha]$, $[\pm\beta]$, etc., that result from decomposing classic inflection classes, and whose cross-classification in turn yields these classes. Such a decomposition of inflection classes will be shown to offer

* For helpful comments and discussion, we would like to thank Asaf Bachrach, John Bailyn, Jim Blevins, Wayles Browne, Jonathan Bobaljik, Alexis Dimitriadis, David Embick, Steven Franks, Jadranka Gvozdanović, Gunlög Josefsson, Fabian Heck, Hans-Heinrich Lieb, Andrew Nevins, Isabel Oltra, Albert Ortmann, David Pesetsky, Frans Plank, Angela Ralli, Milan Rezac, Peter Sells, Wolfgang Sternefeld, Arnim von Stechow, Jochen Trommer, Hubert Truckenbrodt, Anna Volodina, Bernd Wiese, Dieter Wunderlich, Gisela Zifonun, an anonymous reviewer, and audiences at the 26th GLOW meeting at Lunds Universitet (April 2003), the workshop on inflectional paradigms at IDS Mannheim (May 2003), the GGS meeting at Universität Köln (May 2003), and Universität Tübingen (July 2003).

a straightforward explanation of systematic instances of syncretism that hold across inflection classes. As for the function of class features, we propose that they qualify as the device that brings about fusional inflection in the first place: They act as probes on stems, with matching inflection markers as goals, and thus trigger morphological Agree operations that merge stem and inflection marker. This process will be argued to take place before syntax is reached. The underlying rationale is that whereas arbitrary class features emerge as indispensible in morphology (gender, phonological, or semantic features that are independently motivated on noun stems do not suffice to correctly predict the choice of inflection class), they are not visible in syntax and would in fact violate the Legibility Condition (see Chomsky 2000; 2001b) if present in this component. Our conclusion is that class features need to be removed from linguistic expressions in a pre-syntactic morphological component and this is achieved by morphological Agree (i.e., inflection) operations.

The analysis suggested here has repercussions on the organization of grammar, and particularly the question where, and how, morphological operations take place. We will compare the pre-syntactic approach to class-driven fusional inflection adopted here with inner- and post-syntactic approaches (like Distributed Morphology); and we will argue that these alternative conceptions are at variance with either the Legibility Condition (if class features are present in syntax) or the Inclusiveness Condition (if class features are added after syntax).

We will proceed as follows. In section 5.2, we address the systems of noun inflection in Russian, Greek, and German. We show that class features are needed in the morphological systems of all these languages, and that assuming inflection class information to be encoded on binary features of a highly abstract nature offers a simple account of many instances of syncretism. In section 5.3, we move from morphology to syntax and investigate the role of noun class features in syntax. We argue that class features are not visible in syntax, neither as heads of functional projections, nor as features on other heads. By putting the evidence from sections 5.2 (morphology) and 5.3 (syntax) together, we develop the main proposal in section 5.4. In section 5.5, we put the proposal in a wider context and discuss further issues raised by the analysis. Finally, section 5.6 contains concluding remarks.

5.2 Class features in morphology

The noun inflection systems of Russian, Greek, and German exhibit massive syncretism; the notion of syncretism is understood here in a broad sense, as identity of inflection marker forms in different paradigm cells.[1] Such syncretism comes in two varieties. First, syncretism can arise within an inflection class, with two (or more) cases being covered by the same inflection marker; we will refer to this (standard) instance of form identity as *intraparadigmatic syncretism*. Second, syncretism can also show up across inflection classes, with two (or more) inflection classes sharing the same inflection marker (which then may or may not be for the same case specification); we will refer to this instance of form identity as *transparadigmatic syncretism*. The languages considered in this article exhibit both kinds of syncretism in abundance.[2]

The question arises to what extent syncretism should be considered systematic. We adopt the meta-grammatical principle in (5.1).

(5.1) *Syncretism Principle*:
       Identity of form implies identity of function (within a certain domain, and unless there is evidence to the contrary).

We take the Syncretism Principle to be the null hypothesis for the child acquiring a language as well as for the linguist investigating it. In both respects, it plays an important role outside morphology, e.g., in syntax and semantics. The two qualifications in (5.1) are minimal. First, the restriction to a certain empirical domain ensures that, for example, an accidental homonymy of a verbal inflection marker and a nominal inflection marker in a given language (e.g., of s in *ask-s* and s in *cat-s*) does not imply an identity of function of the two markers. Any alternative to this would plainly be untenable. In other cases, the decision about the form of the domain in which all syncretism must be considered systematic may not be that uncontroversial. We will assume that different numbers (singular and plural) create different domains for the purposes of the Syncretism Principle, whereas different classes and cases do not. Consequently, we will try to derive syncretism across classes and cases, but not across numbers; that is, "trans-number" syncretism is not assumed to be systematic (cf. Baerman et al. 2002, and footnote 19 below). This difference between number on the one hand and case and class on the other may ultimately be traced back to whether or not a feature carries semantic information—number features do, whereas class features and case features (at

---

[1] We assume that paradigms do not exist as genuine entities that, for example, constraints can refer to (e.g., the Paradigm Economy Principle in Carstairs (1987), or the No Blur Principle in Carstairs-McCarthy (1994)). On the view adopted here, paradigms are epiphenomena (see Bobaljik 2002, Harley and Noyer 2003, and references cited there); they have the status of empirical generalizations that need to be derived.

[2] A cross-linguistic survey reveals that intra- and transparadigmatic instances of syncretism are pervasive in the class-driven, fusional noun inflection systems of Indo-European and other languages (see Plank 1991 and Baerman et al. 2002, among others).

least those of the languages under consideration in this chapter, which do not exhibit "semantic cases") do not.

The second qualification in (5.1) envisages the possibility that positive counter-evidence may make impossible an analysis of a specific instance of syncretism as systematic. This qualification is arguably also unavoidable, especially in inflectional morphology, where it seems clear that historical accidents play some role in shaping the form of paradigms. Still, we would like to contend that there is much less evidence against assuming instances of syncretism to be systematic than is sometimes made out (see, for example, Carstairs 1987; Zwicky 1991; and Williams 1994). More generally, the Syncretism Principle in (5.1) brings about a shift of perspective from much recent work in inflectional morphology, in that the burden of proof is not on considering a given instance of syncretism as systematic but on considering it to be accidental.[3]

A final caveat before we turn to the noun inflection systems of Russian, Greek, and German. Throughout, we focus on the core systems of noun inflection in these languages. We disregard minor inflection classes, minor cases, stem alternations, stress patterns, pure lexical idiosyncrasies, etc. These issues are ultimately important in comprehensive morphological accounts of the respective systems. However, they do not significantly contribute to the issue of the nature of class features, and we believe that the gist of the analyses of noun inflection in Russian, Greek, and German given below can be carried over into more comprehensive accounts without significant changes.

5.2.1 *Noun inflection in Russian*

5.2.1.1 *Data*   Russian has six cases: nominative (nom), accusative (acc), dative (dat), genitive (gen), instrumental (inst), and locative (loc; also known as prepositional). We assume that there are four noun inflection classes in this language, which are here labeled I–IV.[4]

Consider first inflection class I, which contains only masculine stems. Focusing on the singular for now, three sample paradigms are given in table T_1. The variation in this class is conditioned by two factors. First, inanimate

---

[3] The underlying assumption here is that given a proper level of abstraction, inflectional systems show much more regularity and systematicity than a superficial analysis can reveal; see Chomsky (2005, note 14).

[4] An alternative view recognizes three classes, with classes I and IV subclasses of a single class. Since we will suggest an explicit theory of what a "subclass" is, and will in fact argue for further "subclasses" in the system of Russian noun inflection, this question turns out to be mainly terminological. Relevant literature on Russian noun inflection that the material in this section is based on includes Jakobson (1962a; 1962b), Isačenko (1975), Neidle (1988), Corbett and Fraser (1993), Fraser and Corbett (1994), Halle (1994), Franks (1995), Stump (2001), and Wiese (2004). Müller (2004) is an earlier (and, to some extent, different) version of the analysis of Russian in this section that discusses the empirical evidence in much more detail.

T_1: *Inflection class I, Sg: masc*

	I		
	zavod$_m$ ('factory')	*student$_m$* ('student')	*žitel$_m$* ('inhabitant')
nom/sg	zavod-Ø	student-Ø	žitel'-Ø
acc/sg	zavod-Ø	student-a	žitel-ja
dat/sg	zavod-u	student-u	žitel-ju
gen/sg	zavod-a	student-a	žitel-ja
inst/sg	zavod-om	student-om	žitel-em
loc/sg	zavod-e	student-e	žitel-e

T_2: *Inflection class II, Sg: fem, masc*

	II			
	komnat$_f$ ('room')	*učitel'nic$_f$* ('fem. teacher')	*nedel'$_f$* ('week')	*muščin$_m$* ('man')
nom/sg	komnat-a	učitel'nic-a	nedel-ja	muščin-a
acc/sg	komnat-u	učitel'nic-u	nedel-ju	muščin-u
dat/sg	komnat-e	učitel'nic-e	nedel-e	muščin-e
gen/sg	komnat-y	učitel'nic-y	nedel-i	muščin-y
inst/sg	komnat-oj(u)	učitel'nic-ej(u)	nedel-ej(u)	muščin-oj(u)
loc/sg	komnat-e	učitel'nic-e	nedel-e	muščin-e

noun stems like *zavod* ('factory') take a nominative (null) marker /Ø/ in the accusative, whereas animate noun stems like *student-* ('student') take the genitive marker /a/ in the accusative.[5] Second, there are systematic, morphophonologically predictable differences between nouns whose stem ends in a "hard" (i.e., [+back]) consonant and nouns whose stem ends in a "soft" (i.e., [−back]) consonant: compare *student* ('student') with *žitel'* ('inhabitant').[6]

Inflection class II has mainly feminine stems; it is illustrated in table T_2. This time, there is no animacy effect in the accusative, which employs a uniform marker /u/ for, for example, inanimate *komnat* ('room') and animate *učitel'nic* ('female teacher'). However, as before, there is predictable morphophonological variation that depends on the nature of the stem ending as [±back]; compare, for example, the markers attached to a stem ending in a hard consonant (like *komnat* ('room')), with the endings attached to a stem ending in a soft consonant (like *nedel'* ('week')). Furthermore, this inflection class turns out to be non-gender-specific. In addition to the feminine stems, some masculine stems also belong to this class (like *muščin* ('man')); that is, they trigger masculine agreement but inflect according to the pattern in T_2. Unlike

---

[5] Here and henceforth, the / / notation will be used for markers and segments so as to indicate that these have the status of underlying representations that may undergo changes on the way to PF realization.

[6] Note that softness of the final stem consonant /l/ in *žitel'* is represented by the so-called *mjagkij znak* (') in the nominative and by the nature of the ending in the other cases. This is a matter of orthography that should not be taken to signal stem alternation, here and in the following paradigms.

T_3: *Inflection class III, Sg: fem*

	III		
	tetrad'$_f$ ('notebook')	*myš'$_f$* ('mouse')	*doč'$_f$* ('daughter')
nom/sg	tetrad'-Ø	myš'-Ø	doč'-Ø
acc/sg	tetrad'-Ø	myš'-Ø	doč'-Ø
dat/sg	tetrad-i	myš-i	doč-er-i
gen/sg	tetrad-i	myš-i	doč-er-i
inst/sg	tetrad'-ju	myš'-ju	doč-er'-ju
loc/sg	tetrad-i	myš-i	doč-er-i

the masculine stems in class I, masculine stems in class II exhibit no animacy effect in the accusative.

Next, inflection class III is illustrated in table T_3. Abstracting away from a few exceptions, this class contains only feminine stems. All stems in this class end in a soft consonant. Class III shows fewer case differentiations (consequently, more intraparadigmatic syncretism) than classes I and II; in the singular, it employs only the three markers /Ø/, /i/, and /ju/ for the six cases. Some (highly frequent) nouns in this class exhibit stem alternation (compare *doč'* ('daughter'), *mat'* ('mother')).

Finally, inflection class IV contains only neuter stems; see table T_4. This class is similar to class I but differs in the choice of markers for nominative and accusative in the singular (class IV also differs from class I in the plural; see below). There is no animacy effect in the singular (even though there are some animate stems belonging to this class, like *suščestv* ('creature')); but, as before, there is [±back]-governed morphophonological variation (compare *pol'* ('field')).

The question arises how class membership can be determined for a given stem. Ideally, one might hope that independently motivated features on noun stems suffice for this purpose. However, it turns out that this is not the case. We will briefly discuss three possible candidates in this context: gender features, phonological features, and semantic features. Let us address gender features first. There is a one-to-one correspondence between gender and inflection

T_4: *Inflection class IV, Sg: neut*

	IV			
	mest$_n$ ('place')	*jablok$_n$* ('apple')	*suščestv$_n$* ('creature')	*pol'$_n$* ('field')
nom/sg	mest-o	jablok-o	suščestv-o	pol-e
acc/sg	mest-o	jablok-o	suščestv-o	pol-e
dat/sg	mest-u	jablok-u	suščestv-u	pol-ju
gen/sg	mest-a	jablok-a	suščestv-a	pol-ja
inst/sg	mest-om	jablok-om	suščestv-om	pol-em
loc/sg	mest-e	jablok-e	suščestv-e	pol-e

class in the case of class IV. Neuter stems belong to this class, and this class contains only neuter stems. Unfortunately, things are not as simple for masculine and feminine stems. Masculine stems can belong to class I or to class II (with the former option the unmarked case), and feminine stems can belong to class II or to class III. Hence, gender features on the stem do not suffice to predict inflection class (see Corbett and Fraser 1993; Fraser and Corbett 1994).

Consider next phonological features. The first thing to note is that the nature of the stem ending does not reliably predict class membership. Thus noun stems belonging to classes I, II, and IV may end in either a hard or a soft consonant; and whereas all noun stems in class III end in a soft consonant, this does not not imply that class membership can be predicted for these nouns, not even if gender information is also taken into account. A feminine noun stem ending in a soft consonant can belong to class II or class III (compare *nedel'* ('week') with *tetrad'* ('notebook')). Similarly, there are no theme vowels in modern Russian that might encode inflection class.[7]

Third, semantic features on a noun stem do not suffice to predict its inflection class, that is, none of the four inflection classes correlates unambiguously with a semantic property.[8] Note finally that not even a combination of gender, phonological, and semantic information suffices to fully predict class membership. For instance, a feminine, inanimate noun stem ending in a soft consonant may belong to class II or class III; a masculine, animate noun stem ending in a hard consonant may belong to class I or class II; and so forth. We can conclude from this that arbitrary class features are needed in the system of

---

[7] From a diachronic point of view, theme vowels, as extensions of stems, are ultimately responsible for the creation of the modern inflection classes (historically, classes I and IV employ a theme vowel /o/, class II relies on a theme vowel /a/, and class III chooses a theme vowel /i/); and traces of these theme vowels (as items belonging to the stem rather than to the ending) can still be found in Old Church Slavonic (see, for example, Leskien 1955). However, it seems hard to maintain that there are theme vowels left in modern Russian (see Wurzel 1984; Corbett and Fraser 1993), despite some claims to the contrary (see Wunderlich 1996; 2004). If, for example, class II had a theme vowel /a/, this would imply a structure like *komnat-a-Ø* (with a theme vowel and a null inflection marker for case and number) in the nominative singular, and a structure like *komnat-Ø-u* (with an empty theme vowel and an inflection marker /u/ for case and number) in the accusative singular (and similarly for all the remaining cases). Such an approach would clearly miss the simple generalization that /a/ and /u/ have exactly the same status in class II, as inflection markers that encode case and number. Note that this reasoning does not inherently preclude attempts to break down inflection markers (especially segmentally complex markers) into parts, as long as it is acknowledged that choice of the parts is determined by case/number information throughout, and cannot be independent of this information (as the notion of theme vowel presupposes). Analyses that postulate such a fine structure of Russian inflection markers are developed by Halle (1994) and Wiese (2004) but the underlying hypothesis by necessity leads to extremely abstract analyses (because the positions postulated as available for inflection marker segments are then very often not actually used, given the sheer quantity of monosegmental markers in T_1–T_4), and we will not pursue it here.

[8] Recall that this also holds for class IV. Neuter stems are typically inanimate but there are some neuter stems which are animate, like *suščestv*.

T₅: Syncretism within and across inflection classes in Russian

	I_m	$II_{f,m}$	III_f	IV_n
nom/sg	Ø	a	Ø	o
acc/sg	Ø/a	u	Ø	o
dat/sg	u	e	i	u
gen/sg	a	i	i	a
inst/sg	om	oj	ju	om
loc/sg	e	e	i	e

noun inflection in Russian; these features must be inherently present on noun stems. However, so far it is not quite clear what form these features have. An analysis of instances of syncretism in Russian noun inflection will provide an answer.

5.2.1.2 *Analysis*   Abstracting away from the various interfering factors mentioned above, and assuming that at least the vast majority of variation conditioned by the ending of the stem (hard or soft) can and should be accounted for by morphophonological rules (see in particular Halle 1994), we can extract the system of inflection markers in table T_5 from the paradigms illustrating the four Russian noun inflection classes in the singular in T_1–T_4. This system exhibits both intraparadigmatic syncretism and transparadigmatic syncretism.

Examples of intraparadigmatic syncretism include /o/ as the inflection marker for nominative and accusative singular in class IV; /i/ for dative, genitive, and locative in class III; /e/ for dative and locative in class II; and /Ø/ for nominative and accusative (with inanimate stems) in class I. In addition, there are also many instances of transparadigmatic syncretism. For instance, /i/ is not confined to the dative, genitive, and locative of class III; this marker also shows up in the genitive of class II; similarly, /Ø/ shows up in the nominative and accusative of both class I and class III; /om/ is the instrumental marker for class I and class IV; /u/ is an accusative marker for class II, but also a dative marker for classes I and IV; and so forth.

A simple and elegant method to account for intraparadigmatic syncretism goes back to work by Roman Jakobson and Manfred Bierwisch. The central observation here is that intraparadigmatic syncretism shows that cases can form natural classes, and the basic idea is that these natural classes of cases can be captured straightforwardly by decomposing the standard (privative) case features into more primitive binary case features: full cross-classification of these features then yields the traditional cases (as they are relevant in syntax), and underspecification with respect to these primitive case features captures natural classes of cases. The primitive, underlying case features are mainly semantics-based in Jakobson (1962a; 1962b) (and also in much work on Russian noun inflection that follows the Jakobsonian tradition; see in particular Neidle (1988) and Franks (1995)); in contrast, they are syntax-based in Bierwisch (1967) (and in some subsequent work on German nominal–i.e., pronominal or noun–inflection based on this tradition, like Wiese (1999), Blevins (2000), and Müller (2002)). We adopt the latter view here and suggest that Russian cases are decomposed into combinations of the three privative features [±subject], [±governed], [±oblique], as shown in (5.2).[9]

(5.2)   *Decomposition of cases in Russian*: [±subject], [±governed], [±oblique]

nominative:	[+subj,−gov,−obl]
accusative:	[−subj,+gov,−obl]
dative:	[−subj,+gov,+obl]
genitive:	[+subj,+gov,+obl]
instrumental:	[+subj,−gov,+obl]
locative:	[−subj,−gov,+obl]

It follows from (5.2) that nominative and accusative form a natural class characterized by the feature [−obl]; that accusative and dative form a natural class characterized by the feature combination [−subj,+gov]; that dative and locative form a natural class characterized by [−subj,+obl]; and so on. The choice of the correct inflection marker for any given context can then be determined by underspecified case information capturing a natural class of cases, rather than by fully specified case information that encodes a specific case; this derives instances of intraparadigmatic syncretism.[10]

---

[9]   The features [±governed], [±oblique] go back to Bierwisch's discussion of German; the feature [±subject] is introduced by Wiese (2001) for Latin. Note that the feature combinations that characterize the syntactic cases can to some extent be motivated independently. Nominative, genitive (in DPs), and instrumental (in passives) typically show up on "subject" DPs (with "subject" understood as "last-merged argument of a predicate"); hence, they qualify as [+subj], and the remaining cases as [−subj]. Accusative, dative, and genitive are the prototypical cases of internal arguments of verbs (i.e., arguments governed by V); hence, they are [+gov], and the remaining cases [−gov]. Finally, dative, genitive, instrumental, and locative are oblique cases, which are therefore characterized as [+obl], with nominative and accusative emerging as [−obl].

[10]   We take the feature decomposition approach to syncretism to be well established and will not attempt to justify it here. However, it may be worth noting that many approaches to syncretism that purportedly do without feature decomposition do in fact rely on abstract features that capture the natural classes after all, but only by stipulation–see, for example, the property [oblique] in Blevins (2004, 82) and Wiese (2004, 324), or the property [X] (comprising nom/sg and acc/sg) in Baerman (2005a, 812) (based on Zwicky 2000). The main difference between this type of analysis and a feature decomposition approach then simply is that the former theory is less constrained than the latter. That said, there *is* an open question raised by the feature decomposition approach since its earliest

We propose that transparadigmatic syncretism can be accounted for in the same way, by decomposing privative class features as they are standardly assumed (like [class I], [class II], etc.) into more primitive, binary class features. A cross-classification of primitive class features yields fully specified class information (i.e., the standard inflection classes); underspecification with respect to these features yields natural classes of inflection classes. More specifically, we suggest that the four noun inflection classes of Russian result from the cross-classification of two binary inflection class features, as in (5.3).[11] Inflection class features, whether decomposed or not, are not motivated independently, outside morphology (and, as we will argue in section 5.3, they are in fact uninterpretable in syntax).[12] Accordingly, the decomposed features are

manifestations. Decomposed features, such as the case features currently under consideration, may be accessible in syntax (see the previous footnote), but *not* for case assignment; in other words, there are no case assigners that require an *underspecified* case on the assignee. A solution to this problem is beyond the scope of the present chapter.

[11] There are predecessors of this idea. Relying on standard, privative class features in their account of Russian noun inflection, Corbett and Fraser (1993) suggest a common additional fifth class feature [class 0] that co-occurs with inflection class features I and IV. This "meta-inflection class feature" is invoked in order to account for instances of transparadigmatic syncretism affecting inflection classes I and IV. However, this approach does not extend to other instances of transparadigmatic syncretism; moreover, the existence of a natural class comprising the inflection classes I and IV is simply stipulated (by assuming an additional feature 0), and not derived (by feature decomposition; see the previous footnote). More closely related to the present proposal are three analyses that envisage genuine class feature decomposition. First, Halle (1992, 38) employs the primitive, decomposed features [±marginal], [±marked] (in addition to the "standard" class features A, B) in his analysis of Latvian noun inflection, essentially so as to account for instances of transparadigmatic syncretism. Second, Nesset (1994, 229ff) develops an analysis of Russian noun inflection that uses [±nom-end] and [*a*/igen-end] as primitive class features, again in order to account for instances of transparadigmatic syncretism. The analysis has a limited scope (involving only a few of the attested cases of transparadigmatic syncretism, and no cases of intraparadigmatic syncretism), and stays somewhat informal (e.g., theoretical issues arising with underspecification and competition of inflection markers are not explored—more generally, no attempt is made to account for the whole system of noun inflection in a systematic way); nevertheless, it is clearly guided by the same underlying idea. Third, a decomposition of class features that is very similar to the one suggested here is proposed by Oltra Massuet (1999) in her approach to Catalan verb morphology. (Also see Trommer (2005b) for a more recent version of this idea, applied to Amharic verbs.)

[12] In particular, primitive inflection class features fail to strictly correlate with gender features just like the standard inflection classes do. There is no correlation of $[+\beta]$ or $[-\beta]$ with gender features at all; and even though $[+\alpha]$ classes contain non-feminine stems, and $[-\alpha]$ classes contain predominantly feminine stems, the correlation is not complete because masculine stems may also show up in the $[-\alpha]$ class II. Hence, gender features cannot possibly play the role of primitive inflection class features in Russian. This conclusion will be enforced by evidence from Greek and German below. That said, the situation might be slightly different in Icelandic. Icelandic has many noun inflection classes and exhibits transparadigmatic syncretism in abundance, which again supports a decomposition of inflection classes into combinations of primitive class features (see Müller 2005). Some of these primitive class features then do in fact seem to strictly correlate with gender information. However, others have no such grounding, so the main conclusion remains valid.

given the arbitrary names $[\pm a]$, $[\pm\beta]$ in (5.3), so as to indicate that they have the same (i.e., purely formal, morphology-based) status as traditional class features like [I], [II], etc.

(5.3)   *Decomposition of inflection classes in Russian:* $[\pm a]$, $[\pm\beta]$

   I: $[+a,-\beta]$ *zavod*$_m$ ('factory')
   II: $[-a,+\beta]$ *komnat*$_f$ ('room'), *mušcin*$_m$ ('man')
   III: $[-a,-\beta]$ *tetrad'*$_f$ ('notebook')
   IV: $[+a,+\beta]$ *mest*$_n$ ('place')

It follows from (5.3) that classes I and IV form a natural class (characterized by $[+a]$); the same goes for classes I and III ($[-\beta]$), classes II and III ($[-a]$), and classes II and IV ($[+\beta]$). However, classes I and II do not form a natural class, and classes III and IV do not form a natural class either. Thus, the prediction is that there can be instances of transparadigmatic syncretism that exclusively affect classes I and III, I and IV, II and III, and II and IV, but not classes I and II, and not classes III and IV. This prediction will be shown to be borne out.

As noted, underspecification with respect to case features and inflection class features encodes natural classes of cases and inflection classes, and thus acts as the key to intraparadigmatic and transparadigmatic syncretism, respectively. At this point, the choice of a specific approach to inflectional morphology becomes necessary. We assume that inflection markers as they show up in T_5 are morphemes that are stored in the lexicon.[13] As part of their lexical entry, inflection markers bear morphosyntactic features. The inflection markers currently under consideration can be assumed to bear a categorial feature [+N] that ensures combination with a noun stem. In addition, they bear case and class features; crucially, case and class feature specifications on inflection markers may be–and typically are–underspecified. The inflection markers used in the singular of Russian noun inflection are listed in (5.4).

General questions concerning possible inventories of these primitive inflection class features and their status as universal or acquired on the basis of linguistic input (presumably by invoking general strategies of object perception and object categorization) arise under this view in the same way that they arise under the standard view based on class features like [I] and [II], and we do not have any specific claims to make concerning this issue.

[13] We will motivate this assumption in section 5.4 below. For the time being, the gist of our analysis could equally well be formulated in stem-/word-and-paradigm models in which inflection markers are introduced by rules or schemas (see Anderson 1992; Aronoff 1994; Stump 2001; and references cited in these works), or in a Distributed Morphology approach in which inflection markers are vocabulary items that are postsyntactically inserted into positions provided by designated functional heads (see Halle and Marantz 1993; Harley and Noyer 2003; and references cited there).

(5.4) *Russian inflection markers (singular):*

1. /oj/: $\{[+N],[-\alpha,+\beta],[+subj,-gov,+obl]\}$
2. /ju/: $\{[+N],[-\alpha,-\beta],[+subj,-gov,+obl]\}$
3. /om/: $\{[+N],[\underline{+\alpha}],[+subj,-gov,+obl]\}$
4. /e/: $\{[+N],[-\alpha,+\beta],[-subj,+obl]\}$
5. /e/: $\{[+N],[\underline{+\alpha}],[-subj,-gov,+obl]\}$
6. /o/: $\{[+N],[+\alpha,+\beta],[-obl]\}$
7. /Ø/: $\{[+N],[\underline{-\beta}],[-obl]\}$
8. /i/: $\{[+N],[\underline{-\alpha}],[+obl]\}$
9. /u/: $\{[+N],[-subj,+gov]\}$
10. /a/: $\{[+N]\}$

With the exception of the instrumental markers /oj/, /ju/, and /om/ in (5.4-1.)–(5.4-3.), all inflection markers in (5.4) are underspecified with respect to case. Moreover, many inflection markers are also underspecified with respect to class, that is, /om/ in (5.4-3.); /e/ in (5.4-5.); the null marker /Ø/ in (5.4-7.); and /i/ in (5.4-8.) (here and in what follows, underspecified class information is underlined in inflection marker specifications). Indeed, two markers bear no class information at all: /u/ in (5.4-9.), and the default (or elsewhere) marker /a/ in (5.4-10.).

Suppose now that noun stems, in contrast to inflection markers, always bear fully specified case, class, number, and gender features; for now, we can assume that all these features are inherently present on a noun stem in the lexicon (we will modify this assumption slightly in section 5.4). In a language like Russian, a noun stem must (normally, that is, unless it belongs to the class of indeclinables) combine with an inflection marker in morphology. The choice of inflection marker for a fully specified noun stem can be taken to follow from the Subset Principle, a version of which we have formulated in (5.5).[14]

(5.5) *Subset Principle:*
      An inflection marker *I* is merged with a stem *S* iff (i) and (ii) hold:
      (i)   The morphosyntactic features of *I* are a subset of the
            morphosyntactic features of *S*.
      (ii) *I* is the most specific marker that satisfies (i).

It follows from (5.5-i) that quite often there is a priori more than one inflection marker which could be combined with a given noun stem. To see this,

---

[14] See Kiparsky (1973), Anderson (1992), Lumsden (1992), Noyer (1992), Williams (1994), Halle (1997), Williams (1997), Stump (2001), Gunkel (2003), and Zifonun (2003) for versions of this principle, sometimes under different names. The present formulation is closest to the one Halle (1997) gives.

consider, as an extreme case, the following situation: a noun stem like *komnat* ('room') has been selected from the lexicon, bearing the inherent features [+N] (category: noun), $[-a,+\beta]$ (class: II), [−subj,+gov,+obl] (case: dative), [−pl] (number: singular), and [+fem] (gender: feminine). The inflection markers in (5.4) whose morphosyntactic features are a subset of the morphosyntactic features of this noun stem are /a/ in (5.4-10.)–or, as we will write from now on, $/a/_{10}$–which has no morphosyntactic case or class features and therefore fits with every noun stem; $/u/_9$, which, on the view adopted here, is a general marker for accusative and dative, without class restriction; $/i/_8$, which, under present assumptions, turns out to be a simple obliqueness marker for (the predominantly feminine) classes II and III; and $/e/_4$ (a dative/locative marker for class II). Such a competition is systematically resolved by requirement (5.5-ii), according to which the most specific marker of the competing items must be chosen (in the case at hand, this must be /e/). Specificity of inflection markers is defined in (5.6).

(5.6) *Specificity of inflection markers:*
       An inflection marker I_i is more specific than an inflection marker I_j iff there is a set of features $\mathbb{F}$ such that (i) and (ii) hold.
       (i) I_i bears more features in $\mathbb{F}$ than I_j does.
       (ii) There is no higher-ranked set of features $\mathbb{F}'$ such that I_i and I_j have a different number of features in $\mathbb{F}'$.

(5.6) presupposes a hierarchy of different feature sets (or feature classes); see Lumsden (1992), Noyer (1992). For present purposes, the partial hierarchy in (5.7) is sufficient.

(5.7) *Hierarchy of feature classes:*
       Number ≫ class ≫ case

Simplifying a bit, an inflection marker is more specific than another inflection marker if it has more and higher-ranked features, where quality of the features is more important than quantity.[15] Going back to the above example of the competition among inflection markers in the case of the singular, dative-marked class II noun *komnat*, it is now clear that of the four competing markers $/a/_{10}$, $/u/_9$, $/i/_8$, and $/e/_4$, the last one is most specific, that is, class features outrank case features; therefore, $/a/_{10}$ and $/u/_9$, which have no class features, are less specific than $/i/_8$ and $/e/_4$, which bear class features. Of the

---

[15] This is of course reminiscent of Optimality Theory, and responsible for the fact that the definition of specificity in (5.6) bears an uncanny resemblance to the definition of optimality in Optimality Theory.

T_6: *The interaction of inflection markers in the singular in Russian*

	I: $[+a,-\beta]$	II: $[-a,+\beta]$	III: $[-a,-\beta]$	IV: $[+a,+\beta]$
nom/sg: [+subj,−gov,−obl]	**/Ø/$_7$** (/a/$_{10}$)	/a/$_{10}$	**/Ø/$_7$** (/a/$_{10}$)	/o/$_6$ (/a/$_{10}$)
acc/sg: [−subj,+gov,−obl]	**/Ø/$_7$** (/u/$_9$, /a/$_{10}$)	/u/$_9$ (/a/$_{10}$)	**/Ø/$_7$** (/u/$_9$, /a/$_{10}$)	/o/$_6$ (/u/$_9$, /a/$_{10}$)
dat/sg: [−subj,+gov,+obl]	/u/$_9$ (/a/$_{10}$)	/e/$_4$ (/i/$_8$, /u/$_9$, /a/$_{10}$)	/i/$_8$ (/u/$_9$, /a/$_{10}$)	/u/$_9$ (/a/$_{10}$)
gen/sg: [+subj,+gov,+obl]	/a/$_{10}$	/i/$_8$ (/a/$_{10}$)	/i/$_8$ (/a/$_{10}$)	/a/$_{10}$
inst/sg: [+subj,−gov,+obl]	/om/$_3$ (/a/$_{10}$)	/oj/$_1$ (/i/$_8$, /a/$_{10}$)	/ju/$_2$ (/i/$_8$, /a/$_{10}$)	/om/$_3$ (/a/$_{10}$)
loc/sg: [−subj,−gov,+obl]	/e/$_5$ (/a/$_{10}$)	/e/$_4$ (/i/$_8$, /a/$_{10}$)	/i/$_8$ (/a/$_{10}$)	/e/$_5$ (/a/$_{10}$)

latter two, /i/$_8$ bears fewer class features than /e/$_4$ (that is, $[-a]$ vs. $[-a,+\beta]$); hence, in the absence of any number features in (5.4), /e/$_4$ is chosen as the most specific marker that fits into the morphosyntactic context provided by *komnat* in the case at hand.

More generally (at least as a strong tendency), specificity decreases from top to bottom in (5.4)–the fully specified instrumental markers /oj/$_1$ and /ju/$_2$ are most specific and the radically underspecified marker /a/$_{10}$ is least specific. Table T_6 then illustrates how the assumptions about underspecified morphosyntactic features on inflection markers in (5.4) and the specificity-based Subset Principle in (5.5) interact to derive the system of Russian noun inflection in T_5 (with the exception of the animacy effect in class I, to which we will turn shortly).[16]

As shown in T_6, almost all instances of intra- and transparadigmatic syncretism are now accounted for systematically, in accordance with the meta-grammatical principle (5.1). Thus there is only one lexical entry for /a/, namely, /a/$_{10}$; this marker's distribution is not homogeneous (nominative of class II, genitive of classes I and IV), but this is solely due to the fact that /a/ is an extremely non-specific default marker that fits into every context but can actually emerge in a paradigm cell only if there is no more specific marker available–and this is the only property that unites the contexts in which /a/ does show up. Similarly, there is only one entry each for /u/, /i/, /Ø/, and /o/, as well as for the highly specific instrumental markers /oj/, /ju/, and /om/. The only exception is /e/, for which two entries must be assumed: /e/$_4$ is a dative/locative marker of class II, and /e/$_5$ is a locative marker for classes I and

---

[16] Each paradigm cell contains all markers that fit into a given morphosyntactic context provided by a noun stem. The most specific of competing markers that is chosen by the Subset Principle is given in bold face; the remaining markers are given in the line below in parentheses.

T₇: Inflection classes I–IV in the plural

	I zavod_m ('factory')	II komnat_f ('room')	III tetrad'_f ('notebook')	IV mest_n ('place')
nom/pl	zavod-y	komnat-y	tetrad-i	mest-a
acc/pl	zavod-y	komnat-y	tetrad-i	mest-a
dat/pl	zavod-am	komnat-am	tetrad-jam	mest-am
gen/pl	zavod-ov	komnat-Ø	tetrad-ej	mest-Ø
inst/pl	zavod-ami	komnat-ami	tetrad-jami	mest-ami
loc/pl	zavod-ax	komnat-ax	tetrad-jax	mest-ax

IV. At this point, we wish to leave open the question whether this reflects an imperfection of the analysis or an imperfection of the system as such.[17]

So far we have not yet addressed the plural. Focusing again on the core cases, it turns out that the system of Russian noun inflection is much simpler in the plural than it is in the singular. Table T₇ lists the basic patterns of the four inflection classes (as with the discussion of class I in the singular, for now we abstract away from an animacy effect in accusative contexts).[18]

The inflection markers for dative, instrumental, and locative plural are invariant across inflection classes; in this respect, they resemble agglutinative markers. With respect to the nominative/accusative plural markers, there are two possibilities. The first option is to assume that /i/ is a [–obl] marker not restricted by class information, and to treat /a/ as the special case that is confined to class IV (although there is a substantial drift of /a/ into class I as well–albeit one that goes hand in hand with stress on the suffix). The second option is to assume that /a/ is the more general marker, as it is in the singular, and to treat /i/ as the more special case; this then necessitates the assumption that complements of natural classes can also figure in inflection marker entries (see Zwicky 1970). Although considerations related to iconicity (see footnote 17) might ultimately favor the second option, we will adopt the

---

[17] Closer inspection reveals a further interesting property of the markers in (5.4). A decrease in specificity from top to bottom seems to go hand in hand with an increase in sonority, i.e., the system exhibits iconicity in the sense that similarity of form implies similarity of function. This tendency becomes even stronger when we follow Halle (1994) in analyzing the null marker /Ø/ as an abstract vowel (yer) /O/ that undergoes PF deletion, and also take into account the fact that /e/, unlike all the other vocalic markers, always has an initial glide, which in effect makes this marker quasi-consonantal, and at any rate less sonorous; see Müller (2004) for a detailed account along these lines, incorporating observations in Shapiro (1969, 14) and Plank (1979, 143). Note incidentally that this consideration might ultimately also shed new light on the special behaviour of /e/ just mentioned in the main text: /e/ differs from /i/, /u/, /a/, etc., both with respect to its function and its form.

[18] As before, there is systematic morphophonological variation determined by the characterization of a stem-final consonant as [+back] or [–back]. Thus, /i/ is realized as i in [–back] environments, as y in [+back] environments; and so on. Note in particular that /ov/ is realized as ej after a [–back] consonant (i.e., always in class III, and sometimes in class I); that is, ov and ej are different surface realizations of the same underlying abstract marker /ov/. See Halle (1994, 50).

first, more parsimonious option here, mainly for reasons of simplicity. This leaves the two genitive markers /ov/ (realized as *ov* or *ej*) and /Ø/. The former shows up in classes I and III, the latter in classes II and IV, and this is captured straightforwardly in the respective entries, given that class I and class III form a natural class defined by $[-\beta]$, and that class II and class IV form a natural class defined by $[+\beta]$.[19] The list of markers for the plural of Russian noun inflection is given in (5.8) (as before, underspecified class information is underlined, and specificity decreases from top to bottom among the markers that show interaction).

(5.8) *Russian inflection markers (plural):*

1.	/ax/:	$\{[+N],[+pl],[-subj,-gov,+obl]\}$
2.	/ami/:	$\{[+N],[+pl],[+subj,-gov,+obl]\}$
3.	/am/:	$\{[+N],[+pl],[-subj,+gov,+obl]\}$
4.	/ov/:	$\{[+N],[+pl],[-\beta],[+subj,+gov,+obl]\}$
5.	/Ø/:	$\{[+N],[+pl],\underline{[+\beta]},[+subj,+gov,+obl]\}$
6.	/a/:	$\{[+N],[+pl],[+a,+\beta],[-obl]\}$
7.	/i/:	$\{[+N],[+pl],[-obl]\}$

The (minimal) interaction of plural markers is shown in table T_8. Note that there is no principled reason that would keep the singular markers in (5.4) from competing with plural markers. However, given that the plural markers in (5.8) all bear the feature [+pl], and given that the singular markers in (5.4) no not bear any number feature, singular markers can never become the most specific markers for any given plural environment. Plural features outrank class and case features on the hierarchy of features in (5.7).[20] For this reason, competing singular markers are not listed in T_8.

---

[19] There is a well-known generalization concerning an alternation between nominative singular and genitive plural with respect to the occurrence of /Ø/: an inflection class has /Ø/ in the genitive plural iff it does not have /Ø/ in the nominative singular; classes I, III have /Ø/ in the nominative singular, and classes II, IV in the genitive plural. It is not quite clear whether there could be a simple, conservative way to make this follow under the present set of assumptions (but see footnote 28). In any event, it seems that an account of *all* such "transnumber" syncretisms (including /a/ and /i/) in terms of underspecification of morphosyntactic features must remain out of reach for systematic reasons. Hence, in line with our guiding assumption that there is no systematic syncretism across numbers, we will consider the singular/plural alternation effect with /Ø/ accidental from a purely synchronic perspective. (Incidentally, all systematic accounts of this phenomenon that we know of require a significantly more complex approach, for example, by permitting reference to existing output forms in the determination of markers; see Bailyn and Nevins (this volume) for a recent analysis.)

[20] Conversely, plural markers can never compete in singular environments because their morphosyntactic features include [+pl], which implies that they can never qualify as a subset of the features of a singular noun stem, which includes the feature [-pl].

T_8: *The interaction of inflection markers in the plural in Russian*

	I: $[+a,-\beta]$	II: $[-a,+\beta]$	III: $[-a,-\beta]$	IV: $[+a,+\beta]$
nom/pl: [+subj,−gov,−obl]	$/i/_7$	$/i/_7$	$/i/_7$	$/a/_6$ ($/i/_7$)
acc/pl: [−subj,+gov,−obl]	$/i/_7$	$/i/_7$	$/i/_7$	$/a/_6$ ($/i/_7$)
dat/pl: [−subj,+gov,+obl]	$/am/_3$	$/am/_3$	$/am/_3$	$/am/_3$
gen/pl: [+subj,+gov,+obl]	$/ov/_4$	$/\emptyset/_5$	$/ov/_4$	$/\emptyset/_5$
inst/pl: [+subj,−gov,+obl]	$/ami/_2$	$/ami/_2$	$/ami/_2$	$/ami/_2$
loc/pl: [−subj,−gov,+obl]	$/ax/_1$	$/ax/_1$	$/ax/_1$	$/ax/_1$

Taking the singular and plural paradigms together, we end up with an interesting result. For each natural class of inflection classes that is predicted to be possible under class feature decomposition, there is indeed at least one marker that refers to it. A list of inflection markers that thus refer to underspecified class information is given in (5.9). [21]

---

[21] The reviewer notes that it is a priori unclear why systems do not seem to exist where natural classes of inflection classes are systematically referred to by many more inflection markers, not just by "at least one"; a borderline case would be a system of "Pseudo-Russian" in which class I and class III are identical except for their choice of dative and locative markers (/x/, /y/ vs. /w/, /z/), and class II and class IV are also identical except for their choice of dative and locative markers, with the dative and locative markers of class IV being identical to the corresponding markers of class I (/x/, /y/), and the dative and locative markers of class II being identical to the dative and locative markers of class III (/w/, /z/). Such a system could come into being as a result of class feature decomposition: /x/ and /y/ both happen to refer to the natural class of inflection classes I and IV; /w/ and /z/ both happen to refer to the natural class of inflection classes II and III; and all the other markers refer to either the natural class comprising classes I and III, or the natural class comprising classes II and IV. More generally, it may seem that the present approach suffers from a lack of restrictiveness, in the sense that it does not radically constrain the set of inflection classes that are logically possible on the basis of a given inventory of markers. In this, it differs from approaches that employ constraints like Carstairs's (1987) Paradigm Economy Principle (PEP) or Carstairs-McCarthy's (1994) No Blur Principle, which restrict the number of possible inflection classes by stipulation (essentially, the PEP states that the number of inflection classes cannot be greater than the maximal number of allomorphs for a given morphosyntactic specification in a paradigm; and according to No Blur, only one marker can fail to uniquely identify inflection class, for any given morphosyntactic specification in a paradigm). These constraints cannot be imposed onto the present analysis, and not only because they rely on paradigms (see footnote 1); the main reason is that they are inherently incompatible with a decomposition of inflection class features. Thus, Noyer's (2005) Interclass Syncretism Constraint (itself derivable from more general assumptions in a Distributed Morphology approach, and similar–but not identical–in its effects to No Blur) also crucially presupposes that inflection class features are not decomposed (and natural classes of inflection classes cannot be referred to by inflection markers).

(5.9) $[+\alpha]$ (I, IV):   /om/ (Sg.), /e/ (Sg.)
       $[-\alpha]$ (II, III): /i/ (Sg.)
       $[+\beta]$ (II, IV):   /Ø/ (Pl.)
       $[-\beta]$ (I, III):   /Ø/ (Sg.), /ov/ (Pl.)

Thus far we have not yet said anything about the animacy effect that shows up with class I in the singular, and with all inflection classes in the plural, and that consists of inserting the respective genitive marker in accusative environments with animate stems. The resulting instances of syncretism look very different from the ones addressed so far and we believe that they should therefore not be captured in the same way, by underspecified feature matrices on inflection markers. Thus we would like to suggest that the animacy-induced instances of accusative/genitive syncretism go back to two rules of referral (see Zwicky 1985), i.e., rules that explicitly state (rather than derive) the fact that the marker for a given morphosyntactic context is identical to the marker of some other morphosyntactic context; such a rule may thus override the results of the core system based on underspecification. The following rules of referral are based on similar rules in Corbett and Fraser (1993, 135) and Stump (2001, 229); the suspension of the decomposition- and specificity-based outcome by this rule is reflected in the formulation of the rule (where "$I_{\{\ldots\}}$" stands for "the inflection marker determined by the Subset Principle for context $\{\ldots\}$", and "$\rightarrow$" stands for "is replaced by").[22]

(5.10) a. $I_{\{[+\alpha,-\beta],[-\text{subj},+\text{gov},-\text{obl}]\}} \rightarrow I_{\{[+\alpha,-\beta],[+\text{subj},+\text{gov},+\text{obl}]\}}/[+\text{animate}]\_\_.$

        b. $I_{\{[+\text{pl}],[-\text{subj},+\text{gov},-\text{obl}]\}} \rightarrow I_{\{[+\text{pl}],[+\text{subj},+\text{gov},+\text{obl}]\}}/[+\text{animate}]\_\_.$

A comprehensive discussion of the nature of restrictions on possible inflection classes is beyond the scope of the present investigation. Certain empirical and conceptual problems with constraints like No Blur notwithstanding (see Müller 2005, based on evidence from Icelandic), we will confine ourselves to pointing out that a system like that of Pseudo-Russian is statistically highly unlikely, because not a single marker bears fully specified inflection class information. However, as soon as marker specifications are more mixed with respect to inflection class (some markers are fully specified, some are underspecified, or not specified at all), the resulting system looks completely natural–in fact, not too dissimilar from the system of German declension proposed below, with multiple reference to primitive inflection class features by markers. Finally, it is worth pointing out that the Syncretism Principle can be shown to significantly restrict the number of possible inflection classes by itself (see Müller 2006a). We contend that given a set of n inflection markers, there can only be at most 2^{n-1} inflection classes (= the powerset of the inventory minus one radically underspecified marker), independently of the number of categorizations that the markers have to distribute over (and abstracting away from imperfections like /e/ in Russian). Thus, assuming, say, five markers for a system with six cases, there can only be 16 (2^4) inflection classes, out of the 15.625 (5^6) that would be logically possible without the Syncretism Principle.

[22] One might speculate whether these rules ultimately have a functional motivation, essentially that of ensuring differential object marking (as discussed in Aissen (2003) and literature cited there); see Comrie 1978 and Baerman et al. 2002. Also see Wunderlich 2004, whose Optimality-Theoretic account of the phenomenon incorporates this insight.

T_9: *Inflection class I: masc, fem*

	I	
	$an\theta rop_m$ ('man')	$psif_f$ ('vote')
nom/sg	anθrop-os	psif-os
acc/sg	anθrop-o(n)	psif-o(n)
gen/sg	anθrop-u	psif-u
voc/sg	anθrop-e	(psif-e)
nom/pl	anθrop-i	psif-i
acc/pl	anθrop-us	psif-us
gen/pl	anθrop-on	psif-on
voc/pl	anθrop-i	psif-i

This concludes our discussion of Russian noun inflection. The main result is that class features are indispensable in an account of this system and that there is also good reason to assume that they are quite abstract, binary features. Full specification with respect to these features encodes the standard inflection classes and underspecification with respect to these features yields natural classes of inflection classes, which permits a systematic account of transparadigmatic syncretism. In the next section, we will see that the situation is completely analogous in Greek.

5.2.2 *Noun inflection in Greek*

5.2.2.1 *Data*   Modern Greek has three major cases: nominative, accusative, and genitive. In addition, there is a fourth vocative case.[23] As for the number of inflection classes, a traditional view that is documented in, for example, Ruge (1986) recognizes three inflection classes. In contrast, Ralli (1994) argues that there are eight inflection classes. We adopt the system argued for by Ralli here (and also her numbering of the inflection classes); but it should be clear that class feature decomposition permits the formation of natural classes of inflection classes, which can then accommodate the more traditional view (to the extent that it proves correct).

Let us begin with inflection class I; see table T_9. This class contains masculine and some feminine noun stems. It shows the greatest variety of inflection markers, with only one instance of intraparadigmatic syncretism arising (/i/ in the nominative/vocative plural). This inflection class has also appropriately been called the "declension of the seven forms" (see Ruge 1986, 30).

---

[23] The discussion in this section is mainly based on the following sources: Mackridge (1985), Babiniotis (1986), Ruge (1986), Ralli (1994), Ralli (2002), and Alexiadou (2004); see also the contributions in Anastasiadi-Simeonidi et al. (2003).

T_{10}: *Inflection classes II–IV: masc, fem*

	II *maxit(i)$_m$* ('fighter')	III *avl(i)$_f$* ('yard')	IV *pol(i)(e)$_f$* ('city')
nom/sg	maxit-i-s	avl-i-Ø	pol-i-Ø
acc/sg	maxit-i-Ø	avl-i-Ø	pol-i-Ø
gen/sg	maxit-i-Ø	avl-i-s	pol-i-s
voc/sg	maxit-i-Ø	avl-i-Ø	pol-i-Ø
nom/pl	maxit-es	avl-es	pol-is
acc/pl	maxit-es	avl-es	pol-is
gen/pl	maxit-on	avl-on	pol-e-on
voc/pl	maxit-es	avl-es	pol-is

Next, inflection classes II, III, and IV are illustrated in table T_{10}. Class II contains only masculine stems; class III and class IV are confined to feminine stems. These inflection classes show much more intraparadigmatic syncretism than class I. In addition, there is substantial stem alternation, which, as before, we will remain silent about (note in particular that the examples given here all involve formation of the plural stem by subtraction of the final stem vowel). These three inflection classes are grouped together under the label of "s-principle" in Ruge (1986). Inflection classes that obey the s-principle are characterized by the occurrence of /s/ in the singular, either in the nominative or in the genitive (but never in both cases), with the masculine class II opting for the former and the feminine classes III and IV opting for the latter.

Finally, table T_{11} lists the four neuter classes; these classes share some markers (most notably in the plural) but are otherwise sufficiently different to preclude grouping them under a single inflection class.

As in Russian, class membership cannot be determined on the basis of inherent features of noun stems in Greek. Thus gender features do not suffice

T_{11}: *Inflection classes V–VIII: neut*

	V *vun$_n$* ('mountain')	VI *krat$_n$* ('state')	VII *spiti$_n$* ('house')	VIII *soma(t)$_n$* ('body')
nom/sg	vun-o	krat-os	spiti-Ø	soma-Ø
acc/sg	vun-o	krat-os	spiti-Ø	soma-Ø
gen/sg	vun-u	krat-us	spitj-u	soma-t-os
voc/sg	vun-o	krat-os	spiti-Ø	soma-Ø
nom/pl	vun-a	krat-i	spitj-a	soma-t-a
acc/pl	vun-a	krat-i	spitj-a	soma-t-a
gen/pl	vun-on	krat-on	spitj-on	soma-t-on
voc/pl	vun-a	krat-i	spitj-a	soma-t-a

T_{12}: *Syncretism within and across inflection classes in Greek*

	'7 forms'	's-principle'			'neuter'			
	$I_{m,f}$	II_m	III_f	IV_f	V_n	VI_n	VII_n	VIII_n
nom/sg	os	s	∅	∅	o	os	∅	∅
acc/sg	o(n)	∅	∅	∅	o	os	∅	∅
gen/sg	u	∅	s	s	u	us	u	os
voc/sg	e	∅	∅	∅	o	os	∅	∅
nom/pl	i	es	es	is	a	i	a	a
acc/pl	us	es	es	is	a	i	a	a
gen/pl	on	on	on	on	on	on	on	on
voc/pl	i	es	es	is	a	i	a	a

for this purpose. Masculine noun stems can belong to either class I or class II; feminine noun stems can belong to class I, class III, or class IV; and neuter noun stems can belong to any of the classes in V–VIII. Similarly, phonological features on the noun stem do not suffice to predict inflection class. What one might initially take to be a theme vowel is either a part of the ending, in which case it cannot encode inflection class by definition; or it is a part of the stem, where it fails to unambiguously encode inflection class. Compare, e.g., *maxit(i)* ('fighter'), *papa(δ)* ('priest'), and *papu(δ)* ('grandfather'), all of which belong to class II. Finally, semantic features on the stem (like [±animate]) also fail to predict inflection class. The conclusion to be drawn from this is again that pure class features are indispensable. And, as in Russian, the widespread occurrence of transparadigmatic syncretism provides strong arguments for decomposing these features into more abstract items.

5.2.2.2 *Analysis* The core of the Greek noun inflection system is given in table T_{12}. There is both intraparadigmatic syncretism (see, for example, /o/ in the nominative and accusative singular of class V) and transparadigmatic syncretism (as in the case of /u/, which shows up in genitive singular environments of classes I, V, and VII).

As before, intraparadigmatic syncretism can be traced back to natural classes of cases resulting from case feature decomposition, and lexical entries of inflection markers referring to these natural classes via underspecification. The Greek case system is simpler than the one found in Russian to begin with. Furthermore, we will abstract away from the vocative in what follows (which has a form different from the nominative form only in class I). Decomposition of the three remaining cases in Greek can then be taken to be identical to what we have seen for the respective cases in Russian, except for the absence of the feature [±subject]; see (5.11).[24]

(5.11)   *Decomposition of cases in Greek*: [±governed], [±oblique]
       nominative: [–gov,–obl]
       accusative: [+gov,–obl]
       genitive: [+gov,+obl]

Next, again as before, transparadigmatic syncretism strongly suggests the presence of natural classes of inflection classes and thus motivates the decomposition of class features. Interestingly, although Greek has fewer cases than Russian, it has more noun inflection classes. We propose that the eight classes envisaged by Ralli (1994) result from the cross-classification of the three primitive class features $[\pm a]$, $[\pm \beta]$, and $[\pm \gamma]$, as in (5.12).[25]

(5.12)   *Decomposition of inflection classes in Greek*: $[\pm a]$, $[\pm \beta]$, $[\pm \gamma]$

I:	$[+a,+\beta,+\gamma]$	$an\theta rop_m$ ('man'), $psif_f$ ('vote')
V:	$[+a,+\beta,-\gamma]$	vun_n ('mountain')
VII:	$[+a,-\beta,+\gamma]$	$spiti_n$ ('house')
VIII:	$[+a,-\beta,-\gamma]$	$soma(t)_n$ ('body')
VI:	$[-a,+\beta,+\gamma]$	$krat_n$ ('state')
II:	$[-a,+\beta,-\gamma]$	$maxit(i)_m$ ('fighter')
IV:	$[-a,-\beta,+\gamma]$	$pol(i)(e)_f$ ('city')
III:	$[-a,-\beta,-\gamma]$	$avl(i)_f$ ('yard')

As shown in (5.13), inflection markers for the singular of Greek noun inflections may make crucial use of underspecified case and class information (the latter is again underlined in marker entries). Again, specificity of the markers decreases from top to bottom.

---

[24] The Greek genitive characterization is thus a proper subset of both the Russian genitive and the Russian dative characterizations. This is in accordance with the syntactic evidence. The genitive in Greek, in addition to its prototypical DP-internal role, shows up in many syntactic contexts where other languages employ the dative, such as the indirect object of double object verbs.

[25] The classes are not listed here according to the number they receive in Ralli's analysis but according to shared class features, beginning (somewhat arbitrarily) with the $[\pm a]$ distinction. Note that, as in Russian (see footnote 12), there is no strict correlation between gender information and the primitive class features adopted here. In particular, the four neuter declensions do not form a natural class; for example, $[+a]$ subsumes classes V, VII, and VIII but fails to cover class VI, integrating the masculine/feminine class I instead. Similar conclusions apply in the case of feminine stems; for example, $[-a]$ does not correlate with feminine gender because of the neuter and masculine classes VI and II, respectively; $[-\beta]$ does not correlate with feminine gender because of the neuter classes VII and VIII; and class I, which contains feminine stems, is not characterized by either $[-a]$ or $[-\beta]$. Finally, the same goes for masculine stems. The only feature that class I and class II have in common is $[+\beta]$, which also characterizes the neuter classes V and VI.

(5.13) *Greek inflection markers (singular):*

1. /o(n)/: $\{[+N],[+a,+\beta,+\gamma],[+gov,-obl]\}$
2. /os/: $\{[+N],[+a,-\beta,-\gamma],[+gov,+obl]\}$
3. /us/: $\{[+N],[-a,+\beta,+\gamma],[+gov,+obl]\}$
4. /o/: $\{[+N],[+a,+\beta,-\gamma],[-obl]\}$
5. /os/: $\{[+N],[+\beta,+\gamma],[-obl]\}$
6. /s/: $\{[+N],[-a,\aleph\beta],[-\aleph gov,-\aleph obl]\}$
7. /u/: $\{[+N],[+a],[+gov,+obl]\}$
8. /Ø/: $\{[+N]\}$

The marker /o(n)/$_1$ is fully specified as the accusative marker of class I; the markers /os/$_2$ and /us/$_3$ are fully specified as the genitive markers of classes VIII and VI, respectively. /o/$_4$ is a non-obliqueness marker for class V. /os/$_5$ is the first inflection marker that exhibits underspecified class information: it is the non-obliqueness marker for classes I and VI, which form a natural class characterized by the features $[+\beta,+\gamma]$ (however, /os/$_5$ is blocked in accusative singular contexts of class I by the more specific marker /o(n)/$_1$).

Next, /s/$_6$ emerges a special type of marker. Instead of bearing the features $[-a,+\beta]$ or $[-a,-\beta]$, it is characterized by the feature specification $[-a,\aleph\beta]$; and similarly for its case specification. Here, $\aleph$ is a variable ranging over the feature values $\pm$. Assuming that variables ranging over feature values can show up in morphosyntactic specifications of inflection markers, the two /s/ markers in class II and classes III and IV can emerge as one.[26] Without this option, there would have to be two /s/ markers, one specified as $\{[+N],[-a,+\beta],[-gov,-obl]\}$, and one specified as $\{[+N],[-a,-\beta],[+gov,+obl]\}$, and the covariance of feature values for class and case would be left unaccounted for. In contrast, the use of variables over feature values captures the gist of the s-principle, which incorporates a combined economy/alternation effect (i.e., class II, III, and IV must use /s/ exactly once, in either the nominative or the genitive).[27, 28]

[26] The $\aleph$-notation is originally known as the a-notation, a label that cannot be used here for obvious reasons. The concept was introduced in Chomsky (1965, 175 and 233) and Chomsky and Halle (1968, 83), and has been used in morphology in Noyer (1992) (but see Harley 1994); also compare the rule for /i/-insertion in Halle (1992, 39), and, more generally, Johnston (1996).

[27] It seems plausible to assume that, other things being equal, markers with variables over feature values count as less specific than markers without such variables. Consequently, /s/$_6$ is blocked by a more specific /os/$_5$ in the fourth context in which we would otherwise expect it, namely, in the nominative singular of class VI.

[28] As noted by Jonathan Bobaljik (p.c.) and Alexis Dimitriadis (p.c), the use of variables over feature values increases the number of possible natural classes. This is a welcome result for cases in Greek (because /s/$_6$ may then fit in nominative and genitive contexts), but it potentially undermines the above claim about classes I and II, and III and IV, not forming natural classes in Russian; for instance, a specification $[\aleph a,-\aleph\beta]$ would encode a natural class comprising class I ($[+a,-\beta]$) and class II ($[-a,+\beta]$). More generally, the $\aleph$-notation is a powerful tool that needs to be severely restricted. For the problem

T_{13}: *The interaction of inflection markers in the singular in Greek*

	I: $[+a+\beta+\gamma]$	II: $[-a+\beta-\gamma]$	III: $[-a-\beta-\gamma]$	IV: $[-a-\beta+\gamma]$	V: $[+a+\beta+\gamma]$	VI: $[-a+\beta+\gamma]$	VII: $[+a-\beta+\gamma]$	VIII: $[+a-\beta-\gamma]$
nom/sg: [−gov,−obl], [−pl]	/os/$_5$ (/Ø/$_8$)	/s/$_6$ (/Ø/$_8$)	/Ø/$_8$	/Ø/$_8$	/o/$_4$ (/Ø/$_8$)	/os/$_5$ (/s/$_6$, /Ø/$_8$)	/Ø/$_8$	/Ø/$_8$
acc/sg: [+gov,−obl], [−pl]	/o(n)/$_1$ (/os/$_5$, /Ø/$_8$)	/Ø/$_8$	/Ø/$_8$	/Ø/$_8$	/o/$_4$ (/Ø/$_8$)	/os/$_5$ (/Ø/$_8$)	/Ø/$_8$	/Ø/$_8$
gen/sg: [+gov,+obl], [−pl]	/u/$_7$ (/Ø/$_8$)	/Ø/$_8$	/s/$_6$ (/Ø/$_8$)	/s/$_6$ (/Ø/$_8$)	/u/$_7$ (/Ø/$_8$)	/us/$_3$ (/Ø/$_8$)	/u/$_7$ (/Ø/$_8$)	/os/$_2$ (/u/$_7$, /Ø/$_8$)

The last two markers in (5.13) are /u/$_7$, the genitive marker for $[+a]$-marked classes (which is blocked by more specific /os/$_2$ in class VIII); and finally /Ø/, the default marker that emerges whenever there is no more specific marker present. To conclude, all instances of syncretism in the singular of Greek noun inflection are accounted for, except for that involving /os/, which has two possible sources in the paradigm. As before, the imperfection may lie in the analysis or in the system as such, with the extremely specific distribution of /os/$_2$ (as opposed to that of /os/$_5$) arguably suggesting the latter. The interaction of inflection markers in the singular is illustrated in table T_{13}.[29]

The noun inflection markers for plural environments in Greek are listed in (5.14). /on/$_1$ is an obliqueness marker on a par with its Russian counterparts /am/, /ami/, and /ax/ that is invariant across inflection classes. /is/$_2$ and /us/$_3$ are class-specific markers, indicating non-obliqueness in class IV and accusative in class I, respectively. More interesting in the present context is the observation that some of these markers crucially refer to underspecified class information, that is, natural classes of inflection classes: /es/$_4$ is a non-obliqueness marker for classes II and III, and /i/$_5$ is a non-obliqueness marker for classes I and VI (where /i/$_5$ is blocked by more specific /us/$_3$ in the accusative plural of class I in exactly the same way that the singular marker /os/$_5$ turned out to be blocked by the more specific singular marker /o(n)/$_1$

at hand, we may assume that only one class feature of inflection markers may be specified by a variable over feature values (which ensures that there is no increase in natural classes of inflection classes). In addition, any use of this technique must be linguistically well motivated (as we take it to be in the case of the s-principle in Greek). Note incidentally that the singular/plural alternation effect with /Ø/ in Russian (see footnote 19) might in principle be amenable to an analysis along these lines, given some modifications (with /Ø/ receiving a specification containing [אpl],[אβ]); but we will not pursue the issue here.

[29] Note in passing that the system again seems to show indications of iconicity, with less sonorous markers in general emerging as more specific.

T_{14}: *The interaction of inflection markers in the plural in Greek*

	I: $[+a+\beta+\gamma]$	II: $[-a+\beta-\gamma]$	III: $[-a-\beta-\gamma]$	IV: $[-a-\beta+\gamma]$	V: $[+a+\beta+\gamma]$	VI: $[-a+\beta+\gamma]$	VII: $[+a-\beta+\gamma]$	VIII: $[+a-\beta-\gamma]$
nom/pl: $[-gov,-obl]$, $[+pl]$	/i/$_5$ (/a/$_6$)	/es/$_4$ (/a/$_6$)	/es/$_4$ (/a/$_6$)	/is/$_2$ (/a/$_6$)	/a/$_6$	/i/$_5$ (/a/$_6$)	/a/$_6$	/a/$_6$
acc/pl: $[+gov,-obl]$, $[+pl]$	/us/$_3$ (/i/$_5$, /a/$_6$)	/es/$_4$ (/a/$_6$)	/es/$_4$ (/a/$_6$)	/is/$_2$ (/a/$_6$)	/a/$_6$	/i/$_5$ (/a/$_6$)	/a/$_6$	/a/$_6$
gen/pl: $[+gov,+obl]$, $[+pl]$	/on/$_1$	/on/$_1$	/on/$_1$	/on/$_1$	/on/$_1$	/on/$_1$	/on/$_1$	/on/$_1$

in the accusative singular of class I; see T_{13}). The plural marker /a/$_6$ does not carry any class or case information and thus qualifies as least specific.

(5.14) *Greek inflection markers (plural):*

1. /on/: $\{[+N],[+pl],[+gov,+obl]\}$
2. /is/: $\{[+N],[+pl],[-a,-\beta,+\gamma],[-obl]\}$
3. /us/: $\{[+N],[+pl],[+a,+\beta,+\gamma],[+gov,-obl]\}$
4. /es/: $\{[+N],[+pl],[\underline{-a,-\gamma}],[-obl]\}$
5. /i/ : $\{[+N],[+pl],[\underline{+\beta,+\gamma}],[-obl]\}$
6. /a/: $\{[\underline{+N}],[+pl],[-obl]\}$

Thus, the Syncretism Principle is adhered to without exception in the plural in Greek; the interaction of plural markers is shown in table T_{14}.

5.2.3 *Noun inflection in German*

5.2.3.1 *Data*   As a third and final illustration of the role of decomposed class features in inflectional morphology, we consider German noun inflection.[30] German has four cases: nominative, dative, accusative, and genitive. Inflection marking on nouns is minimal in the singular (quite in contrast to inflection marking on pronouns, determiners, and "strongly" inflected adjectives). However, there are several differences in the plural, which, in interaction with the minimal marking options available in the singular, give rise to a substantial number of inflection classes. We assume that the core system of German noun inflection involves eight major inflection classes.[31]

---

[30] The following discussion draws on Carstairs (1986); Carstairs-McCarthy (1994), Wurzel (1998), Cahill and Gazdar (1999), Blevins (2000), Eisenberg (2000), Wiese (2000), Sternefeld (2004), and literature cited in these works.

[31] In what follows, we disregard plural formation by means of the inflection marker /s/. We believe that a case can be made that /s/-plurals lie outside the system of German noun inflection proper,

T_{15}: *Inflection classes I–IV*

	I		II	III		IV	
	$Hund_m$ ('dog')	$Schaf_n$ ('sheep')	$Baum_m$ ('tree')	$Buch_n$ ('book')	$Mann_m$ ('man')	$Strahl_m$ ('ray')	$Auge_n$ ('eye')
nom/sg	Hund-Ø	Schaf-Ø	Baum-Ø	Buch-Ø	Mann-Ø	Strahl-Ø	Auge-Ø
acc/sg	Hund-Ø	Schaf-Ø	Baum-Ø	Buch-Ø	Mann-Ø	Strahl-Ø	Auge-Ø
dat/sg	Hund-Ø	Schaf-Ø	Baum-Ø	Buch-Ø	Mann-Ø	Strahl-Ø	Auge-Ø
gen/sg	Hund-es	Schaf-es	Baum-es	Buch-es	Mann-es	Strahl-s	Auge-s
nom/pl	Hund-e	Schaf-e	Bäum-e	Büch-er	Männ-er	Strahl-en	Auge-n
acc/pl	Hund-e	Schaf-e	Bäum-e	Büch-er	Männ-er	Strahl-en	Auge-n
dat/pl	Hund-en	Schaf-en	Bäum-en	Büch-ern	Männ-ern	Strahl-en	Auge-n
gen/pl	Hund-e	Schaf-e	Bäum-e	Büch-er	Männ-er	Strahl-en	Auge-n

The first four classes are illustrated by the examples in table T_{15}. Class I contains masculine stems (for which it is the unmarked class) and neuter stems. It exhibits an inflection marker /(e)s/ in the genitive singular (where presence or absence of *e* depends on whether the stem ends in a consonant or in a vowel); otherwise, there is no overt marker in the singular, that is, the marker is /Ø/. In the plural, the marker for non-dative cases is /(e)/ (realization as Ø or *e* is conditioned by whether or not the stem ends in a trochee whose second syllable consists of schwa plus /n/, /l/, or /r/; compare, for example, the nominative plural *Segel* ('sail')); the marker for the dative is /(e)n/ (where *e*-realization obeys the same generalization).[32] Class II is confined to masculine noun stems. It looks exactly like class I, except for the fact that there is umlaut in the plural; following standard practice, we note umlaut as a floating feature" on the inflection marker; thus class II employs the plural markers/"(e)/ and/"(e)n/.[33] Class III is again identical in the singular; the plural markers are /"er/ (with an invariant *e*) for the non-dative cases, and /"ern/ for the dative. This class is arguably an unmarked class for neuter stems, but it also contains some masculine stems. Class IV contains masculine stems and neuter stems;

with /s/ attaching essentially only to those items that resist integration into the regular inflectional system and require to be left unaffected by resyllabification, as it standardly occurs with other inflection markers in the plural (thus, /s/-plural formation primarily affects loan words and proper names, plus stems ending in a non-schwa vowel).

[32] Given that we have assumed throughout that the inflection markers determined in the morphological component may undergo further modification towards PF, these systematic morphophonological alternations would not have to be indicated in the markers; we do so mainly for reasons of compatibility with the existing literature.

[33] See Wiese (1996) and Wunderlich (1999), among others. An alternative that we do not pursue here would be to separate segmental from supra-segmental (umlaut) information; see Carstairs-McCarthy (1994) and Trommer (2006) for analyses of this type. Note also that umlaut in German noun declension differs from stem alternation in Russian and Greek (which we abstracted away from in our analyses) in giving rise to fully systematic inflectional patterns.

T_{16}: *Inflection classes V–VIII*

	V *Planet_m* ('planet')	VI *Ziege_f* ('goat')	VII *Maus_f* ('mouse')	VIII *Drangsal_f* ('distress')
nom/sg	Planet-Ø	Ziege-Ø	Maus-Ø	Drangsal-Ø
acc/sg	Planet-en	Ziege-Ø	Maus-Ø	Drangsal-Ø
dat/sg	Planet-en	Ziege-Ø	Maus-Ø	Drangsal-Ø
gen/sg	Planet-en	Ziege-Ø	Maus-Ø	Drangsal-Ø
nom/pl	Planet-en	Ziege-n	Mäus-e	Drangsal-e
acc/pl	Planet-en	Ziege-n	Mäus-e	Drangsal-e
dat/pl	Planet-en	Ziege-n	Mäus-en	Drangsal-en
gen/pl	Planet-en	Ziege-n	Mäus-e	Drangsal-e

it is marked for both of them. Inflection marking in the singular is as before; in the plural there is a uniform marker /(e)n/, with *e* realization depending on whether the stem ends in a vowel or in a consonant.

The remaining four major classes are illustrated in table T_{16}. Class V contains the so-called weak masculine noun stems; these stems take the inflection marker /(e)n/ in all environments except for nominative singular contexts, where they are not overtly marked. Classes VI, VII, and VIII are relevant only for feminine stems. Of these, class VI is the canonical, unmarked one. The markers are uniformly /Ø/ in the singular and /(e)n/ in the plural. Class VII combines the singular of class VI with the plural of the masculine class II. Finally, class VIII is an extremely marked feminine class that differs from class VII only in having no umlaut in the plural, like the unmarked masculine class I (note that the final vowel in *Drangsal* ('distress') could in principle be subject to umlaut).

As before, the first thing to note is that genuine, arbitrary class features are necessary to correctly assign noun stem to their inflection classes. First, gender features on the stem do not suffice to predict inflection class: Masculine stems can belong to classes I, II, III, IV, or V; feminine stems can belong to classes VI, VII, or VIII; and neuter stems can belong to classes I, III, or IV. Second, phonological features on the stem do not suffice to predict inflection class (this is particularly evident when we take into account that many inflection markers have versions with and without *e*, depending on the nature of the stem-final segment). Third, semantic features on the stem do not suffice to predict inflection class. To take a critical case, even though animacy is often regarded as a typical feature of noun stems in class V (the class of weak masculines), not all members of class V are in fact [+animate] (e.g., the example chosen

T_{17}: *Syncretism within and across inflection classes in German*

	$I_{m,n}$	II_m	$III_{n,m}$	$IV_{m,n}$	V_m	VI_f	VII_f	VIII_f
nom/sg	Ø	Ø	Ø	Ø	Ø	Ø	Ø	Ø
acc/sg	Ø	Ø	Ø	Ø	(e)n	Ø	Ø	Ø
dat/sg	Ø	Ø	Ø	Ø	(e)n	Ø	Ø	Ø
gen/sg	(e)s	(e)s	(e)s	(e)s	(e)n	Ø	Ø	Ø
nom/pl	(e)	"(e)	"er	(e)n	(e)n	(e)n	"(e)	(e)
acc/pl	(e)	"(e)	"er	(e)n	(e)n	(e)n	"(e)	(e)
dat/pl	(e)n	"(e)n	"ern	(e)n	(e)n	(e)n	"(e)n	(e)n
gen/pl	(e)	"(e)	"er	(e)n	(e)n	(e)n	"(e)	(e)

in T_{16} is not), and not all masculine noun stems marked [+animate] are in class V.

5.2.3.2 *Analysis* The system of inflection markers as it can be extracted from T_{15} and T_{16} is given in table T_{17}. The German marker inventory is much smaller than its Russian or Greek counterparts. This implies that there is an enormous amount of syncretism, both of the intraparadigmatic and the transparadigmatic type.

As before, intraparadigmatic syncretism can be traced back to a decomposition of case features. Given that German has four cases, one might think that these result from a cross-classification of two binary features. However, there is one instance where it seems that three cases form a natural class that must be characterized by a common feature not shared by the fourth case because the fourth case exhibits the default marker (which is completely unspecified with respect to case information). The case in point involves the singular of the weak masculine inflection class V. Accusative, dative, and genitive have /(e)n/ but a brief glance at T_{17} reveals that the remaining marker /Ø/ must be the default marker of the system. The only way to permit a systematic reference to three out of four cases in a system based on cross-classification of two binary features would again be to resort to the assumption going back to Zwicky (1970), that complements of natural classes can also be referred to– the cases which are not nominative, in the case at hand (see above, section 5.2.1.2). Although this might well be a viable possibility, we will here make the more straightforward assumption that the cases in German result from a cross-classification of three binary features [±subject], [±governed], and [±oblique], where accusative, dative, and genitive qualify as [+gov]. Thus nominative, accusative, dative, and genitive have a fine structure that is exactly as in Russian (and the syntactic justification is essentially analogous).

(5.15)   *Decomposition of cases in German:* [±subject], [±governed], [±oblique]

    nominative: [+subj,–gov,–obl]
    accusative: [–subj,+gov,–obl]
    dative: [–subj,+gov,+obl]
    genitive: [+subj,+gov,+obl]

Turning next to the classes in German noun inflection, there are three primitive features, as in Greek, whose cross-classification yields the classes in T_{17}; see (5.16).

(5.16)   *Decomposition of inflection classes in German:* $[\pm a]$, $[\pm \beta]$, $[\pm \gamma]$

    I: $[+a,-\beta,+\gamma]$ *Hund$_m$* ('dog'), *Schaf$_n$* ('sheep')
    II: $[+a,-\beta,-\gamma]$ *Baum$_m$* ('tree'), *Nagel$_m$* ('nail')
    III: $[+a,+\beta,+\gamma]$ *Buch$_n$* ('book'), *Kalb$_n$* ('calf'), *Mann$_m$* ('man')
    IV: $[+a,+\beta,-\gamma]$ *Strahl$_m$* ('ray'), *Auge$_n$* ('eye')
    V: $[-a,+\beta,+\gamma]$ *Planet$_m$* ('planet'), *Bote$_m$* ('messenger')
    VI: $[-a,+\beta,-\gamma]$ *Ziege$_f$* ('goat')
    VII: $[-a,-\beta,-\gamma]$ *Maus$_f$* ('mouse')
    VIII: $[-a,-\beta,+\gamma]$ *Drangsal$_f$* ('distress'), *Finsternis$_f$* ('darkness')

There are only three inflection markers for singular environments; these are listed in (5.17): /(e)n/$_1$ is a marker for accusative, dative, and genitive in the weak masculine inflection class V. /(e)s/$_2$ is a marker that shows up in the genitive of $[+a]$ classes, i.e., the masculine or neuter classes I–IV.[34] Finally, /Ø/$_3$ shows up everywhere else.

(5.17)   *German inflection markers (singular):*

    1. /(e)n/:   {[+N],[−a,+β,+γ],[+gov]}
    2. /(e)s/:   {[+N],<u>[+a]</u>,[+subj,+gov,+obl]}
    3. /Ø/:   {[+N]}

The minimal interaction of inflection markers in the singular is shown in table T_{18}.

A list of plural markers is given in (5.18). These markers provide massive evidence for a decomposition of class features because the eight inflection classes in T_{17} exhibit only four distinct patterns. Class III ($[+a,+\beta,+\gamma]$) uses

---

[34] As before, note that none of the primitive class features co-varies fully with a gender feature (see footnotes 12, 25); in particular, even though [−a] typically characterizes a feminine inflection class, and [+a] a non-feminine inflection class, the correlation breaks down in the case of class V, which is marked [−a] but contains only masculine stems. Therefore, the [+a]-specification in /(e)s/$_2$'s lexical entry provides an argument for arbitrary class features and for their decomposition.

T_{18}: *The interaction of inflection markers in the singular in German*

	I: $[+a-\beta+\gamma]$	II: $[+a-\beta-\gamma]$	III: $[+a+\beta+\gamma]$	IV: $[+a+\beta-\gamma]$	V: $[-a+\beta+\gamma]$	VI: $[-a+\beta-\gamma]$	VII: $[-a-\beta-\gamma]$	VIII: $[-a-\beta+\gamma]$
nom/sg	/Ø/$_3$	/Ø/$_3$	/Ø/$_3$	/Ø/$_3$	/Ø/$_3$	/Ø/$_3$	/Ø/$_3$	/Ø/$_3$
acc/sg	/Ø/$_3$	/Ø/$_3$	/Ø/$_3$	/Ø/$_3$	/(e)n/$_1$ (/Ø/$_3$)	/Ø/$_3$	/Ø/$_3$	/Ø/$_3$
dat/sg	/Ø/$_3$	/Ø/$_3$	/Ø/$_3$	/Ø/$_3$	/(e)n/$_1$ (/Ø/$_3$)	/Ø/$_3$	/Ø/$_3$	/Ø/$_3$
gen/sg	/(e)s/$_2$ (/Ø/$_3$)	/(e)s/$_2$ (/Ø/$_3$)	/(e)s/$_2$ (/Ø/$_3$)	/(e)s/$_2$ (/Ø/$_3$)	/(e)n/$_1$ (/Ø/$_3$)	/Ø/$_3$	/Ø/$_3$	/Ø/$_3$

/"ern/$_1$ and /"er/$_2$. Classes I and VIII ($[-\beta,+\gamma]$) employ /(e)n/$_3$ and /(e)/$_4$. Classes II and VII ($[-\beta,-\gamma]$) have /"(e)n/$_5$ and /"(e)/$_6$; and the remaining classes IV, V, and VI (which can be characterized by $[+\beta]$ because the markers for the $[+\beta]$-class III are more specific) resort to a /(e)n/$_7$ throughout.[35]

(5.18)   *German inflection markers (plural):*

1. /"ern/: $\{[+N],[+pl],[+a,+\beta,+\gamma],[-subj,+gov,+obl]\}$
2. /"er/: $\{[+N],[+pl],[+a,+\beta,+\gamma]\}$
3. /(e)n/: $\{[+N],[+pl],\underline{[-\beta,+\gamma]},[-subj,+gov,+obl]\}$
4. /(e)/: $\{[+N],[+pl],\underline{[-\beta,+\gamma]}\}$
5. /"(e)n/: $\{[+N],[+pl],\underline{[-\beta,-\gamma]},[-subj,+gov,+obl]\}$
6. /"(e)/: $\{[+N],[+pl],\underline{[-\beta,-\gamma]}\}$
7. /(e)n/: $\{[+N],[+pl],\underline{[+\beta]}\}$

---

[35] On this approach, the similarity of the dative marker and the general marker in the first three groups is, from a synchronic point of view, accidental. This is incompatible with most of the literature on this issue, where it is assumed that there is a separate dative marker /n/ which attaches to the plural markers /"er/$_2$, /(e)/$_4$, and /"(e)/$_6$. Such a view presupposes that inflection marking in dative plural contexts is truly agglutinative rather than fusional in German. This may or may not be correct; but whatever assumptions one decides to make to reconcile this assumption with the otherwise strictly fusional system of nominal inflection in German will leave our main claim–namely, that plural inflection markers in German refer to natural classes of inflection classes–unaffected. Still, in our view, there is reason to doubt an agglutinative marking of plural and dative in German. First, agglutination does not show up anywhere else in the system of German declensions. Second, it is unclear why it should be just dative plural contexts that are affected by agglutination. (Note also that the dative specification in the pronominal, determiner, and strong adjectival inflections is strictly fusional, with a partition into two separate markers impossible.) Third, it has not yet been shown convincingly that there is a good reason why an alleged agglutinative /n/ dative marker does not attach to other plural markers, like /s/ (as in *Auto-s* vs. **Auto-s-(e)n*, excluded from discussion here) and, in particular, /n/ (as in classes IV, V, and VI) and /Ø/ (in classes I, II, VII, and VIII, in cases where *e* is not realized because the stem ends in *n*); compare *Frau-en*, *Wagen-Ø* with **Frau-en-(e)n*, **Wagen-Ø-(e)n*. Fourth and finally, it seems that the *n* in dative plural contexts is about to disappear in colloquial varieties of German, especially in PP-internal contexts, thereby unifying marking in the four plural contexts; see Gallmann (1998). This would seem to imply a radical shift from agglutination to fusion in dative plural contexts in the standard approach but can be analyzed in terms of simplification and assimilation of a single marker in the present analysis.

T_{19}: *The interaction of inflection markers in the plural in German*

	I: $[+\alpha-\beta+\gamma]$	II: $[+\alpha-\beta-\gamma]$	III: $[+\alpha+\beta+\gamma]$	IV: $[+\alpha+\beta-\gamma]$	V: $[-\alpha+\beta+\gamma]$	VI: $[-\alpha+\beta-\gamma]$	VII: $[-\alpha-\beta-\gamma]$	VIII: $[-\alpha-\beta+\gamma]$
nom/pl	/(e)/$_4$	/ˈ(e)/$_6$	/ˈer/$_2$ (/(e)n/$_7$)	/(e)n/$_7$	/(e)n/$_7$	/(e)n/$_7$	/ˈ(e)/$_6$	/(e)/$_4$
acc/pl	/(e)/$_4$	/ˈ(e)/$_6$	/ˈer/$_2$ (/(e)n/$_7$)	/(e)n/$_7$	/(e)n/$_7$	/(e)n/$_7$	/ˈ(e)/$_6$	/(e)/$_4$
dat/pl	/(e)n/$_3$ (/e/$_4$)	/ˈ(e)n/$_5$ (/ˈe/$_6$)	/ˈern/$_1$ (/ˈer/$_2$, /(e)n/$_7$)	/(e)n/$_7$	/(e)n/$_7$	/(e)n/$_7$	/ˈ(e)n/$_5$ (/ˈe/$_6$)	/(e)n/$_3$ (/e/$_4$)
gen/pl	/(e)/$_4$	/ˈ(e)/$_6$	/ˈer/$_2$ (/(e)n/$_7$)	/(e)n/$_7$	/(e)n/$_7$	/(e)n/$_7$	/ˈ(e)/$_6$	/(e)/$_4$

The interaction of plural markers in the system of German noun inflection is shown in T_{19}.

To sum up, we have argued on the basis of the noun inflection systems of Russian, Greek, and German that inflection class features are indispensable in morphology, and that they must be understood not as privative features directly encoding the class but as more abstract, binary features. Cross-classification of these features yields the standard inflection classes; underspecification with respect to these features yields natural classes of inflection classes, which inflection markers make use of in their lexical entries, thereby accounting for transparadigmatic syncretism. With instances of intraparadigmatic syncretism derived by underspecification with respect to primitive case features ([±subj],[±gov],[±obl]), most instances of syncretism in the three noun inflection systems are explained and the demands imposed by the metagrammatical Syncretism Principle (5.1) can be met.[36]

Let us now turn to the question which role class features play in syntax.

---

[36] Baerman (2005a; 2005b) argues that there are systematic instances of syncretism which cannot be accounted for by underspecification because the paradigm cells that participate in the syncretism do not seem to form a natural class. That is certainly true (and explicitly acknowledged as a possibility in the formulation of the Syncretism Principle). However, we would like to suggest that each pattern of syncretism in a language should be thoroughly investigated from the perspective of feature decomposition and underspecification before the conclusion can be reached that the inflectional system is somehow suboptimal vis-à-vis (5.1); and we contend that closer scrutiny will often reveal that the situation is far from hopeless for an underspecification approach. To name just one example: Baerman (2005a, 824) argues that the syncretism involving comitative singular and locative plural in the nominal declension system of (the Eastern Finnmark variety of) North Sámi involves an "unnatural class"; see the following partial paradigm:

(i)   *North Sámi pronoun declension* (simplified):

	sg	pl
nom	gii	gea-t
acc/gen	gea-n	gea-id
loc	gea-s	gea-inna
com	gea-inna	gea-iguin

5.3 Class features in syntax

There are two ways in which class features might figure in syntax: as features on lexical items, or as separate functional heads. We will argue in this section that neither option is available. Let us begin with the second, more radical possibility, according to which class features project class marker phrases in syntax.

5.3.1 *Class marker phrases*

Bernstein (1993) suggests that the presence of class features in morphology has a syntactic reflex (see Haegeman 1998 for a generalization of this proposal). The assumption is that those languages which provide the morphological evidence for class features, for example, Spanish (see Harris 1991), have a functional projection in the DP that intervenes between NP and Num(ber)P, namely, a "class marker phrase" (CMP) that hosts the respective marker. In contrast to what we have seen to be the case with inflection classes in Russian, Greek, and German, inflection classes in Spanish (which has lost morphological case on nouns) are not needed to provide markers for different cases; their sole task is to provide an invariant theme vowel as an inflection marker, which can be /o/, /a/, or /Ø/ (the last marker may trigger phonologically conditioned *e*-insertion). As shown by Harris, gender features on noun stems in Spanish do not suffice to systematically predict the choice of inflection marker for any given stem; hence, inflection class features are needed, as in Russian, Greek, and German. This is shown in table T_{20}.[37]

However (notwithstanding our above conclusion that instances of transnumber syncretism may be exempted from an analysis in terms of underspecification), this syncretism can straightforwardly be accounted for by decomposition and underspecification. Locative and comitative are both oblique cases; furthermore, they share semantic features. This may plausibly be taken as independent evidence for a shared primitive case feature, which we may refer to as [+loc] for present purposes. On this view, /inna/ would be the general [+loc] marker for singular and plural, with /s/ and /iguin/ emerging as more specific markers for locative singular and comitative plural contexts, respectively. What is more, assuming that inflection markers can have variables over feature values as part of their lexical entries (the ℵ-notation; see the Greek marker /s/ in (5.13)), /inna/ could in fact be specified as a highly specific marker that alternates between singular and plural (see footnote 28). Suppose that [±x] is a feature that distinguishes locative and comitative (where locative = [+loc,−x], and comitative = [+loc,+x]), then /inna/ might be specified as [ℵpl],[+loc,−ℵx], which would account for the syncretism in (i) without even invoking a competition of markers (and the concept of default). Similar conclusions apply to other cases brought up by Baerman—for example, the surprising patterns of syncretism in Dhaasanac paradigms, which may plausibly be taken to instantiate a single homogeneous phonological process of lenition (Jochen Trommer, p.c.).

[37] The class features here are rendered as [class I], [class II], and [class III]. We can ask ourselves whether a decomposition of these features is possible or even necessary. Given the radically impoverished system of noun inflection in Spanish, empirical evidence for decomposition is hard to imagine. However, a decomposition of features like [class I] into combinations of more primitive features is of course possible and can plausibly be assumed for reasons of uniformity alone.

T$_{20}$: Inflection classes I–III in Spanish (based on Harris 1991; Aronoff 1994)

	I		II		III			
	muchach$_m$ ('boy')	man$_f$ ('hand')	di$_m$ ('day')	muchach$_f$ ('girl')	Cid$_m$ ('Cid')	sed$_f$ ('thirst')	padr ('father')	madr ('mother')
inflected	muchach-o	man-o	di-a	muchach-a	Cid-Ø	sed-Ø	padr-Ø[e] (*e* inserted)	madr-Ø[e] (*e* inserted)

Given that Spanish has class features, Bernstein postulates a separate CMP for this language, as in (5.19).

(5.19) [$_{DP}$ D [$_{NumP}$ Num [$_{CMP}$ CM [$_{NP}$ N]]]]

The presence of this CMP in a language is then held responsible for two further properties: (i) the presence of head movement within the DP, resulting in N A order; and (ii) the occurrence of indefinite noun ellipsis. As shown in (5.20), Spanish exhibits both these properties, whereas a language like English, which does not have inflection class features for nouns, does not exhibit either of them.

(5.20) a. [$_{DP}$ la muchacha$_1$ americana t$_1$]
                 the girl   american
        b. [$_{DP}$ uno pequeño [$_N$ –]]
                 a   small   (one)
        c. [$_{DP}$ a red ball]/*[$_{DP}$ a ball$_1$ red t$_1$]
        d. *[$_{DP}$ a small [$_N$ –]]

Assuming that both in English and Spanish adjectives are located in the specifier of NP (see Cinque 1993), in the Spanish example (5.20a) the head noun moves from its base position to a higher head in the functional domain, while it remains in its base position in English. As shown in (5.21), a CMP provides a language with just the right kind of position for this head movement.

(5.21)

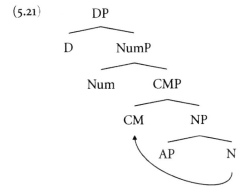

With respect to indefinite noun ellipsis, Bernstein proposes that this operation depends on movement of a noun inflection marker to D, with the indefinite article (which, by assumption, starts out as the specifier of NumP) adjoining to it.

5.3.2 *Problems for Bernstein's correlations*

There is evidence against the two correlations postulated by Bernstein which can be taken to undermine the motivation for class marker phrases.[38] The first problem is that there are languages that exhibit N movement and indefinite noun ellipsis in the absence of distinct class-feature-driven inflectional morphology. Thus French is similar to Spanish with respect to N A order and ellipsis, although its system of noun inflection differs from that of Spanish considerably, that is, it has no obvious noun inflection markers:

(5.22) a. $[_{DP}$ Un cube$_1$ rouge $[_{NP}$ t$_1$]] est sur le coin gauche de cette table
              a   cube   red   is on the left corner of this table

     b. $[_{DP}$ Un bleu $[_N$ e]] est sur le coin droit
              a   blue (one) is on the right corner

Italian is also similar to Spanish with respect to N A order and noun ellipsis, although it is not immediately transparent whether the language can be assumed to have class markers (see Bernstein 1993); consider (5.23a. b.).

(5.23) a. $[_{DP}$ un libro$_1$ grande t$_1$]
              a   book   big

     b. $[_{DP}$ un grande $[_N$ –]]
              a   big   (one)

A final, striking case is that of Modern Hebrew. Hebrew does not have any noun inflection classes (see Aronoff 1994, 75–9). However, there is good evidence for N movement, resulting in N A order and for indefinite noun ellipsis (see Ritter 1991 and Danon 1996). N A order is illustrated in (5.24).[39]

(5.24) $[_{DP}$ ha smalot$_1$ ha yapot t$_1$]]
              the dresses the nice

(5.25) illustrates indefinite noun ellipsis in Hebrew.

(5.25) ra?ti   šloša praxim ?adumim ve $[_{DP}$?arba?a sgulim $[_N$ –]]
              (I) saw three flowers red   and   four   purple

---

[38] Also see Alexiadou et al. (2001) for some of the following observations.

[39] See, however, Shlonsky 2000 and Sichel 2002 for an alternative analysis involving XP fronting.

The second problem for Bernstein's correlation is that there is also evidence against its other direction. There are languages that lack N movement in the presence of class-driven inflection marking. Such counter-evidence comes from the three languages discussed in section 2, namely, Russian, Greek, and German. Let us begin with Greek.

As we have seen, Greek has quite an elaborate system of class-driven noun inflection. However, N movement across adjectives does not seem to take place–the head noun always follows adjectives. This is shown in (5.26).

(5.26) a.   *[$_{DP}$ to spiti$_1$ meghalo/paljo/oreo t$_1$]
             the house big/old/nice

        b.   [$_{DP}$ to meghalo/paljo/oreo spiti$_1$]
             the big/old/nice   house

        c.   *[$_{DP}$ i gineka$_1$ amerikanida t$_1$]
             the woman American

        d.   [$_{DP}$ i amerikanida gineka]
             the American   woman

N ellipsis is possible, though:

(5.27) I Maria   tha agorasi ena prasino vivlio ki   ego [$_{DP}$ ena kokino
        Mary$_{nom}$ fut buy-3sg a   green   book and I   a   red
        [$_N$ –]]
        (one)
        'Mary will buy a green book and I a red one.'

As shown above, German also has class-driven noun inflection. It also has N ellipsis (see (5.29)), but no N movement (see (5.28)).

(5.28) Er hat [$_{DP}$ ein neues Buch$_1$] / *[$_{DP}$ ein Buch$_1$ neues t$_1$] gekauft
        he has   a   new book   a   book new   bought

(5.29) Er hat [$_{DP}$ ein neues [$_N$ –]] gekauft
        he has   a   new (one) bought

As a third language with class-driven noun inflection, let us finally consider Russian. Russian permits indefinite N ellipsis (see (5.31)). N A order is also possible, as shown by the examples in (5.30). However, there is good reason to doubt that this phenomenon involves head movement. The reason is that N may end up in front of numerals (Franks 1995), determiners, and even outside the DP. For this reason, the phenomena in (5.30) are probably better

T$_{21}$: Distribution of class features, ellipsis, and NA order

Language	Indefinite ellipsis	N movement	Inflection classes
Spanish	+	+	+
French	+	+	(−)
Italian	+	+	(−)
Hebrew	+	+	−
Greek	+	−	+
Russian	+	(−)	+
German	+	−	+

analyzed as instances of (potentially remnant) NP scrambling, as indicated here.

(5.30) a. Èto   [$_{NP_1}$ vopros]   složnyj t$_1$
             this is   question$_{nom}$ complicated$_{nom}$

         b. My tam žili   [$_{NP_1}$ goda] dva t$_1$
             we there lived   year$_{gen}$ two

         c. [$_{DP_2}$ [$_{NP_1}$ Razgovor]   ètot t$_1$] ja načal t$_2$ naročno
                           conversation this   I began   intentionally

         d. [$_{NP_1}$ t$_2$ Čelovek] on   [$_{DP}$ neploxoj$_2$ t$_1$]
                       person   he is   not bad

(5.31) U   menja bol'šaja mašina a   u   nego [$_{DP}$ malen'kaja [$_N$ −]
        with me   big   car   and with him   small   (one)

T$_{21}$ summarizes the distribution of N movement and indefinite N ellipsis in the languages considered here. As shown by this table, Bernstein's correlation can hardly be maintained in light of the evidence discussed here and with it goes the argument for class marker phrases. (See Alexiadou 2004 and Alexiadou et al. 2001 for a treatment of indefinite noun ellipsis that capitalizes on gender agreement.)

5.3.3 *General considerations*

We conclude that class features do not project in syntax. Closer inspection supports a stronger claim: There is no evidence for assuming that class features are syntactically active (as features on other categories) at all. To see this, suppose that inflection class features were active in syntax. In that case, we might possibly expect there to be verbs that select inflection class features such that, for example, only inflection class III (i.e., [−α,−β]-marked) nouns were available as objects of these verbs in Russian. Even more to the point, we might expect subject-verb agreement with respect to inflection class (that is, a designated morphological reflex of the subject's inflection class on the verb) or noun-adjective agreement with respect to inflection class. Such things do not seem to occur; see, for example, the lack of noun-adjective agreement with respect to inflection class in Spanish in (5.32).

(5.32)   a.   [_DP la   chica inteligente]
               the girl   intelligent

        b.   [_DP el   chico inteligente]
               the boy   intelligent

Syntactic inertness is exactly the property that distinguishes inflection class features from gender features, which do figure in syntactic agreement relations. However, whereas gender features are syntactically visible, they do not play a central role in the fusional noun inflection systems of Russian, Greek, and German (see section 5.2). More generally, we may speculate that there is a division of labor between class features and gender features. Both are inherent features marked on a noun stem in the lexicon but, whereas class features are relevant only in morphology, gender features are of crucial importance in syntax.[40] To sum up, inflection class features are of no use in syntax; they are not visible in this component. Thus class features are interpretable in morphology but uninterpretable in syntax.[41]

---

[40] In line with this, at least in the type of language currently under consideration, the gender of a noun stem is read off agreement in syntax. Note that this view is not incompatible with the assumption that the language learner's burden can to some extent be reduced by assuming default implicational relations holding between inflection class, gender, semantic, and phonological features of a noun stem, which predict some typical associations of features but can be overriden; see, for example Fraser and Corbett 1994 for Russian, Aronoff 1994 for Spanish and Latin, and Bierkandt 2006 for Diyari. The main point here is, however, that these features ultimately come to co-occur on a given noun stem, they must be kept separate, playing different roles in different components of grammar. Note also that we do not wish to imply that gender features are completely irrelevant in systems of noun inflection. For instance, gender (rather than class) information is needed to predict the right order of derivational affixes in German (see Eisenberg and Sayatz 2004, 110–15). Even more important in the present context is the observation that gender features *are* relevant (in addition to inflection class features) in systems of noun inflection that are historically closely related to the ones discussed here. Thus, as noted above, gender features seem to play an important role in Icelandic noun inflection (see footnote 12). Similarly, the distribution of accusative/genitive syncretisms in the plural in Polish differs from the similar phenomenon in Russian (see (5.10)) in that reference must be made not to the feature [±animate] but to the gender feature [±masculine] (and the feature [±person]); see, for example, Gunkel (2003). For reasons like these, we do not want to contrive ways to exclude gender information systematically from inflectional morphology in the domain of nouns (however, see Bachrach and Wagner 2005 for a different view). Also cf. Ritter 1993 for pertinent discussion.

[41] A clarification may be in order. Many languages, among them, for example, Swahili (see Krifka 1995) and Archi (see Kibrik 1979), exhibit 'noun classes,' and there is syntactic agreement with respect to this information. However, this does not call into question the claim just made because a different

This conclusion has important consequences if we adopt the Legibility Condition (see Chomsky 2000; 2001b), a version of which is given in (5.33).

(5.33)   *Legibility Condition*:
         Morphosyntactic features can be present in some component of grammar only if they are interpretable in this component.

Given (5.33), the further conclusion has to be that class features are not merely syntactically uninterpretable; they must in fact be absent in syntax. This state of affairs is strongly reminiscent of a situation that Chomsky (2000; 2001b) argues to occur in the case of features that are present in syntax but uninterpretable, hence absent, at LF. Chomsky suggests that such features can act as probes and thereby trigger syntactic operations. To capture this convergence of morphology and syntax, we develop a probe-based approach to fusional inflection in the next section.[42]

5.4 Proposal

Given the Legibility Condition in (5.33), features that are uninterpretable at LF must be deleted in syntax. Under the minimalist approach developed in Chomsky (2000; 2001b), which we adopt here, such features can be deleted by participating in an Agree operation. Agree applies under matching of a probe and a goal. Simplifying a bit, the probe is an LF-uninterpretable feature that shows up on a category that (minimally) c-commands a category containing a feature bundle acting as the goal, and Agree takes place if there is both an LF-uninterpretable feature and a matching feature in the goal. Depending on other factors, Agree then may or may not be accompanied by an additional movement operation that displaces a category containing the goal and re-merges it with a category on whose head the probe feature is. We propose that an analogous procedure underlies class-driven fusional inflection: Class features of a noun stem act as probes in morphology in the same way that, say,

phenomenon is involved. The "class" features in question are needed to determine an agglutinative "class" marker for a given noun stem, and for syntactic agreement with the noun; their role is not to determine a fusional marker encoding case and number. Thus "class" in Bantu or Daghestanian languages in fact means gender not inflection class. See (Corbett, 1991, 43–9) for further discussion.

[42] Clearly, (5.33) treats the syntactic and semantic components of the grammar identically and does not differentiate between "interface" components and others. In our view, there is no reason to presuppose that different components manipulate/interpret features in a fundamentally different way. (In particular, this holds if a derivational approach to semantic interpretation is adopted; see Stechow 2005 for preliminary remarks.)

ϕ features of T act as probes in syntax.[43] This presupposes that morphology and syntax are separate components; and indeed, we propose that Agree operates in morphology to remove syntactically uninterpretable features before syntax is reached, in the same way that Agree operates in syntax to remove LF-uninterpretable features before LF is reached.

Let us flesh out this proposal. Suppose that there is a sequence of grammatical components as in (5.34).[44]

(5.34)   Lexicon → Morphology → Syntax → PF, LF

We assume that the lexicon is a mere list of exceptions. Morphology follows the lexicon but precedes syntax. We can plausibly conceive of this component as a more elaborate version of a numeration in the sense that it assembles the material that will be used in the syntactic derivation. The morphological component takes items from the lexicon and turns them into objects that can be interpreted by syntactic operations. Crucially, morphology and syntax employ the same structure-building operations. First, there is simple Merge, which typically applies under selection. Instantiations of simple Merge in morphology could be taken to include certain types of agglutinative inflection and derivational morphology that apply pre-syntactically (with other types applying in the syntax; see section 5.5 below). Second, there is Merge under Agree (pure Agree as such is not structure-building). In syntax, Merge under Agree typically involves movement. However, assuming that the absence of displacement is the remaining fundamental difference between morphology and syntax, this option is not available for Agree in morphology. We suggest that Merge under Agree can take place without any pre-existing structure in morphology, concatenating two items taken directly from the lexicon. Our claim is that fusional inflection driven by class features is an instantiation of this operation.[45]

---

[43] In her analysis of Swedish noun inflection, Josefsson (2001) has independently suggested that class features act as probes. However, abstracting away from identical terminology, her analysis emerges as quite different, as does its underlying rationale. The class feature acting as a probe is assumed to be a separate nominal syntactic head that is merged with a category-neutral root (rather than a feature of a noun stem that triggers pre-syntactic Merge with an inflection marker, as in our proposal; see below).

[44] For present purposes, it is immaterial whether this sequence is run through only once or whether it is (or parts of it are) run through repeatedly, as in multiple spellout approaches with a phase-based cycle.

[45] Note that, on this view, agglutinative noun inflection in morphology and fusional noun inflection in morphology could differ in that the former involves a selection relation between a noun stem and an inflection (e.g., case) marker without a syntactically uninterpretable feature, whereas the latter involves a matching relation involving a syntactically uninterpretable feature. However, throughout

More specifically, we propose that class-driven, fusional noun inflection works as follows. First, a noun stem is selected from the lexicon with its inherent, non-predictable (or not fully predictable, given the qualification in footnote 40) features; these include class and gender features. Second, when the noun stem enters morphology, non-inherent features are added; among these are case and number features. (This conforms exactly to the assumptions made in Chomsky (1965, 171).) All features on a noun stem are fully specified, whether inherent or not. Third, the (syntactically uninterpretable) class feature of a noun stem acts as a probe, looking for a matching goal with which it can undergo Agree. An appropriate feature bundle on an inflection marker can act as such a goal. The class, case, and number features of an inflection marker differ from their counterparts on a noun stem in two respects: They are always inherent; and they can be (and often are) underspecified. Fourth, the only way to provide a matching inflection marker for an Agree operation with the probe on the noun stem is to select it from the lexicon and merge it with the noun stem. Thus the inflection marker determined by the Subset Principle is selected from the lexicon and merged with the noun stem, resulting in Agree.[46] Fifth, the class features of the noun stem are deleted

this article we will remain uncommitted as to the analysis of agglutinative inflection, confining our attention to the analysis of fusional inflection. Agglutinative inflection may well turn out to be an inhomogeneous phenomenon, with instances of both pure Merge (under selection, as speculated in the main text) and Merge under Agree showing up in inflectional systems of the world's languages. Consider passive marking in Maori (we are grateful to the reviewer for bringing this up). In this language, passive forms of verbs are derived by adding agglutinative suffixes to the verb stem; the crucial observation is that this operation involves what looks like a significant number of passive allomorphs (*tia, ia, ina, a, ʔa, kia, nia,* etc.). One possible type of analysis of this phenomenon is morphological (see Hale 1973). We might say that the allomorphy results from inflection class features on verb stems that select passive markers with matching inflection class information. Another possibility is to assume that the variation is essentially phonological in nature. On this view, there is only one passive marker, and the initial segments of the markers are reanalyzed as final segments of the stems that are deleted in active (i.e., suffix-less) forms because the language does not permit codas (e.g., /hopuk/ → [hopu], /hopuk/+/ia/ → [hopukia], with resyllabification). A convincing phonological analysis (based on Optimality Theory) along these lines has recently been developed by de Lacy 2002. He argues that the realization of the passive in Maori is determined by independently observable restrictions on the size of prosodic words in this language. (The default status of passive forms ending in *tia,* which Hale took to support a morphological analysis, is here derived by assuming /t/ to be an epenthetical consonant inserted as a last resort operation rather than a stem-final segment.) Clearly, under the first, morphological analysis, class features would have to be postulated for Maori verbs, and hence for a case of agglutinative inflection; in contrast, under the second (and arguably superior), phonological analysis, inflection class plays no role since it is a single passive marker (/ia/) that shows up in all cases.

[46] It must be independently ensured that such Merge operations result in the inflection marker ending up to the right of the noun stem (that is, that inflection is suffixal in the case at hand).

in morphology. Furthermore, all morphosyntactic features of the inflection marker are deleted.[47] Finally, the inflected noun enters syntax, bearing only fully specified and syntactically interpretable features.[48]

This conception of fusional noun inflection as class feature-driven Merge under Agree is illustrated by two examples each from Russian, Greek, and German in (5.35). The Russian examples in (5.35a. b.) involve a class III noun in the dative singular and a class II noun in the accusative singular, respectively; the Greek examples in (5.35c. d.), a class I noun in the genitive singular and a class VI noun in the nominative plural; and the German examples in (5.35e. f.), a class I noun in the genitive singular and a class V noun in the dative plural. Throughout, features that are deleted under Agree are struck out.

(5.35) a. [N /tetrad'/ ('notebook')   – /i/]
            {[+N],[–anim],[–pl],~~[–α, –γ]~~,[–subj,+gov,+obl]} ~~{[+N],[–α],[+obl]}~~

        b. [N /komnat/ ('room')   – /u/]
            {[+N],[–anim],[–pl],~~[–α,+γ]~~,[–subj,+gov,–obl]} ~~{[+N],[–subj,+gov]}~~

        c. [N /anθrop/ ('man')   – /u/]
            {[+N],[–pl],~~[+α,+β,+γ]~~,[+gov,+obl]} ~~{[+N],[+α],[+gov,+obl]}~~

        d. [N /krat/ ('state')   – /i/]
            {[+N],[+pl],~~[–α,+β,+γ]~~,[–gov,–obl]}   ~~{[+N],[+pl],[+β,+γ],[–obl]}~~

---

[47] The reason for this additional deletion is obvious for class features of an inflection marker (which are no more interpretable in syntax than their counterparts on noun stems). But what about other morphosyntactic features of an inflection marker such as, in particular, case features? Case features of inflection markers must be deleted because their potential underspecification makes them syntactically defective. Syntax needs fully specified case information, not the underspecified case information provided by inflection markers. Thus underspecified case features are uninterpretable in syntax and must therefore be absent, given the Legibility Condition. There is further evidence that underspecified case features of inflection markers must be absent in syntax. Given that the rightmost item of a word that is specified for property $\mathbb{P}$ qualifies as the head with respect to $\mathbb{P}$ in morphology (see DiSciullo and Williams 1987), a simultaneous presence of underspecified case information on an inflection marker and fully specified case information on a noun stem wrongly implies that *only* the former kind of information is accessible in syntax. Problems of this type do not arise if we assume that all morphosyntactic features of an inflection marker are syntactically uninterpretable and are deleted by a morphological inflection operation.

[48] Stump (2001) distinguishes between two basic types of approaches to inflectional morphology, namely, realizational vs. incremental approaches. In incremental approaches, inflection markers contribute information that is not otherwise present; in realizational approaches, all information is there to begin with, and the inflection marker contributes no new information. It is worth pointing out that the present approach qualifies as realizational in this sense, and not as incremental. Despite being a lexical item with morphosyntactic features, an inflection marker does not actually carry any morphosyntactic information that the noun stem would not already have itself; furthermore, all relevant morphosyntactic information on the inflection marker is in fact deleted after pre-syntactic inflection.

    e. [$_N$ /Hund/ ('dog')
        {[+N],[−pl],~~[+α, β,+γ]~~,[+subj,+gov,+obl]}
      − /(e)s/]
      ~~{[+N],[+α],[+subj,+gov,+obl]}~~

    f. [$_N$ /Planet/ ('planet')   − /en/]
        {[+N],[+pl],~~[α,+β,+γ]~~,[−subj,+gov,+obl]} ~~{[+N],[+pl],[+β]}~~

The probe-based approach developed so far goes a long way towards accounting for fusional noun inflection in terms of well-established elementary operations in minimalist grammar. However, there is still one step in the analysis where a special assumption appears to be necessary at first sight: Selection of the correct inflection marker from the lexicon for a given noun stem is determined by the Subset Principle. Recall that the Subset Principle has two parts: one that ensures that an inflection marker must fit (in a given context provided by the noun stem's morphosyntactic features), and one that ensures that, among the markers that satisfy this requirement, the most specific one is chosen. The first requirement does not need to be stipulated anymore in a probe-based approach since Agree presupposes feature matching. If a morphosyntactic feature shows up on an inflection marker without also showing up on the noun stem, there will invariably be a feature mismatch; the reason is that, by assumption, there is no underspecification with respect to morphosyntactic features on noun stems. As for the second requirement, that of specificity, Chomsky (2001b, 15) suggests a principle Maximize Matching Effects for Agree operations in syntax, in order to guarantee that "if local [probe, goal] match [. . .], their uninterpretable features must be eliminated at once, as fully as possible." As such, Maximize Matching Effects is sensitive only to the quantity of features, not to their quality. However, given that there are hierarchies of feature classes, as in (5.7), it is arguably a natural extension of this principle (that leaves its syntactic consequences unaffected) to assume that maximization of feature matching is sensitive to the nature of the features as well, along the lines of (5.6). Under this assumption, a specific Subset Principle can be dispensed with: Selection of the most specific inflection marker follows from a maximization of matching effects. This is shown for the example in (5.35a.) in (5.36): Agree of /tetrad'/ and /i/ maximizes feature matching, as opposed to Agree of /tetrad'/ and /u/ or of /tetrad'/ and /a/, in which fewer, or less highly ranked, uninterpretable features undergo deletion.

(5.36) a. [$_N$ /tetrad'/ ('notebook')   − /i/]
           {[+N],[−anim],[−pl], ~~[α, γ]~~,[−subj,+gov,+obl]} ~~{[+N],[α],[+obl]}~~

b.   *[$_N$ /tetrad'/   ('notebook')
     {[+N],[–anim],[–pl],~~[–α, –γ]~~,[–subj,+gov,+obl]}
   – /u/]
   ~~{[+N],[–subj,+gov]}~~

c.   *[$_N$ /tetrad'/   ('notebook')   – /a/]
     {[+N],[–anim],[–pl],~~[–α, –γ]~~,[–subj,+gov,+obl]}   ~~{[+N]}~~

Thus, fusional noun inflection can fully be accounted for in terms of independently-motivated properties of Agree operations in syntax.

A further interesting consequence of the present approach concerns indeclinables. Russian, Greek, and many other languages that employ fusional noun inflection exhibit the phenomenon of indeclinable noun stems that resist inflection for case and number. These items are usually loan words, e.g., *buržua*$_m$ ("bourgeois"), *kofe*$_m$ ("coffee") in Russian, or *reporter*$_m$ ("reporter"), *plaz*$_f$ ("beach") in Greek.[49] The standard approach to indeclinables is to assign them to a separate inflection class, which effectively treats them on a par with other noun stems and thus denies their special status. In contrast, the present approach permits a maximally simple account of indeclinables. These noun stems have fully specified gender, case, and number features (the latter two types of features are added in morphology), but they simply lack a class feature. Hence, there is no probe on them in morphology that might trigger inflection; consequently, inflection does not take place.

5.5 Further issues

5.5.1 *The timing of inflection*

Let us take a step back. We have argued that (highly abstract, decomposed) class features are needed in fusional noun inflection systems of languages like Russian, Greek, and German. A priori, there are three possibilities concerning the timing of inflection, all of which are compatible with this hypothesis:

(5.37)   a.   Fusional noun inflection applies pre-syntactically.
        b.   Fusional noun inflection applies inner-syntactically.
        c.   Fusional noun inflection applies post-syntactically.

---

[49] Indeclinable noun stems are practically non-existent in German, though, except perhaps for some marginal cases involving abbreviations that are pronounced letterwise, like *PKW* ("Personenkraftwagen", 'car'); however, even in these cases, there is a tendency to assign the stem to a regular inflection class. Loan word nouns that are not (yet) fully integrated into the core inflectional system in German typically take an /s/-plural, which implies an exceptional, marked class (see footnote 31), but a class nevertheless.

Class features play no role in syntax, and the version of the Legibility Condition adopted here actually prohibits their presence in this component. This reasoning makes option (5.37b.) unavailable but it does not necessarily decide between options (5.37a.) and (5.37c.). We have adopted a pre-syntactic approach to noun inflection where class features are deleted before the noun enters syntax. But what about a post-syntactic approach?

Post-syntactic approaches are most prominently pursued within Distributed morphology (see Halle and Marantz 1993 and Harley and Noyer 2003 for overviews). In such an approach, fusional noun inflection has the status of a spellout operation. An inflection marker is a vocabulary item that is inserted post-syntactically into a designated head position (a functional morpheme) in the vicinity of the noun stem. As noted above, the analyses developed in section 5.2 can in principle be reformulated in a Distributed Morphology analysis without much ado. The (often underspecified) morphosyntactic features borne by the inflection markers can be re-interpreted as the insertion contexts associated with vocabulary items; the (fully specified) morphosyntactic features borne by noun stems can be re-interpreted as the features provided by the syntactic context (on the functional morpheme into which vocabulary insertion takes place, and/or on the associated noun stem); and the Subset Principle can act as a condition on vocabulary insertion rather than on merging of inflection markers (which, of course, corresponds to its original formulation; cf. Halle 1997).

However, such a post-syntactic approach turns out to be problematic in view of the argument developed in section 5.3. Basically, there are two possibilities for a class feature to be present post-syntactically and participate in an inflection operation. The first possibility is that the class feature is present in syntax already, even though it becomes relevant only after syntax. This possibility faces the same problems as genuinely inner-syntactic approaches. At the point where a post-syntactic approach to fusional noun inflection needs a class feature, the Legibility Condition has long forced its deletion. This leaves the second possibility. The class feature is not yet present in syntax; rather, it enters the derivation after syntax, but before vocabulary insertion (see, for example, Embick 2000 and Harbour 2003), perhaps by an operation like dissociation (see Embick 1998).[50] This second possibility invariably violates the Inclusiveness Condition (see Chomsky 1995; 2000; 2001b) according

---

[50] Predecessors of such an operation are Halle and Marantz's (1994) redundancy rules that post-syntactically introduce class features for theme vowels of clitic pronouns in Spanish, and Halle and Marantz's (1993) post-syntactic insertion of an AGR-morpheme into a T-adjoined position in English (the latter is an even more radical example since it involves a whole category rather than a single feature).

to which new elements (like features) cannot be introduced in the course of the derivation. Thus a post-syntactic approach will have to violate either the Legibility Condition or the Inclusiveness Condition.[51] We conclude that the present, pre-syntactic approach is the only option that respects both the Legibility Condition and the Inclusiveness Condition, and should therefore, *ceteris paribus*, be preferred to a post-syntactic approach.[52]

In addition to these considerations, the present, pre-syntactic approach to fusional noun inflection has one central property that distinguishes it from a post-syntactic approach in terms of Distributed Morphology and that strikes us as interesting: It relies exclusively on elementary (Merge and

---

[51] Two remarks. First, one might think that a late insertion approach violates the Inclusiveness Condition by definition, given that phonological material is inserted post-syntactically into the derivation (by vocabulary insertion). However, Chomsky (2000, 118) explicitly exempts PF operations from the Inclusiveness Condition. Hence, a late insertion approach could in principle respect this principle– but not if it adopts post-syntactic insertion of a class feature (which is not phonological in nature). Second, as noted by Asaf Bachrach (p.c.), it might technically be possible to respect a version of the Inclusiveness Condition in a post-syntactic approach after all if one assumes (i) that late vocabulary insertion is not confined to functional categories but affects lexical categories as well (see Marantz 1995 for the idea, and Embick 2000 for an argument against it), and (ii) that these vocabulary items can bear features that trigger further operations. Under such a view, a noun stem could be inserted late that in turn carries a class feature, and this class feature would then determine subsequent insertion of an inflection marker. (As a matter of fact, the mechanism of class feature insertion for theme vowels in Spanish pronouns proposed by Halle and Marantz (1994, 282) works more or less like this.) However, even assuming that the Inclusiveness Condition would not prohibit such an instance of "piggy-back" insertion of morphosyntactic features (which is far from clear and depends on subtleties of formulation), we take it that this kind of approach requires an unrestricted concept of vocabulary insertion (and a highly complex notion of vocabulary item) and should therefore be avoided if possible.

[52] Needless to say, it is by no means clear that all other things are indeed equal in all empirical domains, and there may well be cases where a post-syntactic approach to inflectional morphology looks initially advantagous or initially disadvantagous. Consider the first possibility first. Putative morphology/syntax mismatches in feature specifications are a case in point. These have been addressed in Distributed Morphology by post-syntactic (but pre-morphology) operations like impoverishment, which deletes features before morphological spellout (see Bonet 1991; Noyer 1992; Halle and Marantz 1993; Bobaljik 2002; Frampton 2002; also cf. Ackema and Neeleman 2003) or even changes features (see Noyer 1998), and fission, which makes features of a feature bundle individually accessible to spellout (see Noyer 1992; Frampton 2002). There is no need for operations of this type in the present analysis but there may be in other cases. As it turns out, the present approach can be extended to capture such effects (for example, a pre-syntactic version of impoverishment is adopted in Müller (2006b) to account for the interaction of verb inflection and pro-drop).

However, as noted, there may also be empirical domains where a post-syntactic approach faces problems that a pre-syntactic approach manages to avoid. For instance, free relative clauses, across-the-board dependencies, and parasitic gap constructions in languages like Russian (or Polish) (see McCreight 1988; Franks 1995) and German (see Groos and van Riemsdijk 1981; Bayer 1988) obey morphological rather than syntactic case matching requirements in the sense that identity of the morphological output form (i.e., intraparadigmatic syncretism), rather than of the syntactic case feature specification, is decisive in allowing the constructions. In a post-syntactic approach to noun inflection, the relevant information is not yet there at the point where syntax would seem to need it, so capturing these effects is far from straightforward (see Sauerland 1996; but also Trommer 2005a, where such phenomena are accounted for within Distributed Morphology by invoking (i) impoverishment and (ii) an operation of chain reduction).

Agree) operations that are independently motivated, rather than on additional morphology-specific operations like vocabulary insertion which have no syntactic counterpart, and whose properties are very different. We take it that an analysis that employs identical elementary operations in morphology and syntax is preferable to an analysis that employs different sets of elementary operations in the two domains. However, closer inspection reveals that this conceptual difference is not necessarily one between pre- vs. post-syntactic approaches; rather, it separates approaches in which an (actual, non-abstract) inflection marker is merged with a stem from those in which it is not (either because it is inserted, as in Distributed Morphology, or because it is introduced by rules or schemas, as in word-and-paradigm approaches). Thus we might in fact conceive of a variant of our proposal in which class features act as probes in a post-syntactic morphological component, triggering an operation of Merge under Agree with the most specific matching inflection marker, and thus undergo deletion before PF is reached. This would avoid the conceptual problem of introducing additional machinery that is otherwise absent from derivations; but it would not fare any better than a standard Distributed Morphology approach with respect to the task of reconciling the Legibility Condition and the Inclusiveness Condition.

5.5.2 *The status of derivational morphology*

We have argued that fusional noun inflection involves a probe-based Agree operation that takes place pre-syntactically in a morphological component. However, we have been careful not to make any specific claims about particular cases of agglutinative inflection and derivational morphology, except for noting that the present approach is compatible with these operations applying in morphology, in syntax, or in both components. As a case in point, Siloni (1997) (based on Chomsky 1970 and Wasow 1977) argues that there is both pre-syntactic ("lexical", in our approach morphological) and syntactic nominalization in Hebrew: event nominalization is pre-syntactic, gerund formation takes place in syntax. It is worth noting that such an analysis does not contradict the present approach; in particular, there is no reason why nominalization should be precluded from applying in the syntax (see Borer 2004; Alexiadou 2001, and references cited there), for example, via head movement of V to a nominalizing head N (as in van Hout and Roeper 1998). However, if syntactic nominalization occurs in a language with fusional noun inflection, it is clear that head movement of V must go to an N head that is already inflected, as a result of a pre-syntactic Agree operation triggered by N's class feature. This is shown for a Greek example in (5.38).

(5.38)

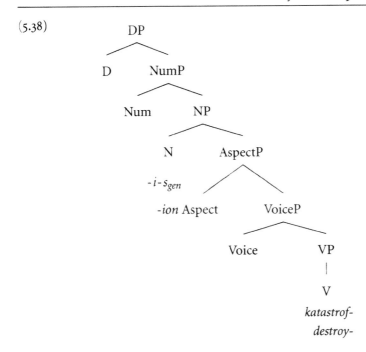

Here, the genitive singular nominalization *katastrof-i-s* ('destruction') results from first merging a nominalization suffix *i* bearing an s-principle class feature probe with the matching genitive singular inflection marker *s* in morphology, and then applying head movement of the verb stem *katastrof* to the inflected noun *i-s* in the syntax. Thus, in this analysis, inflection precedes derivation, which at first sight seems to go against the received wisdom that derivation always precedes inflection (see, for example, Anderson 1992). However, this apparent contradiction is resolved when we take into account that this problem is mainly terminological. Derivation continues to precede inflection when we look at the eventual order of morphemes rather than the order of rule applications.

5.6 Concluding remarks

In the present chapter, we have been concerned with the status of inflection class features in a minimalist grammar. Based on evidence from the fusional noun inflection systems of Indo-European languages (in particular, Russian, Greek, and German), we have tried to shed new light on the form and function of these features. In a nutshell, we have argued that inflection class features are highly abstract, binary features that act as morphological probes. The main payoffs of this hypothesis are that transparadigmatic syncretism can be accounted for (because underspecification with respect to class features yields natural classes of inflection classes), and that fusional inflection emerges as the result of the basic operations envisaged in minimalist grammar (namely, Merge and Agree). The theory has been developed on the basis of noun inflection systems, but the null hypothesis is that it applies more generally to all fusional systems of inflection (for example, to fusional pronominal, determiner, or adjectival inflection, but also to fusional verb inflection).

Thus, we may speculate that all fusional inflection is in fact driven by class features. There are two kinds of problems that may arise for this hypothesis: First, there could be fusional inflectional systems in which there is no partition of the entire domain of the items that need to be inflected into subdomains; and, second, there could be fusional inflectional systems in which the partition of the entire domain is fully predictable by non-arbitrary features. The first kind of problem does not seem to arise, given that fusional inflection typically goes hand in hand with the presence of inflection classes.[53] The second kind of problem looks initially more pressing. Fusional systems like that of adjectival inflection in Russian, or that of pronominal inflection in German, exhibit inflection classes, but these classes seem to be completely determined by gender and number features, with resort to specific inflection class features apparently unnecessary. Since gender and number features are interpretable in syntax, it is clear that they cannot act as pre-syntactic probes. A full-fledged anaylsis of these types of system is beyond the scope of this chapter but we would like to tentatively propose that inflection class features acting as probes underlie these cases as well, with the relevant (syntactically) uninterpretable class features being parasitic on (syntactically) interpretable gender or number features.

These considerations reinforce the conclusion that syntactically uninterpretable inflection class features are apparent imperfections in grammatical systems, in the same way in which LF-uninterpretable features qualify as

---

[53] That said, given a maximally simple notion of inflection classes, it actually follows that a (trivial) inflection class is present even if there is only one inflectional pattern. Compare, for example, the definition of inflection class in Aronoff (1994, 64) ("a set of lexemes whose members each select the same set of inflectional realizations"), from which it follows that "a language whose major lexical categories each have only one inflectional class will still have inflectional classes" (Aronoff 1994, 182, fn. 6). On this view, even if we assume (following the reviewer's suggestion) that it is correct to analyze cases like the variable realization of first person plural specifications in Turkish verb inflection (where there does not appear to be a concomitant inflection class variation) as involving agglutination (*im-iz*) in some tenses and fusion (*ik*) in others, such an instance of fusional inflection would not pose a problem under this definition of inflection classes, as a trivial inflection class feature would have to be postulated anyway.

apparent imperfections in the theory laid out in Chomsky (2000; 2001b) (but not in Chomsky 2001a). In both cases, the imperfection may only be apparent because the features emerge as an optimal means to bring about another property that also initially looks like an imperfection: fusional inflection in one case (which blurs different pieces of grammatical information by encoding them as a single unit), displacement in the other. As for displacement, Chomsky argues that closer inspection may reveal the displacement property not to be an imperfection after all. Fusional inflection, too, might plausibly be argued to be an imperfection that is merely apparent, and might emerge an optimal solution to the conflicting demands of economy of expression and explicitness of encoding grammatical information. However, we will not pursue these matters here any further.

References

Ackema, Peter, and Ad Neeleman (2003) 'Context-sensitive spell-out'. *Natural Language and Linguistic Theory*, 21: 681–735.

Aissen, Judith (2003) 'Differential object marking: Iconicity vs. economy', *Natural Language and Linguistic Theory*, 21: 435–83.

Alexiadou, Artemis (2001) *Functional Structure in Nominals*. Amsterdam: Benjamins.

——(2004) 'Inflectional class, gender, and DP internal structure', in G. Müller, L. Gunkel, and G. Zifonun (eds.), *Explorations in Nominal Inflection*. Berlin: Mouton de Gruyter, pp. 21–49.

——Liliane Haegeman, and Melitta Stavrou (2001) 'On nominal functional projections: Noun morphology, movement and ellipsis', in *Proceedings of the Annual Conference of the Israel Association for Theoretical Linguistics*, vol. 16, pp. 1–8.

Anastasiadi-Simeonidi, Anna, Angela Ralli, and Despoina Hila-Markopoulou (eds.) (2003) *Gender*. Athens: Patakis (In Greek).

Anderson, Stephen (1992) *A-Morphous Morphology*. Cambridge: Cambridge University Press.

Aronoff, Mark (1994) *Morphology by Itself*. Cambridge, MA: MIT Press.

Babiniotis, George (1986) *Brief History of the Greek Language*. Athens: Athens University Press.

Bachrach, Asaf, and Michael Wagner (2005) 'The prosody of adjunction vs. complementation: The case of diminutives in Brazilian Portuguese', Ms., MIT, Cambridge, MA.

Baerman, Matthew (2005a) 'Directionality and (un)natural classes in syncretism'. *Language* 80: 807–24.

——(2005b): 'The limits of morphological underspecification', Ms., University of Surrey.

——Dunstan Brown, and Greville Corbett (2002) 'Case syncretism in and out of Indo-European', in M. Andronis, C. Ball, H. Elston, and S. Neuvel (eds.), *The Main*

Session. Papers from the 37th Meeting, vol. 1, Chicago Linguistic Society, Chicago, pp. 15–28.

Bailyn, John Frederick, and Andrew Nevins (2003) 'The form of Russian genitive plurals', Ms., SUNY at Stony Brook and MIT.

Bayer, Josef (1988) 'Fortschritte der Syntaxtheorie'. *Linguistische Berichte* 117: 410–26.

Bernstein, Judy (1993) Topics in the syntax of nominal structure across Romance. PhD thesis, CUNY.

Bierkandt, Lennart (2006) 'Kasusmorphologie des Diyari. Ein Ansatz im Rahmen der Distribuierten Morphologie', in G. Müller and J. Trommer (eds.), *Subanalysis of Argument Encoding in Distributed Morphology*, vol. 84 of *Linguistische Arbeitsberichte*, Universität Leipzig.

Bierwisch, Manfred (1967) 'Syntactic features in morphology: General problems of so-called pronominal inflection in German', in *To Honor Roman Jakobson*. The Hague/Paris: Mouton, pp. 239–70.

Blevins, James (2000) 'Markedness and blocking in German declensional paradigms', in B. Stiebels and D. Wunderlich (eds.), *Lexicon in Focus*. Berlin: Akademie-Verlag, pp. 83–103.

—— (2004) 'Inflection classes and economy', in G. Müller, L. Gunkel, and G. Zifonun (eds.), *Explorations in Nominal Inflection*. Berlin: Mouton de Gruyter, pp. 51–95.

Bobaljik, Jonathan (2002) 'Syncretism without paradigms: Remarks on Williams 1981, 1994', in G. Booij and J. van Marle (eds.), *Yearbook of Morphology 2001*. Dordrecht: Kluwer, pp. 53–85.

Bonet, Eulália (1991) Morphology after syntax. Ph.D. thesis, MIT, Cambridge, MA.

Borer, Hagit (2004) *Structuring Sense. An Exo-Skeletal Trilogy*, vols 1 and 2. Oxford: Oxford University Press.

Cahill, Lynne, and Gerald Gazdar (1999) 'German noun inflection', *Journal of Linguistics* 35: 1–42.

Carstairs, Andrew (1986) 'Macroclasses and paradigm economy in German nouns'. *Zeitschrift für Phonetik, Sprachwissenschaft und Kommunikationsforschung* 39: 3–11.

—— (1987) *Allomorphy in Inflection*. London: Croom Helm.

Carstairs-McCarthy, Andrew (1994) 'Inflection classes, gender, and the principle of contrast'. *Language* 70: 737–87.

Chomsky, Noam (1965) *Aspects of the Theory of Syntax*. Cambridge, MA: MIT Press.

—— (1970) 'Remarks on nominalization', in R. Jacobs and P. Rosenbaum (eds.), *Readings in English Transformational Grammar*. Waltham, MA: Ginn and Company, pp. 184–221.

—— (1995) *The Minimalist Program*. Cambridge, MA: MIT Press.

—— (2000) 'Minimalist inquiries: The framework', in R. Martin, D. Michaels, and J. Uriagereka (eds.), *Step by Step*. Cambridge, MA: MIT Press, pp. 89–155.

—— (2001a) 'Beyond explanatory adequacy', Ms., MIT, Cambridge, MA.

—— (2001b) 'Derivation by phase', in M. Kenstowicz (ed.), *Ken Hale. A Life in Language*. Cambridge, MA: MIT Press, pp. 1–52.

—— (2005) 'On phases', Ms., MIT, Cambridge, MA.

——and Morris Halle (1968) *The Sound Pattern of English*. Cambridge, MA: MIT Press.

Cinque, Guglielmo (1993) 'On the evidence for partial N-movement in the Romance DP'. *University of Venice Working Papers in Linguistics* 3.2: 21–40.

Comrie, Bernard (1978) 'Morphological classification of cases in the Slavonic languages'. *The Slavonic and East European Review* 56: 177–91.

Corbett, Greville (1991) *Gender*. Cambridge: Cambridge University Press.

——and Norman Fraser (1993) 'Network morphology: A DATR account of Russian nominal inflection'. *Journal of Linguistics* 29: 113–42.

Danon, Gabi (1996) The syntax of determiners in Hebrew. Master's thesis, Tel-Aviv University.

de Lacy, Paul (2002) 'Maximal words and the Maori passive', in J. McCarthy (ed.), *Optimality Theory in Phonology: A Reader*. Oxford: Blackwell, pp. 495–512.

DiSciullo, Anna-Maria, and Edwin Williams (1987) *On the Definition of Word*. Cambridge, MA: MIT Press.

Eisenberg, Peter (2000) *Grundriß der deutschen Grammatik. Band 1: Das Wort*. Stuttgart: Metzler.

——and Ulrike Sayatz (2004) 'Left of number: Animacy and plurality in German nouns', in G. Müller, L. Gunkel, and G. Zifonun (eds.), *Explorations in Nominal Inflection*. Berlin: Mouton de Gruyter, pp. 97–120.

Embick, David (1998) 'Voice systems and the syntax/morphology interface', in H. Harley (ed.), *Papers from the UPenn/MIT Roundtable on Argument Structure and Aspect*, vol. 32, Cambridge, MA: MITWPL, pp. 41–72.

——(2000) 'Features, syntax, and categories in the Latin perfect'. *Linguistic Inquiry* 31: 185–230.

Frampton, John (2002) 'Syncretism, impoverishment, and the structure of person features', in M. Andronis, E. Debenport, A. Pycha, and K. Yoshimura (eds.), *Papers from the Chicago Linguistics Society Meeting*, vol. 38, Chicago, pp. 207–22.

Franks, Steven (1995) *Parameters of Slavic Morphosyntax*. New York and Oxford: Oxford University Press.

Fraser, Norman, and Greville Corbett (1994) 'Gender, animacy, and declensional class assignment: A unified account for Russian', in G. Booij and J. van Marle (eds.), *Yearbook of Morphology 1994*. Dordrecht: Kluwer, pp. 123–50.

Gallmann, Peter (1998) 'Case underspecification in morphology, syntax and the lexicon', in A. Alexiadou and C. Wilder (eds.), *Possessors, Predicates and Movement in the Determiner Phrase*. Amsterdam: Benjamins, pp. 141–75.

Groos, Anneke, and Henk van Riemsdijk (1981) 'Matching effects in free relatives', in A. Belletti, L. Brandi, and L. Rizzi, (eds.), *Theory of Markedness in Generative Grammar*. Pisa: Suola Normale Superiore, pp. 171–216.

Gunkel, Lutz (2003) 'Syncretisms and case underspecification in Polish noun paradigms', in P. Banski and A. Przepiórkowski (eds.), *Generative Linguistics in Poland: Morphosyntactic Investigations (Proceedings of the GLiP-5 Conference held in Warsaw, Poland, 30 November–1 December 2002)*.Warsaw: GLiP, pp. 47–62.

Haegeman, Liliane (1998) 'Gender and word markers in West Flemish', Ms., University of Lille.

Hale, Ken (1973) 'Deep-surface canonical disparities in relation to analysis and change: An Australian example', in T. Sebeok (ed.), *Current Trends in Linguistics 11*. The Hague: Mouton, pp. 401–58.

Halle, Morris (1992) 'The Latvian declension', in G. Booij and J. van Marle (eds.), *Yearbook of Morphology 1991*. Dordrecht: Kluwer, pp. 33–47.

——(1994) 'The Russian declension: An illustration of the theory of Distributed Morphology', in J. Cole and C. Kisseberth (eds.), *Perspectives in Phonology*. CSLI Publications, Stanford, pp. 29–60.

——(1997) 'Distributed Morphology: Impoverishment and fission', in B. Bruening, Y. Kang, and M. McGinnis (eds.), *Papers at the Interface*, vol. 30, MITWPL, pp. 425–49.

——and Alec Marantz (1993) 'Distributed Morphology and the pieces of inflection', in K. Hale and S. J. Keyser (eds.), *The View from Building 20*. Cambridge, MA: MIT Press, pp. 111–76.

——and Alec Marantz (1994) 'Some key features of Distributed Morphology', in A. Carnie, H. Harley, and T. Bures (eds.), *Papers on Phonology and Morphology*, vol. 21 of *MIT Working Papers in Linguistics*, Cambridge, MA: MITWPL, pp. 275–88.

Harbour, Daniel (2003) 'The Kiowa case for feature insertion'. *Natural Language and Linguistic Theory* 21: 543–78.

Harley, Heidi (1994) 'Hug a tree: Deriving the morphosyntactic feature hierarchy', in A. Carnie and H. Harley (eds.), *MITWPL 21: Papers on Phonology and Morphology*. Cambridge, MA: MITWPL, pp. 275–88.

——and Rolf Noyer (2003) 'Distributed Morphology', in L. Cheng and R. Sybesma (eds.), *The Second GLOT International State-of-the-Article Book*. Berlin: Mouton de Gruyter, pp. 463–96.

Harris, James (1991) 'The exponence of gender in Spanish'. *Linguistic Inquiry* 22: 27–62.

Isačenko, Alexander (1975) *Die russische Sprache der Gegenwart*. München: Max Hueber Verlag.

Jakobson, Roman (1962a) 'Beitrag zur allgemeinen Kasuslehre. Gesamtbedeutungen der russischen Kasus', in *Selected Writings*, vol. 2. The Hague and Paris: Mouton, pp. 23–71.

——(1962b) 'Morfologičeskije nabljudenija', in *Selected Writings*, vol. 2. The Hague and Paris: Mouton, pp. 154–81.

Johnston, Jason (1996) Systematic homonymy and the structure of morphological categories. PhD thesis, University of Sydney.

Josefsson, Gunlög (2001) 'The meaning of lexical classes'. *Nordic Journal of Linguistics* 24: 218–31.

Kibrik, Aleksandr (1979) 'Canonical ergativity and Daghestan languages', in F. Plank (ed.), *Ergativity*. London: Academic Press, pp. 61–77.

Kiparsky, Paul (1973) '"Elsewhere" in phonology', in S. Anderson and P. Kiparsky (eds.), *A Festschrift for Morris Halle*. New York: Academic Press, pp. 93–106.

Krifka, Manfred (1995) 'Swahili', in J. Jacobs, A. von Stechow, W. Sternefeld, and T. Vennemann (eds.), *Syntax. Ein internationales Handbuch zeitgenössischer Forschung*, vol. 2. Berlin: de Gruyter, pp. 1397–418.

Leskien, August (1955) *Handbuch der altbulgarischen Sprache*. 7 edn. Heidelberg: Carl Winter Universitätsverlag.

Lumsden, John (1992) 'Underspecification in grammatical and natural gender'. *Linguistic Inquiry* 23: 469–86.

Mackridge, Peter (1985) *Modern Greek*. Oxford: Clarendon Press.

Marantz, Alec (1995) ' "Cat" as a phrasal idiom: Consequences of late insertion in Distributed Morphology', Ms., MIT, Cambridge, MA.

McCreight, Katherine (1988) Multiple case assignments. PhD thesis, MIT, Cambridge, MA.

Müller, Gereon (2002) 'Remarks on nominal inflection in German', in I. Kaufmann and B. Stiebels (eds.), *More than Words: A Festschrift for Dieter Wunderlich*. Berlin: Akademie Verlag, pp. 113–45.

——(2004) 'On decomposing inflection class features: Syncretism in Russian noun inflection', in G. Müller, L. Gunkel, and G. Zifonun (eds.), *Explorations in Nominal Inflection*. Berlin: Mouton de Gruyter, pp. 189–227.

——(2005) 'Syncretism and iconicity in Icelandic noun declensions: A Distributed Morphology approach', in G. Booij and J. van Marle (eds.), *Yearbook of Morphology 2004*. Dordrecht: Springer, pp. 229–71.

——(2006a) 'Notes on paradigm economy', in G. Müller and J. Trommer (eds.), *Subanalysis of Argument Encoding in Distributed Morphology*, vol. 84 of *Linguistische Arbeitsberichte*, Universität Leipzig.

——(2006b) 'Pro-drop and impoverishment', in P. Brandt and E. Fuß (eds.), *Form, Structure, and Grammar. A Festschrift Presented to Günther Grewendorf on Occasion of his 60th Birthday*. Berlin: Akademie Verlag, pp. 93–115.

Neidle, Carol (1988) *The Role of Case in Russian Syntax*. Dordrecht: Kluwer.

Nesset, Tore (1994) 'A feature-based approach to Russian noun inflection'. *Journal of Slavic Linguistics* 2: 214–37.

Noyer, Rolf (1992) Features, positions, and affixes in autonomous morphological structure. PhD thesis, MIT, Cambridge, MA.

——(1998) 'Impoverishment theory and morphosyntactic markedness', in S. Lapointe, D. Brentari, and P. Farrell (eds.), *Morphology and its Relation to Phonology and Syntax*. Palo Alto, CA: CSLI, pp. 264–85.

——(2005) 'A constraint on interclass syncretism', in G. Booij and J. van Marle (eds.), *Yearbook of Morphology 2004*. Dordrecht: Springer, pp. 273–315.

Oltra Massuet, Isabel (1999) On the notion of theme vowel: A new approach to Catalan verbal morphology. Master of science thesis, MIT, Cambridge, MA.

Plank, Frans (1979) 'Ikonisierung und De-Ikonisierung als Prinzipien des Sprachwandels'. *Sprachwissenschaft* 4, 121–58.

——(1991) 'Rasmus Rask's dilemma', in F. Plank (ed.), *Paradigms*. Berlin: Mouton de Gruyter, pp. 161–96.

Ralli, Angela (1994) 'Feature representations and feature-passing operations: The case of Greek nominal inflection', in *Proceedings of the 8th International Symposium on English & Greek*. University of Thessaloniki: School of English, Dept. of Theoretical and Applied Linguistics, pp. 19–46.

—— (2002) 'The role of morphology in gender determination: Evidence from Modern Greek'. *Linguistics* 40: 519–51.

Ritter, Elizabeth (1991) 'Two functional categories in noun phrases: Evidence from Modern Hebrew', in S. Rothstein (ed.), *Syntax and Semantics*, vol. 26. San Diego, CA: Academic Press, pp. 37–62.

—— (1993) 'Where's gender?' *Linguistic Inquiry* 24: 795–803.

Ruge, Hans (1986) *Grammatik des Neugriechischen*. Köln: Romiosini.

Sauerland, Uli (1996) 'The late insertion of Germanic inflection', Generals paper, MIT.

Shapiro, Michael (1969) *Aspects of Russian Morphology*. Cambridge, MA: Slavica Publishers.

Shlonsky, Ur (2000) 'The form of the Semitic noun phrase: An antisymmetric, non N-movement account', Ms., University of Geneva.

Sichel, Ivy (2002) 'Phrasal movement in Hebrew adjectives and possessives', in *Dimensions of Movement: From Remnants to Features*. Amsterdam: Benjamins, pp. 297–339.

Siloni, Tal (1997) *Noun Phrases and Nominalizations*. Dordrecht: Kluwer.

Stechow, Arnim von (2005) 'LF in einem Phasenmodell', Ms., Universität Tübingen.

Sternefeld, Wolfgang (2004) 'Feature checking and case agreement in German DPs', in G. Müller, L. Gunkel, and G. Zifonun (eds.), *Explorations in Nominal Inflection*. Berlin: Mouton de Gruyter, pp. 269–99.

Stump, Gregory (2001) *Inflectional Morphology*. Cambridge: Cambridge University Press.

Trommer, Jochen (2005a) 'A derivational approach to matching effects in free relative constructions', Ms., Universität Leipzig.

—— (2005b) 'A feature-geometric approach to Amharic verb classes', Ms., Universität Leipzig.

—— (2006) 'Head-level and chain-level constraints on spellout', in J. Costa and M. C. F. Silva (eds.), *Studies on Agreement*. Amsterdam: Benjamins.

van Hout, Angelique, and Tom Roeper (1998) 'Events and aspectual structure in Derivational Morphology'. *MIT Working Papers in Linguistics* 32: 175–220.

Wasow, Tom (1977) 'Transformations and the lexicon', in P. Culicover, T. Wasow, and A. Akmajian (eds.), *Formal Syntax*. New York: Academic Press.

Wiese, Bernd (1999) 'Unterspezifizierte Paradigmen. Form und Funktion in der pronominalen Deklination'. *Linguistik Online* 4. (www.linguistik-online.de/3_99).

—— (2000) 'Warum Flexionsklassen? Über die deutsche Substantivdeklination', in R. Thieroff, M. Tamrat, N. Fuhrhop, and O. Teuber (eds.), *Deutsche Grammatik in Theorie und Praxis*. Tübingen: Niemeyer, pp. 139–53.

—— (2001) 'Zur lateinischen Deklination: Die Form-Funktions-Beziehung', Ms., IDS Mannheim.

—— (2004) 'Categories and paradigms: On underspecification in Russian declension', in G. Müller, L. Gunkel, and G. Zifonun (eds.), *Explorations in Nominal Inflection.* Berlin: Mouton de Gruyter, pp. 321–72.

Wiese, Richard (1996) *The Phonology of German.* Oxford: Clarendon Press.

Williams, Edwin (1994) 'Remarks on lexical knowledge'. *Lingua* 92: 7–34.

—— (1997) 'Blocking and anaphora'. *Linguistic Inquiry* 28: 577–628.

Wunderlich, Dieter (1996) 'Minimalist morphology: The role of paradigms', in G. Booij and J. van Marle (eds.), *Yearbook of Morphology 1995.* Dordrecht: Kluwer, pp. 93–114.

—— (1999) 'German noun plural reconsidered', Ms., Universität Düsseldorf.

—— (2004) 'Is there any need for the concept of directional syncretism?' in G. Müller, L. Gunkel, and G. Zifonun (eds.), *Explorations in Nominal Inflection.* Berlin: Mouton de Gruyter, pp. 373–95.

Wurzel, Wolfgang Ullrich (1984) *Flexionsmorphologie und Natürlichkeit.* Berlin: Akademie Verlag.

—— (1998) 'Drei Ebenen der Struktur von Flexionsparadigmen', in R. Fabri, A. Ortmann, and T. Parodi (eds.), *Models of Inflection.* Tübingen: Niemeyer.

Zifonun, Gisela (2003) 'Aspekte deutscher Reflexivkonstruktionen im europäischen Vergleich: Pronominale Paradigmen und NP-interne Reflexiva', in G. Müller, L. Gunkel, and G. Zifonun (eds.), *Arbeiten zur Reflexivierung.* Tübingen: Niemeyer, pp. 267–300.

Zwicky, Arnold (1970) 'Class complements in phonology'. *Linguistic Inquiry* 1: 262–64.

—— (1985) 'How to describe inflection', in M. Niepokuj, M. V. Clay, V. Nikiforidou, and D. Feder (eds.), *Proceedings of the 11th Annual Meeting of the Berkeley Linguistics Society.* BLS, Berkeley, University of California, pp. 372–86.

—— (1991) 'Systematic versus accidental phonological identity', in F. Plank (ed.), *Paradigms.* Mouton de Gruyter, pp. 113–32.

—— (2000) 'Describing syncretism: Rules of referral after 15 years', Ms., Stanford University.

6

On absolute and contextual syncretism: Remarks on the structure of case paradigms and on how to derive them

ANDREA CALABRESE*

6.1 Case paradigms: Introduction

A set of morphologically-related words, each containing the same stem and the morphological realizations of different combinations of the same set of inflectional features–which may represent morphosyntactic properties such as case, gender, number, tense, person, etc.,–is traditionally called a paradigm. In this chapter I will deal with the nature and structure of paradigms in terms of the model of morphology called Distributed Morphology (DM) (Halle and Marantz 1993). The paradigms that will be investigated are those of the case systems of Old French, Sanskrit, Classical Greek, and, in particular, of Latin.

In Distributed Morphology, paradigms are epiphenomenal constructs derived by establishing the feature sets entering the terminal nodes of the morphosyntax and by determining the vocabulary items that are inserted in these terminal nodes. No knowledge of the paradigm as a structured set of fully inflected words is required. A fundamental issue to address in accounting for paradigms is that of their structure, i.e., the system of morphological contrasts characterizing them. Research in Distributed Morphology has focused on the identification of the vocabulary items and on the operation of impoverishment as the means to account for this structure (Halle and Marantz 1993; Noyer 1998; Bobaljik 2001). In this chapter I will propose that this is not enough and that to achieve this goal one must also consider the fundamental role played by the constraints that govern the combinations of features in the terminal nodes of the morphosyntax. These constraints generate the overall structure of the paradigm. I will deal with syncretisms, i.e., with situations in

* I would like to thank Morris Halle, Jonathan Bobaljik, and Andrew Nevins, and two anonymous reviewers for their comments and suggestions on a previous draft of this paper.

which the same morphological realization is assigned to two different morphosyntactic categories. As we will see, two different types of syncretism must be distinguished: contextual syncretism and absolute syncretism. In the case of absolute syncretism two morphosyntactic categories which may have different morphological realization in language A have the same morphological realization across the morphology of language B. Thus, for example, the ablative and the instrumental, which are morphologically distinct in Sanskrit, are both morphologically realized by the ablative in Latin. In the case of contextual syncretism, in a certain morphological context, language A has the same morphological realization for two different morphosyntactic categories that are otherwise morphologically distinct in other contexts in A. For example, whereas Latin distinguishes between the dative and the ablative in singular nouns of the first, second, and fifth declension and in singular non-neuter nouns of the third and fourth declension, such distinction is not present in plural nouns of all declensions and in the neuter singular nouns of third and fourth declension. In this chapter, I will propose an account for contextual and absolute syncretism. Contextual syncretism is accounted for by determining the feature specifications of the vocabulary items and by using the operation of impoverishment. In absolute syncretism, instead, we need to use feature-changing procedures that modify the feature combinations of the terminal nodes of the morphosyntax. These procedures–akin to the rules of referrals of Zwicky (1985) and Stump (1993)–involve repairs triggered by markedness constraints.

The paper is structured as follows. Sections 6.2.1 and 6.2.2 introduce the main facts to be analyzed. Section 6.2.1 illustrates the case paradigms of Old French, Sanskrit, and Classical Greek and explains why the notion of case is needed. It also introduces the concepts of contextual and absolute syncretisms. Section 6.2.2 deals with these two types of syncretism in the case paradigm of Latin and shows how these two types of syncretisms behave differently with respect to concord. This section also discusses the status of the Latin locative case, which is syncretic with the genitive or dative in nouns of towns or small islands and with the ablative in all other nouns. It is shown that in this case we are dealing with an instance of absolute syncretism.

Section 6.3 outlines the model proposed here. Section 6.3.1 introduces the morphological features used in the analysis and illustrates under what formal conditions there is a morphological contrast in a system. Section 6.3.2 analyzes the instances of contextual syncretism found in Old French, Sanskrit, Classical Greek, and Latin; it is hypothesized here that contextual syncretism is accounted for by determining the feature specifications of the vocabulary items forming a paradigm and by using the operation of impoverishment. Underspecification of the vocabulary items is crucial in the analysis of contextual syncretism. In section 6.3.3, I turn to absolute syncretism. The following model is proposed. In the morphological component syntactic grammatical relations and thematic roles are universally mapped into the same set of morphological case features. Vocabulary insertion accesses only a subset of them. This limited feature access is obtained by assuming that there is a set of restrictions that filter out feature combinations that do not have morphological realization in a language and change them into feature combinations that do have this realization in the language. This is absolute syncretism. Section 6.3.3.2 shows that morphosyntactic representations cannot be underspecified to account for this type of syncretism differently than vocabulary items in the case of contextual syncretism. Specifically here I consider the hypothesis that grammar does not generate the feature specifications of cases that are not morphologically realized, i.e., of the cases that undergo absolute syncretism. Such a hypothesis will be rejected. Section 6.3.4 introduces the case restrictions, the markedness constraints that govern the structure of case systems. First, in section 6.3.4.1, the notion of morphological markedness is discussed; it is proposed that the morphological realizations of certain feature specifications, or of certain combinations of feature combinations, as affixes with an idiosyncratic exponent is "marked", i.e. costly. Assuming that a general principle of economy governs language, languages will tend to avoid these marked combinations. I will consider markedness effects in the case of case systems by showing that cases must be ranked into an implicational hierarchy. Section 6.3.4.2 illustrates how markedness effects can be accounted for by ranked negative constraints disallowing configurations of feature specifications. The negative constraints needed to describe case paradigms, the case restrictions, are introduced in this section. Active constraints mark certain feature combinations as illicit. These illicit configurations are removed by repairs. Section 6.3.4.2 illustrates how by using active case restrictions and the related repairs we can account for the cases of absolute syncretism introduced in the first part of the chapter. In particular, an analysis of the syncretic changes affecting the Latin locative case is proposed. Section 6.3.5 shows how diachronic changes in case systems can be accounted for only by changes in the featural specifications of the morphosyntax, as the model proposed here predicts. Section 6.3.6 shows that phonological changes in the case exponents cannot account for diachronic changes in the structure of case systems, as often proposed. Section 6.4 discusses and rejects an alternative model in which there are no constraints and repairs that eliminates illicit feature combinations that do not have morphological realization in a language. In this model all possible syncretic patterns must be encoded in the feature system and the absolute syncretism patterns found in a language must be accounted for only by looking at the feature specifications of the vocabulary items of the language. Finally in the appendix there is discussion of how the feature system used to represent cases in this chapter was chosen.

6.2 Case paradigms

6.2.1 *Basic facts*

I begin with some basic assumptions in morphological analysis. Any morphological analysis begins with the segmentations of words. This segmentation identifies the morphemes, the structural units of words. A morpheme is contrastive with respect to another morpheme if it is associated with different values of at least one feature (see section 6.3.1 for a formal definition of morphological contrast).

Consider two examples of paradigms. These two examples involve case systems–which will be the focus of my investigation of the notion of paradigm–and represent the two polar opposites in the case of these systems: the third nominal declension in Old French and the /-a/ declension of Sanskrit. Old French has a minimally reduced two case system; Sanskrit has a full-fledged seven case system.[1,2] In addition, Sanskrit has a dual number that Old French does not have.

(6.1)   Old French third nominal declension:

	Singular	Plural
Nominative	*chiens*	*chiens* 'dog'
Oblique	*chien*	*chiens*

(6.2)   Sanskrit /-a/ declension:

SING.

N.	*devas*	(/*dev-a-s*/)	'god'
G.	*devasya*	(/*dev-a-sya*/)	
D.	*devāya*	(/*dev-a-ya*/ + thematic vowel lengthening)	
A.	*devam*	(/*dev-a-m*/)	
L.	*deve*	(/*dev-a-i*/)	
Abl.	*devāt*	(/*dev-a-t*/ + thematic vowel lengthening)	
Ins.	*devena*	(/*dev-a-ina*/)	

[1] According to Blake (1994), a seven case system such as that of Sanskrit is the most common maximal case system if differentiations in the local cases such as those found in Uralic or in Caucasian languages are not considered.

[2] Sanskrit has also a vocative case. I assume that this case has morphological and syntactic properties quite different than the other seven cases. I will systematically disregard this case throughout the chapter.

DUAL

N.	*devāu*	(/*dev-a-u*/ + thematic vowel lengthening[3])
G.	*devayos*	(/*dev-a-i-aus*/] + /-i-/ insertion)
D.	*devābhyam*	(/*dev-a-bhyam*/ + thematic vowel lengthening)
A.	*devāu*	(/*dev-a-u*/ + thematic vowel lengthening)
L.	*devayos*	(/*dev-a-i-aus*/] + /-i-/ insertion)
Abl.	*devābhyam*	(/*dev-a-bhyam*/ + thematic vowel lengthening)
Ins.	*devābhyam*	(/*dev-a-bhyam*/] + thematic vowel lengthening)

PLU.

N.	*devās*	(/*dev-a-s*/ + thematic vowel lengthening)
G.	*devānām*	(/*dev-a-nām*/ + thematic vowel lengthening)
D.	*devebhyas*	(/*dev-a-i-bhyas*/] + /-i-/ insertion)
A.	*devān*	(/*dev-a-n*/ + thematic vowel lengthening)
L.	*deveṣu*	(/*dev-a-i-su*/] + /-i-/ insertion)
Abl.	*devebhyas*	(/*dev-a-i-bhyas*/] + /-i-/ insertion)
Ins.	*devāis*	(/*dev-a-is*/ + thematic vowel lengthening)

In comparing the Sanskrit /a/-declension and the Old French third declension, one observes that in Old French, the exponent /-Ø/ of the singular represents seven case functions which in Sanskrit are instead represented by different exponents. In Old French, the exponent /-Ø/ represents the syncretism of six different cases.

Still, when we look at both Sanskrit and Old French, we realize that the phonological exponents of the different grammatical properties characterizing the same paradigm can be identical. Thus, in Old French, /-s/ is the exponent of the nominative, singular and plural, and oblique plural. In Sanskrit, /-u/ is the exponent of the nominative and accusative dual, /-bhyam/ and /-bhyas/ are the exponent of the dative-ablative-instrumental dual, and of the dative-ablative plural, respectively. Again we are seeing a syncretism between these different cases.

It is important at this point to notice that the notion of case was developed by Greek and Latin grammarians mainly as a way of expressing meaningful generalizations on case exponents in systems characterized by massive syncretism. Cases are traditionally recognized on the basis of a distinction of case forms for groups of nouns, i.e., for declensional classes of nouns.

---

[3] In the nominative and accusative dual, the suffixal /-u/ becomes a coda glide because of an independent syllabification process. The fact that the thematic vowel is lengthened prevents the Sandhi operation by which /a/ + /u/ monophthongizes into /o/. Monophthongization affects only short /a/. Examples of this monophthongization process can be seen in the locative and instrumental singular where [a] + [i] monophthongize into [e].

There is no requirement that the distinction be made for all classes of nouns. In Sanskrit, as in Latin (see table (6.7) below) and in other Indo-European case languages, the nominative and accusative have contrastive exponents for masculine and feminine nouns, but there is syncretism of this contrast with neuter nouns (see also the Sanskrit dual above). In Latin, there is also syncretism of nominative and accusative with plural nouns of the fourth and fifth declensions and third declension consonant stems. Nevertheless, we recognize the distinction as applying to all nouns, since it allows us to make exceptionless generalizations about the exponents used for various functions in various syntactic contexts (Blake 1994).

In Latin, for instance, we want to be able to make statements like those in (6.3):

(6.3) (i) The accusative is used to express the direct object.

(ii) The accusative is used to express the object of prepositions such as *ad, per, trans*, etc.

(iii) The accusative is used to express duration: *XXVII annos* 'for 27 years.'

(iv) The accusative is used to express direction of motion: *Romam venit* 'He comes to Rome'.

It does not matter, for the purposes of these rules, that the accusative is realized by a form identical to the nominative in some paradigms. The issue is that the Accusative is identified as a single abstract property, or single set of abstract properties, which is associated with a number of syntactic functions and which is morphologically realized as a set of different exponents. Thus, morphological cases mediate the mapping between syntactic functions and surface case exponents.

This is not the only way of dealing with syncretism. We could recognize only the formally distinct exponents in each paradigm and relate these directly to syntactic functions. For the first declension singular (see table in (6.7) below), there would be the exponents /-∅/, /-m/, and /-i/. For the second declension singular non-neuter, there would be the exponents /-s/, /-m/, /-i/ and /-∅/, and so on. Rules for encoding syntactic functions would have to refer to these exponents. For example, the rule in (6.3i), which states that the direct object is expressed in the accusative case, would have to be changed as in (6.4):

(6.4) The direct object is expressed thus:
With masculine and feminine singular nouns of any declension the exponent /-m/ is used.

With plural nouns of the first and second declensions the exponent /-s / is used.

With plural nouns of the third, fourth, and fifth declensions and with all neuters the exponent /-a/ is used.

In the traditional descriptions the indirect object is described as being in the dative. If we decided not use the notion of case and to directly correlate exponents to syntactic functions, we would have rules like the following:

(6.5)   The indirect object is expressed as follows:

With nouns of first, third, and fourth declensions singular the exponent /-i/ is used.

With nouns of the second declension singular the exponent /Ø/ is used.

With nouns of the first and second declensions plural the exponent /-is/ is used.

With nouns of the third, fourth, and fifth declensions plural the exponent /-ibus/ is used.

The problem with this approach is that the list of case forms given in (6.4) for the direct object would have to be repeated for all the functions of the traditional accusative, of which there are about four. Similarly the list of case forms given in (6.5) for indirect object would have to be repeated for all the functions of the traditional dative, of which there are six or so (Blake 1994).

This shows that an attempt to link exponents directly to syntactic functions results in a quite complex and redundant grammar. By using cases as in (6.3) we achieve a significant simplification of grammar.

Let us consider again the case syncretisms that we observed in Old French and Sanskrit. As noted above, we can clearly distinguish two types of syncretism. In the singular oblique /-Ø/ of Old French, this exponent is representing case functions like the genitive that do not have an overt morphological realization anywhere in the nominal system of this language. In contrast, in the /-bhyam/ of the dative-ablative plural of Sanskrit, we are dealing with a single exponent of two case functions (the dative and the ablative) that otherwise have contrastive exponents in the singular.

Meiser (1992) (see also Ringe 1995 on this distinction) distinguishes between functional syncretism and formal syncretism. Functional syncretism involves the falling together of two morphosyntactic categories into a single one across the morphology of a language. Formal syncretism, in contrast, involves the use of the same form to express morphosyntactic categories that are otherwise morphologically contrasting in a language. Here I will replace this terminology and call the first absolute syncretism and the second contextual syncretism. I will detail their workings by considering case systems.

Absolute syncretism in a case system involves the syncretism between a case that is morphologically realized in the language and a case that is not morphologically expressed in that language but that is morphologically expressed in other languages. For example, this is the situation of the oblique in Old French that realizes cases such as the genitive, the dative, the accusative, and the ablative that were morphologically contrastive in Latin. Likewise, it is the case of the Latin ablative that realizes cases such as the ablative, locative, and instrumental that are contrastive in Sanskrit. Historically, absolute syncretism involves the replacement a given case exponent with another case exponent across all nominal classes and nominal categories.[4] Below I will propose that absolute syncretism is obtained by changing the feature bundles of the terminal nodes of the morphosyntax.

In contrast, contextual syncretism in a case system involves the syncretism between cases that are morphologically realized in this system. It involves replacement of a given case exponent with another case exponent only in certain nominal classes or in certain grammatical categories such as the plural or the dual. In the Old French declension in (6.3) we observe contextual syncretism among the nominative singular, the nominative plural, and the oblique plural where we find the exponent /-s /. In Sanskrit there is contextual syncretism in the dative, ablative, and instrumental dual where we find the same exponent /-bhyam/, in the genitive and locative dual where we find the exponent /-yaus/, and in the dative and ablative plural where we find the exponent /-bhyas/. Below I will propose that contextual syncretism is accounted for by considering the feature assignments of the exponents of the vocabulary items.

To summarize, case systems present two major problems for description. One is the problem of distinguishing the cases; the other is the problem of describing their meaning and function. Distinguishing the cases is a problem, since nouns belonging to different declensional classes may exhibit a different

---

[4] Observe that I am not implying that any two cases that a language L_1 distinguishes will be merged neatly into just one case in another language, L_2, that lacks that distinction. Consider Latin, which lacks the instrumental but has an ablative that has the instrumental among its functions, and Classical Greek, which lacks an ablative as well as an instrumental. What will be proposed here does not predict that the functions of the ablative in a language such as Latin are absorbed by just one case in Classical Greek. In fact, some of the Latin ablative's functions (notably the "instrumental" ones) are fulfilled by the Greek dative while some (notably the "ablative" ones) are fulfilled by the genitive. As discussed below in section 6.3.4.2, this depends on the patterns of absolute syncretism characterizing the diachronic development of Classical Greek that are simply different from those characterizing the diachronic development of Latin.

range of contextual syncretisms. As we saw above, the traditional solution to this problem is to identify cases across declensional classes on the basis of the functions they have in common. Although this solution allows a simplification of grammatical statements as we saw above, it is still not satisfactory from the point of view of morphological analysis, for it categorizes as distinct exponents that are otherwise identical. In fact, traditional grammars of Sanskrit list the /-bhyas/ of the dative plural and the /-bhyas/ of the ablative plural as two different entries. The same occurs in Latin where the /-iː/ of I declension dative (cf. rosae) and the /-iː/ of the I declension genitive (cf. rosae) are treated as different.

Describing the meaning and function of the cases traditionally involves finding a principal meaning, which is reflected in the label of the case, as well as listing a range of separate meanings or functions. When we have absolute syncretism, this solution becomes particularly cumbersome. Consider the Classical Greek /o-/ declension below:

(6.6) SING.

N.   ἀδελφ os   (< adelph -o-s)   'brother'
G.   ἀδελφν   (< adelph -o-io)[5]
D.   ἀδελφῳ   (< adelph -o-i)
         (+thematic vowel lengthening and laxing)
A.   ἀδελφον   (<adelph -o-n)

DUAL

N.   ἀδελφω   (<adelph -o-Ø) (+thematic vowel
         lengthening and laxing)
G.   ἀδελφοιν   (<adelph -o-in)
D.   ἀδελφοιν   (<adelph -o-in)
A.   ἀδελφω   (<adelph -o-Ø) (+thematic vowel
         lengthening and laxing)

PLUR.

N.   ἀδελφοι   (<adelph -o-i)
G.   ἀδελφων   (<adelph -o-ɔːn)
D.   ἀδελφοις   (<adelph -o-is)
A.   ἀδελφους   (<adelph -o-ns)

---

[5] To understand the different surface forms of this declension, one must know the following:

i.   /o/ is the [+ATR] short vowel [o], /ω /is the [−ATR] long vowel [ɔː].

ii.   Adjacent vowels contract in Greek; in (6.6) we have the following contractions: [o + ɔː]→[ɔː], [o + o]→[oː] (written ον) . The long [+ATR] vowel [oː] later became [uː]) (see Noyer 1997 on Greek vowel contractions).

iii.   Intervocalic /i-/ is syllabified as a glide and deleted. Thus in the case of the genitive, we have the following changes: /oio→oyo→oo→oː/. I am assuming that these diachronic changes also hold synchronically. As an alternative synchronic analysis one can assume that the

In Classical Greek there is absolute syncretism between the genitive and the ablative, and between the dative, the locative, and the instrumental. When one attempts to account for the uses of the dative, or those of the genitive, we have to put together meanings and functions that apparently do not have anything in common. Therefore there is no clear way of relating the syntax to the morphological surface of the language other than by a stipulative list of function-case correlations.

6.2.2 Contextual and absolute syncretism in Latin

An investigation of contextual and absolute syncretism in the case paradigms of Latin, which are given in (6.7), will allow us to understand these phenomena better. Two characteristics of Latin are relevant here: the presence of massive contextual syncretisms and the presence of the absolute syncretism between the ablative and instrumental, and the absolute syncretism we observe for the locative which is syncretic with the dative-genitive in nouns of towns and small islands and with the ablative in all other nouns.

The five declensions of Latin:

(6.7)	First	Second			
	porta, -ae	amicus, -i	puer, -i	ager, -gri	donum, i
	f., 'gate'	m., 'friend'	m., 'boy'	m., 'field'	n., 'gift'
SING.					
N.	port-a	amic-u-s	puer	ager	dōn-u-m
G.	port-ae	amic-i	puer-i	agr-i	dōn-i
D.	port-ae	amicō	puer-ō	agr-ō	dōn-ō
A.	port-a-m	amic-u-m	puer-u-m	agr-u-m	dōn-um
Ab.	port-ā	amic-ō	puer-ō	agr-ō	dōn-ō
PLU.					
N.	port-ae	amic-i	puer-i	agr-i	dōn-a
G.	port-ā-r-um	amic-ō-r-um	puer-ō-r-um	agr-ō-r-um	dōn-ō-r-um
D.	port-i-s	amic-i-s	puer-i-s	agr-i-s	dōn-i-s
A.	port-ā-s	amic-ō-s	puer-ō-s	agr-ō-s	dōn-a
Ab.	port-i-s	amic-i-s	puer-i-s	agr-i-s	dōn-i-s

genitive singular ending is /-Ø/ and that there is lengthening of the thematic vowel in this case.

iv. Coda [n] is lost before tautosyllabic [s]. When this occurs, the preceding vowel lengthens. (see the accusative plural: /ons→o:s/). We need to hypothesize this shape for the accusative plural ending because of historical reasons. I assume it to make the synchronic relationship with the accusative singular ending explicit. An alternative synchronic analysis can assume the ending /-s/ for this Case coupled with lengthening of the thematic vowel.

Third

	rēx, rēgis m., 'king'	corpus, -oris n., 'body'	cîvis, -is m., 'citizen'	urbs, -is f., 'city'	mare, -is n., 'sea'
SING.					
N.	rēx	corpus	cîv-i-s	urb-s	mar-e
G.	rēg-i-s	corpor-i-s	cîv-i-s	urb-i-s	mar-i-s
D.	rēg-î	corpor-î	cîv-î	urb-î	mar-î
A.	rēg-e-m	corpus	cîv-e-m	urb-e-m	mar-e
Ab.	rēg-e	corpor-e	cîv-e	urb-e	mar-î
PLU.					
N.	rēg-ē-s	corpor-a	cîv-ē-s	urb-ē-s	mar-i-a
G.	rēg-um	corpor-um	cîv-i-um	urb-i-um	mar-i-um
D.	rēg-i-bu-s	corpor-i-bu-s	cîv-i-bu-s	urb-i-bu-s	mar-i-bu-s
A.	rēg-ē-s	corpora	cîv-ē-s	urb-ēs	mar-i-a
Ab.	rēg-i-bu-s	corpor-i-bu-s	cîv-i-bu-s	urb-i-bu-s	mar-i-bu-s

Fourth   Fifth

	frŭctus, -ūs m., 'fruit'	cornū, -ūs n., 'horn'	di-ē-s, diêî m., 'day'
SING.			
N.	frŭct-u-s	corn-ū	di-ē-s
G.	frŭct-ū-s	corn-ū-s	di-ē-î
D.	frŭct-u-î	corn-ū	di-ē-î
A.	frŭct-u-m	corn-ū	di-e-m
Ab.	frŭct-ū	corn-ū	di-ē
PLU			
N.	frŭct-ū-s	corn-u-a	di-ē-s
G.	frŭct-u-um	corn-u-um	di-ē-r-um
D.	frŭct-i-bu-s	corn-i-bu-s	di-ē-bu-s
A.	frŭct-ū-s	corn-u-a	di-ē-s
Ab.	frŭct-i-bu-s	corn-i-bu-s	di-ē-bu-s

Let us begin with an analysis of the suffixes characterizing Latin inflectional morphology (cf. Halle and Vaux 1997). Each word class is characterized by a common vocalic element that is traditionally called the thematic vowel. The thematic vowels of Latin are given in (6.8):

(6.8) TV → a in the env. [I]
       TV → o in the env. [II]
       TV → i in the env. [III]
       TV → u in the env. [IV]
       TV → eː in the env. [V]

Various processes of lengthening, lowering, raising and deletion affecting the thematic vowel must be unparsed (cf. 31–33).

Once we subtract the thematic vowel from the desinences, we obtain the different case endings. They are listed in (6.9–6.10).

(6.9) Singular:

	a-stems	o-stems	C-stems	mixed	i-stems	u-stems	ē-stems
NOM	-Ø	-s	-s		-s	-s	-s
GEN	-iː	-iː	-s		-s	-s	-s
DAT	-iː	-Ø	-iː		-iː	-iː	-iː
ACC	-m	-m	-m		-m	-m	-m
ABL	-Ø	-Ø	-Ø		-Ø	-Ø	-Ø

(6.10) Plural:

	a-stems	o-stems	C-stems	mixed	i-stems	u-stems	ē-stems
NOM	-iː	-iː	-s		-s	-s	-s
GEN	-r-um	-r-um	-um		-um	-um	-um
ACC	-s	-s	-s		-s	-s	-s
DAT	-iː-s	-iː-s	-bu-s		-bu-s	-bu-s	bu-s

Given the constituent structure in (6.11) produced by the morphology (see Calabrese 1998 for discussion) the suffixes in (6.9–6.10) are inserted in the fused case-number terminal node.

(6.11) [[[stem] + Thematic Vowel]$_N$ + Number-Case]$_N$

Let us now turn to the syncretisms we observe in the Latin system. I consider only the basic cases we find in Indo-European languages and omit from the analysis cases such as the comitative, the purposive, or the locational cases such as the allative, elative that were never morphologically realized in these languages. First of all, there is absolute syncretism between ablative and instrumental. The instrumental is not morphologically realized in Latin, and the ablative is used to represent the grammatical function of the instrumental:

(6.12) *occidere gladio* 'to kill with a sword'

The locative is also not morphologically realized in Latin. I consider the absolute syncretism that we observe in this case below.

Secondly, we also observe various cases of contextual syncretism, among which are:

(6.13) (i)   between nominative and accusative in neuters

(ii) between the genitive and the dative in the singular of I and V declensions

(iii)   between the dative and the ablative in the II declension

(iv)   between the dative and the ablative in the plural of all declensions

(v)   between nominative and accusative in the plural of III, IV, V declensions

In the analysis developed below in sections 6.3.2 and 6.3.3, contextual syncretism is accounted for by the feature assignments of the exponents or of morphophonological changes, while absolute syncretism involves changing the feature bundles of the terminal nodes of the morphology.

The difference between these two types of syncretism is shown in concord. In Latin adjectives agree with their head noun in case, number, and gender. Adjectives belong either to the first and second declensions (e.g., *bonus* (masc), *bona* (fem), *bonum* (neuter)) or to the third (e.g., *tristis* (masc and fem., third declension adjectives do not distinguish gender), *triste* (neuter)). Now, when an adjective makes more distinctions than the noun it modifies, the appropriate case form of the adjective is chosen. Thus, we have the following situation (*tristis* III decl., *puella, puellae* I decl., *rex, regis* III decl., *diēs, diēi* V decl.):

(6.14)   Genitive: *tristis puellae / regis / diei* 'of the sad girl/king/day'

(6.15)   Dative: *tristī puellae / regī/ diei* 'to the sad girl/king/day'

In the word form *puellae* of I declension, for instance, there is contextual syncretism between genitive and dative: the ending of /-ae/ can realize the genitive or the dative. If it is modified by a third declension adjective like *tristis*, which distinguishes between genitive *tristis* and dative *tristī*, the form of the adjective which is appropriate to the syntactic context is chosen. Therefore, we have to say that concord copies only the features of the terminal node of the morphosyntax, i.e., the output of absolute syncretism.[6] The presence of contextual syncretism–a type of syncretism that is determined by lexical features such as declensional class membership–in the forms of the head noun does not matter.

One outstanding problem of Latin grammar involves deciding whether or not there is a locative case. For now I will show that a solution of this problem can be found only if we rely on the notion of absolute syncretism. Later in section 6.3.4.2, I will propose a formal analysis of what happens in this case.

---

[6] Since absolute syncretism is a post-syntactic operation, it follows that the operation of adjectival concord we see here must also be post-syntactic. The consequences of this result cannot be discussed here since they are not directly relevant to the topic of this chapter. I leave this issue to future research.

Location in Latin is normally expressed by the ablative and usually governed by the preposition *in*. However, with singular names of towns and small islands, where no preposition is used, location is expressed by case forms identical to the genitive/dative of names belonging to the first or second declension singular: *Rōmae* 'at Roma', *Milēti* 'at Miletus' (and nouns such as *proximae* 'in proximity'). There are a few third declension singular names with forms the same as the dative: *Karthāgini* 'in Carthage' (although the ablative *Karthāgine* is an alternative). There is also *rūri* (third declension) 'in the country' and *domi* 'at home'. *Domus* 'home' has a mixture of second and fourth declension forms. In all of these cases we can say that we are dealing with the vocabulary item /-i:/ identical to that of the dative-genitive singular (see (6.26)).

Since the expression of location involves different patterns of syncretism in different declensions, we could assume the following: 1) Latin has a locative case; 2) there is contextual syncretism between this case and the genitive/dative in singular nouns of towns and small islands (in addition to *rūri* and *domi*, *proximae*.) In all other nouns and in the plural nouns, instead, there would be contextual syncretism between the locative and the ablative.

This hypothesis, however, is easily rejected when we consider concord in the phrases in (6.16):

(6.16)   *meae domi (Pl. Au 432)* 'at my home'   vs. *villā meā*
           domi suae (Cic. N.D. 381) 'at his home' vs. *urbe copiosā*
           'at my villa'
           'in a wealthy town'
           proximae viciniae habitat (Pl. Ba 205–6) 'he lives very close'

Consider the first two phrases *meae domi* and *villā meā*. The case form *villā* is ablative; *domi* is a genitive/dative "locative".

If we account for the contrast between *domi* and *villā* in terms of contextual syncretism, we are assuming that both forms are inserted in a terminal node characterized by the same feature bundle, the locative in this case. Therefore, we expect only one form of the adjective to appear insofar as concord depends only of the features of the terminal node. However, then we have to explain the opposition between the two forms of the adjective: *meae*, which is required by *domi*, and *meā*, which is required by *villā*. They cannot be due to contextual syncretism since, as shown in (6.13), contextual syncretism patterns found in the head noun are not transmitted to the modifying adjective. Therefore, we have to conclude that the contrast between *domi* and *villā* must be accounted for by changing the feature bundle of the terminal node of the head noun. We are dealing with a case of absolute syncretism.

6.3 Analysis

6.3.1 *Features, morphological contrast and the notion of paradigm*

All possible morphological contrasts in any language must be expressible in terms of features. These "morphosyntactic" features are universal; the human mind is one and categorizes life experience and reality in the same way. These features provide a range of possible feature combinations that languages can make use of. Therefore, I assume that if a language has a particular morphological contrast, this contrast must be expressible in terms of these universal features. This also holds for unusual morphological properties. Take an unusual case such as the "evitative" found in Australian languages (Blake 1994) or the contrast between the "reportative" and the "eyewitness" past tense in Turkish; they must be accounted for by reducing them to known features or a new universal feature must be introduced. It is the duty of markedness theory to account for why these morphological categories are rarely used across languages. It is the same in phonology. All possible phonological contrasts in any language must be expressible in terms of universal features. Suppose that we observe a phonological contrast between two segments in a particular language, say between the protruded round front vowel /y/ and the non-protruded rounded front vowel [ʉ] of Swedish. If we cannot reduce this contrast to an already known feature, i.e., to the feature [ATR], for example, we have to postulate a new feature, [Lip Protrusion] and assume that this feature belongs to UG. Markedness theory must then account for why this feature is rarely used across languages.

Before introducing the feature system used in this chapter to account for cases, I want to look into the formal conditions under which morphological features determine morphological contrast. Consider three features X, Z, Y, of a given terminal node of the morphosyntax in a language L. We have the combinations in (6.17):

$$(6.17) \quad \begin{array}{cccccccc} | & | & | & | & | & | & | & | \\ +X & +X & -X & -X & +X & +X & -X & -X \\ +Z & -Z & +Z & -Z & +Z & -Z & +Z & -Z \\ +Y & +Y & +Y & +Y & -Y & -Y & -Y & -Y \end{array}$$

Assume that each terminal node in (6.17) has a different exponent as in (6.18) (where $\Phi_n \neq \Phi_{n+1}$):

$$(6.18) \quad \begin{array}{cccccccc} | & | & | & | & | & | & | & | \\ +X & +X & -X & -X & +X & +X & -X & -X \\ +Z & -Z & +Z & -Z & +Z & -Z & +Z & -Z \\ +Y & +Y & +Y & +Y & -Y & -Y & -Y & -Y \\ \Phi_1 & \Phi_2 & \Phi_3 & \Phi_4 & \Phi_5 & \Phi_6 & \Phi_7 & \Phi_8 \end{array}$$

A morphological contrast exists in a language under the following condition:

(6.19)   A morphological feature X is contrastive in L

(i.)   if there is at least a phonological exponent S in L, where S is inserted in a terminal node containing $[aX, \beta Z]$ and there is a phonological exponent T $(S \neq T)$ where T is inserted in a terminal node containing $[-aX, \beta Z]$; or

(ii.)   there is at least one readjustment rule in L that includes either $[aX]$ or $[-aX]$ in its structural description (see later discussion).

The vocabulary items and the outputs of the readjustment rules associated with contrastive morphosyntactic features are the *morphological realizations* of these features.

Because of (6.19), all of the features in (6.18) are contrastive and $\{\Phi^1, \ldots \Phi^8\}$ are the morphological realizations of the features $\{X, Y, Z\}$. Let us exemplify (6.19) in the case of the case systems discussed above.

I assume the following case feature system (see Appendix for discussion).

(6.20)

	Nom.	Acc.	Gen.	Dat.	Loc.	Abl.	Inst.
Peripheral	−	−	+	+	+	+	+
Source	−	−	+	−	−	+	−
Location	−	−	−	−	+	+	+
Motion	−	+	−	+	−	+	+

Given the case features in (6.20), the presence of the exponent /-Ø/ in the singular oblique of *chien-/-Ø/* (as opposed to /-s/ of *chien-s* in the oblique plural, in the nominative singular/plural) indicates that the features [motion] and [plural] are contrastive in Old French. The oblique, i.e, the non-nominative case, is [+motion]. The cases of Sanskrit and Latin are obviously more complex. The same is true for Classical Greek. If we consider the ablative forms of Latin and Sanskrit, we need to say that the features [source, location] and [motion] are contrastive in both languages. In the case of the dative in Classical Greek only the feature [source] is contrastive. Observe that in Latin it is not the presence of actual idiosyncratic exponents that make the features [source, location] and [motion] contrastive but the presence of the readjustment rules of lengthening and lowering which apply to the thematic vowels in singular ablative forms (see (6.31) below).

Given the notions just introduced, the notion of paradigm can now be formally defined: a paradigm is the set of the morphological realizations of the contrastive features of a given terminal node of the morphosyntax. Thus, $(\Phi^1, \ldots \Phi^8\}$ is the paradigm formed by the features $\{X, Y, Z\}$ in (6.18).

6.3.2 *Vocabulary items and contextual syncretism*

In the case systems considered before, there is contextual syncretism: the phonological exponents of the different terminal nodes in a paradigm are often identical. In Distributed Morphology, the phonological exponents of the different morphemes are listed in the vocabulary as parts of the vocabulary items. A vocabulary item consists of a phonological exponent and an associated set of features that governs its insertion in the terminal nodes of the morphosyntax. A fundamental hypothesis in DM is that only a subset of the morphological features provided by the terminal nodes of the morphosyntax is required for selecting the correct phonological exponent, i.e., vocabulary items must be underspecified. The principle that governs feature assignments to vocabulary items, originally proposed in Calabrese (1998), is given in (6.21):[7]

(6.21)   For each vocabulary item I in a paradigm P, the minimal set of features able to account for the maximal distribution of I in P is assigned to I.

Once the feature assignments of the vocabulary items is determined, we can account for how their phonological exponents are inserted in the terminal nodes of the morphosyntax. This insertion is governed by the Subset Principle (6.22):

(6.22)   The phonological exponent of a Vocabulary item is inserted into a morpheme in the terminal string if the item matches all or a subset of the grammatical features specified in the terminal morpheme. Insertion does not take place if the Vocabulary item contains features not present in the morpheme. Where several Vocabulary items meet the conditions for insertion, the item matching the greatest number of features specified in the terminal morpheme must be chosen. (Halle 1997)

Given (6.22), only the phonological exponent /-Ø/ of Old French in (6.1) needs to be maximally specified as in (6.23). The exponent /-s/ instead will not have any features; it is what is called the elsewhere item, the item whose distribution cannot be captured by any subset of the features relevant for the other items of the list. This item will be inserted when no other item of the list can be inserted.

(6.23)   Old French:

      a.   Ø ↔ [+motion, −plural]

      b. /-s/ ↔ Ø (Elsewhere)

---

[7] Adger (2005) proposes a similar approach to the assignment of feature specifications to lexical items. According to him, they are assigned by a procedure governed by "an evaluation metric [seeking] maximal generalizations (hence minimally specified lexical items)" (Adger 2005: 18).

In the case of Sanskrit /a/-declension, we need the vocabulary items in (6.24):[8]

(6.24)   Sanskrit:

a. /-bhyam/ ↔ [+peripheral, +motion, −singular, −plural] (D,A&I Du)
b. /-yaus/   ↔ [+peripheral, −singular, −plural]   (G&LDu)
c. /-u/   ↔ [−singular, −plural]   (N&ADu)
d. /-is/   ↔ [−source, +location, +motion, +plural]   (IPl)
e. /-su/   ↔ [+peripheral, +location, −motion, +plural]   (LPl)
f. /-bhyas/ ↔ [+peripheral, +motion, +plural]   (D&AblPl)
g. /-naːm/   ↔ [+source, −location, +plural]   (GPl)
h. /-n/   ↔ [+motion, +plural]   (APl)
i. /-ina/   ↔ [−source, +location, +motion]   (ISg)
j. /-ya/   ↔ [+peripheral, −source, −location]   (DSg)
k. /-t/   ↔ [+source, +location]   (AblSg)
l. /-i/   ↔ [+peripheral, +location]   (LSg)
m. /-sya/   ↔ [+source]   (GSg)
n. /-m/   ↔ [+motion]   (ASg)
p. /-s/   ↔ Ø   (NSg &P)

For the Classical Greek /o/-declension, we need the vocabulary items in (6.25):[9]

(6.25)   Classical Greek:

a. /-in/ ↔ [+peripheral, −singular, −plural]   (G&DDu)
b. /-Ø/   ↔ [−singular, −plural]   (N&ADu)
c. /-is/ ↔ [+peripheral, −source, +plural]   (DPl)

---

[8] I assume that the dual is characterized by the feature specifications [−singular, −plural], the singular is [+singular, −plural], the Plural [−singular, +plural]. The combination [+singular, +plural] is not allowed.

[9] The somewhat simpler list of vocabulary items in (i) can be proposed if we segment the endings /-is/ of the dative plural and /-ns/ of the accusative plural into /-i+s/ and /-n+s/, respectively. Under this analysis, we can extract the /-n/ of the accusative singular and the /-i/ of the dative singular from their respective plural counterparts. The remaining /s/ would be the elsewhere /-s/ in (6.25j.) which could fill an extra insertion site created by fission (see Halle and Vaux 1998 for a similar analysis for Latin /-bu-s/ and /-r-um < s-um/)).

(i) Greek :
   a. /-in/ ↔ [+peripheral, −singular, −plural] (G&DDu)
   b. /-Ø/   ↔ [−singular, −plural]   (N&ADu)
   c. /-ɔːn/ ↔ [+peripheral, +plural]   (GPl)
   d. /-i/   ↔ [+peripheral, −source]   (D)
   e. /-i/   ↔ [+plural]   (NPl)
   f. /-io/ ↔ [+peripheral]   (GSg)
   g. /-n/   ↔ [+motion]   (A)
   h. /-s/   ↔ Ø   (NSg)

d. /-ɔːn/   ↔   [+peripheral, +plural]   (GPl)
e. /-ns/   ↔   [+motion, +plural]   (ASg)
f. /-i/   ↔   [+plural]   (NPl)
g. /-i/   ↔   [+peripheral, −source]   (DSg)
h. /-io/   ↔   [+peripheral]   (GSg)
i. /-n/   ↔   [+motion]   (ASg)
l. /-s/   ↔   Ø   (NSg)

The vocabulary items for all Latin declensions are listed in (6.26):

(6.26)
a. /-um/   ↔   [+peripheral, −motion, +plural]   (GPl)
b. /-iː/   ↔   [−peripheral, −motion, +plural]/[−neut, I, II] +_   (NPl I, II)
c. /-bu-/ ↔   [+peripheral, +motion, +plural]/[III, IV, V] +_   (D&AbPl. III-V)
d. /iː/   ↔   [+peripheral, −location, −plural]   (G&DSg)
e. /a/   ↔   [−peripheral, +plural]/[+neuter]+_   (N&APl. Nt)
f. /-m/   ↔   [+motion, −plural]   (ASg)
g. Ø   ↔   [−plural]   (Sg default)
h. /s/   ↔   [Ø]   Elsewhere

The ending [r-um](<-s-um) and [bu-s] are produced by a fission process whose discussion I omit here (see Halle and Vaux 1998, 228–29 for details).

The fact that /s/ is the elsewhere case in Latin allows us to account for the shape of the nominative and genitive singular. According to the list in (6.26), in these cases we should always expect the null exponent Ø, the default ending of the singular in the case of the nominative, and the morpheme /iː/ in the case of the genitive singular. This is not what we observe in the nominative of the II–IV declensions and in the genitive of the III–IV declensions. Following Halle and Vaux (1998), in these cases morphological impoverishment prevents the insertion of this exponent by deleting the feature [−pl][10]

(6.27)   a. The feature [−plural] is deleted in the nominative of the II, III–IV declensions.

         b. The feature [−plural] is deleted in the genitive of III–IV declensions.

Impoverishment operates in the following way. The terminal node of a genitive singular of the third declension nominal in Latin morphosyntax is given

---

[10] In Calabrese (2002), I propose a different approach to impoverishment. According to that proposal, impoverishment does not involve deletion of a feature but simply an operation that makes a given feature temporarily inaccessible during a certain insertion cycle. Therefore, during that cycle, a vocabulary item characterized by that feature cannot be inserted and a less specified item must be instead inserted, as in the traditional DM account. However, that feature can be accessed in later insertion cycles, and therefore it can be used by other vocabulary items or by other readjustment rules. (See Calabrese 2002 for examples and more discussion).

in (6.28). In (6.28) the vocabulary item in (6.26d.), i.e, /iː/↔[+peripheral, −location, −plural], should be inserted.

(6.28)   a.

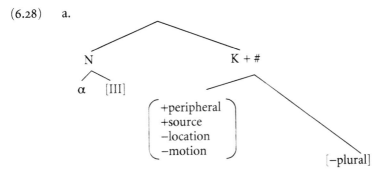

Given (6.27b.), the feature [−plural] is deleted as in (6.29). Therefore, neither the null morpheme Ø or the morpheme /iː/ of the list in (6.26) can be inserted in these cases. The elsewhere case /-s/ is instead inserted as in (6.28b.):

(6.28)   b.

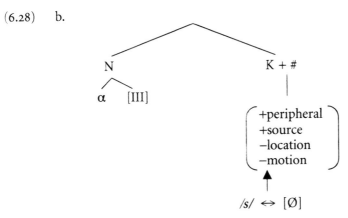

Another impoverishment operation is needed to account for the insertion of /Ø/ in the dative singular of the II declension.

(6.29)   a.   The feature [−location] is deleted in the environment [__ +peripheral] of the II declension.

b.   The feature [−location] is deleted in the environment [__ +peripheral] of the neuters of the IV declension.

Assuming the vocabulary items in (6.26) and impoverishment, we have an account of contextual syncretism in the Latin case endings.

In addition, a set of readjustment rules is needed to account for the surface shape of the Latin case forms. This is of particular relevance here to account for how the ablative is morphologically realized in Latin. The different forms of the ablative are provided below:

(6.30) a.

	First	Second	Third	Third	Fourth	Fifth
	porta, -ae	*amîcus, -î*	*rēx, regis*	*mare, -is*	*frūctus,-ūs*	*di-ē-s, ē î*
	f., 'gate'	m., 'friend'	m., 'king'	n., 'sea'	m., 'fruit'	m.'day'
SING.						
Ab.	*port-ā*	*amîc-ō*	*rēg-e*	*mar-î*	*frūct-ū*	*di-ē*
PLU.						
Ab.	*port-î-s*	*amîc-î-s*	*rēg-i-bu-s*	*mar-i-bu-s*	*frūct-i-bu-s*	*di-ē-bu-s*

Given the analysis just proposed in (6.26), the case forms in (6.29) should have the shape in (6.30b.) where Ø is the default exponent of the singular and /-s/ is the elsewhere item. The complex ending /-bu-s/ is created through fission (not discussed here; see Halle and Vaux 1997 for more details):

(6.30) b.

SING.

Ab.	*port-a-Ø*	*amîc-o-Ø*	*rēg-i-Ø*	*mar-i-Ø*	*frūct-u-Ø*	*di-ē-Ø*

PLU.

Ab.	*port-a-s*	*amîc-o-s*	*rēg-i-bu-s*	*mar-i-bu-s*	*frūct-u-bu-s*	*di-ē-bu-s*

The following readjustment rules (Halle 1997) account for the surface shape we observe in (6.29):

(6.31) a. Rules lengthening the thematic vowel:

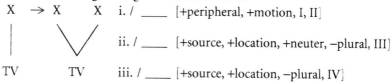

i. / _____ [+peripheral, +motion, I, II]

ii. / _____ [+source, +location, +neuter, −plural, III]

iii. / _____ [+source, +location, −plural, IV]

b. A rule fronting the thematic vowel of the dative/ablative in the I, II, and IV plural:

$$X \rightarrow X \quad / \underline{\quad\quad} \text{[+peripheral, +motion, +plural, I, II, IV]}$$
$$|\qquad\; |$$
$$\text{TV}\quad \text{TV} \searrow$$
$$\text{[−back]}$$
$$\text{[+high]}$$

c. A rule lowering the thematic /i/ in the ablative in the non-neuters of the III declension:

[−back] → [−high]/ [TV_____][+source, +location, −neuter, −plural, III]

6.3.3 *Absolute syncretism*

6.3.3.1 *The basic idea* Let us turn to the issue of absolute syncretism. In the model I put forth here, after the mapping of syntactic grammatical relations and thematic roles into case features, we first establish what feature combinations are contrastively realized in the morphology. Only these feature combinations are relevant in the analysis of the system; all other combinations are not relevant–i.e., not used in the morphology. I will assume that they are disallowed by specific morphological constraints that will be discussed below. The disallowed feature combinations are then removed by featural repairs that change them into allowed combinations. These repairs are the processes that bring about absolute syncretism.[11] The feature specifications of vocabulary items and of the structural description of readjustment rules is established only by considering the relevant (allowed) feature combinations. The consequence of this is that only patterns of contextual syncretism, and not of absolute syncretism, are considered in the determination of these feature specifications. This is the analysis proposed above for the Old French, Sanskrit, Classical Greek, and Latin vocabulary items which was based on the tacit assumption that the only case feature combinations that ought to be considered in establishing the pattern of distribution of the different items are those in (6.32). The feature systems in (6.32) include only the feature specifications that are morphologically contrastive in the respective languages:

(6.32)   i.   For Old French:

	Nom.	Acc.
Peripheral	–	–
Source	–	–
Location	–	–
Motion	–	+

ii.   For Sanskrit:

	Nom.	Acc.	Gen.	Dat.	Loc.	Abl.	Inst.
Peripheral	–	–	+	+	+	+	+
Source	–	–	+	–	–	+	–
Location	–	–	–	–	+	+	+
Motion	–	+	–	+	–	+	+

---

[11] An alternative model in which all possible feature combinations mapped from syntax are accessed during vocabulary insertion and where absolute syncretism is accounted for by assigning common feature specifications to the syncretic cases directly in the mapping from syntax to morphology will be discussed later in section 6.4.

iii. For Classical Greek:

	Nom.	Acc.	Gen.	Dat.
Peripheral	–	–	+	+
Source	–	–	+	–
Location	–	–	–	–
Motion	–	+	–	+

iv. For Latin:

	Nom.	Acc.	Gen.	Dat.	Abl.
Peripheral	–	–	+	+	+
Source	–	–	+	–	+
Location	–	–	–	–	+
Motion	–	+	–	+	+

In this way, all irrelevant non-contrastive feature combinations are eliminated and vocabulary items need to refer only to the limited set of contrastive features. A simplification of the feature specifications of the vocabulary items can, therefore, be achieved. Notice that such simplification cannot be obtained in a model such as that discussed below in section 6.4 in which all features specifications mapped from the syntax are accessed regardless of whether or not they are contrastive.

The issue is then to account for the different patterns of absolute syncretism: in the case of the oblique in Old French we have absolute syncretism among the accusative, the dative, the genitive, the ablative, the locative, and the instrumental; in the case of the dative of Classical Greek we have absolute syncretism among the dative, the locative, and the instrumental, whereas in the case of the genitive, that between the genitive and the ablative; in the case of Latin, we have absolute syncretism ablative–instrumental, locative–dative, or locative–ablative.

Consider Classical Greek. Given the universal set of features mapped from the syntax into the morphology (see (6.33)), I assume that there are feature-changing operations–similar to the rules of referral of Zwicky (1985) and Stump (1993)–which change the feature bundle of the instrumental and the locative of (6.33) into that of the dative, and the feature bundle of the ablative in (6.33) into that of the genitive. As discussed below in section 6.3.4.2, these operations–the operations that lead to absolute syncretism–are repairs triggered by the negative constraints on case feature combinations. We thus obtain (6.32iii.). The same occurs in Old French: these repair operations change the feature bundles of the dative, the genitive, the ablative, the locative, and the instrumental into that of the accusative (see 6.3.4.2 below for discussion of

Latin and a detailed analysis of absolute syncretism in Classical Greek and Old French).

(6.33)		Nom.	Acc.	Gen.	Dat.	Loc.	Abl.	Inst.
	Peripheral	−	−	+	+	+	+	+
	Source	−	−	+	−	−	+	−
	Location	−	−	−	−	+	+	+
	Motion	−	+	−	+	−	+	+

For example, consider the Greek instrumental construction in (6.34a.) τοῖς ὀφθαλμοῖς 'with the eyes'. It contains the case form /-is/ which is identical to that found in the dative construction in (6.34b.). I assume that in both cases we have the same case terminal nodes in (6.35) in the morphosyntax. As discussed below, these two terminal nodes are initially different–with instrumental feature specifications in (6.36a.) and dative ones in (6.36b.)–when case features are mapped from the syntax into the morphosyntax. However, the instrumental in (6.36a.) is then changed into the dative in (6.36b.) by the feature change in (6.36c.) before vocabulary item insertion, as discussed below in section 6.3.4.2.

(6.34)   a.   τοῖς ὀφθαλμοῖς ὁρῶμεν 'we see with the eyes'
             the-PlDat. eye-PlDat. see-1pl.

         b.   τοῖς θεοῖς ευχομαι 'we pray to the gods'
             the-PlDat. god-PlDat pray-1pl.

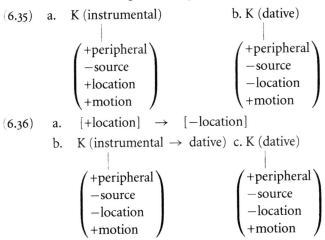

(6.35)   a.   K (instrumental)   b. K (dative)

$$\begin{pmatrix} +\text{peripheral} \\ -\text{source} \\ +\text{location} \\ +\text{motion} \end{pmatrix} \qquad \begin{pmatrix} +\text{peripheral} \\ -\text{source} \\ -\text{location} \\ +\text{motion} \end{pmatrix}$$

(6.36)   a.   [+location] → [−location]

         b.   K (instrumental → dative) c. K (dative)

$$\begin{pmatrix} +\text{peripheral} \\ -\text{source} \\ -\text{location} \\ +\text{motion} \end{pmatrix} \qquad \begin{pmatrix} +\text{peripheral} \\ -\text{source} \\ -\text{location} \\ +\text{motion} \end{pmatrix}$$

Before discussing the nature of the constraints that govern case paradigms and detailing the repair operations that these constraints trigger, I want to exclude a possible account for absolute syncretism based on the notion of underspecification. This is done in the next subsection.

6.3.3.2 *Against underspecification of absent cases*   Before going on, I want to reject the hypothesis that the structure of a morphological paradigm with its patterns of absolute syncretism is accounted for by underspecifying morphosyntactic representations. This underspecification could be obtained by assuming that only the features of morphologically realized cases are active, and specified, in morphosyntactic representations. In contrast, those of the case that are not morphologically realized–i.e, those that undergo absolute syncretism–would be not active, and therefore left unspecified. This is a commonly accepted, albeit implicit, hypothesis: when traditional grammars state that Classical Greek has only four cases the implicit assumption is that the missing cases are simply not generated in the morphosyntax. This hypothesis has never been thought through adequately in the light of absolute syncretism patterns.

Let us consider Classical Greek. In Classical Greek we have four cases: the nominative, the accusative, the genitive, and the dative. We could account for this four-case system by assuming that only the features of these cases, but not of cases such as the ablative, the locative, the instrumental, etc., are specified in morphosyntactic representations. The featural representations of the cases are given in (6.37) where I assume the minimal amount of specifications:

(6.37)   Feature specifications of Classical Greek morphosyntactic representations (with underspecification):

	Nom.	Acc.	Gen.	Dat.	Loc.	Abl.	Inst. ...
Peripheral			+	+			
Motion		+		+			

Given (6.37), the relevant vocabulary items of the Classical Greek *o*-declension could be specified as follows:

(6.38)   Classical Greek:
   a. /*-in*/   ↔   [+peripheral, −singular, −plural]   (G&DDu)
   b. /*-Ø*/   ↔   [−singular, −plural]   (N&ADu)
   c. /*-is*/   ↔   [+peripheral, +motion, +plural]   (DPl)
   d. /*-ɔːn*/   ↔   [+peripheral, +plural]   (GPl)
   e. /*-ns*/   ↔   [+motion, +plural]   (ASg)
   f. /*-i*/   ↔   [+plural]   (NPl)
   g. /*-i*/   ↔   [+peripheral, +motion]   (DSg)
   h. /*-io*/   ↔   [+peripheral]   (GSg)
   i. /*-n*/   ↔   [+motion]   (ASg)
   j. /*-s*/   ↔   Ø   (NSg)

But, as already mentioned, in Classical Greek there is absolute syncretism between the genitive and the ablative, and between the dative, the locative, and the instrumental. This means that we have to insert the vocabulary items in (6.38c.) and (6.38g.)–the "dative endings"–also into the case terminal nodes of phrases with the syntactic functions of "instrumental" and "locative", and the vocabulary items in (6.38d.) and (6.38i.)–the "genitive" endings–also into the case terminal nodes of phrases with the syntactic functions of "ablative." However, given (6.37) and (6.38), this is not what we obtain. Instead, we predict insertion of (6.38j.)–the elsewhere ending. Playing with the feature specifications in (6.38) will not solve this problem: given that the case terminal nodes of the instrumental, locative, and ablative do not contain feature specifications, they will always be assigned the elsewhere case ending, contrary to the facts. Eliminating the elsewhere item in (6.38), together with assigning a feature specification to the nominative in (6.37) (say [−motion]) does not solve the problem either. If we do that, the result is that no vocabulary item would be inserted in the terminal nodes of the instrumental, locative, and ablative, which is again contrary to the facts. It follows that we cannot leave unspecified the terminal nodes of these syntactic functions. I assume that morphosyntactic representations are always fully specified. Only vocabulary items can be underspecified to account for distribution in paradigms and for the patterns of contextual syncretisms.

6.3.4 *Markedness theory and case systems*

6.3.4.1 *Morphological markedness* Before turning to an analysis of absolute syncretism, I need to discuss the issue of morphological markedness. The main proposal put forth here, in fact, assumes that the processes leading to absolute syncretism are due to markedness effects. It is a fact that the exponents[12] of certain morphological categories are more likely to disappear and be replaced by other exponents by absolute syncretism. I assume that these categories are to be characterized as being morphologically marked. Greenberg (1963) observes that languages seem to prefer affixal realization for categories such as the singular (here [+singular, −plural] in terms of features) or the plural ([−singular, +plural]) but not for the [dual] (−singular, −plural). I assume that this fact must be dealt with by a theory of morphological markedness. This theory should identify certain morphological features or combinations of morphological features as marked. I assume that the realization of marked morphological configurations as affixes with an idiosyncratic exponence is costly. Assuming that a general principle of economy governs language (see Calabrese 2005), languages should tend to avoid these costly morphological configurations. For example, although the

---

[12] Notice that with the term "exponent" here I am simplifying a little insofar as, in addition to exponents, morphophonological changes triggered by morphological features–i.e., readjustment processes (see section 6.3.2)— must also be included in the processes of absolute syncretism.

dual (featurally [−singular, −plural]) is morphologically realized with an idiosyncratic exponence in languages such as Classical Greek and Sanskrit, the common situation is that of Latin and Old French where plural forms are simply used for this number. Languages with a dual are much less common than languages without one. I assume that this is a markedness effect.

As for case systems, Blake (1994) observes that there are clear implicational relationships between the different cases. An implicational hierarchy of cases is given in (6.39). If we assume that the presence of more marked entities implies the presence of less marked ones, as originally proposed by Jakobson (1941), the hierarchy in (6.39) tells us that the nominative is the least marked case and the locative the most marked one:[13, 14]

(6.39)   NOM < ACC < GEN < DAT < ABL < INST < LOC < OTHERS

The implicational hierarchy in (6.39) is supported by the typology of case systems in (6.40).

(6.40)   Case systems:
    a.   Two cases:
        NOM - ACC(Obl) (e.g., in Old French, Chemehuevi, Kabardian)
    b.   Three cases:
        NOM - ACC - GEN (e.g., in Classical Arabic, Modern Greek)
    c.   Four cases:
        NOM - ACC - GEN - DAT (e.g., in Classical Greek, Nuer)
    d.   Five cases:
        NOM - ACC - GEN - DAT - ABL(Obl) (e.g., in Latin)
        NOM - ACC - GEN - DAT - INST(Obl) (e.g., in O. H. German)
    e.   Six cases:
        NOM - ACC - GEN - DAT - ABL - LOC (e.g., in Turkish)
        NOM - ACC - GEN - DAT - INST - LOC (e.g., in Slavic lgs)
    f.   Seven cases:
        NOM - ACC - GEN - DAT - ABL - INST - LOC (e.g., in Sanskrit, C. Armenian)

---

[13] See 6.3.4.2 for brief discussion of the ergative case.

[14] The implicational hierarchy in (6.39) is different from that proposed by Blake (1994). First of all, I propose that the locative is more marked than the ablative and the instrumental. Evidence for this is provided by the systems in (6.40) that show that it is the presence of the locative that implies the presence of the ablative and the instrumental and not vice versa. Secondly, to avoid ambiguity, I assume that each case can imply only one other case. No branching in the hierarchy is allowed. This assumption forces me to decide which case between the ablative and the instrumental is less marked. I propose that it is the ablative to be the least marked of the two. This hypothesis must be tested by further research.

g. Systems with more cases may include differentiations in the local cases (allative/perlative, etc.), the comitative, the purposive, the comparative, and some other special cases: e.g., Tamil:
NOM - ACC - GEN - DAT - LOC - ABL - INST - COM
Toda:
NOM - ACC - GEN - DAT - LOC - ABL - INST - COM - PURP

Languages seem to prefer idiosyncratic case-marking for grammatical relations such as subject and object but not for grammatical relations expressing location or instrument. In terms of the theory of morphological markedness, cases such as the ablative, locative, instrumental, or the comitative and purposive are morphologically marked so that their realization as affixes with an idiosyncratic exponence tends to be avoided.

6.3.4.2 *A theory of morphological markedness, morphological repairs and an analysis of absolute syncretism* I assume that languages differ in their exploitation of morphological features and combinations of morphological features, just as languages differ in their exploitation of phonological features. Given a language L, the morphological features–or better the combinations of morphological features–that can appear in merged terminal nodes characterizing affixes are limited.

I propose that the restrictions on the exploitation of features in the terminal nodes of the morphosyntax result from constraints on combinations of morphological features (see the seminal work of Noyer 1992 on this issue). These feature constraints target the feature combinations of terminal nodes merged with stems into words.

Many feature combinations are excluded by universal prohibitions. Prohibitions are always active across languages. (I mark them with two asterisks.)

(6.41)   **[+singular, +plural]

Other combinations are excluded by marking statements that characterize as costly the morphological realization of certain feature combinations as affixes. Marking statements may be active or deactivated on a language-specific basis. If a marking statement is active, the relevant combination of features must be changed.

I assume that the following marking statement characterizes morphological realization of duality in affixes as costly.

(6.42)   *[−singular, −plural]/ [[ ]$_{root}$ (...)+ ___]$_w$

In Latin (and Old French) the marking statement in (6.42) is active. In contrast, (6.42) is deactivated in Classical Greek or Sanskrit. In Latin (and Old

French) only the unmarked configuration [+singular, −plural], [−singular, +plural] are morphologically realized in merged terminal nodes as affixes.

Calabrese (1998) proposed that each case is characteristically identified by a marking condition that constrains a case features combination (a case restriction from now on; see (6.43)). These case restrictions represent case feature combinations whose affixal realization is marked as costly. These case restrictions may be active or inactive in a language. If a case restriction is active in a language the relevant case is not present in the language. If it is inactive, the relevant case is present. The case restrictions are organized hierarchically. The lower a restriction in the hierarchy, the more probable is that it is active across languages. Thus the restriction characterizing the instrumental is in a low position in the hierarchy. This expresses the fact that the instrumental is more rarely found across languages. In their natural state, case restrictions are active. A case restriction is deactivated in a language L only if there is evidence that the relevant case is morphologically realized in L. Furthermore, I assume that a case restriction can be deactivated in a language only if case restrictions in higher position in the hierarchy are also deactivated. Nominative–accusative systems are characterized by the activity of the case restriction in (6.45a.) disallowing the ergative. Ergative systems are instead characterized by the activity of the case restriction in (6.45b.) disallowing the nominative.[15]

(6.43)   The case restrictions:

a. i.   *Locative: *[+location, −source]/[_____, −motion]
    ii. *Instrumental: *[−source, +location]/[_____, +motion]
    iii. *Ablative: *[+location, +source]
    iv   *Dative: *[−location, −source] /[___, +peripheral]
    v.   *Genitive: *[+peripheral]
    vi. *Accusative: *[−peripheral, +motion]

The ranking is given in (6.44):

(6.44)   vi ← v ← iv ← iii ← ii ← i

---

[15] In the case of the Salishan or Australian languages that display a nominative–accusative system in pronouns and an ergative system in nouns, we need to assume that the deactivation of a case restriction may be limited only to certain grammatical subsystems. Specifically, in the case of these languages one must say that (6.45b.) is deactivated only in the pronominal subsystem and that (6.45a.) is deactivated only in the nominal subsystem. In languages such as in Hindi and Georgian where the split nominative–accusative system vs. ergative system is across aspectual lines, (6.45a.b.) need to be (de)activated in the presence of certain aspectual nodes. Further research on these types of issues is obviously needed.

(6.45) a. Nominative–accusative systems:
            *Ergative: *[−peripheral, +source]
        b. Ergative systems:
            *Nominative: *[−peripheral, −motion]

Observe that given the analysis proposed here we have to say that the case restrictions in (6.43) constrain case feature bundles only when they are merged with other constituents, that is, when they are morphologically realized as affixes, i.e., in the context [[ ]$_{root}$ (...)+ ___]w.

I propose that absolute case syncretisms are due to active case restrictions. These active case restrictions trigger repair operations that adjust the disallowed feature configurations of the terminal nodes of the morphosyntax.[16, 17]

I now consider how case restrictions operate synchronically and how their deactivation is detected. A case restriction is deactivated in a language L if its feature specifications are morphologically realized in L. There are situations in which the feature specifications of more than one case restriction have the same morphological realization. These situations are the outcomes of absolute syncretism processes. I propose that in such cases it is the least marked case restriction that gets deactivated. The other case restrictions remain active and trigger repairs converting by feature change operations (see below for discussion) their target feature bundles into that of the now deactivated feature bundle. Take the "dative" case forms in Classical Greek. They morphologically realize the dative, the locative (in most nouns), and the instrumental. In this situation, it is the dative case restriction that is deactivated. The feature bundles of the locative and instrumental are then repaired into that of the dative. The same occurs in the case of the "genitive" case forms in Classical Greek, which morphologically realize the genitive and the ablative. I assume that in this case the genitive case restriction is deactivated and a repair changes the ablative feature bundles into those of the genitive.

Observe that I am hypothesizing that the repair operations trigger feature changes in the terminal nodes and are not the result of impoverishment, which is the only operation that has been recognized as operating on feature specifications in Distributed Morphology (Halle and Marantz 1993; Noyer 1998;

---

[16] The historical development leading to an absolute syncretism is obviously due to the activation of a deactivated case restriction and the subsequent adjustment of the feature bundles of the morphosyntax by a repair rule. As a consequence the vocabulary item characterized by the disallowed configurations can no longer be inserted. Instead, the vocabulary item characterized by the configuration that is the output of the repair rule is inserted. Thus the exponent identified by the disallowed feature configuration is eliminated and replaced by the exponent of the allowed configuration. The relevant morphological contrast is therefore eliminated.

[17] See Calabrese (2005) for a systematic theory of markedness constraints and repair operations in phonology.

Bobalijk 2001). Impoverishment can only account for why a given vocabulary item is not inserted in a certain terminal node, but cannot account for why a case is replaced by another case across vocabulary items regardless of their exponence and their feature specifications. This is what happens in the case of absolute syncretism. Hence impoverishment cannot be used to account for this phenomenon. It can deal only with the distribution of exponents and in particular with the retreat from a more specified exponent to a less specified one. This is not what we observe in the case of absolute syncretism. Take the syncretism between the genitive and the ablative in Classical Greek. By removing a feature from the feature bundle of the ablative—as required by impoverishment—we cannot get the fact that genitive case forms, regardless of their exponence, must be systematically used for this case. What we should expect instead are default or unspecified forms such as /-s/, not the exponent /-io/ of the genitive. Impoverishment governs only vocabulary insertion; changes of a case into another are beyond its reach. Impoverishment plays a role only in contextual syncretism and its function is that of preventing the insertion of existing vocabulary items.

Let us consider how syncretic processes occur. First of all, syntactic grammatical relations and thematic rules are mapped into case features bundles in the morphology, as proposed above. However, active case restrictions will filter out those illicit feature combinations of cases that do not have an idiosyncratic suffixal exponent. Repair operations triggered by these active restrictions change the disallowed feature bundle into allowed ones. A diagrammatic representation of how this occurs is provided below.

(6.46)

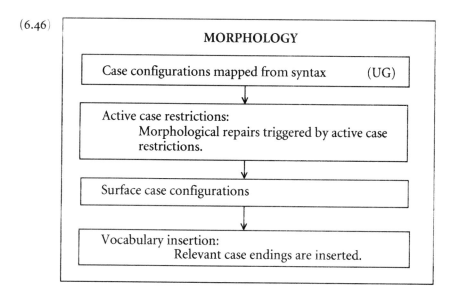

MORPHOLOGY

Case configurations mapped from syntax   (UG)

Active case restrictions:
  Morphological repairs triggered by active case restrictions.

Surface case configurations

Vocabulary insertion:
  Relevant case endings are inserted.

Consider what happens in the case of the ablative in Latin. The so-called "ablative" case forms of Latin morphologically realize the ablative, the locative, and the instrumental. I assumed that the Ablative is the least marked of the three; therefore, the case restriction governing the ablative is deactivated synchronically in Latin. The other feature bundles must then be converted into the feature bundle of the ablative by repairs.

Let us consider what happens in the case of the instrumental. A syntactic "instrumental" configuration is mapped into the case configuration in (6.47):

(6.47)   *Instrumental*
         +peripheral
         −source
         +location
         +motion

However, the morphological component of this language contains the active case restriction in (6.48):

(6.48)   *[+location, −source]/ [___, +motion]

This active restriction triggers the repairing feature change in (6.49a.):[18]

(6.49)   a.   [−source] → [+source]/ [_____, +location, +motion]

The operation in (6.49a.) changes the feature bundle of the instrumental into that of the ablative as in (6.49b.):

(6.49)   b.   *Instrumental* → *Ablative*
              +peripheral   +peripheral
              −source   +source
              +location   +location
              +motion   +motion

The case feature bundle that is the outcome of the change in (6.49b.) is that of the ablative. Thus, by feature change, the instrumental case mapped from the syntax is replaced by the ablative in the morphological component. This is a

---

[18] As proposed in Calabrese (2005), feature change operations are obtained by deletion of the relevant feature followed by automatic insertion of the same feature with an opposite value. This insertion is required by a principle enforcing fully specified representations.

Impoverishment is also an operation of deletion and one can wonder if the operation of deletion behind (6.49) is also "impoverishment". In my view, despite their apparent formal similarity, this operation of deletion and the operation of impoverishment are quite different. Impoverishment as used in Distributed Morphology (see section 6.3.2) leaves morphosyntactic representations underspecified. Only in this way can it block vocabulary insertion (but see note 9 for a different formulation of impoverishment). In contrast, after the application of the deletion operation behind (6.49), morphosyntactic representations must be specified again. This results in a feature change operation.

case of absolute syncretism. The operations leading to the feature systems in (6.32) are due to repairs like this (see below for discussion).

One could propose that activation of case restrictions such as (6.48) and repairs such as (6.49), i.e., cases of absolute syncretisms, are only diachronic phenomena or adjustments occurring in the process of learning a language. In this case they would not have an active role in the synchrony of a grammar. However, I would like to propose that they do. Consider the Latin locative phrases in (6.16) again. I repeat them in (6.50).

(6.50)   *meae domī (Pl. Au 432)* 'at my home'   *villā meā* 'at my villa'
         domī suae (Cic. N.D. 381) 'at his home' *urbe copiosā* 'in a wealthy
                                                                        town'
         proximae viciniae habitat (Pl. Ba 205–6)
         'he lives very close'

As discussed above, in the phrases in the right column, the case of the head noun is ablative. In those of the left column, the case is a genitive/dative "locative". The issue is that the grammatical, thematic and semantic functions of the phrases in (6.50) are identical; we are dealing with "locatives". If the different case forms we see on the head noun were just the outcome of contextual syncretism, that is, due to the different distributional properties of the vocabulary items, we should expect an identical case form on the adjective (see discussion above in section 6.2). As already observed, this is not what we find. The case forms of the adjective are different: genitive/dative in the left column, ablative in the right one. This indicates that the distribution of vocabulary items (i.e., contextual syncretism) does not play any role here. We are instead dealing with absolute syncretism, in particular synchronic absolute syncretism, an operation changing the feature bundle of one case into another one.

I propose that the most adequate analysis is the following. First of all, I assume that a syntactic locational phrase is mapped into a "locative" feature bundle. This feature bundle is disallowed by the active case restriction in (6.51).

(6.51)   *[+location, −source]/[___, −motion]

This active restriction leads to the repairs in the feature bundles of the terminal nodes of the locative in the morphosyntax. The first repair occurs in singular nouns of towns and small islands and changes the locative into a dative; the other–most general–repair occurs in all other nouns and changes the locative into the ablative.

A problem that must be solved is that this analysis requires access to the lexical properties of the head nouns–one must know whether or not they are names of towns and small islands–before the insertion of the case exponent. To solve this problem I have to assume a cyclic model in which modifications of the feature bundles of the terminal nodes in outer morphological cycles occur after vocabulary insertion in the inner cycles (see Bobaljik 2000). In this way the idiosyncratic morphological properties of nouns of towns and small islands can be made available for the repairs. The repairs triggered by (6.51) are given in (6.52)–(6.53).

(6.52)   a.   [+location]   →   [−location]/[___, −source, −plural] X +__ where X = a name of
                                                                          a town or a small
                                                                          (island.

   b.   Locative   →   Dative
        +peripheral   +peripheral
        −source   −source
        +location   −location
        −motion   +motion[19]

   Otherwise:

(6.53)   a.   [−source]   →   [+source]/ [___ +location]
   b.   Locative   →   Ablative
        +peripheral   +peripheral
        −source   +source
        +location   +location
        −motion   +motion[20]

Observe that the absolute syncretism in (6.52) is characteristic of Classical Greek. (6.53) is obviously the common case in Latin.[21] An account of the changes we see in Latin locational phrases can thus be achieved.

To conclude I will consider the absolute syncretisms we observe in Classical Greek and in Old French. A schematic account of the changes accounting for the absolute syncretisms of Classical Greek are given in (6.54)).

[19] In most of the cases discussed below there must be some further adjustments in feature specifications. They mostly involve the feature [motion]. This feature is contrastive only in the Nominative/Accusative and Locative/Instrumental, otherwise its value is predictable from the other feature specifications in the feature bundle. The following repairs account for its distribution:

(i)   [asource, alocation] → [+motion]/ [___, +peripheral]
(ii)   [4−source, −location] → [−motion]]/ [___,+peripheral]
(iii) [+source] → [+motion]]/ [___, −peripheral]

It is the rule in (i) that applies in (6.52b) and changes the original feature specification [- motion] of the Locative into the feature specification [+motion] of the Dative, The status of these adjustments is unclear to me at this point They could indicate that the feature [motion] is problematic and needs to be changed; however, it works well in identify at this point. Further research is needed.

[20] The change of [−motion] to [+motion] in (6.53) is due to (i) of footnote 19.

[21] The following reconstruction for the situation we observe in Latin can be proposed: the locative case was a short /i/(cf. Watkins 1993 for Indo-European). This /-i/ was preserved in the case of nouns of towns and small islands. In contrast the locative was replaced by the ablative in the case of all other nouns. I propose that the short /i/ of the special local nouns was merged with the long /i:/ of the genitive-dative and that in this case the underlying case was reinterpreted as being genitive–dative. This led to the system that we observe in Latin.

(6.54) Active case restrictions in Classical Greek:[22]

    a.   i.   *Instrumental: *[−source, +location]/[_____ , +motion]

          ii. Repair:

              [+location] →   [−location]/[_____, −source, +motion]

         iii. *Instrumental* → *Dative*

             +peripheral   +peripheral

             −source   −source

             +location   −location

             +motion   +motion

    b.   i.   *Ablative: *[+location, +source]

          ii. Repair:

              [+location] →   [−location]/ [_____ , +source]

         iii. *Ablative* → *Genitive*

             +peripheral   +peripheral

             +source   +source

             +location   −location

             +motion   −motion

    c.   i.   *Locative: *[+location, −source]

          ii. Repair:

              [+location] →   [−location]/[___, −source]

         iii. *Locative* → b. *Dative*

             +peripheral   +peripheral

              −source   −source

             +location   −location

              −motion   +motion

Accounting for what happens in Old French is not so straightforward. In Calabrese (1998) I proposed a detailed analysis of the different diachronic steps that led to this system. I cannot discuss this analysis here and refer the interested reader to that work. However, to assume that all these historical syncretic steps are still active in Old French would lead to a quite cumbersome analysis. I therefore propose that the best way to account for the Old French system is to hypothesize that the genitive case restriction is active in this language. (6.55a.) triggers the repair in (6.55b.):

(6.55)   a. *Genitive: *[+peripheral]

         b. Repair: [+peripheral] → [−peripheral]

---

[22] The change in feature motion in (6.54b iii) is due to (11) of Note 19; that in (6.54c iii) to (i) of Note 19.

The adjustments in (6.57) are then needed to remove configurations disallowed by the constraints in (6.56). They transform all of the non-nominative cases into the accusative as shown in (6.58):[23]

(6.56) i. *[−peripheral, +source]
       ii. *[−peripheral, +location]

(6.57) i. [−peripheral] → [−source]
       ii. [−peripheral] → [−location]

(6.58) Input:

		Nom.	Acc.	Gen.	Dat.	Loc.	Abl.	Inst.
	Peripheral	−	−	+	+	+	+	+
	Source	−	−	+	−	−	+	−
	Location	−	−	−	−	+	+	+
	Motion	−	+	−	+	−	+	+

(by 6.55b.):

		Nom.	Acc.	Gen.	Dat.	Loc.	Abl.	Inst.
	Peripheral	−	−	−	−	−	−	−
	Source	−	−	+	−	−	+	−
	Location	−	−	−	−	+	+	+
	Motion	−	+	+[24]	+	−	+	+

(by 6.57):

		Nom.	Acc.	Gen.	Dat.	Loc.	Abl.	Inst.
	Peripheral	−	−	−	−	−	−	−
	Source	−	−	−	−	−	−	−
	Location	−	−	−	−	−	−	−
	Motion	−	+	+	+	+	+	+

6.3.5 The evolution of the Latin case system

Evidence for hypothesizing that feature changes are needed to account for absolute syncretism is provided by historical changes implementing this type of syncretism. The case system of Latin underwent major changes in Late Latin. As discussed in Calabrese (1998) one of these changes was the widespread syncretism between the genitive and the dative.

---

[23] The change in the feature [motion] is due to rule (iii) of note 19 Therefore, I am predicting that in an ergative system, the genitive may become ergative once (6.55b.) applies. This appears to be correct (see Blake 1994: 122). A closer investigation of this issue is needed, something that I cannot do at present.

[24] All of the case restrictions in (6.43) are active with the exception of those against the accusative and the nominative. To obtain the correct result the active case restriction against the locative must trigger a repair changing this case into either the dative or the ablative so that it will obtain the feature [+motion].

Characteristically it was the genitive that replaced the dative, as we can see in (6.59):[25]

(6.59)   *quod vinclum, quaeso, deest nostrae coniunctionis* (instead of *nostrae coniunctionii*) (Cic. ad Fam. v, 15, 2)
'What bond, I ask, is absent from our relationship?'
ille tunc imber...mortem intulit corporum (instead of *corporibus*) (Chrisost. Ho. 7, 7)
'...the rain brought death to their bodies'
qui eorum (instead of *eis*) *auxiliare presumpserat* (Fredeg., sec. VI or VIII, 3, 51)
'he who had taken help to them'
viriliter eorum (instead of *eis*) *resistens* (Chronicum Salernitanum, 747–974)
'... resisting courageously to them'

We have seen the fundamental role that impoverishment and replacement by a less specified vocabulary item plays in the account of contextual syncretism. We could then try to extend the same type of analysis to the cases of absolute

---

[25] Two other important changes cannot be discussed here: one is the appearance of the accusative after prepositions that took the ablative in the classical language. This is illustrated in (i):

(i)   cum:
cum filios suos tres (CIL, VIII, 3933)   'with his three children'
(instead of *filiis suis tribus*)
ab:
posita a fratres (CIL, VIII, 20296)   'put by the brothers'
(instead of *fratribus*)
pro:
pro se et suos (CIL, XII, 1185)   'for himself and his'
(instead of *se et suis*)

In the other, all prepositionless case-marked NPs were replaced with prepositional constructions as shown in (ii):

(ii)   *ad carnuficem dabo*   in place of   *carnufici dabo*
'I will give ___ to the executioner'
dixit Iesus ad discipulos   *dixit Iesus discipulis*
'Jesus said to the disciples'
ostentare ad digitum   *ostentare digito*
'to indicate with the finger'
  monasterium de castas (Theodosius De situ terrae sanctae)
'monastery of young girls'
in hoc tempore   *hoc tempore*
'at this time'

As discussed in Calabrese (1998), these two changes are not due to feature change, the type of repair operation which is used in the text, but to a different type of repair operation, fission, and to a consequent change in the status of prepositions in morphosyntactic representations of Late Latin. Discussion of these changes would take too long and I am forced to refer the reader to Calabrese (1998) for an analysis of them.

syncretism we saw above. Specifically, we could hypothesize that the feature bundles of the cases that are eliminated are impoverished so that the relevant vocabulary items can no longer be inserted. Less specified vocabulary items would then be inserted.

Given what was proposed earlier, the ending /-s/ has a special status in Latin being the elsewhere case, the least marked vocabulary item. If we assume that syncretic changes are due to impoverishment of features in terminal nodes, we should expect this ending to play a crucial role in the development of the system and we should then expect the ending /-s/ to be extended to uses that it did not have before. For example, it should have become the exponent of the genitive of the second declension or of the dative, or of the genitive plural. No such change is attested or can be reconstructed in the history of the Romance nominal system.

The changes that we observe in this case do not involve exponents but the actual cases. Thus, we have syncretic changes between genitive and dative, regardless of the exponents that they have. For example, the genitive plural /-ōrum/ replaces the dative plural /-īs/ in the second declension, regardless of the internal constituency and featural assignments of these exponents.

The evolution of the Latin case system seems to operate only through operations on case feature bundles, regardless of the exponents realizing these case features. The best way of representing these changes is therefore by modifications in the morphosyntactic component, that is, through the activation of case restrictions and subsequent featural repairs. I hypothesize that this is one of the major ways in which case systems evolve.

6.3.6 *Absolute syncretism is not obtained by phonological changes*

A widely held explanation of the loss of the case system in a language argues that it is due to the phonological developments that this language underwent (see Blake 1994: 177–82, for example). In the case of Latin, the sound changes in (6.60) could have affected the case system. By these changes, the case distinctions in (6.61) can be phonologically neutralized.

(6.60) a. Loss of /m/ in word final position.

   b. Merging of short /ĭ, ŭ/ with /long / ē, ō/.

   c. Loss of quantity (Thus, Romă(nom.) can no longer be distinguished from Romā(abl.)).

(6.61) NOM ACC ABL
   terra terram terrā → *terra* 'earth'
   campus campum campō → *campo* 'field'
   panis panem pane → *pane* 'bread'

However, a purely phonological explanation of the loss of the case system in Latin does not work. First of all, observe that the system of inflectional endings in verbs was not lost, although these endings were affected by the changes in (6.60) in the same way as the nominal ones. Furthermore, given the changes in (6.60) in a language like Spanish where final vowels and final /s/ were preserved, all the case distinctions in the plural should have been maintained, as we can see in (6.62). If they were lost, it must have been because of some non-phonological reason.

(6.62)   Latin:
Plural

Nominative	Genitive	Dative/Ablative	Accusative	
terrae	*terrarum*	*terrīs*	*terrās*	'earth'
campi	*camporum*	*campīs*	*campōs*	'field'

(6.63)   **terre *terraro *terris *terras*
         *campi *camporo *campis *campos

The same is true for the genitives and datives characterized by a long /-ī/ in languages like Italian where final vowels were preserved.

In Old French, where low vowels were raised but not lost in word-final position, in contrast with non-low vowels that were lost, we should find an alternation between /Ø∼e/ to realize a genitive–dative of the Romanian type, as in (6.64):

(6.64)   *rose* < Lat. ROSA and ROSAM 'rose'
         *ros < Lat. ROSAE/ROSE

The absence of this case contrast in Old French, as well as the other arguments mentioned above, demonstrates that a purely phonological account of the evolution of the Latin case system is not satisfactory (see Renzi 1993 for more discussion of these points).

Finally it is important to point out that phonological changes similar to those that occurred in the development from Latin to Romance also affected the Slavic languages. Thus, we have loss of coda consonants (e.g., Proto-Slavic **greb-tēi, *greb-ām, *grēb-s-am* > Common Slavic *greti, grebǫ, grěsŭ*) and lowering and surface disappearance of the short high vowels (e.g., Proto-Slavic **dĭn-ĭ-x, *sŭp-na-x* > Common Slavic **dĭn-ĭ, *sŭnŭ* > Russian *den', son*). Despite these changes, the original case system of Proto-Slavic is fully preserved in most of the Slavic languages. The six cases system of reconstructed Proto-Slavic (see the /-o-/ declension in (6.65)) is still present in Russian, after more than two thousand years, despite the radical changes in the phonological exponents of the different cases. This clearly indicates that syncretic changes are not due to modifications in the phonological shape of exponents even if they can lead to phonological neutralizations between exponents. If case restrictions remain deactivated, then readjustments in the morphological system will restore the morphological contrasts.

(6.65)   Proto-Slavic /-o-/ declension: Russian /-o-/ declension:

SING.

N.	*stal-a-x*	'table'	*stol*	'table'
G.	*stal-a-at*		*stol-á*	
D.	*stal-u?*		*stol-ú*	
A.	*stal-a-m*		*stol*	
L.	*stal-a-i*		*stol-é*	
Ins.	*stal-ā*		*stol-am*	

DUAL

N.-A	*stal-ā*
G.-L.	*stal-au*
D.-Ins.	*stal-a-mā*

PLU.

N.	*stal-ai*		*stol-i*
G.	*stal-am*		*stol-ov*
D.	*stal-a-max*		*stol-a-m*
A.	*stal-ans*		*stol-i*
L.	*stal-ai-xu*		*stol-a-x*
Ins.	*stal-(?)*		*stol-a-mi*

6.4 A model without restrictions and repairs

Finally, I deal with another possible way of accounting for the morphological realization of case in a language. In this approach, the morphological realization of case is accounted for by determining the feature specifications of the vocabulary items and by resorting to operations–such as impoverishment–that control the distribution of these items in the system. The feature combinations of the terminal nodes are free. Only the morphological exponence is limited. Therefore, all of the case feature combinations mapped from the syntax must be taken into consideration during vocabulary insertion and the feature assignments of vocabulary items must be established by considering all of them. All possible cases are present in morphosyntactic representations. Therefore, we have to say that the morphology of Latin includes the locative, the instrumental, the comitative, the purposive, all of the locational cases such as the elative, translative, and so on. This model, thus, does not recognize the existence of absolute syncretism, only of contextual syncretism. Variations in the morphological realization of a given case can be accounted for only by referring to the feature specification of the vocabulary items and to impoverishment.

A first problem for this approach arises in situations in which there could be a contradiction between a vocabulary item that is elsewhere because of its pattern of contextual syncretism and a vocabulary item that is elsewhere because it is the sole exponent of different cases, that is, because it enters a situation of absolute syncretism according to the model outlined in the previous sections.

For example, consider Old French in (6.1). The exponent /Ø/ represents all non-nominative cases in the singular. Given the feature system in (6.20), there is no common feature in all of these cases. Therefore /-Ø/ should be an elsewhere item. But /s/ has a wider distribution in the system because of its pattern of contextual syncretism. According to this criterion, /s/ should be the elsewhere item. Hence we have a problem to solve.

The solution involves selecting an adequate set of features. For example, we can introduce a new feature, say [oblique]. All non-nominative cases would be [+oblique]; so Old French /Ø/ could be assigned the feature [+oblique, −plural]; /s/ remains the elsewhere item. This is shown in (6.66):

(6.66)   Ø ↔ [+oblique, −plural]
         s ↔ [Ø]

Given that /-Ø/ is [+oblique], it can be inserted in the feature bundles of all cases, with the exception of the nominative, without any problem.

The selection of an adequate set of features is fundamental in this model. Here I explore one such feature system. Let us suppose that cases are organized in a hierarchical structure such as that in (6.67). In (6.67), each case, with exception of the nominative, which contains only negative feature specifications, is obtained by adding a positive feature specification to the feature bundle of the case on its left: in the instrumental [+means] is added, in the ablative [+origin] is added and so on. The features here are just classificatory devices and self-explanatory).[26]

(6.67)		N	A	G	D	L	Abl.	I
	Oblique	−	+	+	+	+	+	+
	Peripheral	−	−	+	+	+	+	+
	Inherent	−	−	−	+	+	+	+
	Location	−	−	−	−	+	+	+
	Origin	−	−	−	−	−	+	+
	Means	−	−	−	−	−	−	+

[26] Here I am again assuming that morphosyntactic representations are fully specified and my arguments here use fully specified representations. However, as the reader can try by him/herself, the same arguments would hold if one were to adopt underspecified morphosyntactic representations.

In this approach, each vocabulary item is assigned this feature: thus an instrumental form would be [+means], an ablative form [+source] and so on. The nominative is [−oblique]. The feature assignments of the different case exponents in a hypothetical system without syncretism would be as in (6.68):

(6.68) $a_{Nom.}$ ↔   [−oblique]
          $\beta_{Acc.}$ ↔   [+oblique]
          $\gamma_{Gen.}$ ↔   [+peripheral]
          $\delta_{Dat.}$ ↔   [+inherent]
          $\varepsilon_{Loc.}$ ↔   [+location]
          $\eta_{Abl.}$ ↔   [+source]
          $\zeta_{Inst.}$ ↔   [+means]

One could now propose that syncretism involves simple loss of a vocabulary item. If this occurs, the vocabulary item of an adjacent feature bundle in (6.67) would be inserted in the terminal node of the lost item. For example, given (6.68), if the vocabulary item of the instrumental is lost, the vocabulary item of the ablative would be inserted in the terminal node of the instrumental since this terminal node also contains the feature [+source]. This solution complicates the feature system but simplifies the morphology that does not need to have feature-changing operations like those used in section 6.3.4.2.

In (6.67) for each case there is a feature. However, there are syncretic relationships that require the introduction of new features. Let us look back at the singular of the Classical Greek /o-/ declension. It is repeated in (6.69):

(6.69)   SING.
          N.   ἀδελφos   (<*adelph -o-s*)   'brother'
          G.   ἀδελφου   (<*adelph -o-io*)
          D.   ἀδελφῳ   (<*adelph -o-i*) (+thematic vowel lengthening
                              and laxing)
          A.   ἀδελφον   (<*adelph -o-n*)

In Classical Greek there is absolute syncretism between the genitive and the ablative, and between the dative, the locative, and the instrumental. In this model, when a speaker is faced with accounting for the distribution of the vocabulary items, he/she must also consider the cases that are not morphologically realized in the system, in addition to those that are morphologically realized in it. Therefore, what we call the genitive in (6.66) is actually a genitive–ablative in the sense that the exponent of this vocabulary item must be inserted in the feature bundles of the genitive, as well as of the ablative. In the same way, what we call a dative is actually a dative–locative–instrumental.

Now observe that assuming (6.67) there is no feature set or subset ordering that can account for the distribution of the items. The feature system in (6.67) fails to account for Classical Greek. The correct result is achieved by adding a further feature to (6.67) where there is a common feature specification between the genitive and the ablative and hypothesizing the feature system in (6.70). The appropriate vocabulary items for Classical Greek are given in (6.71):

(6.70)

	N	A	G	D	L	Abl.	I
Oblique	−	+	+	+	+	+	+
Peripheral	−	−	+	+	+	+	+
Inherent	−	−	−	+	+	+	+
Location	−	−	−	−	+	+	+
Origin	−	−	−	−	−	+	+
Means	−	−	−	−	−	−	+
Source	−	−	+	−	−	+	−

(6.71)   Classical Greek:

g. /-i/ ↔ [+peripheral, −source]   (D/L/I Sg)
h. /-n/ ↔ [+oblique, −peripheral]   (AccSg)
i. /-io/ ↔ [+source]   (G/AbSg)
j. /-s/ ↔ Ø   (NSg)

One of the problems of this model is thus that it requires a quite complex set of features. This becomes obvious when we start considering other cases such as the different locational cases, the comitative, the purposive, the ergative, and so on. For each of these cases, we will need a new feature. This obviously leads to a sizable expansion of the feature system in (6.70).

However, the most fundamental problem for this approach is another one. As mentioned above, in this model, there are only the feature bundles of the morphosyntax, the vocabulary items, and the operation of impoverishment.[27] Therefore, there is no way of dealing with absolute syncretism. This leads to various failures.

First of all, we know that there are syncretic operations that operate across vocabulary items. Thus, in section 6.3.5 where we considered the evolution of the Latin case system, we have seen that when a case is replaced

---

[27] I omit discussion of operations such as fission that do not play a role in syncretic processes.

by another case in the history of a language, this occurs across declension classes regardless of the different exponents of the cases. The exponents that represent the case in the different declension classes are simply replaced by the different exponents of the other case. This is an instance of what I called absolute syncretism. Now this model is able to account only for changes in the distribution of single lexical items, but not of classes of lexical items as it happens in the case of absolute syncretism. Therefore, this model fails to deal with across-the-board case replacements.

Secondly, this model cannot deal with what we observe in the case of the Latin locative in which we found a case form that was syncretic to that of genitive/datives in singular nouns of towns and small islands and another one that was syncretic to ablatives elsewhere. In fact, in this model variations in the morphological realization of a given case, as are those seen in the Latin locative, can be accounted for only by referring to the feature specifications of the vocabulary items and to impoverishment. Therefore, we must say that in Latin there is contextual syncretism between locative and the genitive/dative in singular nouns of towns and small islands (in addition to *rūrī* and *domī*). In all other nouns, instead, there would be contextual syncretism between the locative and the ablative. We have already seen that this leads to problems. Here I will try to see if we can find a better solution in this model.

Formally, the following analysis could be proposed: in the mapping from syntax, the features of the locative case are assigned to locational phrases. This locative case is preserved throughout the morphology in the relevant terminal node of the morphosyntax, and the appropriate vocabulary items must be inserted in this terminal node.

We have to decide which is the basic vocabulary item for the locative. There are two possibilities: 1) /Ø/ which is syncretic with the ablative (plus the relevant readjustments); 2) /i:/ which is syncretic with the genitive/dative. The basic item to select should be the most specified one of the two. The insertion of other one would be accounted for by impoverishment. The first possibility is easy to reject. The distribution of the exponent /Ø/ is less restricted than that of /i:/, therefore it must be less specified than /i:/. We then select /i:/. Now, we have to decide if this exponent is the same as that of the genitive/dative or a different one, and accept two different homonymous /i:/ in the singular, in addition to the other one in the plural. If we assume that the /i:/ we see in the locative is identical to the other one found in the genitive/dative, we need a new feature common to these three cases. I would prefer not to complicate the case feature system in (6.70) further, and instead propose that there is a high degree of homonymy among Latin case exponents. The list of the case vocabulary items in Latin would be that in (6.72). (The feature system used is that in (6.70).)

(6.72) a. */-um/* ↔ [+peripheral, −inherent, +plural]   (GPl)
        b. */-i:/* ↔ [−oblique, −peripheral, +plural]/
                       [−neut, I, II] +__   (NPl, I, II)
        c. */i:/* ↔ [+peripheral, −location, −plural]   (G&DSg)
        d. */i:/* ↔ [+location, −association, −plural]   (LSg)
        e. */ə/* ↔ [−peripheral, +plural]/[+neuter]+___   (N&APl. Nt)
        f. */−m/* ↔ [+oblique, −peripheral, −plural]   (ASg)
        g. */-bu-/* ↔ [+inherent, +plural]/[III, IV, V] +__   (D&Ab, L, I,
                                                           Pl. III–V)
        h. Ø   ↔ [−plural]   (Sg default)
        i. */s/* ↔ [Ø]   Elsewhere

To account for the appearance of /Ø/ with nouns that are not nouns of towns and small islands, we have to assume an operation of impoverishment such as that in (6.73). This operation accounts for the insertion of /Ø/ in the locative of most nouns.

(6.73)   The feature [−association] is deleted in the environment [__+loca-
         tion] in nouns that are not names of towns and of small islands.

Assuming the vocabulary items in (6.72) and impoverishment we have an account of contextual syncretism in the Latin case endings.

   An immediate problem for this analysis arises from the fact that the appearance of Ø is associated with the application of certain readjustment rules in the ablative (see section 6.3.2). Crucially these rules do not apply when the exponent */-i:/* occurs. Somehow we have to say that the operation of impoverishment must also affect the application of the readjustment rules. It is unclear to me how we can implement this.

   However, a worse problem arises in this approach when we have to account for the morphological variations we see in concord between an adjective and a head noun in locational phrases. As we see in (6.74), a genitive/dative form appears in the adjective if the head noun has a form syncretic with the genitive/dative case, and an ablative form if the head noun has a form syncretic with the ablative case.

(6.74)   *meae domî* (Pl. Au 432) 'at my home' *villā meā* 'at my villa'

In this model there is no way of manipulating the feature complexes of the terminal nodes to obtain changes in case identity. Therefore, we must assume that both the adjective and the noun of both phrases in (6.74) are character-ized by the locative case. It follows that the variations in the morphological realization of this case that we see in (6.74) must be due to manipulations of the feature specifications of the vocabulary items and to the operation of impoverishment, the only means that this model has to account for syncretic changes.

Now we know that that contextual syncretism patterns do not play a role in concord. In concord the lexical properties of the root noun such as declension class are not transmitted/copied onto the dependent adjective as shown again in (6.75):

(6.75)   Genitive: *tristis puellae* 'of the sad girl'
   Dative: *tristī puellae* 'to the sad girl'

The fact that, in the first declension class, the dative and the genitive have the same case exponent does not matter in the selection of the case exponent of the adjective. Concord looks only at grammatical properties such as case, gender, and number.

We also know that lexical properties triggering impoverishment cannot be transmitted from the head noun to the adjective. An impoverishment operation that applies in the head noun does not apply in the modifying adjective. We see this in (6.76).

(6.76)   *bonī regis* 'of the good king'

The presence of /-s/ in the genitive *regis* indicates that impoverishment has applied. This property of the head noun, a characteristic feature of the third declension to which the word for king belongs, is not transmitted to the adjective *bonus* of the II declension which then shows up with /-i:/ in the genitive.

In the model just proposed to account for the case variation we observe in (6.74) we have to assume that an operation of impoverishment must also apply when the case exponent of the adjective is inserted. This means that a lexical property of the head noun must be copied or transmitted during concord. However, as shown above, the idiosyncratic properties of the head noun are not copied/transmitted in concord. Therefore we have to conclude that this analysis cannot be pursued. The model fails to account for what happens in (6.74). I put forth that to have an adequate analysis of what happens in the phrases in (6.74) one must distinguish between absolute and contextual syncretism, and I propose that in the case of locational phrases in Latin we are dealing with absolute syncretism: the underlying locative is changed into the ablative and locative as proposed in section 6.3.

The fact is that absolute and contextual syncretism must be recognized to exist. They are different phenomena. Contextual syncretism accounts for the distribution of items with respect to other items realizing different specification of the same set of features. Contextual syncretism directly deals with the phonological aspects of these items. As such, it is the result of the historical interaction between the phonological and morphological properties of the vocabulary items. Absolute syncretism is much more abstract: a case is replaced by another case regardless of the vocabulary items that realize them. Being different phenomena, they must be treated independently, and not uniquely by manipulating the features of the lexical items. The model discussed in this section fails to do that.

6.5 Conclusions

In this chapter I proposed that the structure of paradigms is accounted for by the constraints on feature combinations of the terminal nodes of the morphosyntax.

If this is correct, one could propose the following principle:

(6.77)   An allowed feature combination of a language L must be morphologically realized in L at least once.

From (6.77) it follows that neutralization of phonological contrast does not lead to neutralization of morphological contrasts. Thus, if we have a phonological neutralization between exponents in a paradigm, but the relevant morphological contrast is maintained–that is, if the relevant morphological marking statement is not activated–the morphological contrast will be realized by other phonological means. This is what occurred in the Slavic languages.

Given the paradigmatic structure established by (6.77), the feature assignment of vocabulary items accounts for the distribution of exponents in the structure and for the contextual syncretism we observe in it. Both synchronic and diachronic absolute syncretism would instead require changes of the feature assignments of the terminal nodes of the morphosyntax.

Appendix: Case features

In this section I provide motivation for the case feature system I use in the text. Behind all of the assumptions of this chapter is the idea that case syncretisms, both contextual and absolute ones, are not accidental or random, but follow precise generalizations. The goal of case features is to account for syncretic patterns.

I propose the feature system in (6.79). It was obtained in the following way. I decided to use the minimal number of features required to account for the cases of contextual syncretism[28] we observe in Old French, Sanskrit, Classical Greek, and Latin. No less than four features must be used. I focused on the peripheral cases: the genitive, the dative, the locative, the ablative, and the instrumental. One observes the following contextual syncretism between these cases: a. between genitive and dative (cf. Latin); b. between dative and ablative (cf. Latin); c. between dative, ablative, and instrumental (cf. Sanskrit); d. between genitive and locative (cf. Sanskrit). I first freely assigned positive and negative specification of arbitrary labels such as Z, X, Y, W and then I tried to establish patterns of insertion. To insert the same exponent in the genitive and the dative, the feature bundles of these two cases must have some common feature specifications, at least two.[29] Subsequently I fine-tuned the feature assignments of the different cases, trying to account for the absolute syncretisms in the languages under consideration by changing the minimal number of feature specifications. The system that resulted is that in the non-shaded part of (6.78).[30] Starting from the non-shaded part I then tried to give a name to the arbitrary labels Z, X, Y, W by considering their possible meaning and function. At this point I tried to give appropriate specification for the nominative, accusative, and ergative (the shaded part of (6.78)), keeping in mind the contextual syncretism between nominative and accusative found in Latin neuters. This led to the system in (6.79). The different names have the following rationale: [Z] is [Peripheral]. [Z] is common to the genitive, dative, locative, ablative, and instrumental, which are often called the peripheral cases in contrast to the nominative and accusative, which are called the core cases. [Y] is [Location]. The positive specification of [Y] identifies the locative and the ablative, which are the locational cases. I also assigned it to the instrumental. [W] is [Motion]. A positive specification of [W] contrasts the dative, ablative, instrumental against the genitive, locative. I assumed that what is common to

---

[28] I considered only cases of syncretism involving features, that is, I disregarded all the cases of syncretism that can be accounted for by using an elsewhere or default exponent such as Latin /-s/ or /-Ø/.

[29] G–D = [+Z, − Y], G–L = [+Z, − W], D–Abl–Ins = [+Z, +W]. The feature X was required to distinguish the instrumental from the other peripheral cases. Its specifications are more arbitrary and in function of the name I later gave to this feature.

[30] There is some editing. To simplify the exposition, I reverted + and − specifications in function of the names I will later give; for example, the feature Y came first out with the assignments in (i):

(i)   Gen.   Dat.   Loc.   Abl.   Inst.

        Y   +   +   −   −   −

I   reverted   +   and   −   as   in   (ii)   when   I   decided   to   call   it   [Location]:

(ii)   Gen.   Dat.   Loc.   Abl.   Inst.

        Location   −   −   +   +   +

The same feature specification for the Abl. and the Inst. was required by the need to simplify the operation accounting for the absolute syncretism between these two cases.

these cases with respect to the locative is that their semantics involve motion (to or from). I extended this feature specification to the accusative and the ergative. Finally [X] is [Source]. I needed this feature to distinguish the instrumental [−X] from the ablative [+X]. I also assigned [+source] to the genitive, which is often syncretic with the ablative (see Classical Greek), and to the ergative.

(6.78)

	Erg.	Nom.	Acc.	Gen.	Dat.	Loc.	Abl.	Inst.
Z				+	+	+	+	+
X				+	−	−	+	−
Y				−	−	+	+	+
W				−	+	−	+	+

(6.79)

	Erg.	Nom.	Acc.	Gen.	Dat.	Loc.	Abl.	Inst.
Z (Peripheral)	−	−	−	+	+	+	+	+
X (Source)	+	−	−	+	−	−	+	−
Y (Location)	−	−	−	−	−	+	+	+
W (Motion)	+	−	+	+	+	−	+	+

References

Adger, D. (2005) 'Combinatorial variability', Ms., Queen Mary, Universty of London.

Blake, B. (1994) *Case.* Cambridge: Cambridge University Press.

Bobalijk, J. (2000) 'The ins and outs of contextual allomorphy', in K. K. Grohmann and C. Struijke (eds.), *University of Maryland Working Papers in Linguistics*, vol. 10, 35–71.

—— (2001) 'Syncretism without paradigms: Remarks on Williams 1981, 1994'. *Yearbook of Morphology 2001.*

Calabrese, A. (1998) 'Some remarks on the Latin case system and its development in Romance', in J. Lema and E. Trevino (eds.), *Theoretical Advances on Romance Languages.* Amsterdam: John Benjamins, pp. 71–126.

—— (2002) 'On impoverishment and fission in the verbal morphology of the dialect of Livinallongo', in Christina Tortora (ed.), *Studies on Italian Dialects*. Oxford: Oxford University Press, pp. 3–33.

—— (2005) *Markedness and Economy in a Derivational Model of Phonology*. Berlin: Mouton de Gruyter.

Greenberg, J. H. (1963) 'Some universals of grammar with particular reference to the order of meaningful elements', in J. H. Greenberg (ed.), *Universals of Language*. Cambridge, MA: MIT Press, pp. 58–90.

Halle, M. (1997) 'Distributed Morphology: Impoverishment and fission', *MIT Working Papers in Linguistics* 30: 425–49.

—— and A. Marantz (1993) 'Distributed Morphology and the pieces of inflection', in K. Hale and S. J. Keyser (eds.), *The View from Building 20: Linguistic Essays in Honor of Sylvain Bromberger*. Cambridge, MA: MIT Press.

—— —— (1994) 'Some key features of Distributed Morphology', *MIT Working Papers in Linguistics* 21: 275–88.

—— and B. Vaux (1997) 'Theoretical aspects of Indo-European nominal morphology: The nominal declensions of Latin and Armenian', in C. Melchert, J. Jasanoff, and L. Oliver (eds.), *Mir Curad. A Festschrift in honor of Calvert Watkins*.

Meillet, A., and J. Vendryes (1966) *Traité de grammaire comparée des langues classiques*. Paris: Champion.

Meiser, G. (1992) 'Syncretism in Indo-European languages–Motives, processes, and results'. *Transactions of the Philological Society* 90: 187–218.

Noyer, R. (1992) Features, positions, and affixes in autonomous morphological structure. PhD dissertation, MIT.

—— (1997) 'Attic Greek accentuation and intermediate derivational representations,' in I. Roca (ed.), *Derivations and Constraints in Phonology*. Oxford: Oxford University Press, pp. 501–29.

—— (1998) 'Impoverishment theory and morphosyntactic markedness', in Steven G. Lapointe, Diane K. Brentari, and Patrick M. Farrell (eds.), *Morphology and Its Relation to Phonology and Syntax*, CSLI, Stanford, pp. 264–85.

Renzi, L. (1993) 'Vestiges de la flexion casuelle dans les langues romanes', *XXe Congrés International de Linguistique et Philologie romanes*, t. II, Sect. 6. Bern: Francke.

Ringe, D. (1995) 'Nominative-accusative syncretism and syntactic case'. *Penn Working Papers in Linguistics* 2: 45–81.

Stump, G. T. (2001) 'On rules of referral'. *Language* 69.3: 449–79.

Watkins, C. (1993) 'Il Proto-Indo-Europeo. Comparazione e Ricostruzione'. in A. Giacalone and P. Ramat (eds.), *Le lingue Indo-europee*, Bologna: Il Mulino.

Zwicky, A. M. (1985) 'How to describe inflection', in Proceedings of the Berkeley Linguistics Society, pp. 372–86.

7

A feature-geometric approach to Amharic verb classes

JOCHEN TROMMER

7.1 Introduction

It is well known that Ethiopian Semitic languages have different verb classes which determine root shape in different paradigms (Leslau 1995, 2000; Amberber 2002). Thus verbal roots with three consonants (called "triradicals" in the Semitistic literature) in Amharic are traditionally divided into three classes, A, B, and C, which differ by the vowel and gemination patterns in different paradigms. In type A roots, the medial consonant geminates only in the perfect, in type C roots in the perfect and the imperfect, and in type B roots there is gemination throughout all paradigms (**säbbära**, 'break'; **fällägä**, 'seek, want'; **marräkä**, 'take prisoner'; affixes are in gray):[1,2]

(7.1) Verb Classes for Triradicals

	Type A	Type B	Type C
Perfect	säbbärä	fällägä	marräkä
Imperfect	yəsäbər	yəfälləg	yəmarrək
Participle	säbari	fällagi	maraki

Class C verbs also differ from the other two classes by using the vowel **a** instead of **ä** after the second-to-last radical. The same type of difference can be observed with quadriradicals (roots with four consonants), which are

---

[1] All forms except the participle are third person singular masculine forms. Apart from the participle suffix -i, the indicated affixes are agreement affixes. While different tense/aspect paradigms, e.g., perfect and imperfect, differ in the sets of agreement affixes they take, the only other difference between these paradigms are their different gemination and vowel patterns.

[2] All Amharic data, the basic verb classification and the Amharic orthography in this paper are taken from (1995; 2000); ä is a central mid-vowel, ə a central high vowel, and a a central low vowel.

usually divided into two classes (type 1 and type 2), where type 2 roots take a after the second-to-last radical in most paradigms while type 1 roots do not (mäsäkkärä, 'testify'; däballäqä, 'mix'):

(7.2) Verb Classes for Quadriradicals

	Type 1	Type 2
Perfect	mäsäkkärä	däballäqä
Imperfect	yəmäsäkkər	yədäballəq
Participle	mäskari	däbalaqi

Thus for both major types of roots, triradicals and quadriradicals, the distribution of gemination and of vowels in the stem can be completely predicted once the class membership of the root is known.[3] Crucially, verb classes cannot be completely reduced to syntactic, semantic, or phonological features of the respective roots. While it could be assumed that constant gemination of type B verbs corresponds to an underlying phonological feature of these roots, this is not true for gemination in specific morphological contexts such as for all the other verb classes. For example, it is unlikely that the restriction of gemination to the perfect in type A roots is due to a phonological feature of these roots. The fact that the inflectional class of Amharic verb roots is not predictable has been stated, e.g., by Leslau (2000) as follows (see also Bender and Fulass 1978; Amberber 2002):

(7.3) There are three types of triradicals: type A, type B, and type C. These types are conditioned neither by the nature of the consonants nor by the meanings of the verb. Indeed, verbs in any of these types may be active, transitive, verbs of state and so on, and may consist of any kind of consonants. The types are therefore to be considered lexical items. (Leslau 2000: 57)

In this chapter, I show, in line with Müller's (2003) analysis of noun classes in Russian, that Amharic verb classes have a fine-grained internal structure, and must be decomposed in different, more basic diacritic features. These features correspond roughly to properties like "gemination in the perfect" or "a after the penultimate root consonant", which characterize together traditional verb classes (e.g., "A, B, C" for triradical and "1, 2" for quadriradical verbs). I argue

---

[3] Amharic also has roots with five radicals which behave in all crucial respects like quadriradicals and will not be discussed here. Roots which apparently have only two radicals are traditionally analyzed as underlyingly triradical roots where one root consonant is deleted by (morpho)phonological processes (Leslau 1995) and are also outside of the scope of this chapter.

that class features are organized in a feature-geometric tree as has been proposed for pronominal features in Harley and Ritter (2003). Both assumptions are important to account for the phenomenon of class syncretism which is a pervasive feature of Amharic inflection. Thus, in the so-called **as**-derivation the distinction between type A and type B verbs collapses and both types assume the gemination pattern of type B (näggärä, 'tell', affixes are omitted here and in the following tables):

(7.4)   Class Syncretism in *as*-Stems

	Type A/B		Type C
Perfect	näggär	fälläg	marräk
Imperfect	näggər	fälləg	marrək
Participle	näggar	fällagi	marak

Assuming that syncretism generally follows from impoverishment, i.e., feature deletion, this means that the diacritic features of type A roots form a superset of those of type B roots, and as-derivation triggers deletion of the features which are specific for type A. This entails necessarily that class features for specific verb classes can be decomposed. I will show below that the unidirectionality of class syncretisms in Amharic verb inflection follows straightforwardly from the assumed feature geometry.

The remainder of this chapter is structured as follows. In section 7.2, I introduce Minimalist Distributed Morphology, the formal framework I will assume throughout. I lay out my proposal for the decomposition of verb class features for Amharic in section 7.3 and show how they are organized in a feature-geometric tree in section 7.4. After demonstrating that this geometry derives important restrictions on possible verb classes in the language, section 7.5 shows that it makes possible a simple analysis of class syncretism in terms of impoverishment operations. Finally, section 7.6 compares the feature-geometric approach with an alternative one using unordered feature bundles and contains a short summary of the chapter.

7.2 The framework: Minimalist Distributed Morphology

The framework I adopt in this paper is Minimalist Distributed Morphology (MDM, Trommer 1999; 2003a,b). In MDM, as in standard Distributed Morphology (DM, Halle and Marantz 1993), morphology interprets the output of syntax which operates on abstract feature bundles ("heads") without phonological content. Thus the Amharic sentence *anči tə-fälləg-i*, 'you (fem sg) wish', is represented syntactically as follows:

(7.5)   Syntactic Structure of *anči tə-fälləg-i*, 'you (fem sg) wish'

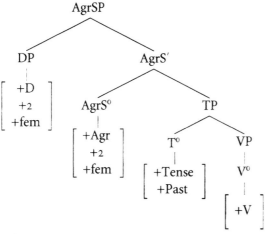

At morphological structure (MS), so-called vocabulary items (VIs), pairing underspecified morphosyntactic features with phonological content, are inserted into heads. Crucially, each inserted vocabulary item corresponds to exactly one head. (7.6) lists the VIs to be inserted in (7.5) to result in *anč-i təfälləgi*. Into the verb node **flg** is inserted, into the Agr head **tə-** and **-i**, and into the D head **ant** and **-i**.[4] The mechanisms which derive *fälləg* from the root **flg** will be discussed in detail in the following sections and will also shed light on the spellout of Tense.

(7.6)   ant: $\begin{bmatrix} +D \\ +2 \end{bmatrix}$ -i: $\begin{bmatrix} +\text{fem} \end{bmatrix}$

   tə-: $\begin{bmatrix} +\text{Agr} \\ +2 \end{bmatrix}$ flg: $\begin{bmatrix} +V \end{bmatrix}$

While standard DM assumes a great wealth of operations which manipulate the output of syntax before vocabulary insertion, in MDM vocabulary insertion apart from morphophonology is the *only* morphological operation. Systematic neutralization and "splitting" of syntactic heads into different affixes (VIs) which require separate rule formats in standard DM are captured as the by-product of vocabulary insertion itself. Formally, vocabulary insertion in MDM involves two conceptually virtually inescapable aspects of spell out: Syntactic features specified in the VI are deleted from the targeted syntactic head and the phonological representation is concatenated with the

---

[4]   Concatenation of **ant** and **i** leads to palatalization of **t**.

corresponding stem. With Halle (1997), I assume that more than one VI can be inserted into one syntactic head as long as the head still has undeleted features. Thus, as the form tə-säbr-i shows, in Amharic the feminine feature in 2sg forms is expressed by an affix (-*i*:[+fem]) separate from the person affix (*tə*-:[+2]). Data like this are expressed in classical DM by a fission operation which distributes the underlying heads into two partial heads and subsequent vocabulary insertion in the resulting positions:

(7.7)   Fission and Vocabulary Insertion in Classical DM

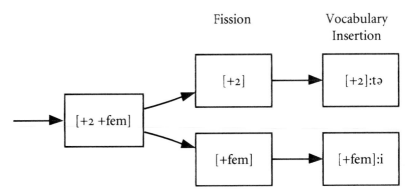

In MDM, fission is superfluous. Insertion of tə:[+2] deletes the second person feature and still allows insertion of i:[+fem] into the remaining feminine feature. At this point vocabulary insertion halts since there are no features left to trigger insertion:

(7.8)   Fission and Vocabulary Insertion in Minimalist DM

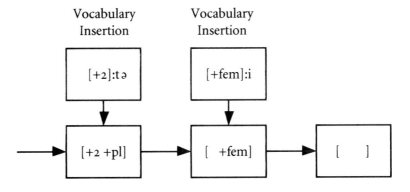

Syncretism is captured by insertion of VIs which are phonologically zero. Take as an example the gender distinction in Amharic imperfect forms which leads to different forms for masculine and feminine subjects in the second and third person singular, but which is syncretized in the plural (yə-säbər, 'he breaks'):

(7.9)   Gender Syncretism in Amharic Imperfect Forms

	Singular	Plural
1. sg	ə-säbər	ənnə-säbər
2. sg fem	tə-säbr-i	tə-säbr-u
2. sg masc	tə-säbər	
3. sg fem	tə-säbər	yə-säbr-u
3. sg masc	yə-säbər	

In classical DM, syncretisms of this type are usually captured by impover-ishment rules such as (7.10) which deletes feminine features in the context of plural agreement. Since impoverishment generally precedes vocabulary insertion, the syntactic feature specification [+fem] is invisible to insertion and -i:[+fem] is never inserted in plural forms:

(7.10)   [+/–fem] → Ø   / [__ +pl]

MDM maintains that syncretism results from feature deletion but denies the existence of a separate rule format to derive it. Instead data of this type are captured by insertion of VIs with zero phonology. (7.10) is thus replaced by (7.11):

(7.11)   Ø:[+fem]   / [__ +pl]

Since non-zero VIs also allow context restrictions in DM (classical and min-imalist), it implies no additional machinery to use them for zero VIs. That (7.11) is inserted before -i:[+fem] follows from the general principle that more specific VIs are inserted before less specific ones which is a basic tenet of DM (see section 7.4.1 for discussion). Note finally that zero vocabulary insertion again allows subsequent insertion of non-zero VIs if this spells out features which have not been deleted. Hence insertion of tə-:[$^{+Agr}_{+2}$] can and actually must follow insertion of (7.11).

7.3 Decomposing verb classes

Class syncretisms similar to the ones observed in Amharic also occur in the noun inflection of Russian. Müller (2003a,b) observes that syncretism in case endings in Russian occurs both inside single noun classes and across these classes. Thus, while the suffix -oj is restricted to class III nouns, -i occurs in specific contexts with both class II and class III nouns:

(7.12)   Case Syncretism in Russian Noun Suffixes

	I	II	III	IV
nom	Ø	a	Ø	o
acc	Ø/a	u	Ø	o
dat	u	e	i	u
gen	a	i	i	a
inst	om	oj	ju	om
loc	e	e	i	e

To capture the fact that -i is not restricted to a specific class, Müller proposes to decompose the noun classes by the features $+/-\alpha$ and $+/-\beta$ as follows:

(7.13)   Russian Noun Classes Decomposed

I $[+\alpha - \beta]$
II $[-\alpha + \beta]$
III $[-\alpha - \beta]$
IV $[+\alpha + \beta]$

The VIs in (7.14) now correctly capture the class restrictions for the markers -i and -oj. Restricting an affix to a single class is still possible as in the case of the full feature specification for -oj, but crucially an adequate characterization for the class distribution of -i is only possible by underspecification which is based on the decomposition of classes into atomic features:

(7.14)   Vocabulary Items for Russian

a.   oj:$[-\alpha - \beta \ldots]$
b.   i:$[-\alpha \ldots]$

In the following, I will show that a decomposition approach reveals crucial aspects of the verb class system of Amharic. Let us first review the distribution of gemination in triradicals and quadriradicals. The tables in (7.15) and (7.16) summarize the distribution of gemination for the penultimate root consonants from the data in (7.1) and (7.2):

(7.15)   Gemination in Triradicals

	Type A	Type B	Type C
Perfect	Gemination	Gemination	Gemination
Imperfect	No Gemination	Gemination	Gemination
Participle	No Gemination	Gemination	No Gemination

(7.16)   Gemination in Quadriradicals

	Type 1	Type 2
Perfect	Gemination	Gemination
Imperfect	Gemination	Gemination
Participle	No Gemination	No Gemination

Interestingly enough, the five verb classes have only three distinct distributions of gemination. Type C, type 1 and type 2 all have gemination in the perfect and imperfect but not in the other paradigms. This observation can be captured by assigning class features which correspond to the distribution of gemination: 1 is the class feature of roots having gemination only in the perfect, **all** characterizes roots with gemination throughout, and 2 is assigned to roots with gemination in perfect and imperfect. (7.17) illustrates this with a slightly bigger range of forms:

(7.17)   Gemination Classes

	Type A	Type B	Type 1	Type 2	Type C
Perfect	s bb r	f ll g	m s kk r	m rr k	d b ll q
Imperfect	s b r	f ll g	m s kk r	m rr k	d b ll q
Imperative	s b r	f ll g	m s k r	m r k	d b l q
Gerund	s b r	f ll g	m s k r	m r k	d b l q
Participle	s b r	f ll g	m s k r	m r k	d b l q
Verbal Noun	s b r	f ll g	m s k r	m r k	d b l q
Gemination Class	1	all	2		

While gemination classes 1 and **all** seem to be restricted to verb types A and B respectively, as we have seen above at least gemination class **all** also extends to other verbs in cases of class syncretism. Note that the names for gemination class features are mnemonic but in principle arbitrary and could be replaced by more neutral designators (such as α and β in Müller's analysis of Russian). While the morphological realization of all three features is related to gemination, they are diacritic features and none of them (except perhaps **all**) can be equated with a specific phonological realization throughout different paradigms.

That specific patterns cross-classify the traditional verb classes holds also true for vowel patterns. (7.18) and (7.19) show the distribution of the vowel preceding the second to last root consonant across different verb classes for tri- and quadriradicals. Type C and type 2 roots have consistently **a** in this position while types A, B and 1 have ä if the following root consonant is geminated, and otherwise either ä, ə or no vowel at all:

(7.18)   Class

	Type A	Type B	Type 1	Type C	Type 2
Perfect	säbbär	fälläg	mäsäkkär	marräk	d balläq
Imperfect	säb r	fälləg	mäsäkkər	marrək	d balləq
Imperative	səb är	fälləg	mäs k ər	mar k	d bal q
Gerund	säb r	fälləg	mäs k ər	mar k	d bal q
Participle	säb ar	fällag	mäs k ar	mar ak	d bal aq
Verbal Noun	səb är	fälläg	mäs k är	mar äk	d bal äq
Vowel Class		ä			a

I will show in section 7.4.2 that the different distributions of vowels in classes A/B/1 in this position is due to an complex interplay of different morphological processes and phonological epenthesis. What is of importance here is that all verb classes fall in one of two more general vowel classes, one characterized by ä and one characterized by a. Taking the subclassifications for gemination and vowels together now each of the traditional verb classes can be defined as the combination of a specific gemination class with a specific vowel class and the radical number as follows:

(7.19)   Vowel Classes Decomposed

	Type A	Type B	Type 1	Type C	Type 2
Gemination Class	1	all	2	2	2
Vowel Class	ä	ä	ä	a	a
Radical Number	3	3	4	3	4

However, not all combinations of vowel and gemination classes correspond to an existing verb class. Thus, there are no verbs (and hence no corresponding verb classes) which geminate only in the perfect (as type A) or throughout their paradigms (as type B) and have the characteristic a- vowel of vowel class **a**. This gap is indicated by "*" in (7.20):

(7.20)   (Non-)Co-occurrence of Decomposed Classes

Gemination Class	Vowel Class	
	ä	a
1	Type A	*
All	Type B	
2	Type 1	Type C Type 2

Similarly, not all combinations of vowel and gemination class combine with both numbers of radicals (3 and 4). Actually, only the combination 2/a occurs with 3 and 4 radicals (resulting in verb classes C and 2), but other combinations are restricted either to triradicals or to quadriradicals:

(7.21)   Vowel Classes Decomposed

Gemination/Vowel Class	1/ä	all/ä	2/ä	2/a
3 Radicals	Type A	Type B	*	Type C
4 Radicals	*	3	Type 1	Type 2

In section 7.4, I will show that both types of restrictions follow from the combination of a feature-geometric representation for vowel class and gemination class features and impoverishment rules.

7.4 The feature geometry of verb classes

Structuring features in hierarchical trees has a long tradition in generative phonology (cf. Clements 1985; Sagey 1986). Harley and Ritter (2002) show that a similar geometry of features is also able to capture important crosslinguistic generalizations if applied to morphosyntactic features (cf. also Bonet 1991; Nevins 2003; Trommer 2003a). More specifically, they propose a geometry for person and number features which is here exemplified by the representations for the number features singular, plural, and dual:

(7.22)   Feature Geometry in Morphosyntax (Harley and Ritter 2002)

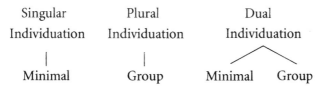

The fact that dual is represented by conjoining the features characteristic for singular and plural allows a simple account of the fact that languages which have a grammaticalized plural category also have a singular/plural distinction (Greenberg's universal 34; Greenberg 1963: 94). In the context of Minimalist Distributed Morphology, this geometry predicts strong restrictions on possible syncretisms. Thus, as argued in Trommer (2003a), this geometry allows for syncretisms of dual to plural or singular but not for syncretisms where singular levels to plural forms. This follows if all syncretism is caused by impoverishment, that is, zero VIs causing deletion of features. Hence syncretism can be caused by transforming the structure for dual into the one for singular as in (7.23), but the converse derivation in (7.23) which would involve feature insertion is excluded:[5]

(7.23)   Dual → Singular Syncretism (Possible)

(7.24)   Singular → Dual Syncretism (Excluded)

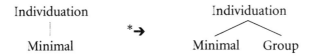

While Harley and Ritter (2002) argue that the features for person and number and their geometrical organization are universal,[6] I will show that the feature-geometric approach is also crucial for an account of language-specific, and more specifically diacritic, class features. In particular, I will argue that the gemination and vowel class features introduced in section 7.3 are structured as in (7.25):

(7.25)   Distinguishing Verb Classes Geometrically

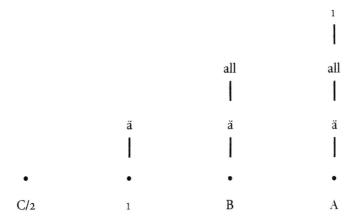

---

[5] The argument is slightly more intricate since underspecified vocabulary items must be taken into account. See Trommer 2003a for details.

[6] Parametrization among different feature systems in single languages is due the fact that not all languages use all features in all combinations and certain categories (e.g., singular) might be represented by underspecified feature geometries.

Note that the trees in (7.25) and in the following are depicted bottom-up not upside down as in the preceding examples since this allows a more transparent representation of derivations involving feature deletion. The traditional class names (1, 2, A, B, and C) are added for expository convenience but are not part of the tree structures, and in fact do not have any theoretical status in the analysis. The bullet ("•") represents the root node of the class features which links them to other morphosyntactic features of roots. It might be identified with a specific root feature but I will remain agnostic on this question here.

Now assuming that every node in a geometry is restricted to a single node which can immediately dominate it, that is, cannot be immediately dominated by any other node (e.g., all must always be dominated by ä and ä must always be dominated by the root node), this geometry by itself restricts the possible verb classes of Amharic to four. In other words, assuming the same features and the same conditions on immediate dominance, no other representations are possible. Structures as the ones in (7.26) are excluded since single nodes are immediately dominated by inappropriate mother nodes:

(7.26)   Excluded Class Representations

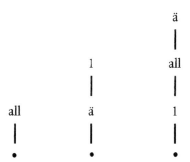

In the following two subsections, I will discuss how gemination and vowel patterns are derived by different VIs realizing class features through consonant gemination or vocalic features.

7.4.1 *Deriving gemination patterns*

I will assume that gemination or non-gemination of the penultimate root consonant is triggered by VIs specified for autosegmental skeleton structures, which are associated at vocabulary insertion with the melodic content of the penultimate root consonant. Hence these vocabulary items either specify CC (for gemination) or C for non-gemination.

I assume further that association of a specific segment happens only once during the derivation. For example, if one vocabulary item has associated the penultimate consonant with C, insertion of a following VI specifying CC will have no visible phonological effect. Vocabulary Insertion deletes, that is, delinks the morphosyntactic features the inserted VI specifies. Following standard assumptions of autosegmental phonology and morphology (Goldsmith 1990; Bonet 1991; Nevins 2003), delinking of a feature F automatically also delinks all features which are dominated by F. Thus, inserting the hypothetical VI (7.27b.) into the tree (7.27a.) results in (7.27c.) (the bare root node) not in (7.27d):

(7.27)   Autosegmental Conditioning of Vocabulary Insertion

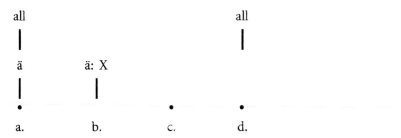

(7.28) now shows all VIs (G1–G3) which are responsible for gemination patterns in Amharic verbs and two default statements for the penultimate root consonants (D1 and D2), which govern gemination if none of the VIs is inserted:

(7.28)   Gemination Patterns by Vocabulary Items

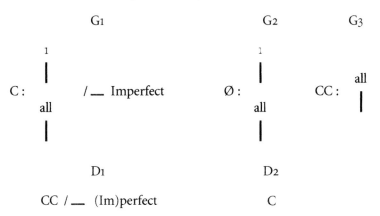

G3 is responsible for consistent gemination of type B roots which have **all** as the highest node of the feature tree. D1 ensures that in the default case imperfect and perfect forms have gemination. That type A verbs are exceptional

to the latter pattern in the imperfect is ensured by G1 which associates the penultimate root consonant with C before D1 can be applied. G2 has the effect that type A verbs in all remaining verb paradigms participate in the default patterns. Which VI is inserted first is determined by the three principles listed in (7.29):

(7.29) a. VIs associated with lower syntactic domains
            are inserted before VIs associated with higher syntactic domains
        b. VIs targeting less embedded features
            are inserted before VIs targeting more embedded features
        c. More specific VIs are inserted before less specific VIs

VIs can be associated to three domains, the root, vP, or CP, i.e., the root alone and the strong phases in the sense of Chomsky (2001). All VIs in (7.28) belong to the CP domain but we will see later VIs which are linked to one of the other two domains. Crucially VIs can spell out features from a lower syntactic domain (if this has not happened in that domain), but their context cannot be restricted by features already spelled out in the lower domain. (7.29b.) for example would prefer insertion of the hypothetic VI in (7.30) over G3 because (7.30) targets the less embedded feature 1:

$$
(7.30) \quad \text{Hypothetical VI:} \quad \overset{1}{\underset{|}{|}} : X
$$

Finally, (7.29c.) prefers insertion of VIs which are more specific either because they specify more features or because they have a context restriction. Thus G1 is prefered over G2 because, while everything else is equal, G1 has a context restriction and G2 has none. Similarly G2 is prefered over G3 since it specifies two features while G3 specifies only one. The principles in (7.29) are ordered in the sense that if they contradict each other (7.29a.) has precedence over (7.29b.) and (7.29c.), and (7.29b.) has precedence over (7.29c.). We will see examples for this point in later sections but for the VIs introduced so far the principles converge. For example, G2 is more specific than G3 but also targets a higher feature.

Let us now turn to concrete derivations. I will discuss derivations for type A, B, and C. Types 1 and 2 are crucially derived in the same way as type C. (7.31) shows how gemination in representative forms of type B verbs is derived. The penultimate consonant is represented by **b**, the preceding vowel by **V**. G1 and G2 do not match the initial class representation of these verbs, which do not contain the feature 1. Therefore, the first VI matching in all three forms is G3, which deletes the feature **all** and associates the penultimate consonant with gemination (CC). Since association for a given segment happens only once, no further VI has any effect on these forms and we get consistent gemination:

(7.31)   Deriving Type B Stems

		G1	G2	G3	D1	D2	
all ❘ ä ❘ •	Vb			all CC V			Perfect
	Vb	—	—	Vb			
				all CC V			Imperfect
	Vb	—	—	Vb			
				all CC V			Participle
	Vb	—	—	Vb			

Type C roots are maximally underspecified for class features, hence G1, G2, and G3 do not match them. Gemination is governed by the default statements resulting in gemination by D1 in the context of perfect and imperfect. In all other forms such as the participle, D2 applies and we get C, i.e., no gemination:

(7.32)   Deriving Gemination in Type C Stems

		G1	G2	G3	D1	D2	
•	Vb	—	—	—	CC V Vb		Perfect
	Vb	—	—	—	CC V Vb		Imperfect
	Vb	—	—	—		C ❘ Vb	Participle

The most complex derivations arise with type A roots. In the non-imperfect forms, G2 is inserted and deletes 1 and **all** but, since its phonological content is zero, there is no association with the penultimate root consonant and, in the perfect, D1 applies leading to gemination while in other non-imperfect forms such as the participle D2 results in non-gemination. G1 bleeds G2 for the imperfect form. Since G1 introduces a non-zero consonantal pattern, no further phonological effect of other VIs or default statements encoding the penultimate consonant is possible:

(7.33)   Deriving Gemination for Type A Stems

	G1	G2	G3	D1	D2	
		~~+all~~				
				CC		Perfect
				V		
	V b	—		—	V b	
		~~+all~~				
		C				Imperfect
		|				
	V b	V b				
			~~+all~~			
					C	Participle
					|	
	V b	—	—	—	V b	

The left margin shows: 1 | all | ä | •

7.4.2 *Deriving vowel patterns*

A specific complication with vowel patterns consists in the fact that, except by root class, vowels interspersed between the root are also partially governed by Tense, the category label of verbs and purely phonological vowel epenthesis. Let us consider each of these factors in turn. (7.34) contains again representative stem forms for all relevant classes. The vowels for each root column are aligned (resulting in spaces without significance) to ease comparison of vowels in corresponding positions:

(7.34)   Vowel Classes

	Type A	Type B	Type 1	Type C	Type 2
Perfect	säbbär	fälläg	mäsäkkär	marräk	däballäq
Imperfect	säb r	fälləg	mäsäkkər	marrək	däballəq
Imperative	səb är	fälləg	mäs k ər	mar k	däbal q
Gerund	säb r	fälləg	mäs k ər	mar k	däbal q
Participle	säb ar	fällag	mäs k ar	mar ak	däbal aq
Verbal Noun	səb är	fälläg	mäs k är	mar äk	däbal äq

Crucially, the last vowel of the stem can be almost completely predicted from Tense/aspect (or related categories as non-finiteness in participles). All perfect forms have ä in their last position, all participle forms a and all imperative forms either no vowel or ə after a geminate which is obviously phono-logically conditioned. I will therefore assume that–apart from phonological epenthesis–the last verbal stem vowel in Amharic is always the spellout of the Tense/aspect head. The only exception to the generalization that the last vowel is the same for a given Tense/aspect across verb classes are the type A forms in the imperative and the verbal noun. I assume that in these cases Tense is expressed by specific allomorphs (more specific VIs restricted to the context of type A, i.e., 1 - **all** - ä - a). Note that it is predicted by the feature-geometric approach that type A should be the locus of idiosyncratic allomorphy. If an allomorph were restricted to **all** - ä or to ä this would include type B but also other classes. This type of allomorphy also provides evidence that spellout of Tense happens before spellout of class features since if the opposite were true the features characteristic for type A would be deleted before spellout of Tense, and hence be invisible for allomorphy of Tense. I will assume that Tense spellout actually applies to bare roots resulting in the derivations shown in (7.35) with the vowels inserted by Tense spellout in bold face:

(7.35)   Tense

	Type A	Type B	Type 1	Type C	Type 2
Perfect	s b **är**	f l **äg**	m säk **är**	m rräk	d b l **äq**
Imperfect	s b **r**	f l **g**	m säkk **r**	m rr k	d b l **q**
Imperative	s**ə**b **är**	f l **g**	m s k **r**	m r k	d b l **q**
Gerund	s b **r**	f l **g**	m s k **r**	m r k	d b l **q**
Participle	s b **ar**	f l **ag**	m s k **ar**	m r ak	d b l **aq**
Verbal Noun	s**ə**b **är**	f l **äg**	m s k **är**	m r **äk**	d b l **äq**

Spellout of class features follows spellout of Tense. Due to the principle in (7.29b.) which has the effect that deeper embedded features are spelled out after less embedded features, VIs for gemination class features apply before VIs for vowel class features. (7.36) summarizes the effects of the derivations discussed in 7.4.1 on the stems in (7.35):

(7.36)   Gemination Class Features

	Type A	Type B	Type 1	Type C	Type 2
Perfect	s **bb**är	f **ll**äg	m säk är	m rräk	d b **ll**äq
Imperfect	s b r	f **ll** g	m säkk r	m rr k	d b **ll** q
Imperative	sə b är	f **ll** g	m s k r	m r k	d b l q
Gerund	s b r	f **ll** g	m s k r	m r k	d b l q
Participle	s b ar	f **ll**ag	m s k ar	m r ak	d b l aq
Verbal Noun	sə b är	f **ll**äg	m s k är	m r äk	d b l äq

As we have seen above, type C and type 2 verbs have a (hence vowel class a) in the second to last vowel position while all other types have ä (hence vowel class ä) if the following root consonant is geminated (we will see below why ä occurs also before some non-geminated penultimate root consonants). That the spellout of vowel class features presupposes information on gemination of the following consonant provides further evidence that the derivation of gemination precedes the determination of vowel patterns which follows crucially from the deeper embedding of vowel class features in the geometry.[7] (7.37) shows the effect I assume for the spellout of vowel class features, a for class a and ä before geminates in class ä roots.

(7.37)   Class

	Type A	Type B	Type 1	Type C	Type 2
Perfect	säbbär	fälläg	m säkkär	marräk	d balläq
Imperfect	s b r	fäll g	m säkk r	marr k	d ball q
Imperative	səb är	fäll g	m s k r	mar k	d bal q
Gerund	s b r	fäll g	m s k r	mar k	d bal q
Participle	s b ar	fällag	m s k ar	mar ak	d bal aq
Verbal Noun	səb är	fälläg	m s k är	mar äk	d bal äq

Finally, all verb classes show occurrence of ä in the position after the first root consonant if this is not already filled by another category as by Tense in the type A imperative or the class vowel a as in all type C roots. I will assume that ä here is the spellout of the categorial head, little v which dominates all verb roots:

(7.38)   v

	Type A	Type B	Type 1	Type C	Type 2
Perfect	säbbär	fälläg	mäsäkkär	marräk	däballäq
Imperfect	säb r	fäll g	mäsäkk r	marr k	däball q
Imperative	səb är	fäll g	mäs k r	mar k	däbal q
Gerund	säb r	fäll g	mäs k r	mar k	däbal q
Participle	säb ar	fällag	mäs k ar	mar ak	däbal aq
Verbal Noun	səb är	fälläg	mäs k är	mar äk	däbal äq

Under the assumption that, as with gemination, insertion of vowels into the root is feature-filling, hence cannot replace previously inserted vowels, this

---

[7] Note that gemination does not correspond one by one to any of the atomic or composed verb classes. Thus, the context dependency of vowel realization in this case seems to be truly phonological.

follows naturally if spellout of little v occurs after the spellout of class and Tense. Taken together the whole derivation implies the hierarchical order Tense ≻ Class ≻ v which also corresponds to the linear order of the root vowels. Tense vowels are final, class vowels roughly medial, and vowels corresponding to little v initial. Importantly, this order is the mirror image of the structure of verbs proposed for verbs in Romance languages by Oltra-Massuet (1999) and Oltra-Massuet and Arregi (2005)[8] suggesting that there are principled syntactic reasons for the ordering of root vowels:

(7.39) a. Amharic: Tense ≻ Class ≻ v
        b. Romance: v ≻ Class ≻ Tense

Finally, in specific positions epenthetic ə is inserted, especially after geminate consonants, but optionally also in specific other positions as in the imperfect form **säbr**, which can optionally be realized as **säbər**. (7.40) shows the cases of obligatory ə-epenthesis:

(7.40) ə-Epenthesis

	Type A	Type B	Type 1	Type C	Type 2
Perfect	säbbär	fälläg	mäsäkkär	marräk	däballäq
Imperfect	säb r	fälləg	mäsäkkər	marrək	däballəq
Imperative	səb är	fälləg	mäs k ər	mar k	däbal q
Gerund	säb r	fälləg	mäs k ər	mar k	däbal q
Participle	säb ar	fällag	mäs k ar	mar ak	däbal aq
Verbal Noun	səb är	fälläg	mäs k är	mar äk	däbal äq

Let us now return to the spellout of the vowel class features themselves. I assume that this is due to the three VIs in (7.41). Note that V1 is restricted to the context of penultimate root geminates:

(7.41) Vowel Patterns by Vocabulary Items

$$V_1 \qquad\qquad V_2 \qquad\qquad V_3$$

$$\text{ä:} \ \begin{matrix} \ddot{a} \\ | \\ \bullet \end{matrix} \ / CC \qquad \varnothing: \ \begin{matrix} \ddot{a} \\ | \\ \bullet \end{matrix} \qquad \text{a:} \ \bullet$$

---

[8] These authors treat the position I term "Class" as "Theme". However in their analysis the theme position expresses–by contextual allomorphy–almost exclusively class features of the verb. A further difference to my analysis here is that they assume for Romance additional theme positions following other functional heads (e.g., Tense).

After the spellout of gemination class features, type A and type B roots have the same feature structures (• dominated by ä). Hence the only distinction which is relevant in both classes is the (non-)presence of a root geminate. If a geminate is present in this position, V1 is inserted, otherwise V2. Since both VIs are more specific and target a less embedded feature, they bleed insertion of V3, which is only inserted in the maximally underspecified type C/2 structures:

(7.42)   Deriving Class Vowels

	V1	V2	V3	
ä | •	•—ä ä | V bb	V b b		Type A/B with Gemination
ä | •	V b	•—ä ä | —	V b	Type A without Gemination
• V b	—	—	• a | V b(b)	Type C

7.4.3 *Explaining co-occurrence restrictions*

Recall that there are substantial restrictions on the co-occurrence of vowel and gemination patterns, but also on the possible combinations of root class and the number of root consonants. The first of these restrictions already follows from the analysis proposed so far. The fact that roots with gemination patterns 1 and **all** never have vowel pattern a follows from the fact that the VIs responsible for the spellout of these classes reduce them uniformly to the structure ä – •, and, as we saw, the VIs for vowel class feature realize this structure as ä bleeding realization as **a**.

Since neither the feature geometry nor the VIs so far make any reference to radical number, the co-occurrence restrictions which treat triradicals and quadriradicals differently still remain to be accounted for. Impoverishment implemented by insertion of zero VIs accounts straightforwardly for these facts. Recall from section 7.3 that there are no quadriradicals which behave like type A triradicals in showing only gemination in the perfect. Similarly, there are no triradicals which have gemination in the perfect and imperfect, and the ä vowel pattern, while there is a root class which has just these properties in quadriradicals (class 1).

The VI in (7.43) is associated with the root level and is inserted before all VIs from vP and CP level (cf. the discussion of (7.29a.)). It applies to all roots with four consonants and the feature specifications of (triradical) class A and B verbs. While quadriradicals with these specifications are possible in the lexicon, (7.43) has the effect that the relevant features are deleted before any other VI is inserted.

(7.43)   CR1

Ø :   all   / __ CCCC

       |

The VI targets the feature **all** which by the general working of autosegmental rules leads for type A roots also to delinking of 1 which is dominated by **all**. The resulting feature structures are identical to the one characteristic of type 1 verbs. Thus, on the surface, quadriradical type A and B verbs are indistinguishable from type C roots:[9]

(7.44)   Neutralization of Quadriradical Type A and B Roots to Type 1

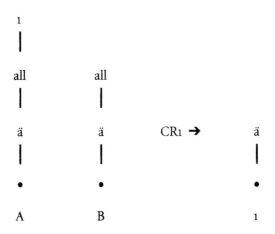

---

[9] Of course, language learners when acquiring a quadriradical root which can either be interpreted as type 2 or A/B will probably choose type 2 since this minimizes the derivational steps necessary to derive verb forms involving this root.

In an analogous way, triradicals of type 1 are excluded by the zero VI in (7.45). The bar above ä indicates that the VI targets only trees where ä is a terminal node (i.e., does not dominate anything else).[10]

(7.45)   CR2

$$\varnothing : \quad \overset{\rule{1em}{0.4pt}}{\underset{|}{ä}} \qquad / \underline{\ \ } \ \text{CCC}$$

Since type 1 roots are characterized underlyingly by undominated ä, this is deleted with triradical verbs, and in this way all such roots will be reduced to the root node, hence type C. (7.46) summarizes how CR1 and CR2 effectively derive the observed inventory of radical number/root type combinations:

(7.46)   Combinations

	Triradicals				Quadriradicals			
Lexical	C/2	1	A	B	C/2	1	A	B
		CR2					CR1	
Surfacing	C/2		A	B	C/2		1	

7.5 Class syncretism as impoverishment

As shown in section 7.1, in stems derived by as-, which express causativity, the distinction between type A and type B roots disappears and both types are inflected throughout as type B roots. The tables in (7.47) and (7.48) illustrate this case of class syncretism:[11]

(7.47)   Basic Stem (Repeated)

	Type A	Type B	Type 1	Type C
Perfect	näggär	fälläg	mänäzzär	marräk
Imperfect	nägər	fälləg	mänäzzər	marrək
Participle	nägar	fällag	mänzar	marak

---

[10] It is also necessary to ensure that "CCC" matches only triradicals and not three consonants in quadriradicals. This might be achieved by boundary symbols, e.g., "+CCC+".

[11] The prefix as- and other derivational prefixes are omitted here and in the following tables.

(7.48) *as*-Stem

	Type A/B		Type 1	Type C
Perfect	näggär	fälläg	mänäzzär	marräk
Imperfect	näggər	fälləg	mänäzzər	marrək
Participle	näggar	fällagi	mänzar	marak

The feature-geometric approach to class features gives us now an easy handle on this phenomenon. Since the features representing class B form a proper subtree of the features for type A, syncretism leveling type A to type B can be simply captured by feature deletion, which in the current framework is implemented as insertion of zero VIs. The VI in (7.49) deletes the feature 1 in the context of an **as**- prefix and has exactly this effect as shown in (7.50):

(7.49) CS1: $\Big|$: ∅   / as- ⎯

(7.50) Class Syncretism in *as*-Stems by Impoverishment

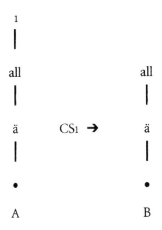

Given the proposed feature geometry in (7.25), in principle any class L can be neutralized to one of the classes which are represented by feature trees forming proper subtrees of the one for L. Indeed all of these possibilities are attested in other derivational patterns of Amharic. Thus, in the at-stem which involves prefixation of at- and expresses causativity of reciprocity (Leslau 1995: 486), all verb classes behave as type C or type 2 roots, that is, they exhibit **a** before the penultimate root consonant and geminate only in the perfect and imperfect as shown in (7.51):

(7.51)   at-Stems

	Type A/B		Type 1	Type C
Perfect	naggär	falläg	mänazzär	marräk
Imperfect	naggər	falləg	mänazzər	marrək
Participle	nagar	falagi	mänazar	marak

The same class syncretism occurs in derivations formed by internal reduplication of the penultimate root consonant, which expresses repetition, frequency, or intensivity of action (Leslau 1995: 456). The vowel preceding the second instance of the doubled consonant is always a, while the penultimate root consonant itself is doubled in the perfect and imperfect and shows otherwise no gemination. Geminated triradical roots hence behave in every respect as quadriradical type 2 roots.[12]

(7.52)   Class Syncretism in Reduplicated Stems

	Type A	Type B	Type C
Perfect	säbabbär	fälalläg	märarräk
Imperfect	säbabbər	fälalləg	märarrək
Participle	säbabar	fälalag	märarak

In terms of the feature geometry for class features, in both types of derivation (at- and frequentative), all features above the root node are deleted in the context of at- or the reduplicative morpheme. This can be accomplished by the VI in (7.53) which targets ä, but by the usual autosegmental delinking conventions delinks, i.e., deletes also all nodes dominated by ä:

(7.53)   CS2 $\begin{vmatrix} \ddot{a} \\ | \\ \bullet \end{vmatrix}$: Ø / __ {at-, RED}

Hence, all occurring feature structures are reduced to the bare root node:

---

[12] In Amharic only triradical roots can reduplicate in this manner. However, in related Ethiosemitic languages such as Tigre, quadriradicals can also reduplicate, resulting in quinqueradicals. Interestingly, these also behave as specific classes of non-derived quinqueradicals (Rose 2003).

(7.54)   Class Syncretism in *at*-Stems and Reduplicated Stems by Impoverishment

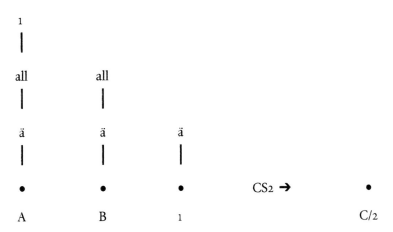

Note that in order to bleed the VIs for type A verbs (G1 and G2 in (7.28)), CS2 has to be associated with an earlier syntactic domain than those. I will assume that all zero VIs relevant for class syncretism are assigned to the vP domain which fits well with the fact that the derivational categories which trigger them manipulate at least partly argument structure.

A third type of class syncretism is found in the tä-derivation which derives passive verbs. Here type A and type B verbs pattern with type 1 verbs in the imperfect and jussive but not in other forms such as participles,[13] that is, in the imperfect and jussive they show the typical vowel distribution of class ä, and geminate in the imperfect but not in the jussive:

(7.55)   Class Syncretism in *tä*-Stems

	Type A	Type B	Type 1	Type C
Perfect	säbbär	fälläg	mäsäkkär	marräk
Imperfect	säbbär	fälläg	mäsäkkär	marräk
Jussive	säbär	fäläg	mäskär	maräk
Participle	säbari	fällag	mäskar	maraki

This behavior follows from the VI in (7.56), which is not only restricted to a specific derivational affix but also to the relevant Tense/aspect categories:

$$(7.56) \quad CS3 \quad \begin{array}{c} \text{all} \\ | \\ \emptyset \end{array} \quad : \quad / \quad \text{tä-} \underline{\quad} \{ \text{Impf/Juss} \}$$

---

[13] Perfect forms are geminated throughout all classes; therefore, that different classes share this pattern is not an indication for syncretism.

(7.57) shows how **CS3** in effect reduces type A and type B roots to type 1:

(7.57)   Class Syncretism in *tä*-Stems by Impoverishment

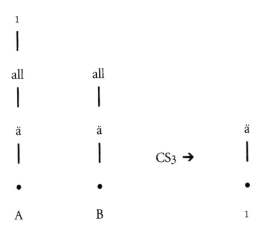

Note that the tä-derivation creates (although only in a restricted part of the paradigms) triradicals which pattern like type 1 roots, which was excluded in section 7.4.3 by **CR2**. However, **CR2** applies at the root cycle, i.e., before **CS3**. This has the–empirically correct–consequence that the constraint against triradical type 1 roots holds only for roots which are type 1 via lexical specification but not for roots where this class is derived by derivational processes.

(7.58) summarizes now the neutralization processes occurring in Amharic root derivations:

(7.58)   Class Syncretisms

A	B	1	C/2	
A ➜ B				(*as-*)
A ➜ 1				
	B ➜ 1			(*tä-*)
A ➜ C				
	B ➜ C			(*at-*)
		1 ➜ C		

Crucially, all the observed class syncretisms follow the hierarchy in (7.59a.) in the sense that syncretism can level a verb class higher in the hierarchy to a lower one but not the other way around. In other words, syncretisms as in (7.59b.) are excluded:

(7.59) a. Hierarchy: $A \succ B \succ 1 \succ C/2$
        b. Excluded: $B \rightarrow A, 1 \rightarrow A, 1 \rightarrow B, C \rightarrow A, C \rightarrow B, 1 \rightarrow C$

This unidirectionality of class syncretism follows from the combination of feature geometry and the assumption that syncretism is always due to strictly feature-deleting zero VI insertion. Since the hierarchy in (7.59a.) corresponds to the complexity of the feature trees in their representation, each class in (7.59a.) is a proper subtree of the next higher class. Syncretism leveling B to A would involve inserting the feature 1 which is excluded in MDM.

Note finally that pervasive implicational patterns in stem-forming morphology are not an idiosyncratic pattern of Amharic root-and-pattern morphology. Related observations have been made explicitly for stem alternants in Polish by Cameron-Faulkner and Carstairs-McCarthy (2000) and Carstairs-McCarthy (2002) (cf. also Wurzel 1984; Bittner 1985; Carstairs-McCarthy 1991). Wiese (2004) notes that in German, despite a bewildering variety of ablaut patterns, ablaut in finite past tense forms always implies ablaut in the past participle (see also section 7.6). Bobaljik (2006) observes on the basis of a cross-linguistic survey and in line with Ultan (1972) that suppletion in the superlative of a given root always implies suppletion in the comparative of this root. Bobaljik's analysis of this implicational generalization is actually quite similar to the analysis of Amharic provided here. He assumes that superlative constructions build syntactically generally on the structure also employed by comparatives; in other words, comparatives are substructures of a phrase headed by a (hierarchically higher) superlative head. Based on similar assumptions about the architecture of morphosyntax as the ones assumed here, this derives the superlative–comparative implication.[14]

---

[14] A feature–geometric account of the superlative-comparative implication seems to be in principle possible, while it is probably problematic to assume that the hierarchy of class features in Amharic is due to internal syntactic structure for these features. Anyway, the conceptual and empirical boundaries between (hierarchical) feature geometry and (hierarchical) syntactic structure are in general a largely unresolved topic awaiting thorough investigation in future research.

7.6 Discussion and summary

The analysis of class syncretism in section 7.5 could in principle be mimicked by a theory which uses unordered feature bundles if verb types are represented by combinations of unary features as in (7.60):[15]

(7.60)   Unordered Feature System for Amharic Verb Types

A	=	[1 ä all]
B	=	[ä all]
1	=	[ä]
C/2	=	[ ]

A similar analysis of implications in the distribution of German ablaut patterns is proposed in Wiese (2004). However, for the Amharic data, this approach has three serious shortcomings. First, it also predicts a number of unattested classes, namely the ones in (7.61):

(7.61)   Additional Verb Classes Predicted by an Unordered Feature System

??	=	[1]
??	=	[all]
??	=	[1 all]

Second, the approach based on unordered features does not predict that gemination class features are spelled out before vowel class features. Thus, nothing under such an approach blocks spellout of ä before spellout of 1 and **all**. However, as we have seen in section 7.4.2, the correct derivational order of feature types is crucial for the appropriate insertion of vowel class VIs in the context of (non-)gemination, and follows straightforwardly from general constraints on vocabulary insertion in the feature-geometric approach.

Third and most importantly, under an unordered feature approach, impoverishment cannot be captured in a natural way. Recall that with tä-derivation, type A and type B reduce to type 1, which I have captured by a VI referring to **all** causing also delinking of 1 if present:

---

[15]   A similar analysis could be stated with binary features but this would make the comparison more complex without changing the general points.

(7.62)   Class Syncretism in *tä*-Stems by Impoverishment

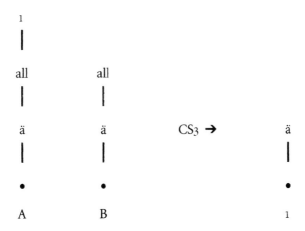

In a unary feature approach, there is no inherent reason why deletion of **all** and 1 should co-occur. This would have to be stipulated by disjunction in the VI carrying out impoverishment or by different VIs referring to the same context (the presence of **tä**). In any way, an important generalization would be missed. Similar observations hold for most of the zero VIs causing impoverishment which I have discussed in this chapter.

Thus, the feature-geometric approach captures important generalizations, both on possible classes (and their derivations) and the working of class syncretisms which are not available in a system with unordered features.

References

Amberber, M. (2002) *Verb Classes and Transitivity in Amharic*. München: LINCOM Europa.

Bender, M. L., and H. Fulass, (1978) *Amharic Verb Morphology: A Generative Approach*. African Studies Center, Michigan State University.

Bittner, A. (1985) 'Implikative Hierarchien in der Morphologie: Das "Stark-schwach-Kontinuum" der neuhochdeutschen Verben'. *Acta Linguistica Academiae Scientiarum Hungaricae* 35: 31–42.

Bobaljik, J. D. (2007) 'Comparative suppletion: Generalizations and implications', Ms., University of Connnecticut, available under http://ling.auf.net/lingBuzz/000443.

Bonet, E. (1991) Morphology after syntax: Pronominal clitics in Romance. PhD thesis, MIT.

Cameron-Faulkner, T., and A. Carstairs-McCarthy (2000) 'Stem alternants as morphological signata: Evidence from blur avoidance in Polish nouns'. *Natural Language and Linguistic Theory*, 18: 813–35.

Carstairs-McCarthy, A. (1991) 'Inflection classes: Two questions with one answer', in F. Plank (ed.), *Paradigms: The Economy of Inflection*, Berlin: Mouton de Gruyter, pp. 213–53.

—— (2002) 'How stems and affixes interact: Stem alternants as morphological signata', in S. Bendjaballah, W. Dressler, O. Pfeiffer, and M. Voeikova (eds.), *Morphology 2000: Selected papers from the 9th Morphology Meeting, Vienna, 24–28 February 2000*, Amsterdam: John Benjamins, pp. 49–57.

Chomsky, N. (2001) 'Derivation by phase', in M. Kenstowicz (ed.), *Ken Hale: A life in Language*, Cambridge, MA: MIT Press, pp. 1–52.

Clements, G. N. (1985) 'The geometry of phonological features'. *Phonology Yearbook*, 2: 225–52.

Goldsmith, J. (1990) (ed.) *Autosegmental and Metrical Phonology*. Oxford: Blackwell.

Greenberg, J. H. (1963) 'Some universals of grammar with special reference to the order of meaningful elements', in J. H. Greenberg (ed.), *Universals of Language*, Cambridge, MA: MIT Press, pp. 58–90.

Halle, M. (1997) 'Distributed Morphology: Impoverishment and fission', in Y. Kang, B. Bruening and M. McGinnis (eds.), *Papers at the Interface*, vol. 30 of *MIT Working Papers in Linguistics*, Cambridge, MA: MITWPL, pp. 425–49.

—— and A. Marantz (1993) 'Distributed Morphology and the pieces of inflection', in K. Hale and S. J. Keyser (ed.), *The View from Building 20*, Cambridge, MA: MIT Press, pp. 111–76.

Harley, H., and E. Ritter (2002) 'A feature-geometric analysis of person and number'. *Language*, 78(3): 482–526.

Leslau, W. (1995) *Reference Grammar of Amharic*. Wiesbaden: Harrassowitz.

—— (2000) *Introductory Grammar of Amharic*. Wiesbaden: Harrassowitz.

Müller, G. (2003a) 'A Distributed Morphology approach to syncretism in Russian noun inflection', in O. Arnaudova, W. Browne, M. L. Rivero, and D. Stojanovic (eds.), *Proceedings of FASL 12*.

—— (2003b) 'On decomposing inflection class features: Syncretism in Russian noun inflection', in L. Gunkel, G. Müller, and G. Zifonun (eds.), *Explorations in Nominal Inflection*, Berlin: Mouton de Gruyter, pp. 189–228.

Nevins, A. I. (2003) 'Do person/number syncretisms refer to negative values?' handout of a talk at the LSA meeting, Atlanta, GA, January 2003.

Oltra-Massuet, M. I. (1999) 'On the constituent structure of Catalan verbs', in V. Lin, C. Krause, B. Bruening, and K. Arregi (eds.), *Papers on Morphology and Syntax: Cycle Two*, vol. 34 of *MIT Working Papers in Linguistics*, Cambridge, MA: MITWPL, pp. 279–322.

—— and K. Arregi (2005) 'Stress-by-structure in Spanish'. *Linguistic Inquiry*, 36(1): 43–84.

Rose, S. (2003) 'Triple take: Tigre and the case of internal reduplication', in *San Diego Linguistics Papers*, Oxford: Oxford University Press, pp. 109–28.

Sagey, E. (1986) The representation of features and relations in non-linear phonology. PhD thesis, MIT.

Trommer, J. (1999) 'Morphology consuming syntax' resources: Generation and parsing in a minimalist version of Distributed Morphology', in *Proceedings of the ESSLI Workshop on Resource Logics and Minimalist Grammars*.

—— (2003a) 'Feature (non-)insertion in a minimalist approach to spellout', in *Proceedings of CLS 39*, pp. 469–80.

—— (2003b) 'Hungarian has no portmanteau agreement', in P. Siptár and C. Pinón (eds.), *Approaches to Hungarian*, vol. 9, pp. 283–302 Akadémiai Kiadó.

Ultan, R. (1972) 'Some features of basic comparative constructions', *Working Papers on Linguistic Universals*, 9: 117–62.

Wiese, B. (2004) 'Unterspezifizierte Stammparadigmen: Zur Systematik des Verbablauts im Gegenwartsdeutschen', Ms., IDS Mannheim; available under http://www.ids-mannheim.de/gra/texte/wi3.pdf.

Wurzel, W. U. (1984) *Flexionsmorphologie und Natürlichkeit*. Berlin: AkademieVerlag.

8

Russian genitive plurals
are impostors

JOHN F. BAILYN AND ANDREW NEVINS

8.1 Markedness and allomorphy within Distributed Morphology

Our primary focus in this chapter is on the distribution of allomorphs for the Russian genitive plural. The Russian genitive plural has been a topic of interest to morphological theory because various authors have claimed that its derivation involves some or all of the following grammatical principles:

(8.1) a. Inflectional paradigms aspire to "avoid homophony". The Russian nominative singular and genitive plural endings reflect a transderivational attempt to minimize homophony across inflectional endings.

  b. Inflectional paradigms require transderivational reference: one cannot compute the Russian genitive plural without knowing what the nominative singular ending is.

  c. Markedness-based neutralization may not hold: the genitive plural ending in Russian, unlike other oblique plurals, shows distinct gender inflection.

The goal of this chapter is to show that, counter to appearances, the Russian genitive plural does not instantiate any of the principles in (8.1). In regards to (8.1a.), it would be opportunistic and in fact false to claim that homophony-avoidance plays a role in Russian inflection across the nominative and genitive cases. Feminine nouns show identical endings for nominative plural and genitive singular:[1]

---

[1] We mark palatalization on each consonant, rather than following the more widely-used orthographic tradition that does not mark soft (palatalized) consonants when before front vowels.

(8.2)	Nom Sg	Nom Pl	Gen Sg	Gen Pl		
	kn'iga	kn'ig'i	kn'ig'i	kn'ig	'book' (fem)
	gaz'eta	gaz'ety	gaz'ety	gaz'et	'newspaper' (fem)
	dv'er'	dv'er'i	dv'er'i	dv'er'ej	'beast' (fem)

An Identical ending across nominative plural and genitive singular occurs in addition for all neuter nouns with fixed stress.[2]

(8.3)	Nom Sg	Nom Pl	Gen Sg	Gen Pl
	gosudárstvo	gosudárstva	gosudárstva	gosudárstv
	zdán'ije	zdán'ija	zdán'ija	zdán'ij

We thus do not consider (8.1a.) in our discussion of the genitive plurals any further. The focus of this chapter will be on (8.1b.–c.) as they relate to principles of inflection within the theory of Distributed Morphology. This chapter is concerned with two core principles of Distributed Morphology (DM): markedness-based syncretism and locally-conditioned allomorphy. These two principles are somewhat novel to DM and distinguish it from other approaches to inflectional morphology. In the course of this chapter, we examine the oblique plural forms of Russian nouns as a case study to examine both of these principles.

8.1.1 *Markedness and impoverishment lead to syncretism*

Within DM, there is an important source of syncretism and of systematic absences of overt featural distinctions within a given category when they occur. This source is feature-deletion prior to morphosyntactic realization. Consider, for example, the fact that first person pronouns never bear gender distinctions in many languages, exemplified here by Russian. Clearly the gender features are present within the syntax in order to condition adjectival agreement in (8.4).

(8.4) Ja   budu   rada
       1st-Nom. be-fut-1.sg glad-fem.sing.
       'I will be glad' (feminine)

The feature [+feminine] must be present on the subject pronoun in order to trigger feminine agreement on the adjective. However, it fails to show up on the agreeing auxiliary or on the pronoun itself. Notably both of these items are ones where the feature of first person (call it [+Author]) is present. Rather

---

[2] Moreover, due to vowel reduction in the final unstressed vowel, the nominative singular is phonetically identical to the nominative plural and genitive singular as well.

than it being an accident of Russian that all environments where [+Author] occurs are ones where there is no distinction made for the gender feature [±feminine], we may view this instead as the consequence of a systematic rule of feature deletion that applies to the output of syntax:

(8.5)   Impoverishment Rule:
        Delete the feature [feminine] on all terminal nodes that bear the feature [+Author]

Since the adjective in (8.4) does not agree in person, it will be exempt from (8.5). However, we know that the feature [+feminine] must be present on the pronominal DP at some earlier point in the syntactic derivation in order to trigger agreement. The featural deletion rule in (8.5) thus yields syncretism: when a feature is deleted prior to morphological realization, there is no way that the morphology can show differentiation for that feature and the effect is identical realization of syntactic terminals that were either [+feminine] or [−feminine].

The observation that syncretism arises because a particular feature (in this case gender) systematically fails to be realized–i.e., is neutralized–in a certain "column/row of a paradigm" is not unique to DM. However, what is unique is the attempt to understand rules such as (8.5) within the context of morphological markedness (see Calabrese (this volume) for an application of markedness-based neutralization to case syncretisms).

Thus, the rule in (8.5) can be viewed as a consequence of the inherent markedness of the feature [+Author] among the person features. This aspect of markedness, leading to fewer subdistinctions within a marked category, is dubbed the syncretizational aspect of markedness by Greenberg (1966). For the purposes of this chapter, we may view the following morphological environments as marked:

(8.6)   Marked environments, where impoverishment is likely to occur:[3]
        a. First Person
        b. Plural Number
        c. Feminine Gender
        d. Oblique Cases (i.e., not Nominative or Accusative)
        e. Non-Present Tense

---

[3] An interesting tendency is that marked environments may be more morphologically "marked" – i.e, show more overt morphology for the category they are expressing–at the same time that they show fewer subdistinctions for other categories. Thus, "marked" often has both "more morphology" on an overt level and "fewer morphosyntactic featural distinctions" at an abstract, featural level. Our discussion here, as that of Greenberg (1966) and most work on morphosyntactic markedness, focuses strictly on the latter.

In many instances, one of these features will be neutralized in the context of another. For example, consider Russian. In the past tense, person is neutralized: cf. *igrala* 'she played, you (fem.) played, I (fem.) played'. On syntactic nodes with the first person feature [+author], gender is neutralized. In the feminine gender, dative and locative (two oblique cases) are neutralized. Finally, our concern with this chapter will be with the plural, where gender is, we argue, neutralized. Plural adjectives in Russian show no gender distinctions. Plural forms of locative, dative, instrumental, and, as we ultimately argue, genitive, show no gender distinctions. In a theory like DM, that has "impoverishment" rules deleting/neutralizing features, syncretisms like this are formally analyzable as more than accidental. This markedness-based approach to neutralization is unique to DM, and does not form a core part of the understanding of syncretisms in alternative approaches to morphology that do not have rules of "impoverishment" that delete/neutralize features.

Given these two sources of syncretism, one can state a fairly restrictive constraint on syncretism within inflectional paradigms:[4]

(8.7) The Least-Marked/Least-Specified Constraint on Syncretisms:

> Let A and B be distinct morphosyntactic categories with respect to a common superordinate category C (e.g., "number"), where the (set of) feature(s) F distinguishes B from A. If A and B are expressed by the same phonological piece a, then either (i) a is the default phonological affix for the superordinate category or (ii) A is the morphosyntactically least marked category within the superordinate category.
>
> a. Case (i): A and B are both expressed by an "elsewhere" item: a phonological piece that realizes C but is underspecified and compatible with either A or B.
>   *Emergence of the Least-Specified*:
> $/a/ \leftrightarrow$ C, where C $\subseteq$ A and C $\subseteq$ B
> b. Case (ii): B undergoes *impoverishment* and becomes featurally identical to A during the syntax-to-phonology mapping.

Crucially, in understanding (8.7), the affix that is the elsewhere item need not be identical to the affix realizing the least marked item. Though sometimes conflated, the two properties of *least marked within a given representational vocabulary* and *widest distribution within a paradigm* are logically independent. The former is a consequence of markedness as defined within a

---

[4] Noyer (2005) reaches a similar conclusion for cross-conjugation class syncretisms in Greek, with syncretism as the result of either (and only) default conjugation class insertion following impoverishment or elsewhere insertion.

featural system, the latter is an accident of a sparse vocabulary in the language at hand.

From a learner's perspective, the elsewhere item will be deduced through its heterogeneous distribution within a paradigm.[5] The least-marked featural complex, on the other hand, is given by the representation, which is based on an explicit theory of markedness. The constraint in (8.7) is not an "axiom" but a consequence of the more general formal restriction that postsyntactic morphological operations simplify the output of syntax: they can delete but not add features.

It is this second source of syncretism, namely markedness-based feature-impoverishment, that will play a role when we turn to our examination of the genitive plural in Russian in the body of this chapter.

(8.8)   **DM Hypothesis I**: Neutralization occurs in *marked* environments; that is, there should not be an inflectional paradigm which shows more gender distinctions in the plural than in the singular, more gender distinctions in the first person than in the third person, and so forth, as governed by a theory of markedness of featural categories.

8.1.2 *Locally-conditioned allomorphy*

One of the most striking things about the mental lexicon is not how many items we memorize but the fact that we have to memorize so many different environments in which the same item will have different realizations. This is the well-known situation of allomorphy:

(8.9)   *Allomorphy*: When a set of features F on a single syntactic terminal has more than one distinct phonological realization

Let us consider a relatively simple case of phonologically-conditioned allomorphy: the nominative case suffix in Korean.

(8.10)   Korean allomorphy: [Nom] ↔ /-ka/ when stem is V-final; /-i/ when stem is C-final

Within DM, allomorphic effects may only arise as a function of elements within the current derivation. Thus, by hypothesis, no effects can arise due to the phonology of "related words".

---

[5] Here and elsewhere, "paradigm" refers to a group of featural complexes that share a superordinate feature (e.g., "Past"). The present framework, however, ascribes no psychological reality to the row-and-column arrangement that is graphically used to display distinctions within a featural space.

(8.11)   **DM Hypothesis II:** Allomorphy can only be conditioned by the phonology in the current derivation, not by the phonology of other derivations

In other words, the choice of which allomorph will realize Korean nominative case is not dependent on which allomorph realizes dative case for that stem.

Having outlined these two core principles of DM, we proceed to the empirical focus of the chapter: the Russian case system. The Russian case system supports both hypotheses: (I) gender and class distinctions are neutralized in the marked environment: [+Oblique, +Pl], and (II) allomorphy is locally determined by the phonological form of the stem. However, as we will go to some lengths in discussing, the genitive plural presents an apparent conundrum, as existing accounts of its realization either violate Hypothesis I (8.8) or II (8.11). In the next section, we turn to a basic outline of Russian inflection. In section 8.3, we introduce the genitive plural conundrum. In sections 8.4 and 8.5, we discuss the solution to the problem. Section 8.6 discusses the productivity of allomorphy in the genitive plural. Section 8.7 turns to an interesting complication with the so-called "paucal" numbers of Russian. Section 8.8 concludes.

8.2 The organization of Russian inflection

Before turning to the conundrum represented by genitive plural formation in Russian, it is necessary to provide some general background on the word formation system of the language and the productive rules that are involved in the organization of Russian inflected words. To do this, we begin with the verbal paradigm, relying on what has been the standard analysis since Jakobson 1948, reflected also in Levin 1978, and assumed to be uncontroversial in most works on Russian morphology. The crucial elements of Russian word formation are (i) theme vowels and (ii) "Jakobson's Rule", a productive truncation rule that systematically applies in all relevant cases of word formation. We will see in the verbal paradigm how these rules apply, and then will turn to the apparently simpler nominal paradigm, where theme vowels appear to be absent, thus setting the table for the appearance of genitive plural as a conundrum with regard to the markedness generalizations discussed above.

8.2.1 *Verbal paradigms*

Russian verbal morphology works in a very systematic fashion. Every verb form consists of three basic parts: a root (always ending in a consonant and usually CVC or CVCVC in form), a theme constituent (which can be a vowel, a sequence of segments, or zero), and an inflectional complex as determined by the particular usage at hand. The root + theme together make up the stem. The inflectional suffixes (e.g., tense and agreement) are added directly to the stem, subject to Jakobson's Rule (see directly below). (8.12) provides a full list of the verbal themes available in the language:[6]

(8.12) Russian verbal themes (Levin 1978):[7]
      -A-   e.g., p'is+a 'write'
      -AJ-   e.g., p'is+aj 'piss'
      -I-   e.g., govor+i 'speak'
      -E-   e.g., bol'+e 'hurt'
      -EJ-   e.g., bol'+ej 'be sick'
      -NU-   e.g., v'er+nu 'return'
      -O-   e.g., kol+o 'stab'
      -OVA-   e.g., r'is+ova 'draw'
      -Ø-   e.g., stan+Ø'become'

Tense suffixes come in many forms but an important generalization exists that helps to elucidate the patterns found: present tense morphemes all begin with vowels, in both conjugations, whereas past tense and infinitival morphemes begin with consonants. Thus, for every verb type, there will be instances where the morpheme begins with V and instances where it begins with C. This is of direct relevance to Jakobson's Rule, which is provided below.

(8.13) Truncation Rules (Jakobson 1948; Halle 1994):
      a. $V \rightarrow \emptyset / \_ V$
      b. $C \rightarrow \emptyset / \_ C$

Examples of resulting derivations are given below.[8]

(8.14) p'is + A (*'to write'*)
      a. p'is + A   + u = p'išu [1sg] (A **truncates**)
                     + ot = p'išot [3sg] (A **truncates**)
                     + ut = p'išut [3pl] (A **truncates**)
      b. p'is + A   + t', l = p'isat' [infin.] / p'isal [past-masc.sg]

---

[6] There are also three verbal suffixes (-AJ, -VAJ and -IVAJ) that can be added to the stem in imperfective derivation to form a new, imperfective stem. Jakobson's Rule applies to these combinations as well, and the resulting new stem always ends in -AJ, thus reducing these cases to instances of (8.1b.). We will therefore not discuss these further here, although see Levin 1978 for discussion.

[7] There are two subclasses of -*nu*-: in one, the theme does not appear in the past tense.

[8] A further consonant mutation takes place in the first conjugation when a theme vowel is deleted in the present tense, changing s → š in the case of 'to write'. This is a productive process which is irrelevant to the discussion at hand (but see Levin 1978).

(8.15) p'is + AJ (*'to piss'*)
    a. p'is + AJ + u = p'isaju [1sg]
                      + ot = p'isajot [3sg]
                      + ut = p'isajut [3pl]
    b. p'is + AJ + t', l = p'isat' [infin.] / p'isal
                    [past-masc.sg] (J **truncates**)

(8.16) govor + I (*'to speak'*)
    a. govor + I   + u = govor'u [1sg] (I **truncates**)
                      + it = govor'it [3sg] (I **truncates**)
                      + at = govor'at [3pl] (I **truncates**)
    b. govor + I   + t', l = govor'it' [infin.] / govor'il
                    [past-masc.sg]

(8.17) bol' + E (*'to hurt'*)
    a. bol' + E   + it = bol'it [3sg] (E **truncates**)
                      + at = bol'at [3pl] (E **truncates**)
    b. bol' + E   + t', l = bol'et' [infin.] / bol'el [past-masc.sg]

(8.18) bol' + EJ (*'to be sick'*)
    a. bol' + EJ + u = bol'eju [1sg]
                      + ot = bol'ejot [3sg]
                      + ut = bol'ejut [3pl]
    b. bol' + EJ + t', l = bol'et' [infin.] / bol'el
                    [past-masc.sg] (J **truncates**)

Notice that, because of the effects of the truncation rule deleting the first of a sequence of consonants, the infinitives and past tenses of the verbs 'to write' and 'to piss' are the same since the theme ending /-j/ in the latter deletes in contact with the /-t'/ ending of the infinitive or /-l/ ending of the past tense, rendering the forms identical (except for stress). Similarly, the verbs 'to hurt' and 'to be sick' will also have the same infinitive and past tense forms. In both cases, however, the difference in theme is reflected in the present tense forms, where the full theme -AJ- or -EJ- is retained, whereas the themes -A- and -E- are truncated as the first V of a V+V sequence.

8.2.2 *Nominal paradigms*

Many readers will be familiar with *yers*, a class of short vowels that were found throughout earlier forms of Slavic and that dropped out historically, either disappearing entirely or merging with full vowels. The historical rule of *yer drop* is maintained in the synchronic grammar of the language (see Lightner 1972), by virtue of the *yer* deletion rule, which acts now as it did historically.

Under *yer* deletion, *yers* will delete in "weak" positions, namely everywhere except when the following syllable itself contains a *yer*. A *yer* is "strong" if the following syllable contains a *yer*. Strong *yers* are retained and, in surfacing, they merge with another phoneme, by a rule of *yer* realization, which results in the mid vowel *e* or *o*.[9]

(8.19) *Yer realization rule* (operative throughout Russian):
ь,ъ → e, o if the next σ contains a ь or ъ

(8.20) *Yer deletion rule* (operative throughout Russian):
ь,ъ → Ø unless the next σ contains a ь or ъ

The relevance of *yers* for the discussion of Russian nominal paradigms arises when one of the case endings contains a *yer*, such as the nominative singular of many nouns. If there is a *yer* in the stem, it will be realized, as in (8.19). On the other hand, if the case ending does not contain a *yer* in the first syllable, the stem *yer* will not surface, due to (8.20). The effect of these two rules yields vowel-zero alternations for stems that contain a *yer*, such as the masculine noun *l'*(ь)*v* 'lion':

(8.21) a. *l'*(ь)v + ъ (nominative singular) → l'ev (by (8.19) of first *yer* and (8.20) of second *yer*)
l'(ь)v + a (genitive singular) → l'va (by (8.20) of first *yer*)

There are three genders in Russian (masc, fem, and neut) as well as three nominal classes, which we call I, II, and III.[10] Note that gender still needs to be specified for classes one and two under this system. It is important to distinguish gender from class in the analysis of Russian nominals, and this distinction is crucial for what follows. We take class to determine a paradigm of endings, whereas gender determines agreement. There is a fairly systematic correlation between the two, but the examples in (8.22) and (8.23) show that neither class nor gender can be eliminated in the description of the nominal system because the correlation is not absolute.[11]

---

[9] In Halle and Nevins (2006) the ordering of vowel truncation and *yer* rules receives a complete treatment; in brief, both a cyclic and post-cyclic version of *yer* realization exist; the former is applied before Jakobson's Rule (which is cyclic), and the latter is applied post-cyclically, after all applications of Jakobson's Rule.

[10] These classes are based on Levin 1978, who labels the classes as "non-neuter", "non-feminine", and "feminine".

[11] We note the existence of examples such as *d'evuška* 'girl', which is Class I and female, and *d'ad'a* 'uncle', which is Class I and male. While both inflect identically in terms of their own case-number endings (determined by declension class), only the latter triggers masculine verbal agreement on a verb. Such examples demonstrate the need for adopting a distinction between declension class and gender, and necessitate revisions to analyses such as Rice (2005), which only discuss conflict in terms

(8.22) Fem. Adj:

    a. prostaja   kn'iga
        simple-fem.sg   book-fem.sg-Class I

    b. prostaja   dv'er'
        simple-fem.sg   door-fem.sg-Class III

(8.23) Masc. Adj:

    a. prostoj   stol
        simple-masc.sg   table-masc.sg-Class II

    b. prostoj   starosta
        simple-masc.sg   leader-masc.sg-Class I

(8.22) and (8.23) show that adjectival agreement within a nominal depends on gender and not class. Thus, Class I nouns can be feminine, as in (8.22a.), or masculine, as in (8.23b.). Conversely, Class III nouns are feminine, thus sharing agreement patterns with most (but not all) Class I nouns (compare identical agreement patterns in (8.22a.b.). The overall possibilities are summarized in the two tables below:

(8.24) Class/Gender relations on left; Gender/Class correlations on right:[12]

Class	Gender
I	MASC or FEM
II	MASC or NEUT (M = IIa, N, = IIb)
III	FEM

Gender	Class
FEM	I or III
MASC	I or II
NEUT	II

The situation with nominal paradigms appears to be simpler than that of verbal paradigms only because nominals appear to contain no theme (on traditional analyses). Thus, nominal forms consist only of a root (always

---

of semantic gender and biological reality. As Harris (1991) has pointed out, declension class is an additional source of conflicting demands on morphological form. Finally we note that DP-internal concord and verbal agreement may differ, in that the latter may reflect biological gender while the former cannot. Thus, a female president's arrival may be reported as (i) but never as (ii) (see Comrie et al. 1996 for additional discussion):

(i)   Novyj   pr'ez'id'ent   pr'ijexala
        New-masc. president-masc. arrived-**fem.**
        "The new (female) president arrived"

(ii)   *Novaja pr'ez'id'ent   pr'ijexala
        New-**fem.** president-masc. arrived-**fem.**

Rappaport (2006) offers a recent syntactic analysis of these facts.

[12] Class III is often said to include one masculine noun *put'* 'path'; however, as its instrumental ending is that of Class II, it appears to be in the process of reanalysis.

C-final, as in verbal roots) and an ending, which are nearly always V-initial.[13] Thus, we do not expect Jakobson's Rule to apply in these cases, which therefore show simple concatenation. Examples are given in (8.25).

(8.25)

(Trad.) Stem	Gender	Class	Nom Sg	Dat Sg	Gen Sg	Instr Sg	Dat Pl
kn'ig- *book*	F	Class I	kn'iga	kn'ig'e	kn'ig'i	kn'igoj	kn'igam
stol- *table*	M	Class IIa	stol	stolu	stola	stolom	stolam
zv'er'- *beast*	M	Class IIa	zv'er'	zv'er'u	zv'er'a	zv'er'om	zv'er'am
nož- *knife*	M	Class IIa	nož	nožu	noža	nožom	nožam
ok(ъ)n- *window*	N	Class IIb	okno	oknu	okna	oknom	oknam
dv'er'- *door*	F	Class III	dv'er'	dv'er'i	dv'er'i	dv'er'ju	dv'er'am

In the traditional analysis of nominals, the root and the stem are identical (as shown in the left column of (8.25). Simple concatenation then produces the inflected forms found throughout the chart.[14] Notice that the Class IIa and Class III nominative singular endings are the only Ø endings in the paradigms. (The chart also shows that Classes IIa and IIb form a unified paradigm in all cases other than the nominative (and accusative, not shown here), hence their treatment as subclasses.)

(8.26)   Traditional Classification of Endings:

	Nom Sg	Dat Sg	Gen Sg	Instr Sg	Dat Pl
Class I	-a	-e	-i	-oj	-am
Class IIa	-Ø	-u	-a	-om	-am
Class IIb	-o	-u	-a	-om	am
Class III	-Ø	-i	-i	-ju	-am

We next turn to a generalization about syncretism in the nominal paradigm. Notice that (8.26) also provides the gender and class information for each of these examples. Only one plural ending is provided in the chart of nominal

---

[13] The consonantal truncation rule applies to any C+C combination except for the instrumental singular of Class III nouns, where a root ending in a soft consonant (/dv'er'-/, 'door') meets the only nominal ending beginning with a consonant, /-ju/. No truncation results in such cases. In order to allow for such cases, we should limit the C truncation rule to instances where C2 is not a glide.

[14] There are certain stems, such as *sos'ed* 'neighbor, nom sg' that have palatalization in the plural: *sos'ed'i* 'nom pl' (not the expected *sos'edy*), *sos'ed'am* 'dat pl', etc. As a result of this palatalization of the final consonant in plural stems, the genitive plural is *sos'ed'ej*, and not expected *sos'edov*. The existence of this genitive plural will be clearly problematic for an output-based derivation based on the nominative singular. In the treatment offered in the text, the existence of plural number features trigger local allomorphy on the root noun, with subsequent effects for genitive plural allomorph selection based on the adjacent phonology of the stem.

paradigms in (8.25), but the generalization about syncretism we can draw from it applies to the other oblique plurals as well (instrumental and prepositional), namely that all class and gender information is neutralized in the plural. This is widely known: "It is a general property of Russian that gender is never distinguished morphologically in the plural" (Bobaljik 2002: 11), although the generalization should presumably make reference to class rather than (or in addition to) gender. The appropriate generalization is given in (8.27).

(8.27) Russian Syncretism Generalizations:
    a. *Markedness*: Gender and class distinctions are neutralized in oblique plural forms
    b. *Locally-Determined Allomorphy*: All case-endings can be determined by the concatenation of stem+affix, with allomorphy determined by regular phonologically-conditioned rules. No reference to output forms or other derivations is required.

Before turning to the discussion of the apparent genitive plural conundrum, we provide the following examples of how the nominal declensions otherwise maintain the transparent combinations in accordance with (8.27):[15, 16]

(8.28) DAT   dv'er'am   kn'igam   stolam   oknam   (all /am/)
       PREP   dv'er'ax   kn'igax   stolax   oknax   (all /ax/)
       INST   dv'er'am'i   kn'igam'i   stolam'i   oknam'i   (all /am'i/)

It is worth noting at this point that adjectival paradigms are generally similar to nominal paradigms and can be analyzed using similar grammatical mechanisms for allomorphy and syncretisms (Matushansky and Halle 2006). If this is the case, we would expect (8.27) to hold for adjectival paradigms as well, and it does, in fact in slightly stronger form, not being sensitive to the oblique vs. non-oblique distinction. This is shown in (8.29):

---

[15] Syncretism has also been handled using a system of binary features (Müller 2003) rather than through markedness neutralization conditions of the kind given in (8.27). Müller argues, for example, that Classes I and III share the Gen Sg ending /-i/ because I and III both consist of a more primitive feature /-a/. However, the features proposed do not really have independent semantic or morphological justification, and this system has no way to handle the genitive plural facts discussed below. We do not therefore address feature systems for syncretism further in this chapter. Interested readers are referred to Müller 2003.

[16] There are a few exceptions to the instrumental plural ending -am'i, such as *lošad'm'i* 'horses' (inst pl). We assume these allomorphs are lexically specified.

(8.29) Class distinction is also neutralized in plural adjectives:

NOM PL	↔	-ije (prostyje okna, kn'ig'i, dv'er'i, doma, starosty)
PREP/GEN PL	↔	-ix
DAT PL	↔	-im
INST PL	↔	-im'i

In the next section we will see that the forms of the genitive plural in Russian appear to contradict both generalizations given in (8.27), the problem that is the central concern of this chapter. The analysis we propose will allow a form of (8.27) to be maintained, as is desirable.

8.3 The genitive plural conundrum

At first glance, the genitive plural paradigm in Russian indicates that neither the markedness nor the locally-derived halves of the syncretism generalization given in (8.27) hold. This is shown in (8.30), where there are three different endings for the genitive plural, which appear to be based on the gender and class of the noun.

(8.30)

(Trad.) Stem	Gender	Class	Nom Sg	Gen Pl	"Ending"
kn'ig *book*	F	CLASS I	kn'iga	kn'ig	-Ø
stol *table*	M	CLASS IIA	stol	stolov	-ov
zv'er' *beast*	M	CLASS IIA	zv'er'	zv'er'ej	-ej
nož *knife*	M	CLASS IIA	nož	nožej	-ej
ok(ъ)n *window*	N	CLASS IIB	okno	okon	-Ø
dv'er' *door*	F	CLASS III	dv'er'	dv'er'ej	-ej
noč *night*	F	CLASS III	noč	nočej	-ej

In (8.30), there appear to be three distinct Gen Pl endings in the language: /-Ø/, /-ov/, and /-ej/. There are some initially tempting gender-based generalizations that one can make, such as the fact that neuter nouns always take the zero ending.[17] However, it is also clear that neither class nor gender information alone is sufficient to predict the distribution of the genitive plural

---

[17] There are some exceptions, such as *pol'o* nom sg, *pol'ej* gen pl, 'field', and *oblako* nom sg, *oblakov* gen pl 'cloud'.

endings. For example, we may observe that Class I shares the /-Ø/ ending with Class IIb. We may also observe that, while Class III shares the /-ej/ ending with some nouns of Class IIa, there are other members of Class IIa that are unique in having the /-ov/ ending. Thus, a completely transparent mapping of these three endings to a corresponding gender/class category does not hold, as it does for other inflectional endings that really depend on gender/class features, such as the singular endings of (8.25).

There are two classes of approaches to characterizing the conditions on selection of these three endings. The first class of approaches requires abandoning the otherwise well-motivated neutralization hypothesis of (8.27). The second class of approaches requires abandoning the otherwise restrictive condition on locally-determined allomorphy introduced in section 8.1.3. After presenting and discussing existing analyses that abandon each of these hypotheses, we turn to our own proposal, which is able to maintain both.

8.3.1 *Models that abandon the gender neutralization hypothesis*

Certain accounts, such as Zaliznjak (1967:207), state the distribution of genitive plural endings in terms of both gender and phonological properties of the stem, and thus single out the genitive as the only oblique plural that refers to gender features. Halle (1994) presents an interesting account in which there is in fact only one allomorph. He proposes that the apparent allomorphy shown by the genitive plural endings is in fact the result of morphologically-determined phonological rules. In Halle's system, there is a single, uniform ending for the genitive plural which is a back *yer* /-ъ/.

Halle's derivation of the genitive plural is shown in (8.31) for the noun *guba* 'lip', The theme vowel *-a-* deletes in pre-vocalic position (due to Jakobson's Rule), as *yer* is, by hypothesis, a vowel. In the next rule application, the *yer* itself deletes as the result of (8.20).

(8.31)   Genitive Plural: gub+a+ъ→ gub+ъ→ gub 'lip' (gen pl)

Halle derives the varying surface forms of the genitive plural phonologically, through a complex series of insertion and deletion rules, as follows: The ordinary state of affairs is as in (8.31), where the stem *guba* becomes *gub* through addition of the Gen Pl *yer*, which yields the surface appearance of a zero ending.

However, Halle's most important addition to this account is a morphologically-conditioned rule of glide insertion, in order to derive the instances where the Gen Pl ending does not end up as /-Ø/. The conditions on glide insertion are provided in (8.32).

(8.32) Glide insertion contexts from Halle 1994:
- A glide is inserted after all Class III stems.
- After Class II stems the glide is generally inserted after masculine, but not after neuter stems. There are however exceptions in both directions.
- After Class I stems the glide is inserted after stems ending in clusters consisting of a consonant followed by a soft liquid /r,l/ or by /č,š,ž/.

In other words, glide insertion serves to place a glide (which is a consonant) in between the final stem vowel and the Gen Pl *yer*, thus blocking the context for Jakobson's Rule of vowel deletion. In Halle's words, "[When glide insertion occurs], the theme vowel surfaces as either /o/ or /e/ [according to readjustment rules]. The theme vowel surfaces because of the insertion of the glide after the theme." A sample derivation under Halle's account is illustrated below:

(8.33) a. um+o+ъ → um+o+j+ъ → um+o+v+ъ → umov 'reason'
         b. car'+e+ъ → car'+e+j+ъ → car'ej 'tsar'

First, a glide /j/ is inserted after the nominal theme vowel. This glide may be changed to /v/ in certain circumstances (Flier 1972). Then, the Gen Pl ending *yer* is added. Finally, it is deleted by the rule of *yer* deletion. Clearly, the most important work is being done by the rule of glide insertion.

The account is thus able to derive the three endings identified above for the Gen Pl, not as a set of allomorphs but as the result of a single ending (*yer*), that is supplemented by two highly specific additional morphologically conditioned rules (glide insertion and the j∼v alternation). However, it requires strong violation of the (otherwise) exceptionless generalization of markedness stated in (8.27) above. In particular, as can be seen in (8.32), Halle's Glide Insertion Rule requires reference to both class and gender information. (Note that this would be the only ending in Russian that required referring to both class and gender). In particular, a glide is inserted in all classes except Classes I and IIb (a non-natural class of declension classes). Thus, glide insertion occurs in exactly those instances where the eventual result is not a /-Ø/ allomorph. Furthermore, the two classes that trigger glide insertion, in addition to being themselves an unnatural class, happen to be the two classes where the Nom Sg ending is not /-Ø/. In short, Halle's account not only requires reference to class and gender information in order to determine the realization of an oblique plural but it does so in a way that seems to be missing a generalization about the phonological form of the stems prior to genitive plural formation. This latter observation forms the basis of a different kind of account, to which we turn below. The next class of approaches to be examined uphold the markedness constraint (8.27), although they do so at the expense of violating the restriction on allomorphic conditioning identified in (8.11).

8.3.2 *Models that violate locally-determined allomorphy*

Another approach to explaining the distribution of genitive plural endings relies on a transderivational condition, as found in Jakobson (1957) and, later, Levin (1978). Intuitively, this condition is simple: nouns whose nominative singular form ends in a vowel have a Ø ending in the genitive plural; whereas those with a zero ending in the nominative singular select either /-ej/ or /-ov/, a subdistribution that can be handled in purely phonological terms. This approach is summarized in (8.34)–(8.35).

(8.34) *Transderivational analysis*: The phonological form of the genitive plural is predictable based on the phonological form of nominative singular (somehow available):

(8.35)

Structural Description	Structural Change	Example	Gender	Class
Nom Sg ends in V	Suffix Ø	kn'iga → kn'ig, zdan'ijo → zdan'ij	M, F, N	I, IIb
Nom Sg ends in C' or palatal fric.	Suffix /-ej/	zv'er' → zv'er'ej	M, F	IIa, III
Nom Sg ends in C or /j/	Suffix /-ov/	stol → stolov	M	IIa

The primary problem with the approach outlined in (8.34)–(8.35), of course, is its direct reference to the nominative singular form in deriving the genitive plural form, which violates DM Hypothesis 2, given in (8.11), repeated below:

(8.36) **DM Hypothesis II**: Allomorphy can only be conditioned by the phonology in the current derivation, not by the phonology of other derivations

Abandonment of (8.36) results in a theory with very little restrictiveness and predicts the existence of languages in which, say, the dative singular is determined by examining the form of the accusative plural and performing some operations on the output of that other derivation. Therefore, we seek a solution to the genitive plural conundrum that violates neither of the leading DM hypotheses and which allows us to maintain the markedness hierarchy proposed earlier, and presented for Russian in (8.27). Before turning to our proposal, however, a brief discussion of the possible privileged status of the nominative singular is in order. Some readers, for example, may object that the reference to the nominative singular countenanced in (8.35) does not represent a wholesale abandonment of (8.36), because the nominative singular has a privileged status within the inflectional paradigm. The idea would be that the genitive plural can reference the nominative singular because there is some unique relation between these two. We examine the status of the nominative singular in the next subsection.

8.3.3 *Does the Nom Sg have a privileged status?*

When two morphologically-related forms A and B show shared phonological behavior in the sense that the phonological form of B is somehow determined by A, there are two grammatical sources that may be posited for this shared behavior.

8.3.3.1 *Pre-derivational relations between forms*   The first mechanism is that there is a pre-derivational source for the shared behavior; in other words, a subsumption relation between the morphosyntactic features (MSF) of A and B, so that $MSF(A) \subset MSF(B)$. Usually, when $MSF(A) \subset MSF(B)$, then A itself is represented as a "subtree" of B, where Z represents possible intermediate derivational material:

(8.37)

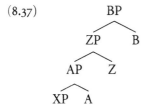

Examples of a morphosyntactic subtree/subsumption effect on phonological form include standard cyclicity effects as discussed in Chomsky and Halle 1968, such as the fact that *cycle* [sajk.l̩] may retain its syllabic liquid even in the gerundive form *cycling* [sajk.l̩.iŋ], even though there is no phonological reason for the [l] to remain syllabic when a vowel-initial suffix is added. In this case, we may think of "A" as the verb *cycle* and "B" as the additional structure added by the gerundive suffix. The phonological "overapplication" of the nuclear syllabification of a liquid consonant is thus viewed as the result of the derivational history of B.

This mechanism might seem initially plausible as a means of understanding how the derivation of the genitive plural would have access to the nominative singular, an "earlier" stage of its derivation, by hypothesis:

(8.38)

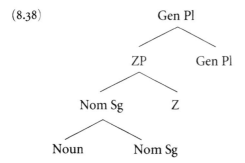

In this case, however, it is implausible to imagine a subtree-based derivational relationship between nominative singular and genitive plural that does not include as an intermediate stage the forms of nominative plural or genitive singular. That is to say, what could "Z" in (8.38) possibly consist of, such that it would take nominative to genitive and singular to plural, without passing through the intermediate derivational stages of Nom Pl and Gen Sg? Nonetheless, as has been discussed above, Nom Pl and Gen Sg show no such apparent phonological dependence on the nominative singular to account for their form (and moreover, as pointed out in the introduction, for almost all feminine nouns, the Nom Pl and Gen Sg are identical to each other to the exclusion of both the Nom Sg and Gen Pl). A subsumption-based mechanism, therefore, regardless of its merits elsewhere in the grammar of natural languages, is not sufficient to explain the genitive plural conundrum.

8.3.3.2 *Transderivational relations between forms*   The second grammatical mechanism that is employed to explain asymmetric phonological dependence between forms is transderivational in nature, and usually is instantiated in Optimality-Theoretic terms by output-output correspondence. According to Kager 1999, output-output correspondence relations, in which the derivation of a form B depends on the derivation of another form A, are limited to cases in which A and B differ by only one morphosyntactic feature, in other words, where $|MSF(A)-MSF(B)| = 1$. This restriction makes strong predictions about where output-output correspondence is possible. Taken literally, the putative phonological dependence of the genitive plural on the nominative singular thus cannot be the result of output-output correspondence, since it is implausible, again, that the nominative singular could differ from the genitive plural by a single morphosyntactic feature. An intermediate route of transderivational correspondence through either the nominative plural or the genitive singular would also predict phonological dependence of these forms on the nominative singular, counter to fact.

We thus conclude that morphosyntactically-based accounts of phonological dependence, either through pre-derivational or transderivational sources, are at present appropriately restrictive and constrained in grammatical theory, and hence we will not attempt to modify these accounts in the hopes of solving the Russian genitive plural conundrum. Rather, we will seek an account in which it is not the nominative singular at all on which the genitive plural depends. We now turn to our proposal.

8.4 The proposal

Having determined that nominative singular does not have a privileged status in Russian that would lead us to expect phonological effects on the genitive plural to the exclusion of all other case–number combinations, we turn now to our own proposal for the proper analysis of genitive plural formation in Russian.

Our proposal is quite simple. First, we preserve the intuition of Halle's account in positing a *yer* (ь) genitive plural form in some (but not all) instances of genitive plural realization. This *yer* is crucial in the derivation–since it is a vowel, it provides the environment for the phonological truncation of a preceding vowel, dubbed Jakobson's Rule above. Thus, as we will see, Halle's (1994) intuition that *yers* are at play in this derivation is thus maintained in the proposal but without any reference made to class or gender information in deriving genitive plurals. Second, with Levin 1978, we share the intuition that the phonological form of the input to the derivation is relevant, rather than any reference at all to the inflectional features of gender and class. In fact, gender and class features still may undergo impoverishment in the environment of oblique plural, with no effect on the mechanism we will require to derive the distribution of allomorphs.

The core of the proposal is this: what appears to be the nominative singular form of Russian nouns is actually the STEM. More precisely, in all cases the nominative singular is phonologically identical to the STEM (though not morphologically identical, as the STEM, i.e., ROOT + THEME, contains no case or number features). Since the phonological form of the nominative singular is the stem, a version of (8.35) can be used in producing the genitive plural forms without reference to the nominative singular form directly. The core of this possibility rests on the proposal that like verbs and adjectives, Russian nouns also contain THEME vowels. This claim runs counter to many structuralist and generative analyses of certain noun classes, where what we claim are theme vowels have been identified as nominative singular endings. This claim is presented in (8.39):

(8.39) *Theme vowels in nouns:* Just as in verbs, all Russian nouns require a theme vowel: A, O, or Ø.

In particular, Class I nouns are exactly defined by being those nouns that have an /-A-/ THEME (rather than those with no THEME) and an /-a/ ending in the nominative singular. Thus, what was previously analyzed as /kn'ig-/ + /-a/, with /-a/ as a case–number allomorph for Class I nouns, is a misanalysis. The proper analysis should be /kn'ig + A / + /Ø/, where the case–number ending for nominative singular is a zero morpheme. Similarly, Class IIb nouns have an /-o-/ THEME and a Ø ending, rather than a Ø THEME and an /-o-/ ending. All other nouns (Class IIa and III) will have Ø THEMES, and either Ø or ь endings. In particular, Class IIa nouns like *ot*(ь)*c* or *d'*(ь)*n'* will have zero themes and *yer* nominative singular endings, which will trigger *yer* vocalization of the root, e.g., [ot'ec, d'en'] (nom.sg.) vs. [otca, d'n'a] (gen.sg.). While theme vowel content must refer to the inherent gender and class features of the noun, plural case endings do not refer to inherent gender or class. This analysis allows us to maintain a version of (8.35), which contained the right intuition, in our view, but the wrong implementation. Now, the distribution of genitive plural endings will depend on the form of the stem (that is, on the phonological nature of the theme) and the genitive plural ending emerges with no reference necessary to class or gender information per se, nor to any other output forms in the nominal paradigm, thus preserving both of the major DM hypotheses presented in section 8.1.

(8.40) Purely phonologically-determined allomorphy in genitive plural; upholds (8.7):

Environment	GEN PL Allomorph
STEM ends in V	Suffix /-ь/ (*YER*)
STEM ends in C' or palatal fric.	Suffix /-ej/
STEM ends [elsewhere]	Suffix /-ov/

In the first instance (Classes I and IIb), a STEM ending in a vowel will take a *yer* ending. Phonology-as-usual will apply, and deliver an output that is identical to the bare noun ROOT itself–without the theme vowel formative. This occurs as follows: By suffixation of a *yer*, the environment for Jakobson's truncation rule is met (V meets V), and the first V is therefore truncated. We have thus reduced the morphological truncation apparently found in genitive plurals to the independently motivated phonological truncation rule in the language, attested throughout the verbal system, as shown above. In such instances, the genitive plural emerges as a form identical to the ROOT, the THEME having been truncated by Jakobson's Rule, and the *yer* dropped by the standard *yer* dropping rule.

In all other instances, namely those where the STEM ends in a C, purely phonological factors alone determine which allomorph surfaces. Recall that this phonological subregularity existed in Levin's account already but required reference to the nominative singular to determine whether it was active or not. Now, the choice can be motivated on purely phonological grounds within the local derivation, as desired. (Derivations will be given below).

Before showing full derivations, however, it is important to point out the effect of this reanalysis on the rest of the declension system. Under this approach, nouns with Ø nominative singular endings wear their theme vowels on their sleeves, as it were, but in the nominative singular only. In all other instances, the required (and phonologically contentful) case+number ending begins with a vowel, causing truncation of the theme vowel, and deriving the exact set of forms expected, as they would come out in the system that does not claim theme vowels for nouns. Thus, the reanalysis does not cause any further complications elsewhere in the declension system.

We turn to derivations of nouns of various classes, in the genitive plural, nominative singular, dative singular, and dative plural forms. The dative plural is included to show that the markedness reduction claimed for oblique plurals in (8.27) remains fully intact in this system.

(8.41) Nominative Singular Revisited:

[ROOT	THEME]	CASE+NUM	SURFACE
kn'ig	+A	+Ø	kn'iga
stol	+Ø	+ъ	stol (*YER* deletes)
zv'er'	+Ø	+ь	zv'er' (*YER* deletes)
ot(ь)c	+Ø	+ъ	ot'ec (first *YER* undergoes realization, second *YER* deletes)
ok(ъ) n	+o	+Ø	okno (root *YER* deletes)
dv'er'	+Ø	+Ø	dv'er'

(8.42) Genitive Singular Derivations:

[ROOT	THEME]	CASE + NUM	SURFACE
kn'ig	+A	+i	kn'ig'i (THEME truncates)
stol	+Ø	+a	stola
zv'er'	+Ø	+a	zv'er'a
ot(ь)c	+Ø	+a	otca (root YER deletes)
ok(ь) n	+o	+a	okna (THEME truncates, root YER deletes)
dv'er'	+Ø	+i	dv'er'i

(8.43) Genitive Plural Derivations:

[ROOT	THEME]	CASE + NUM	SURFACE
kn'ig	+A	+ь	kn'ig (THEME truncates, then YER deletes)
stol	+Ø	+ov	stolov
zv'er'	+Ø	+ej	zv'er'ej
ot(ь)c	+Ø	+ov	(root YER deletes)
ok(ь) n	+o	+ь	okon (THEME truncates, root YER is realized, then second YER deletes)
dv'er'	+Ø	+ej	dv'er'ej

Exemplifying further derivations for completeness:

(8.44) Dative Endings:
/-e/ ↔ Class I, singular
/-u/ ↔ Class II, singular
/-i/ ↔ Class III, singular
/-am/ ↔ plural

(8.45) Dative Singular Derivations:

[ROOT	THEME]	CASE + NUM	SURFACE
kn'ig	+A	+e	kn'ig'e (A truncates)
stol	+Ø	+u	stolu
zv'er'	+Ø	+u	zv'er'u
nož	+Ø	+u	nožu
ok(ь) n	+o	+u	oknu (o truncates, root YER deletes)
dv'er'	+Ø	+i	dv'er'i

(8.46) Dative Plural Derivations:

[ROOT	THEME]	CASE + NUM	SURFACE
kn'ig	+A	+am	kn'igam (A truncates)
stol	+Ø	+am	stolam
zv'er'	+Ø	+am	zv'er'am
nož	+Ø	+am	nožam
ok(ъ) n	+o	+am	oknam (o truncates)
dv'er'	+Ø	+am	dv'er'am

The first advantage of this account is that it unifies the derivational morphology of the nominal system with what is already known about the verbal
system. In particular, all basic categories (N,V,A) are required to have THEMES.
The status of the nominal system alone as not having any THEMES in certain
analyses is an anomaly that our system allows us to overcome. Second, Class
type can now be determined directly from the THEME, with one instance being
split between two classes. This is shown in (8.47):

(8.47) Nominal Class type as determined by THEME type (our account):

THEME	CLASS
-A-	I
-Ø-	IIa or III
-o-	IIb

In those stems with a Ø THEME, class can be further determined by the phonological shape of the end of the stem (which in such cases is of course the end of
the root). In particular, only soft stems and sibilants can be Class III, whereas
all others must be Class IIa.[18]

This is consistent with what is generally accepted about the language's
derivational morphology–theme type determines class membership to a high
degree of certainty. Thus, in the verbal system, verbs with THEMES /-I-/ and
/-E-/ are second conjugation, those with /-AJ-/, /-EJ-/, /-OVA-/, /-NU-/, /-o-/,
are first conjugation, and only those with /-A-/ can be either, with a subregularity about the preceding consonant being the determining factor. In short, class

---

[18] No rules of correspondence will be able to predict that a minimal pair such as *dv'er'* ('door')
and *zv'er'* ('beast') will differ in class, the former being Class III and the latter Class IIa. This will
be true in any theory. (Note that *zv'er'* is Class III in Belorussian.) Thus, any root ending in a soft
consonant containing a zero THEME will be undetermined as to whether it is Class III or Class IIa. This
information will have to be specified lexically in most cases. Crucially, however, only our system will
be able to explain on a purely phonological basis what genitive plural to expect for all cases; in this
case, since both have a Ø THEME, the end of the root will predict the /-ej/ form, which is in fact attested
(*dv'er'ej, zv'er'ej*). Thus, even this lexically underdetermined case lends strength to our analysis.

type being related to theme becomes as transparent in the nominal system as it is in the verbal system under our reanalysis.

To conclude this section, we will once more reiterate the point that, under the proposal here, the derivation of the genitive plural is determined entirely locally–without reference to the output of other case output forms, and entirely without reference to the morphosyntactic features of class and gender, which can be impoverished, in accordance with (8.27), in the presence of oblique-plural morphosyntax, prior to any selection of the allomorphic exponents of the genitive plural.

8.5 Productivity and the wug test

There are several kinds of genitive plurals that appear to be exceptions to the conditions on allomorphic distribution in (8.40). A representative sample is presented below, where a * represents an output that is unexpected under our account thus far.

(8.48)

STEM	NOM PL	GEN PL (Expected)	GEN PL (Actual)	
dýn'a	dýn'i	dýn'	dýn'	*melon (f.)*
pól'o	pol'á	pol'	*pol'éj	*field (n.)*
mór'o	mor'á	mor'	*mor'éj	*sea (n.)*
óblako	oblaká	oblak	*oblakóv	*cloud (n.)*
soldát	soldáty	soldátov	*soldát	*soldier (n.)*

The first form shows the effects of Jakobson's Rule when V meets V as expected in our system. However, the final four forms are exceptions. In the first two of the starred exceptional cases, the expected forms *pol'* and *mor'* are not found. Instead, we find the exceptional forms *pol'éj* and *mor'éj*. This is unexpected in any of the accounts discussed thus far. (We return to the final two cases below.) For cases such as these, it has been claimed in Pertsova (2004) that the relevant factor in the determination of the actual genitive plural form in Russian involves stress. Pertsova's account claims that it is the existence of end stress throughout the plural paradigms of these nouns that leads us to the attested form; that is, she claims that nouns must not have the (apparent) Ø Gen Pl ending if all other forms in the plural paradigm are end-stressed: "Nouns of the I and IIb declensions will not have a zero ending in genitive plural if they have stress on the ending in the (oblique) plural" (Pertsova 2004). (Note that there are nouns with mixed plural patterns in terms of stress, which on this account would allow the zero ending.)

However, Pertsova's claim is clearly too strong, as shown by the following forms (from Levin 1978).

(8.49)

Nom Sg	Nom Pl	Dat Pl	Gen Pl		(Gen Pl ending)
vod'ít'el'	vod'ít'el'i	vod'ít'el'am	vod'ít'el'	*driver (m.)*	-ej
dom	domá	domám	domóv	*house (m.)*	-ov
zdán'ijo	zdán'ija	zdán'ijam	zdán'ij+∅	*building (n.)*	-∅
stat'(ь)já	stat'jí	stat'jám	stat'éj+∅	*article (f.)*	-∅
kočer(ь)gá	kočerg'í	kočergám	kočer'óg+∅	*poker (f.)*	-∅
kn'až(ь)ná	kn'ažný	kn'ažnám	kn'ažón+∅	*princess (f.)*	-∅
kol'ejá	kol'ejí	kol'ejám	kol'éj+∅	*gauge (f.)*	-∅
čertá	čertý	čertám	čert	*feature (f.)*	-∅

Notice that the final five forms in (8.49) all show end stress throughout the plural paradigm, and yet they have the apparently ∅ form (derived from the *yer* deletion rule plus truncation of the theme vowel) resulting in a stem vowel being stressed in the genitive plural form only (a direct counterexample to Pertsova's claim).[19] Thus, the words for 'article', 'poker', 'princess', 'gauge', and 'feature' are end-stressed throughout the plural but the gen pl still shows truncation of the theme vowel and thus stress on an earlier syllable. Clearly Pertsova would have to consider those forms the exceptions rather than the forms in (8.48).

In an attempt to determine which of the two sets of forms are productive, we created a "wug" test, whose details are given below:

---

[19] The words for 'article', 'poker', and 'princess' end up with stress falling on the surfacing strong *yer* in the genitive plural (this vowel remains, according to the productive *yer* realization rule given above, due to the presence of the genitive plural *yer* (which itself deletes). It could be argued that these forms do not counterexemplify Pertsova's claims, since the stress could be said not to fall on the stem, in a system whereby such vowels surface by a rule of epenthesis rather than as realization as an underlying vowel present in the stem. (See Levin 1978 for an attempt to derive all vowel/zero alternations as phonologically determined.) However, there are clear minimal pairs indicating that vowel/zero alternations cannot be determined purely phonologically. Thus the Class I noun *laska* has two meanings, 'caress' and 'weasel' and two different genitive plural forms: *lask* for the former meaning and *lások* for the latter. Clearly, no purely phonological rule can account for this distinction. Therefore, it must be lexically determined and the lexical determination involves a different stem, the former without a *yer* and the latter with one, which then surfaces as expected in the Gen Pl form. (There are also unexpected palatalization effects that can also not be predicted by a purely phonological epenthesis rule but which are derived from the presence of an underlying *yer*.) Therefore, the vowels that surface in forms like *lások*, as well as those in (8.48) above, are stem vowels and their ability to take stress in the Gen Pl form alone stands as a counterexample to Pertsova's claim.

(8.50) Wug test: "This is a Wug-NOM.SG. I like wugs-ACC.PL. I live with wugs-INSTR.PL. I have a lot of __GEN.PL." Conducted with parallel Cyrillic and English transcription, with stress indicated but not gender.

Seventeen native speaking respondents were given the forms in the following chart, with the Nom Sg, Acc Sg and Instr Pl they heard. They were asked to provide the Gen Pl. The results are given in (8.51). "Ineffable" means that the speaker thought there was no possible output.[20]

(8.51) Pilot Wug Test Results with Novel Word Formation

Nom Sg	Acc Pl	Instr Pl (predicted)	Gen Pl Experimental Result	percent	other productions
grapá	grapý	grapám'i	grap	80%	2 grapov, 1 grap'ev (2 ineffable)
k'ingá	k'ing'í	k'ingám'i	k'ing	93%	1 k'in'og (note *yer*!) (1 ineffable)
p'it'á	p'ít'i	p'ít'am'i	p'i't'	67%	5 p'it'ej, 1 p'it'jev (1 ineffable)
tr'aló	tr'ála	tr'álam'i	tr'al	65%	4 tr'álov, 2 tr'ál'ej
čúrko	čurká	čurkám'i	čurok	47%	7 čurkóv, 1 čúrkov (2 ineffable)
Total (Post-accenting)			70% 74%		

Of relevance to the discussion of stress at hand are the first two forms and the last form (all of which are end-stressed in the plural). In all those cases, Pertsova's account predicts that the *yer*+deletion form (leading to an Ø ending) should not be preferred. However, in the first two forms, this choice is the overwhelming favorite (80% and 93%). Only the fifth form does not strongly prefer the (apparently) zero ending, but neither is the other alternative preferred (47%). Thus, the overall results of this pilot wug test indicate that stress may not be the crucial factor and in future work these trends should be confirmed by more extensive testing. Should these trends persist, the forms

---

[20] A famous short story called *Kocherga* by Zoshchenko narrates an argument between office clerks putting in a requisition for five fireplace pokers. The numeral "five" in Russian requires the genitive plural, which would be stem-stressed only in the genitive plural (cf. *kočer'óg* above). Despondent that they cannot unanimously agree on what the correct form they should write is (in other words, they suffered from "group ineffability"), the clerks employ a circumlocution to avoid the genitive plural.

shown in (8.48) then remain as lexical exceptions to an otherwise productive rule that can be maintained without reference to stress or to other forms in the paradigm.

8.6 A possible counterexample to gender impoverishment: Paucals

There is one environment in Russian which displays properties that might render it a potential counterexample to the claim that all gender information is neutralized in non-singular contexts, namely the behavior of adjectival forms in expressions with the numbers 2,3,4. (Let us refer to the numerals that induce these genitive singular endings as the *paucal* numbers.) To see the potential problem paucal constructions raise for our markedness claim, consider first the examples in (8.52):

(8.52) tr'i stola   tr'i kn'ig'i   tr'i dv'er'i   tr'i okna   tr'i zv'er'a
        three tables three books   three doors   three windows three beasts

In (8.52) we see the endings that appear on nominals following paucals.[21] The endings on the nominals appear identical to the normal genitive singular endings. When the head noun is modified by an adjective, however, as in (8.53)–(8.54), a gender (and number) difference emerges (for many speakers), namely the adjective in question appears in the genitive plural for masculine and neuter head nouns and in the nominative plural for feminines:

(8.53) tr'i   prostyx   stud'enta
        three simple-gen.pl. student-masc.gen.sg. (TRADITIONAL GLOSS)

(8.54) tr'i   prostyje   kn'ig'i
        three simple-nom.pl. book-fem.gen.sg.

In (8.53), then, we have a genitive plural adjective with a genitive singular masculine noun, whereas in (8.54) we have a nominative plural adjective with a genitive singular feminine noun.[22] Such a state of affairs is completely

---

[21] In fact, this behavior is limited to direct case contexts, that is contexts where the entire phrase is in a nominative or accusative position. In oblique contexts, such as that required by a preposition taking, say, dative case, both the numeral and the nominal following it appear in the Dat Pl. In those cases, adjectives modifying the nominal will also be dative plural, and as usual there will be no gender distinctions on either the nouns or adjectives involved, thus rendering these examples consistent with the markedness generalization and irrelevant for present purposes.

[22] A reviewer points out that some speakers allow *prostyx* (i.e., the alleged genitive plural) in (8.54), whereas the opposite (i.e., usage of *prostyje* in (8.53)) is unattested, suggesting that Borras and Christian (1971) are correct in observing that the genitive plural form of adjectives may be spreading for all genders. Such a development does not undermine the paucal analysis in the text (as such speakers still

unknown in the Russian agreement and concord system, where concord is regular within a DP: adjectives always agree with their head noun for number, and for gender in the singular only (our markedness generalization). Here, however, in paucal constructions, we have a case where there is a number mismatch (a singular head noun with a plural adjective) and the case of the plural adjective is sensitive to the gender of the head noun. This last point is also the potential problem for our markedness generalization–how can there be a gender distinction in a plural context? Granted, it is marked through the use of a distinct case form (genitive for masculine and nominative for feminine), but it still amounts to a counterexample to our claim that in plural contexts gender is neutralized.

Of course, the traditional analysis of paucals as genitive singular encounters more serious problems than just violating a markedness constraint. In particular, if correct, it violates a basic morphosyntactic law of Russian concerning subject–verb agreement, as follows. When paucal constructions are in subject position, there can be plural agreement marked on the verb. This is shown in (8.55) and (8.56):

(8.55) tr'i   stud'enta   byl'i   na koncert'e
        three students-**masc.gen.sg.** were-**pl.** in the-concert
        'Three students were in the concert'

(8.56) tr'i   kn'ig'i   byl'i   na stol'e
        three books-**fem.gen.sg.** were-**pl.** on the-table
        'Three books were on the table'

If the head nouns are genitive singular, as in the traditional glosses above, the question arises as to what accounts for the plural agreement in (8.55) and (8.56).[23] Two possibilities come to mind: the agreement is with the head noun, or it is agreement with the head of the quantified expression itself, that is, with the paucal numeral. In the first case, the claim is that the genitive singular head noun (*stud'enta* in (8.55)) determines plural agreement. Immediately there is the feature mismatch in number (a singular nominal with a plural

show genitive plural on an adjective and "genitive singular" on the noun, showing a number mismatch on standard accounts, but not on our paucal analysis), and moreover supports the general trend of gender neutralization in non-singular contexts.

[23] With all quantificational indefinite subjects (paucals, numerals from five upwards, *mnogo* 'many'), neuter singular agreement is possible, particularly in post-verbal contexts. The theoretical issue we are treating here, however, is the existence of the agreeing forms. Non-agreement, whether analyzed as the result of a null expletive or NP/DP distinction, is irrelevant to the issues posed by plural agreement with putatively "genitive singular" subjects (which we analyze as nominative paucal in the text).

verb). Secondly, there is the problem that verbal agreement in Russian is systematically restricted to nominative subjects. To our knowledge, other than in controversial quantified expressions such as those under discussion, there are no cases of verbal agreement with non-nominative subjects. Indeed, in the well-known nominative/genitive alternations with negation (Babby 1980; Brown 1999; Borschev and Partee 2002), agreement systematically appears with the nominative and is impossible with the genitive.

(8.57) moroz   n'e čuvstvovalsja
        frost.masc-Nom neg melt-3.masc.sg.

(8.58) moroza   n'e čuvstvovalos'
        frost.masc-Gen neg melt-3.neut.sg. (default)

Nominative case and verbal agreement are biconditional in Russian. To allow plural agreement to be triggered by a genitive singular head noun would thus run counter to one of the language's strongest exceptionless morphosyntactic generalizations. A more plausible alternative would be that the verb agrees with the paucal numeral itself and not the head noun. The paucals could be claimed to have plural features and, when the noun phrase is a subject, to be in the nominative case. Indeed, in our solution, outlined directly below, the spirit of this account is maintained, namely the idea that paucal number is compatible with plural verbal morphology. However, the claim that there is direct agreement between the paucal and the verb runs into problems of its own. First, there is the adjectival behavior of the paucals themselves. One piece of evidence to this effect is given in (8.59) vs. (8.60), where we see the form of the paucal itself showing gender agreement with the head noun:

(8.59) dv'e   kn'ig'i
        two-fem books-fem

(8.60) dva   stola
        two-masc tables-masc

If *kn'ig'i* determines gender agreement on the numeral *dv'e* in ((8.59)), then it appears *kn'ig'i* is the head of the phrase and the numeral is a modifier that undergoes concord with it. This gender-based allomorphy on the numeral strengthens the evidence that *kn'ig'i* is in fact the head of the phrase, which we have already witnessed with the adjectival gender concord in (8.53) and (8.54).

Thus, we reach an apparent paradox. The head noun of the phrase is clearly *kn'ig'i* and not *dv'e*, and yet it is only *dv'e* that might have the right case and number features to trigger verbal agreement with the verb. The solution to this apparent paradox lies in the claim that the head noun is genitive singular. We claim, instead, that the endings we see in these constructions are number morphology and not case morphology (see Rakhlin 2003 for a similar proposal):

(8.61) *Paucal Morphology Proposal*: The apparent genitive singular morphology in paucal constructions is actually (nominative) paucal morphology, a number category distinct from singular and plural.

If (8.61) is true, we would expect there to be instances where nominative-paucal morphology is distinct from genitive-singular morphology. Such examples are found with some Class I nouns, as shown in (8.62):

(8.62) b'ez   šága
        without step-gen.sg.

(8.63) tr'i   šagá/*šága
        three step-pauc/*step-gen.sg.

In (8.62) we see a normal genitive singular ending for this noun. In (8.63) we see the paucal ending. The two are distinct for stress (as occurs often in the language; Russian has a distinctive stress system) and not interchangeable. This is totally unexpected on the traditional analysis.[24] Thus, we argue that the proper analyses of examples such as (8.53) and (8.54) are given in (8.64) and (8.65):

(8.64) dva   prostyx   stud'enta   byl'i   na
        two-masc simple-**masc.pauc** student-**masc.nom.pauc** were-pauc in
        koncert'e
        the concert
        'Two simple students were in the concert'

(8.65) dv'e   prostyje   kn'ig'i   byl'i   na stol'e
        two-fem simple-**fem.pauc** books-**fem.nom.pauc** were-pl on the-table
        'Two simple books were on the table'

---

[24] Note that Zaliznjak (1967, 46–8), while not discussing the problem of verbal agreement with paucals, presents an interesting set of analytic possibilities in terms of the overall case+number system of Russian, ultimately favoring one in which the paucals represent an altogether different "ninth" case category.

This analysis solves the agreement problems noted above. The head nouns in (8.64) and (8.65) are in the nominative case. They have paucal features, required in the context of the numerical adjectives 2/3/4. We argue that paucals shared with plurals the morphosyntactic feature [−singular], but differ in the presence of a feature [−augmented] (cf. Harbour 2006):

(8.66) Singular: [+singular]
        Paucal: [−singular, −augmented]
        Plural: [−singular]

There is concord for both number and case between adjectives and the head nouns. On verbs, paucal and plural verbal features are syncretic. This is of course fully consistent with the historical loss of the paucal morphologically and with a markedness-based impoverishment rule deleting the feature [−augmented] on verbs. However, the feature [paucal] does appear to be syntactically active prior to its impoverishment on verbal agreement. The numeral *dva/dv'e* agrees with the head noun for gender (masculine in (8.65) and feminine in (8.66)). Adjectives also agree for gender in the paucal–but use case forms syncretic with nominative or genitive to show it (cf. (8.53) and (8.54)). So the adjectives in (8.64), (8.65) are paucal in number with gender agreement. All forms within the DP are nominative. This allows for subject–verb agreement. The paucal number solution accounts for all the facts at hand without undermining the general picture of subject–verb agreement in Russian. The full paradigm of paucals in the language, impoverished though it is morphologically, is given in (8.67). Note that plural is distinguished from paucal only in the direct cases, which is an independent instance of the markedness generalization: the distinction for the feature [Paucal] is neutralized everywhere outside of the unmarked nominative and accusative cases.

(8.67) Number Endings in the Nominative:

NOUNS-Nom	Sing	Paucal	Plural
Class I	Ø	-i	-i
Class IIa	ъ	-a	-i
Class IIb	Ø	-a	-a
Class III	Ø	-i	-i

ADJECTIVES-Nom	Sing	Paucal	Plural
Fem	-aja	-ije	-ije
Neut	-oje	-ix	-ije
Masc	-ij	-ix	-ije

A final piece of evidence in favor of our approach to paucals comes from Serbo-Croatian, where there still is gender marking in plural contexts. Consider (8.68):

(8.68) Studenti   su   bili   tamo
       students-**masc**.nom.pl. aux-3.pl. were-pl.**masc**. there
       'Students were there'

(8.69) Devojke   su   bile   tamo
       girls-fem.nom.pl. aux-3.pl. were-pl.**fem**. there
       'Girls were there'

Nominative paucal agreement for masculine nouns is distinct from nominative plural; compare (8.68) with (8.70). Nominative paucal agreement and nominative plural are identical for feminine nouns (8.69) vs. (8.71).

(8.70) Tri studenta   su   bila   tamo
       three student-masc.nom.pauc aux-3.pl. were-pauc.masc. there
       'Three students were there'

(8.71) Tri devojke   su   bile   tamo
       three girls.nom.pauc aux-3.pl. were-pauc.fem. there
       'Three girls were there'

In (8.70) we see distinct verbal agreement for nominative paucal. Note that if paucal is analyzed as the result of special genitive case, the same problem arises as with Russian: why should a genitive subject trigger verbal agreement? Moreover, the verbal agreement in (8.70) cannot be reduced to "default" agreement with a non-nominative subject, as a clear gender distinction exists between (8.70) and (8.71). The proposal that nominative paucal is an instance of nominative case, thereby able to trigger verbal agreement, and paucal number, which is syncretic with plural in feminine but distinct in masculine, is able to explain the Serbo-Croatian pattern under natural assumptions about subject–verb agreement. As the Serbo-Croatian participle still shows gender agreement in paucal and plural contexts, and the only verbal agreement possible in (8.70) is /-a/, that is the paucal masculine form.

8.7 Conclusion

To the extent that the form of the Russian genitive plural appears to be an instance of transderivational derivation or gender-sensitivity in the oblique plural, it is an impostor. Closer scrutiny reveals that no transderivational account of the distribution of genitive plural allomorphs is required once a decomposition of nouns into root and theme vowel is adopted, and that this distribution may be stated purely phonologically and thus without reference to gender. The basic tenets of markedness-based neutralization of gender distinctions may be upheld within a model of locally-determined allomorphy.

References

Babby, Leonard (1980) *Existential Sentences and Negation in Russian*. Ann Arbor, MI: Karoma Publishers.

Borras, F., and R. Christian (1971) *Russian Syntax*. Oxford: Oxford University Press.

Borschev, Vladimir, and Barbara Partee (2002) 'Genitive of negation and scope of negation in Russian existential sentences', in Jindrich Toman (ed.), *Tenth Meeting on Formal Approaches to Slavic Linguistics: The Ann Arbor Meeting*, Ann Arbor, MI: Michigan Slavic Publications, pp. 181–200.

Brown, Sue (1999) *The Syntax of Negation in Russian: A Minimalist Approach*. Palo Alto, CA: CSLI.

Chomsky, Noam, and Morris Halle (1968) *The Sound Pattern of English*. New York: Harper and Row.

Comrie, Bernard, Gerald Stone, and Maria Polinsky (1996) *The Russian Language in the Twentieth Century*. Oxford: Oxford University Press.

Flier, Michael (1972) 'On the source of derived imperfectives in Russian', in D. S. Worth (ed.), *The Slavic Word*, The Hague: Mouton, pp. 236–60.

Greenberg, Joseph (1966) *Language Universals, with Special Reference to Feature Hierarchies*. Janua Linguarum, Series Minor, 59. The Hague: Mouton.

Halle, Morris (1994) 'The Russian declension', in *Perspectives in Phonology*. CSLI.

——— and Andrew Nevins (2006) 'Rule application in phonology', Ms, MIT and Harvard University.

Harbour, Daniel (2006) *Morphosemantic Number: From Kiowa Noun Classes to UG Number Features*. Dordrecht: Springer.

Harris, James (1991) 'The exponence of gender in Spanish'. *Linguistic Inquiry*.

Jakobson, Roman (1948) 'Russian conjugation'. *Word* 4.

——— (1957) 'The relationship between genitive and plural in the declension of Russian nouns'. *Scando-Slavica* 3.

Kager, Rene (1999) *Optimality Theory*. Cambridge: Cambridge University Press.

Levin, Maurice I. (1978) *Russian Declension and Conjugation*. Columbus, OH: Slavica.

Lightner, Theodore (1972) *Problems in the Theory of Phonology, Volume I: Russian Phonology and Turkish Phonology*. Edmonton, AB-Champaign, IL: Linguistic Research, Inc.

Matushansky, Ora, and Morris Halle (2006) 'The morphophonology of adjectival inflection in Russian'. *Linguistic Inquiry*.

Müller, Gereon (2003) 'A Distributed Morphology approach to syncretism in Russian noun inflection', in Olga Arnaudova, Wayles Browne, María Luisa Rivero, and Danijela Stojanović (eds.), *Twelfth Meeting on Formal Approaches to Slavic Linguistics: The Ottawa Meeting.* Ann Arbor, MI: Michigan Slavic Publications, pp. 353–73.

Noyer, Rolf (2005) 'A constraint on interclass syncretisms', in *Yearbook of Morphology 2004.* Springer.

Pertsova, Katya (2004) Distribtion of genitive plural allomorphs in the Russian lexicon and in the internal grammar of native speakers. Master's thesis, UCLA.

Rakhlin, Natalia (2003) 'Genitive of quantification in Russian: The role of morphology', in Marjo van Koppen, Joanna Sio, and Mark de Vos (eds.), *Proceedings of Console XI.* Student Organization of Linguistics in Europe.

Rappaport, Gilbert (2006) 'Towards a theory of the grammatical use of lexical information', in Hana Filip, Steven Franks, James Lavine, and Mila Tasseva-Kurktchieva (eds.), *Fourteenth Meeting on Formal Approaches to Slavic Linguistics: The Princeton Meeting.* Ann Arbor, MI: Michigan Slavic Publications.

Rice, Curt (2005) 'Optimizing Russian gender: A preliminary analysis', in Steven Franks, Frank Gladney, and Mila Tasseva-Kurktchieva (eds.), *Thirteenth Meeting on Formal Approaches to Slavic Linguistics: The South Carolina Meeting.* Ann Arbor, MI: Michigan Slavic Publications, pp. 265–75.

Zaliznjak, Andrej A. (1967) *Russkoe Imennoe Slovoizmenenie.* Moscow: Nauka.

9

Inflectional paradigms have bases too: Arguments from Yiddish

ADAM ALBRIGHT*

9.1 Introduction

It is well known that the phonological form of a word can depend on its morphological structure. In serial approaches, this follows naturally from the fact that words have derivational histories: morphologically complex words undergo successive levels of phonological derivation as they are constructed, making them eligible for different phonological processes along the way. A crucial distinction is typically made, however, between derivational and inflectional morphology. Whereas derived forms usually have clear "bases of affixation", inflected forms are usually not obviously constructed from one another. For this reason, they are generally not held to have the same formal influence on one another.

(9.1)   Traditional inflectional/derivation distinction:

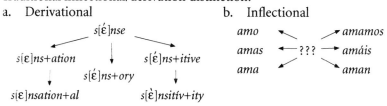

In a fully parallel model such as standard OT (Prince and Smolensky 2004), morphological structure influences phonology not by stages of derivation but by constraints on relations between forms—for example, via output-output (OO) constraints demanding identity to morphologically related

* This work has benefited greatly from the helpful comments and suggestions of many people, including especially the editors, Michael Becker, Bruce Hayes, Junko Itô, Michael Kenstowicz, Armin Mester, Jaye Padgett, Jerry Sadock, Donca Steriade, Jochen Trommer, Michael Wagner, and audiences at MIT and WCCFL 23. All remaining errors and oversights are, of course, my own.

forms (Burzio 1996; Benua 1997; Steriade 2000; Kenstowicz 2005). OO constraints are widely used in the literature, but there is no agreement as to how to evaluate them. Within derivational paradigms, it is clear that derived forms should be constrained to match their bases (Benua 1997). In inflectional paradigms, however, there have been conflicting approaches. Some have argued that inflectional paradigms may also have privileged bases which the remaining forms must be faithful to, as in (9.2a.) (e.g., Kenstowicz 1996; Benua 1997), while others have assumed the more egalitarian structure in (9.2b.) (Burzio 1996; Steriade 2000).

(9.2)   Two approaches to OO correspondence in inflectional paradigms:
    a.   Base Identity   b.   Uniform Exponence

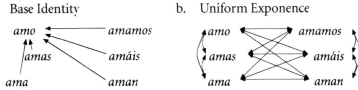

McCarthy's recent "Optimal Paradigms" (OP) proposal aims to resolve the issue by codifying the traditional distinction between inflection and derivation. Derivational paradigms, which have intuitive bases of affixation, have a hierarchical structure as is traditionally assumed ((9.1a.)), while inflectional paradigms have the democratic structure in (9.2b.) (McCarthy 2005, 173ff.). McCarthy formulates OO constraints for inflectional paradigms (called OP constraints) such that every member of the paradigm must match every other member. No member of the paradigm is designated as a privileged base form (ibid.).

The OP hypothesis has several apparent advantages. First, it avoids the need to assign privileged bases in inflectional paradigms, where there are often no obvious "derived from" relations. In addition, it leads to strong and novel predictions. In particular, it predicts that if a phonological process affects one member of the paradigm (markedness ≫ input-output faithfulness), it may potentially spread to the rest of the paradigm through paradigm leveling (overapplication) by means of a high-ranked OP constraint. By contrast, the only way for phonology to underapply (or for marked allomorphs to spread) is by losing the process altogether (input-output faithfulness ≫ markedness). McCarthy calls these effects "attraction to the unmarked" and "overapplication only", respectively.

In order to see why these predictions hold, consider the final devoicing example in (9.3). (Here and elsewhere, I use a final devoicing constraint FINDEVOI as a shorthand for whatever constraint motivates final devoicing, e.g., *VOICEDOBSTRUENT/___#, or more generally, *VOICEDOBSTRUENT/*not before sonorant* (Steriade 1997; Kenstowicz, Abu-Mansour, and Törkenczy 2003).[1] When final devoicing applies without any additional OP effect (FINDEVOI ≫ IO-IDENT(voi), OP-IDENT(voi) ranked low), the paradigm with voicing alternations wins. When an OP effect is introduced (OP-IDENT(voi) reranked high), the paradigm with devoicing throughout (candidate (b)) is selected. Thus, the OP constraint causes final devoicing to overapply, and the less marked allomorph prevails ((9.3b.)). Crucially, the only way for candidate (c) (underapplication) to win is by reranking IO-IDENT ≫ FINDEVOI, that is, by allowing voiced obstruents everywhere (blanket loss of final devoicing).

(9.3)   A language with final devoicing:

a.   No OP effect

/bund/, /bund-ə/	FINDEVOI	IO-ID(voi)	OP-ID(voi)
☞ a. [bunt], [bundə]		*	* (t~d)
b. [bunt], [buntə]		**!	
c. [bund], [bundə]	*!		

b.   OP effect

/bund/, /bund-ə/	OP-ID(voi)	FINDEVOI	IO-ID(voi)
a. [bunt], [bundə]	*! (t~d)		*
☞ b. [bunt], [buntə]			**
c. [bund], [bundə]		*!	

The first goal of this chapter is to show that the overapplication-only prediction, though appealing in its strength, is incorrect. The counterexample comes from a change in the history of Yiddish, involving the "loss of final devoicing". I will show that this change, of the *bunt, bunde* ⇒ *bund, bunde* type, was in fact paradigmatically motivated and represents an example of underapplication and extension of marked forms. The second aim of this chapter is to show that although such a change is unexpected under the OP approach, it follows naturally from a theory in which inflectional paradigms have bases, just like derivational paradigms. In a theory with inflectional bases, the direction of leveling is determined not by markedness or global harmony but by which form in the paradigm serves as the base (in this case, the inflected plural

---

[1] It does not matter for present purposes whether final devoicing is analyzed via positional markedness (*VOICEDOBSTRUENT/___#, *VOICEDOBSTRUENT/___[−son] ≫ IDENT(voi) ≫ *VOICEDOBSTRUENT/___V) or constraint conjunction (*VOICEDOBSTRUENT & *CODA; Ito and Mester 1997; 2003). A positional faithfulness approach (Lombardi 1999; Padgett, to appear) is also compatible with the analysis that I will propose here, but it crucially changes the predictions of the Optimal Paradigms approach; see section 9.4 for discussion.

form). Finally, I will sketch how the choice of base in inflectional paradigms can be determined externally and non-circularly, using a procedure proposed in Albright (2002b), namely, by selecting the maximally informative member of the paradigm as the base. I will show that this procedure correctly predicts the use of a suffixed form as the base form in Yiddish.

9.2 Paradigm leveling in Yiddish nouns: Loss of final devoicing

9.2.1 *Description of the change*

Middle High German (MHG), the primary ancestor of Modern Yiddish, had a regular process of final devoicing (Paul, Wiehl, and Grosse 1989, §62).[2] This can be seen by comparing the forms in (9.4a.), in which stem-final voiced stops surface as voiceless word-finally, against the forms in (9.4b.), which are voiceless throughout.[3]

(9.4)   Final devoicing in Middle High German (MHG):

    a.   Voiced obstruents are devoiced in singular:

	Stem	Nom Sg	Gen Sg	Nom Pl	Gloss
/b/	lob-	lop	lobes	lobe	'praise'
	wîb-	wîp	wîbes	wîber	'woman'
/d/	rad-	rat	rades	reder	'wheel'
	held-	helt	heldes	helde	'hero'
/g/	wëg-	wëc [k]	wëges	wëge	'way'
	tag-	tac [k]	tages	tage	'day'
	ding-	dinc [k]	dinges	dinge	'thing'
	honeg-	honec [k]	honeges	—	'honey'
/z/	hûs-	hûs [s]	hûses [z]	hiuser [z]	'house'
/v/	briev-	brief	brieves	brieve	'letter'

---

[2] The MHG contrast between *p,t,k* and *b,d,g* is generally thought to have involved aspiration and only secondarily voicing; see Paul, Wiehl, and Grosse (1989, §54) or Wright (1950, §33) for discussion. Paul et al. observe that although the alternation was phonologically a fortition (from lenis/sonant to fortis/surd), it was nonetheless motivated by loss of voicing in syllable-final position.

[3] Throughout this chapter, I will use the abbreviations MHG for Middle High German, NHG for Modern (Standard) German, and NEY for Northeast Yiddish. For MHG examples, I will use the standardized orthography of Paul, Wiehl, and Grosse (1989, §§18–20), in which ˆ marks long vowels, *ë* is a short open [e], and *ʒ* is a coronal sibilant fricative, possibly fortis, possibly post-alveolar (Paul et al, §151). For Yiddish forms, I will use YIVO transliteration (http://www.yivoinstitute.org/yiddish/alefbeys.htm), with a few minor modifications: I use the IPA symbol ɔ instead of YIVO *o* for *komets-aleph*, and *-ən* instead of *-en/-n* for syllabic [ņ]. In YIVO transcription, *sh* represents [ʃ], *zh* [ʒ], *kh* [x], *ay* [aɪ], *ey* [eɪ], and *oy* [ɔɪ].

b. Voiceless obstruents throughout the paradigm:

	Stem	Nom Sg	Gen Sg	Nom Pl	Gloss
/t/	blat-	blat	blates	bleter	'leaf'
/k/	roc-	roc	rockes	röcke	'overcoat'
	druc-	druc	druckes	drucke	'pressure'
/s/	sloẓ- [s]	sloẓ[s]	sloẓes [s]	sloẓe [s]	'lock'
/f/	schif-	schif	schiffes [f]	schiffe [f]	'ship'

In its earliest stages, Yiddish also apparently had final devoicing, as seen in
13th–14th century spellings like *tak* 'day' (MHG *tac*), *vip* 'wife' (MHG *wîb*),
etc., written with Hebrew letters indicating voiceless stops (King 1980, 374).
In Modern Northeast Yiddish (NEY), however, there is no general process of
final devoicing (Sapir 1915, 237; Vennemann 1972, 188–9; Sadock 1973). Thus,
words that showed alternations in MHG (9.4a.) and early Yiddish are now
consistently voiced in Modern NEY:

(9.5)   Modern Northeast Yiddish (NEY) shows no final devoicing:

	Stem	Sg	Pl	Gloss	cf: MHG Sg
/b/	loyb-	loyb	loybən	'praise'	lop
	vayb-	vayb	vaybər	'woman'	wîp
/d/	rɔd-	rɔd	reder	'wheel'	rat
	held-	held	heldən	'hero'	helt
/g/	veg-	veg	vegən	'way'	wëc
	tɔg-	tɔg	teg	'day'	tac
/z/	hoyz-	hoyz	hayzər	'house'	hûs
/v/	briv-	briv	briv	'letter'	brief

As King (1980, 383) states, "[g]enerally speaking NEY has restored phonetically
a final voiced obstruent wherever MHG had a voiceless obstruent alternating
morphophonemically with a voiced obstruent." Words which were consistently voiceless-final in MHG (9.4b.) remain voiceless in NEY (*blat, rɔk, druk,
shlɔs, shif*), as did words with no paradigmatically-related forms, e.g., *honik*
'honey' (no plural), *avek* 'away' (etymologically, but not paradigmatically
related to *veg* 'way').

How did words like [vek] come to be pronounced as [veg]? One possibility
is that the change was simply caused by a blanket loss of final devoicing–
that is, through the demotion of FinDevoi. Under such an account, words
like *veg* came to be pronounced with surface [g] simply because the relevant
faithfulness constraint (IO-Ident(voi)) was reranked above FinDevoi. Words

like *druk* and *avek* never had a voiced allomorph in MHG, and thus had under-lyingly voiceless final segments, due to the Alternation Condition (Kiparsky 1982) or Lexicon Optimization (Prince and Smolensky 2004). Hence, they remained voiceless even after the change. I will call this the "markedness demotion" account, since it is based on the idea that the change in NEY involved an increased tolerance of final voiced stops. This is parallel to the "rule loss" account that made the Yiddish case famous in the early generative literature on historical change (Kiparsky 1968, 177; King 1969, 46–8; see also King 1980).

This can be contrasted with a paradigmatic account in which the change of *vek* to *veg* was due to leveling of voicing from the plural to the singular, leading only secondarily to the demotion of FinDevoi. Under this view, words like [vek] imported voicing from the plural and came to be pronounced as [veg]. Words like *druk* were voiceless in the plural, while words like *avek* had no plurals. Therefore, neither group was eligible to become voiced in NEY.

The markedness demotion and paradigmatic accounts seem quite similar since in both cases, the restoration of final voicing is enabled by the presence of alternations. The difference is the mechanism. In the markedness demotion account, alternations are the evidence for the underlying form, while the mechanism for change is increased tolerance for final voiced obstruents. In the paradigmatic account, learners fail to learn or stop tolerating the alternations, and the markedness consequences are only secondary.

In fact, most treatments of the Yiddish change have pursued a paradigmatic explanation. In an early analytical discussion of the change, Sapir (1915) hypothesized that leveling happened quite early in the history of NEY and was followed by other changes affecting the shape of noun paradigms, such as final apocope and adding additional plural endings. This account, found also in Sadock (1973), is illustrated in (9.6). An alternate possibility, shown in (9.7), is that the the change was precipitated by apocope of final -ə suffixes ([vegə] > [veg]), which rendered final devoicing opaque and eventually led to leveling (Stampe 1969, 453; Vennemann 1972, 189).

(9.6) Early leveling from the plural:

		Sg.		Pl.	
Stage 1:	MHG		vek		vegə
Stage 2:	Leveling of voicing		veg		vegə
Stage 3:	Apocope of final schwa		veg		veg
Stage 4:	Plural marking restored		veg		vegən

(9.7) Leveling induced by apocope:

			Sg.		Pl.	
Stage 1:	MHG		Sg.	vek	Pl.	vegə
Stage 2:	Apocope of final schwa			vek		veg
	***Final devoicing is active but counterfed by apocope					
Stage 3:	Leveling of voicing			veg		veg
Stage 4:	Plural marking restored			veg		vegən

Either way, the hypothesized leveling leads to underapplication of final devoicing and creates more marked paradigms–that is, paradigms in which more forms contain voiced stops, and voiced stops occur even in final position. Thus, if the traditional paradigmatic explanation is correct, the Yiddish change represents a counterexample to the "overapplication only" and "attraction to the unmarked" predictions of the OP hypothesis.

My goal in the following sections is to show that the paradigmatic account is indeed correct and that the Yiddish change cannot be attributed to a simple loss of final devoicing. In particular, I will show that the "loss of final devoicing" did not introduce voicing contrasts in all positions, as might be expected from simple rule loss or markedness demotion. Even in modern NEY, coda voicing is contrastive only in places where there was paradigmatic pressure from the plural for voicing, while elsewhere devoicing prevails.

9.2.2 *Persistence of final devoicing in forms outside the paradigm*

Discussions of Modern NEY often emphasize that although final voicing was restored to noun paradigms, derivationally-related forms continued to end in voiceless obstruents. Some examples are shown in the last column of (9.8).

(9.8) Persistence of devoicing in derivationally-related forms

Gloss	NEY Sg.	NEY Pl.	Related to
'way'	veg	vegən	avek 'away'
'enemy'	faynd	faynd	faynt həbən 'hate'; faynt krigən 'come to hate'
'friend'	fraynd	fraynd	(ge)fraynt 'relatives'
'love'	libə	libəs	*Dial.* lip həbən 'love'[4]

The logic of the argument is that the relation between *veg* and *avek* is transparent enough to set up the UR /a+veg/ (supported also by other pairs, such as *heym* 'home' ~ *aheym* 'homewards', *hinter* 'behind' ~ *ahinter* 'backward',

---

[4] On the geographic distribution of *lip* vs. *lib* in this phrase, see Herzog (1965, 222).

durkh 'through' ~ *adurkh* 'through (adv.)', *ponim* 'face' ~ *aponim* 'apparently', etc.), but since 'away' is not part of the inflectional paradigm of 'way' it is protected from leveling and continues to undergo final devoicing. If this is right, it constitutes strong evidence that the change from [vek] to [veg] is not purely phonotactic but is due to paradigmatic pressure.

The same argument can also be made from the opposite direction. If forms outside the paradigm did not participate in leveling, then the existence of voiced forms outside the paradigm should also not have been sufficient to restore final voicing in cases where all of the members of the paradigm happened to be devoiced. This is, in fact, true: the words for the numbers 11 and 12, for example, both end in [f] (*el(ə)f*, *tsvel(ə)f*) but have related forms ending in [v]: *eləvə, tsveləve* '11 o'clock, 12 o'clock'. These related forms retained voicing but were evidently not able to influence the voicing of the simple cardinal numbers (*tsvel(ə)f* remained *tsvel(ə)f*, and did not change to *tsvel(ə)v*). Thus, the only forms that regained voicing were those that had a paradigmatically related form (such as a plural) that showed voicing. This could be taken as evidence that the voicing change was due to leveling within the paradigm, while final devoicing continues to apply in *tsvelf*, as in *avek*.

An important caveat is that these arguments rest crucially on the assumption that even though the related forms in question are not part of the same inflectional paradigm, they do share a stem with the same underlying form. The voiceless [k] in *avek* would be uninteresting for present purposes if it had simply been relexicalized (i.e., /avek/ rather than /a+veg/) by the time of the change, since if *avek* was no longer derived synchronically from /veg/, then there is no reason why changes in the paradigm of /veg/ would have affected *avek*. Certainly there is an intuition that the *a*- prefix is transparent enough to make the relation between *vek* and *avek* clear (and similarly *tsveləf* ~ *tsveləvə*), but any argument based on derivationally-related words must be treated cautiously, since we have no direct evidence about the underlying composition of *avek*. (Plank 2000 discusses a parallel reanalysis of the adverb *weg* and similar words in Modern German.) Fortunately, there are a number of additional arguments that the loss of final devoicing was paradigmatically restricted, which do not rest on assumptions about the underlying form of words like *avek*.

9.2.3 *Persistence of final devoicing in affixes*

A related argument comes from the fact that although voicing contrasts were reintroduced at the ends of lexical roots, affixes went in the opposite direction, leveling to the voiceless variant. The MHG adjectival suffix -*ic*, -*ige* (with [k] ∼ [g]) alternations) yielded NEY -*ik*, -*ike*, with [k] throughout–so, for example, the inflected forms of *ruik* 'calm' include *ruike*, *ruikən*, and *ruiker*. The same is also true of a suffix -*ig*- that appears in verbs: compare Modern German *end-ig-en* 'put an end to', *beteil-ig-en* 'participate' vs. NEY *end-ik-n*, *bateyl-ik-n*. (It is not clear whether this should be treated as the same suffix as adjectival -*ik* or not.[5]) Similarly, the numeric suffix -*(t)sik* (as in *draysik* '30', *akhtsik* '80', *nayntsik* '90') showed [k] ∼ [g] alternations in MHG (*zweinzic* 'twenty' ∼ *zweinzigest* 'twentieth'), but has invariant [k] in NEY: *tsvantsik* ∼ *di tsvantsike yorn* 'the 20's'. Likewise, the MHG preposition/prefix *abe-/ab-/ap-* yielded NEY *ɔp* in all positions (e.g., *ɔpesn* 'eat up'), rather than restoring the voiced [b] on the basis of either the *abe-* variant or the prevocalic voiced variant *ab-*.[6] This is unexpected under the markedness demotion account, since these affixes had alternations and for this reason must have had underlying voiced obstruents (/-ig/, /ab-/). A general loss of final devoicing should have allowed them to surface faithfully.

More generally, a survey of Katz (1987) reveals that although Yiddish has a fair number of affixes ending in consonants, none of these end in final voiced obstruents.[7]

---

[5] In many cases, verbs in -*ik-n* do correspond to adjectives in -*ik*-: e.g., *zindik* 'sinful', *zindikn* 'sin' (see Lieber 1981 for a discussion of the equivalent facts in German). There are, however, also -*ik-n* verbs with no corresponding adjective (*end-ik-n* 'put an end to', but no **end-ik*), and even -*ik-n* verbs for stems that take different (non-*ik*) adjectives: *reyn* 'clean (adj.)' ∼ *reyn-ik-n* 'to clean' (the adjective is *reyn*, not **reynik*), and *payn* 'torture' ∼ *payn-ik-n* 'to torture' (the related adjective is *payn-lɔkh*, not **paynik*). The same facts hold for NHG (*endigen* but no **endig*, *reinigen* but no **reinig*, and *peinigen* but *peinlich*, not **peinig*), and make it difficult to unite the two -*ig*- suffixes.

[6] We cannot exclude the possibility that devoicing of *abe-/ab-/ap-* to *op-* was simply the consequence of a syllabification preference to align the left edge of verb stems with a syllable boundary, as in NHG: *a*[p].[ʔ]*arbeiten*. If Yiddish first lost the *abe-* variant by syncope and then passed through a stage of morpheme-aligned syllabification, then all [b] variants of the prefix would have been lost prior to the restoration of final devoicing. This seems somewhat unlikely, since we independently know that either *abe-* or resyllabified *a.bV* had to have remained long enough to condition open syllable lengthening > *aːb-* in order to yield the [ɔ] in NEY *ɔp-*; see section 9.2.8. Furthermore, it presupposes a brief change in syllabification which is not seen either in MHG or in Modern Yiddish; this is certainly not impossible but there is no evidence to support it.

[7] An ambiguous case is the element *varg* 'equipment, gear, ... ware', found in words such as *esɔnvarg* 'food' (lit. 'eating-ware'), *zisvarg* 'candy' (lit. 'sweet-ware'), *kleynvarg* 'youngsters' (lit. 'small-ware') or *kosvarg* 'stemware' (lit. 'cup-ware'). It seems likely that *varg* is related to English and German *ware* (cf. German *Süßwaren* 'candy'), but I am unable to determine the source of the final [g] in Yiddish. (The MHG source of Modern German *Ware* is *war*, *ware* (fem.).) Whatever its origin, if *varg* is a suffix, then the [g] would be an exception to the claim that affixes never end in voiced obstruents. I would argue, however, that words like *zisvarg* and *kleynvarg* are actually compounds, confirmed by the fact that they have two stresses (*zísvàrg*). Thus, *varg* acts as a (bound) stem and does not constitute an exception.

(9.9) Basic inventory of Yiddish affixes:
    a. Inflectional suffixes
        • Verbal: Ø, *-st, -t, -ən, -n, -əndik*
        • Nominal: Ø, *-ən, -s, -s, -ɪm, -ər, -əkh*
        • Adjectival: Ø, *-ər, -ə, -ən, -əm, -s, ər, ət*
    b. Inflectional prefixes
        • Verbal: *ge-*
    c. Derivational suffixes
        • Verbal: *-kə-, -əvə-*
        • Nominal: *-hayt, -kayt, -ung* [uŋ]*, -ur, -ik, -enish, -ents, -ek, -eray, -shaft, -s, -tum, -əl(ə), -ələkh, -ke, -əkhts, -ɪm, -izm, -ist, -er, -or, -nik/-nitsə, -ent, -ets, -uk, -yak, -tshik, -in, -tə, təl/stəl*
        • Adjectival/adverbial: *-ərheyt, -ləkh*
    d. Derivational prefixes
        • Verbal: *ant-, ba-, der-, far-, tse-, oys-, uf-, um-, unter-, iber-, ayn-, on-, op-, bay-, for-, tsu-, adurkh-, ahin-, aher-, avek-, mit-, antkegən-, anider-, arop-, aroys-, aruf-, arum-, arayn-, arunter-, ariber-, nokh-, farbay-, faroys-, funander-, tsuzamen-, tsunoyf-*
        • Adverbial: *a-, am-*

We are faced, then, with a Richness of the Base issue (Smolensky 1996). In principle, ranking IDENT-IO(voi) ≫ FINDEVOI should allow the possibility of a voicing contrast anywhere, including in affixes. Even while acknowledging the fact that languages do not create or acquire new affixes all that often (and, furthermore, that the primary source languages for Yiddish have had final devoicing during much of the contact period), we must contend with the fact that in the three or four affixes in which NEY should have inherited final voiced stops, we find devoicing: [-ik], [op-]. It appears that the restoration of final voicing was blocked in all of the affixes where it is expected, leaving a language with no voiced-final affixes.

If final voicing was restored by such a reranking, then affixes like *-ig* and *ab-* should have yielded [-ig] and [ɔb-], and, more generally, voiced-final affixes should have become possible. Since they did not, we must conclude that devoicing remained active outside of roots. Distinctions between the phonotactics of roots and affixes are not uncommon and, in particular, it has frequently been noted that roots may allow a greater range of marked structures than affixes. A common recipe for handling such cases within OT is to posit special faithfulness constraints that apply only to roots (or lexical categories): IDENT-IO$_{\text{LexCat}}$(voi) (Casali 1997; Beckman 1998; Alderete 2001; Alderete 2003). A description of the Yiddish change, therefore, would have to involve reranking FINDEVOI with respect to IDENT-IO$_{\text{LexCat}}$(voi), but not with respect to the more general IDENT-IO(voi) constraint:

(9.10)   Reranking to allow final voiced obstruents within roots:
         Stage 1: FINDEVOI ≫ IDENT-IO(voi), IDENT-IO$_{\text{LexCat}}$(voi)
         Stage 2: IDENT-IO$_{\text{LexCat}}$(voi) ≫ FINDEVOI ≫ IDENT-IO(voi)

The "loss of final devoicing" was thus subject to a curious restriction: why was voicing restored only in roots? The older stage of the language provided no evidence for the relative ranking of IDENT-IO$_{\text{LexCat}}$(voi) and IDENT-IO(voi)— in fact, prior to the change, both roots and affixes underwent devoicing and showed active alternations. Therefore, we have no particular reason to expect that a demotion of the ban on voiced codas should have placed it below one constraint but not the other.[8] What we actually observe is a more subtle morphologically-restricted change, in which final devoicing remains active in affixes. This is most easily explained if the mechanism of change was leveling the form of the root within paradigms, preserving the allomorph found in the plural.

9.2.4 *Persistence of devoicing in word-final obstruent clusters*

Another respect in which devoicing persists in NEY is in determining the direction of assimilation in obstruent clusters. This can be seen, for example, in the paradigm of the verb 'to love' (Katz 1987, 29), which shows that although a single voiced obstruent is allowed to surface faithfully (1sg *lib*), when the suffixes -*st* and -*t* are added, the voicing disagreement is resolved by devoicing:

(9.11)   Devoicing in 2sg, 3sg, and 2pl:
1sg	lib	1pl	libən
2sg	lipst	2pl	lipt
3sg	lipt	3pl	libən

---

[8] Note that the observed change does obey the principle of demoting markedness below the most specific available faithfulness constraint, rather than a more general one (Hayes 2004; Tessier 2006). The principle of favoring specificity is intended to decide among different possible analyses of a language that already has marked segments in some positions—not to favor incorrectly permissive grammars. If some external force managed to create voiced obstruents just at the end of stems, but not affixes, this principle would indeed learn exactly the right grammar (attested in Modern Yiddish). However, it does not straightforwardly explain why voiced codas should be created in the first place.

How should this pattern be captured? It is instructive to compare Yiddish with two similar but crucially different languages: English and German. In English, there is no general process of final devoicing, meaning that faithfulness for voicing must outrank the ban on voiced obstruents: IDENT(voi) ≫ *VOICEDOBSTRUENT. Furthermore, when a suffix consisting of a single obstruent is added, the root controls the voicing of the suffix: *swapped* [swap-t] vs. *swabbed* [swab-d]. This pattern can be handled by a constraint against disagreeing sequences like *[bt], *[pd] (AGREE; Lombardi 1999), combined with greater faithfulness to roots than to affixes (IDENT-IO$_{LexCat}$(voi) ≫ IDENT-IO(voi)).

(9.12) IDENT$_{LexCat}$(voi) and AGREE force suffix to assimilate in English:

a. Simple voiced codas surface faithfully

/swab/		AGREE	ID$_{LexCat}$(voi)	ID(voi)	FINDEVOI
☞ a.	[swab]				*
b.	[swap]		*!	*	

b. Voiced+voiced sequences surface faithfully

/swab-d/		AGREE	ID$_{LexCat}$(voi)	ID(voi)	FINDEVOI
☞ a.	[swabd]				**
b.	[swapt]		*!	**	

c. Voiced+voiceless sequences assimilate to root (voiced+voiced)

/swap-d/		AGREE	ID$_{LexCat}$(voi)	ID(voi)	FINDEVOI
a.	[swapd]	*!			*
b.	[swabd]		*!	*	**
☞ c.	[swapt]			*	

In German, by contrast, the opposite pattern holds: there is a general process of final devoicing, so final voiced obstruents surface as voiceless (/liːb/ → [liːp] 'dear'). Furthermore, the 3sg suffix is voiceless (-*t*), and root-final obstruents devoice to agree with the suffix (*klappt* [klapt] 'knock-3sg' vs. *liebt* [liːpt] 'love-3sg'). Superficially, it appears that the choice of [liːpt] over *[liːbd] displays an unnatural preference to maintain suffix faithfulness over root faithfulness, contrary to the usual preference to preserve root specifications. This is only a side effect of the more general process of final devoicing, however, which independently rules out *[liːbd] and favors [liːpt].

The constraints in (9.13) show that the only difference between English and German is the high ranking of FINDEVOI, which rules out both simplex *[liːb] and derived *[liːbd]:

(9.13)   FINDEVOI forces final devoicing in German:

a.   Simple voiced codas are devoiced

/liːb/		FINDEVOI	AGREE	ID$_{LexCat}$(voi)	ID(voi)
a.	[liːb]	*!			
☞ b.	[liːp]			*	*

b.   Voiceless+voiceless sequences surface faithfully

/klap-t/		FINDEVOI	AGREE	ID$_{LexCat}$(voi)	ID(voi)
☞ a.	[klapt]				
b.	[klabd]	*!*		*	**

c.   Voiced+voiceless sequences assimilate to voiceless, by final devoicing

/liːb-t/		FINDEVOI	AGREE	ID$_{LexCat}$(voi)	ID(voi)
a.	[liːbt]	*!	*		
b.	[liːbd]	*!*			*
☞ c.	[liːpt]			*	*

Returning to the Yiddish pattern in (9.11), we see that NEY is like English in lacking final devoicing (e.g., [lib] 'dear'), but is like German in repairing AGREE violations by regressive devoicing. Since there is no final devoicing (*zog, vayb, held, veg* surface faithfully), we infer that some version of faithfulness for voicing (IDENT$_{LexCat}$(voi), IDENT(voi)) must outrank the ban on coda voicing (FINDEVOI). This is compatible with the ranking argued for in the previous section, of IDENT$_{LexCat}$(voi) ≫ FINDEVOI ≫ IDENT(voi). This ranking allows simple voiced codas to surface faithfully:

(9.14)   Simple voiced codas surface faithfully in Yiddish

/lib/		ID$_{LexCat}$(voi)	FINDEVOI	ID(voi)
☞ a.	[lib]		*	
b.	[lip]	*!		*

Turning next to forms with complex codas, we find that adding AGREE to this ranking produces an incorrect prediction for inputs like /lib-t/ 'love-3sg', since IDENT$_{\text{LexCat}}$(voi) eliminates the desired winner [lipt] (indicated by ☠), favoring instead the output [libd]:

(9.15) Ranking incorrectly predicts English-like assimilation for disagreeing complex clusters

/lib-t/			AGREE	ID$_{\text{LexCat}}$(voi)	FINDEVOI	ID(voi)
	a.	[libt]	*!		*	
☞	b.	[libd]			**	*
☠	c.	[lipt]		*!		*

Previous analyses of Yiddish (Lombardi 1999, 294; Baković 1999, 2) have sidestepped this problem because they did not differentiate faithfulness violations in roots vs. affixes. If only a single IDENT(voi) constraint is employed, then both [libd] and [lipt] incur a single faithfulness violation; the decision then falls to *VoiObst, which prefers the less marked output [lipt]. The data from the previous section show that this is too simplistic, however, and that IDENT(voi) must actually be ranked too low to eliminate (9.15b.) [libd], since voiced codas are, in fact, not allowed outside roots. This candidate can, however, be ruled out on general phonotactic grounds.[9] As both Lombardi and Baković correctly observe, Yiddish words never end in sequences of voiced obstruents, no matter whether they are monomorphemic or suffixed. Thus, I will assume that [libd] is eliminated by a high-ranking constraint banning word-final voiced obstruent clusters, which for expedience I will call *DD#. Adding this constraint allows the Yiddish pattern to be derived correctly, as shown in (9.16).

(9.16) Final voiced+voiced sequences are blocked:
a. In monomorphemic words

/tabd/		*DD#	AGREE	ID$_{\text{LexCat}}$(voi)	FINDEVOI	ID(voi)
	a. [tabt]		*!	*	*	*
	b. [tabd]	*!			**	
☞	c. [tapt]			**		**

---

[9] Borowsky (2000) suggests another possible motivation, that suffixes consisting of a single consonant demand greater faithfulness than those consisting of multiple suffixes. This idea has intuitive appeal but fails to distinguish Yiddish /-t/ from English /-d/.

b. Or derived by suffixation

/lib-t/		*DD#	AGREE	ID$_{LexCat}$(voi)	FINDEVOI	ID(voi)
a.	[libt]		*!		*	
b.	[libd]	*!			**	*
☞ c.	[lipt]			*		*

How did Yiddish end up with the ranking shown in (9.16)? In particular, why did a language with the German-like ranking *DD], FINDEVOI ≫ IDENT(voi) change to a language with the ranking *DD] ≫ IDENT(voi) ≫ FINDEVOI, rather than the English-like ranking IDENT(voi) ≫ *DD], FINDEVOI? There is nothing that specifically predicts one outcome or the other, under an account that relies on the spontaneous promotion of the relevant faithfulness constraint (=loss of the phonological process by purely phonological change). Under a leveling account, on the other hand, the reason is simple: there were noun stems that ended in single underlyingly voiced obstruents (*tak* ∼ *tage*), but no stems ending in sequences of voiced obstruents (hypothetical *takt* ∼ **tagde*). Thus, there was no paradigmatic pressure to produce final DD sequences, and the *DD] markedness constraint was free to remain highly ranked, under the general preference for markedness constraints to remain as high as possible (Tesar and Prince 2004; Hayes 2004).

To summarize sections 9.2.3–9.2.4, we see that the restoration of final voiced obstruents in Yiddish was quite restricted, namely, only a single root-final voiced obstruent is allowed. When seen from the point of view of constraint reranking, the end result appears to be complex rearrangement of contextual faithfulness and specific markedness constraints, none of which could have been uniquely predicted from the earlier stage in the language. When seen from the point of view of paradigm uniformity, on the other hand, the result is clear: the language changed in the minimum way necessary to allow paradigms with invariant voicing.

9.2.5 *Resistance to voicing in word-internal clusters*

Further evidence that voiced obstruents are not freely allowed in codas in NEY comes from the way that voicing disagreements are resolved in intervocalic clusters. According to the standard description, obstruent clusters are subject to regressive voicing assimilation, both within words and (to a lesser extent) across word boundaries (Katz 1987, 29–30; Lombardi 1999, 279; Baković 1999):

(9.17) Regressive devoicing:

a.	/vɔg + shɔl/	→ [vɔkshɔl]	'weight-scale'
b.	/briv + treger/	→ [briftregər]	'letter carrier'
c.	/ayz + kastən/	→ [ayskastən]	'ice box'

(9.18) Regressive voicing:

a.	/bak + beyn/	→ [bagbeyn]	'cheek-bone'
b.	/kɔp + veytik/	→ [kɔbveytik]	'head-ache'
c.	/zis + varg/	→ [zizvarg]	'sweet-ware' (candy)

Recent OT discussions of regressive voicing and devoicing in Yiddish (e.g., Lombardi 1999) have treated them as fully parallel, providing a unified analysis of both processes. In point of fact, regressive voicing is weaker and less frequent than regressive devoicing. Katz states: "voiced consonants *usually* undergo devoicing," but "voiceless consonants *may* undergo voicing" (emphasis mine). He elaborates further: "voicing assimilation [i.e., regressive voicing] is less consistent than devoicing assimilation, but it is frequently heard in natural speech."

The most direct test of this claimed asymmetry would be to measure the rate and phonetic degree of assimilatory voicing and devoicing across word boundaries under various syntactic conditions, using a corpus study of spoken Yiddish. Although the necessary corpus does not exist, Yiddish does provide another valuable source of information about the propensity to assimilate, in the form of large numbers of words from Hebrew that contain obstruent clusters with disagreeing voicing underlyingly. Thus, in order to get a quantitative estimate of the asymmetry between voicing and devoicing, we can look to Hebrew words in Yiddish.

Hebrew words are a good test case for the productivity of assimilation, since Hebrew permits a large assortment of disagreeing word-internal clusters. In fact, since clusters in Hebrew generally arise through templatic morphology–e.g., *kadosh* 'holy' ~ *mikdash* 'sanctuary'–voicing disagreements probably arise more often than they would in a non-templatic language that allows such clusters. Furthermore, Hebrew words in Yiddish are unusual among cases of adaptation, in that they have been borrowed heavily through texts rather than through contact with speakers of a different language, and are thus relatively free from effects of bilingualism or the influence of detailed knowledge of the phonology of the source language (Veynger 1913).[10] As a result, to the extent

---

[10] According to many scholars, the Hebrew/Aramaic component of Yiddish should be viewed not as a set of borrowings but rather as a substrate with a continuous spoken history (Weinreich 1973, §§99–112; Jacobs 2005, 41). The relation between the reconstructed history of German vs. Semitic-component elements in Yiddish is intricate (see Jacobs for a thorough overview). Certainly, many Hebrew words have been an integral part of Yiddish for centuries, including in the everyday speech

that such words undergo assimilation in Yiddish, we can be certain that this is a result of Yiddish phonology, and not, say, the way that Hebrew voiced stops are perceived by Yiddish listeners hearing speakers of a different language.

There is one other fact about Hebrew words in Yiddish which facilitates the study of assimilation, and that is the fact that the two languages differ in how they represent vowels: Yiddish uses separate letters, while Hebrew, for the most part, does not. Under current orthographic practice, Hebrew words in Yiddish are written faithfully to the Hebrew spelling (i.e., without separate letters for vowels), meaning that for unfamiliar words, Yiddish speakers may often be uncertain about the pronunciation (in particular, where the vowels go, and what they should be). Weinreich's (1968) dictionary solves this problem by including romanized transcriptions of Hebrew words, with the purpose of revealing the vowels, but with the side effect of also marking the assimilation pattern, at least as found in the educated speech of Weinreich and his editors/assistants. For example, a word written <BDKENEN> ('inspect slaughtered animals') in Hebrew letters is transcribed as [batkenen] (with assimilation), whereas the morphologically-related word <BDIKH> 'inspection of slaughtered animals' is transcribed as [bdike] (no context for assimilation).

I compiled a database of all Hebrew words in Weinreich (1990) containing disagreeing obstruent clusters, along with their transcriptions. In some cases, the root occurred in multiple words—e.g., S,G,L in *hisgales* 'revelation' and *nisgale* 'revealed', or SH,G,KH in *mazhgiekh* 'custodian' and *hazhgokhe* 'supervision'. In such cases, only one instance was counted to avoid the risk of inflated counts due to a lexicalized allomorph. In addition, clusters involving [x] were removed, since the standard romanization includes no symbol for [ɣ], leaving no way to indicate voicing in such cases.

---

of millions of illiterate speakers. At the same time, written Hebrew texts have served as a source of continual reborrowing or updating ("scooping anew from the open Hebrew well"; Weinreich 1973, vol. 2, p. 7). Knowledge of Hebrew orthography and reborrowing have been sufficient to eradicate virtually all traces of final devoicing, even among Hebrew words that must have been present since MHG times–and, by the same token, must provide a certain amount of evidence about the underlying voicing values of obstruents in clusters. The many layers of Hebrew loans also raises another issue which I am not able to address here, concerning the relative recency of different loans and how this might affect their degree of nativization. Differences between various portions of the lexicon have been a major focus of studies on loanwords (see, for example, Ito and Mester 2002), and it seems plausible that more recent (or, less frequent or familiar) loans would be relatively more protected from assimilation. This is an important question and it is difficult to give it the treatment it deserves without an etymological dictionary (including dates of attestation) and a frequency dictionary for the language. Fortunately, the question here is simply whether there is a difference between voiced+voiceless inputs and voiceless+voiced ones. It seems unlikely that words with certain types of clusters have entered Yiddish systematically earlier than others.

TABLE 9.1. Obstruent clusters with and without assimilation

C₁	C₂	Pattern	Example		
[+voi]	[−voi]	Assim.	/plugte/	[pluktə]	'dispute'
		No assim.	/kodshe/	[kodshə]	'Holy of'
[−voi]	[+voi]	Assim.	/hekdesh/	[hegdəsh]	'poorhouse'
		No assim.	/makdim/	[makdəm]	'ahead'

Among the remaining cases, we see in Table 9.1 that assimilation is not absolute in either voiceless+voiced or voiced+voiceless combinations. (That is, there are both assimilating and unassimilating examples of both types of input sequences.) However, as the graph in Figure 9.1 shows, devoicing (on the right) is far more common than voicing: 13/15 vs. 9/38 cases. Although the numbers are somewhat small and it is not a categorical effect, we see that even in Modern NEY, voiced obstruents are dispreferred in coda (really, not pre-sonorant) position.

This effect can be seen even more strongly in onset clusters, where voiced+voiceless sequences generally assimilate in Weinreich's transcriptions, but voiceless+voiced clusters never do ((9.19)):

(9.19) Assimilation in word-initial obstruent clusters:
   a. Voiced+voiceless sequences generally assimilate
        a. /bsule/   [psulə]   'maiden'
        b. /bkhor/   [pkhor]   'first-born son'
        c. /dkhak/   [tkhak]   'dire need'
        d. /zkeynim/ [skeynəm] 'old men'
      though non-assimilating examples also occur:
        e. /bshas/   [b(ə)shas] 'during'

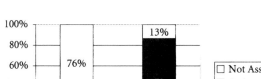

FIGURE 9.1. Relative occurrence of regressive voicing and devoicing

b. Voiceless+voiced sequences do not assimilate
   a. /kdushe/   [k(ə)dushə]   'sanctity'
   b. /pgam/   [p(ə)gam]   'dent, blemish'
   c. /shvue/   [sh(ə)vuə]   'oath'

It should be reiterated that when obstruent clusters agree in the input, they are always pronounced with faithful voicing values (/hagbe/ → [hagbe], /bdike/ → [bdike] 'ritual inspection'). That is, there is no general process eliminating voiced+voiced sequences intervocalically–there is merely a reluctance to create them through voicing assimilation.

Several approaches to such "grandfathering" effects have been proposed in the literature (Baković 1999; Łubowicz 2002; Ito and Mester 2003; McCarthy 2003). What they all have in common is that they differentiate between markedness violations that are present underlyingly, as opposed to those that are created by changing an underlying value. Following McCarthy (2003), I will state this distinction by splitting FinDevoi into a comparative constraint $_N$FinDevoi, which penalizes new instances of voiced codas (not voiced underlyingly), and $_O$FinDevoi, which penalizes coda obstruents that were voiced underlyingly and remain voiced on the surface.[11] In an idealized version of Yiddish in which the asymmetry between [+voi][−voi] and [−voi][+voi] clusters is absolute and categorical, the effect could be captured by placing $_N$FinDevoi above Agree, blocking voicing assimilation specifically in case it involves voicing an underlyingly voiced obstruent. (This is also the pattern found in Mekkan Arabic, as discussed by McCarthy, and by Kenstowicz, Abu-Mansour, and Törkenczy 2003.) Note that we also need a positional faithfulness constraint preserving voicing in onsets (Ident$_{Onset}$(voi)) in order to assure that assimilation is exclusively regressive.

(9.20)   a.   Regressive devoicing in /abta/

/abta/		Id$_{Ons}$(voi)	$_N$FinDevoi	Agree	Id$_{LexCat}$(voi)	$_O$FinDevoi	Id(voi)
a.	[abta]			*!		*	
b.	[abda]	*!			*	*	*
☞ c.	[apta]				*		*

---

[11] The Yiddish facts could just as well be handled by a conjoined markedness and faithfulness constraint, following Łubowicz (2002): FinDevoi & Ident(voi) (will not be both a voiced coda obstruent and an Ident violation). See McCarthy (2003) for discussion of some issues surrounding this use of constraint conjunction. Yet another option that would work for these data is to split FinDevoi to distinguish between voicing contrasts before voiced vs. voiceless obstruents, as proposed by Kenstowicz, Abu-Mansour, and Törkenczy (2003).

b. No regressive voicing in /apda/

/apda/	ID_{Ons}(voi)	_NFINDEVOI	AGREE	ID_{LexCat} (voi)	_OFINDEVOI	ID(voi)
☞ a. [apda]			*			
b. [abda]		*!		*		*
c. [apta]	*!			*!		*

In actuality, the effect is not all-or-nothing but is rather a statistical tendency
(devoice 87% of the time, voice 24%). The probabilistic nature of the pattern
can be captured using stochastic constraint ranking procedure, such as the
Gradual Learning Algorithm (GLA: Boersma 1997; Boersma and Hayes 2001).
In a stochastic version of OT, constraints do not receive absolute rankings
but rather ranges of possible ranking values. When the grammar is invoked
to derive an output, each constraint is probabilistically assigned a specific
ranking value. This means that if two constraints (C1, C2) have overlap-
ping ranges, their relative ranking may differ from utterance to utterance,
with the probability that C1 ≫ C2 depending on the degree of overlap. (See
Boersma 1997 for further details.) In the case of Yiddish, what is required is for
AGREE to be ranked in such a way that it usually (but not always) dominates
IDENT_{LexCat}(voi), producing regressive devoicing most of the time. At the same
time, the comparative constraint _NFINDEVOI must usually outrank AGREE,
blocking regressive voicing on a majority of occasions. A ranking that achieves
these relative proportions is shown in Figure 9.2.

When applied to input forms with disagreeing sequences, the constraint
ranking in Figure 9.2 will produce assimilation at the rates shown in Figure 9.1.
A fact that this cannot account for, however, is the stability of individual lexical
items amid global gradience. Although many of the words listed in Weinreich
(1990) show variation (occurring both with and without assimilation), some
tend to occur more often in their assimilated form, while others rarely or never

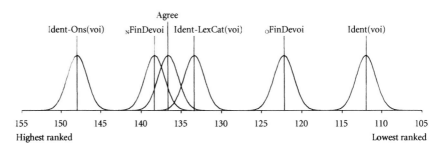

FIGURE 9.2. Stochastic constraint ranking for regressive voicing assimilation

do. A full analysis of the pattern would therefore require two components: a constraint ranking that produces assimilation at the expected rates, and knowledge about the behavior of individual lexical items. For a proposal regarding how learners acquire both types of knowledge simultaneously and deploy them in a grammar of stochastically ranked constraints, see Zuraw (2000). For present purposes, it is enough to observe that constraints eliminating voiced codas play an active role in driving the gradient pattern of voicing assimilation that is observed in intervocalic obstruent clusters.

There is one final observation that is relevant to the analysis of assimilation in Yiddish. King (1980, 387), in his discussion of final devoicing, notes that regressive voicing assimilation across word boundaries may not be fully neutralizing: "My own impression is that a sound like the *t* in *halt zi* [dz] is not identical with the [d] in *vald* 'forest'; rather, it is a semivoiced (or even voiceless) lenis." Similar effects have been observed in other languages, such as Taiwanese (Hsu 1997) and Dutch (Ernestus 2000; Jansen 2004), and have been taken as evidence that assimilation involves deleting the voicing specification rather than copying the neighboring specification: /[−voice][+voice]/ → [Ø voice][+voice]. Under such an analysis, the first consonant loses contrastive voicing, but may still receive coarticulatory/passive voicing from the preceding vowel. This would be fully in line with King's observation of partial voicing. A prediction of this underspecification account, however, is that neutralized segments should receive passive voicing from the preceding vowel regardless of the voicing of the following consonant—and indeed, this is what Jansen (2004) observes for Dutch. Impressionistically, what one finds in Yiddish, however, is that C_1 has intermediate voicing only in underlying voiceless+voiced sequences; in voiced+voiceless sequences, it is fully devoiced. Interestingly, this is also what Kenstowicz, Abu-Mansour, and Törkenczy (2003) report for Mekkan Arabic. Clearly, careful phonetic studies are needed to determine whether assimilation across word boundaries in Yiddish is amenable to an underspecification analysis. An additional complication is that, unlike in Arabic, assimilation within words in Yiddish appears to yield fully voiced or voiceless outcomes (though this too requires investigation). Further data may change the precise formulation of the analysis, but what is important here is that the rate (and possibly degree) of assimilation differs depending on whether one must voice or devoice to satisfy AGREE.

In sum, this section presents yet another suspicious restriction. If the loss of final devoicing was accomplished by demoting the ban on voiced codas, why is there a reluctance to create voiced codas root-internally through regressive assimilation?

9.2.6 *Capturing this distribution with gradient constraint ranking*

The previous sections have shown that although Modern NEY lacks final devoicing, voiced obstruents do not occur freely in codas; rather, they are avoided in affixes, in final clusters, and, to a certain extent, in medial and initial clusters as well. In this section, I sketch an analysis of these facts using the Gradual Learning Algorithm (GLA; Boersma 1997; Boersma and Hayes 2001) to capture the gradient nature of assimilation observed above.

As seen in the previous sections, the analysis of Modern NEY requires a variety of contextual constraints to capture the distribution of voiced obstruents. These reflect the fact that voicing contrasts are maintained more consistently before sonorants and within lexical roots than before obstruents and outside of roots. In addition, the assimilation pattern requires a constraint that bans the voicing of underlyingly voiceless codas, such as $_N$IDENT(voi). The full set of constraints employed thus far are summarized in (9.21):

(9.21)   Constraints needed for the analysis of Modern NEY:

    a.   Faithfulness constraints

IDENT(voi)	Preserve underlying voicing value
IDENT$_{Onset}$(voi)	Preserve voicing in onset (really, pre-sonorant) position
IDENT$_{LexCat}$(voi)	Preserve voicing within roots of lexical categories

    b.   Markedness constraints

$_O$FINDEVOI	No faithfully voiced obstruents in coda position
$_N$FINDEVOI	No derived (new) voiced obstruents in coda position
*DD#	No word-final sequences of voiced obstruents
AGREE	Consecutive obstruents may not have conflicting [voice] specifications

By combining the rankings given in (9.10), (9.16), and Figure 9.2, it appears that it would be possible to yield a single ranking which yields all of the Yiddish data. A small complication arises, however, from the fact that regressive devoicing is not absolute word-internally (87%), while it does occur consistently at the ends of words (/lib-t/ → [lipt]). The stochastic ranking in Figure 9.2 predicts that AGREE may be violated a certain proportion of the time, favoring outcomes that are more faithful to the underlying voicing of the root. Thus, a ranking that yields word-internal variation also predicts a small but unacceptable amount of variation word-finally ([libt]). There is no ranking of the given constraints which can produce [abta] 13% of the time,

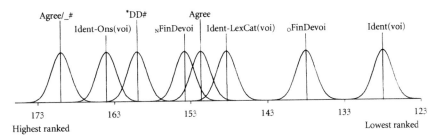

FIGURE 9.3. Overall ranking of constraints

while never producing * [libt]. In order to solve this problem, I added one more constraint, designed to enforce voicing agreement specifically at the ends of words: AGREE/___ #. This context-specific AGREE constraint is never violated in Yiddish and can thus be ranked on top, stamping out any [libt]-type errors that would otherwise be produced by the gradient ranking of regular AGREE.

I submitted these constraints to the GLA using the OTSoft software package (Hayes, Tesar, and Zuraw 2003). The input forms included: (1) monomorphemic pseudowords ending in voiced and voiceless obstruents, which always surface faithfully ([tak], [tag], [dak], [dag]), (2) suffixed pseudowords showing absolute regressive assimilation (/zok-t/, /zog-t/ → [zokt]), and (3) monomorphemic pseudowords with disagreeing obstruent clusters, showing assimilation in the observed ratios (/abta/ → [apta] or [abta], /apda/ → [apda] or [abda]). Since the main goal of the simulation was simply to show that all of the data could be captured by a single consistent constraint ranking, the model was provided with the clear, categorical rankings ahead of time; its task was to discover the correct stochastic ranking of AGREE relative to ${}_N$Fin Devoi and IDENT$_{LexCat}$(voi). Training was run for 10,000,000 trials, using an initial plasticity of 2 and a final plasticity of .002. The resulting grammar was then tested on all of the input forms, along with hypothetical monomorphemic inputs like /tagd/ and /tagt/ (which never occur in the training data but should nonetheless be repaired by the grammar).

A ranking that can produce all of the Yiddish forms in the correct proportion is shown in Figure 9.3. The difference in absolute values between Figures 9.2 and 9.3 are meaningless; it is only the degree of overlap between the constraints that matters. This ranking not only produces assimilation to the same degree that it is observed in the lexicon (variably word-internally, invariably word-finally), but it also generalizes correctly to hypothetical inputs with final /DD/ or /DT/ sequences (fixing them by devoicing).

There are two things to observe here. The first is that the distribution of voicing in Modern NEY is considerably more complex than either simple devoicing or simple lack of devoicing—a point also made by Sadock (1973, 793). Although it is true that Yiddish differs from German in allowing voiced obstruents in coda position, the "loss of final devoicing" did *not* yield a language that freely allows them in all positions. In fact, even in the modern language, there are only two places where voiced obstruents freely occur: (1) before sonorants, where they have always been possible, and (2) in root-final position, where there were paradigmatic alternations (and even then not in clusters with other obstruents). The ranking in Figure 9.3 is hardly a phonological simplification; the only thing that got simpler about Yiddish is that paradigms lack alternations, with modern forms preserving the voicing values previously seen only in affixed forms.

9.2.7 *The fate of* -nd *and* -ld *clusters*

One additional complication that does not seem to play a role in the synchronic grammar of NEY, but does provide further support for the paradigmatic account, concerns the fate of MHG stems ending in *nd* or *ld*. In many such cases, [d] was restored as expected, as seen in (9.22):

(9.22)   Restoration of [d] in /nd/, /ld/ clusters

	MHG sg, pl	Yiddish sg	Yiddish pl
'picture'	bilt, bilder	bild	bilder
'land'	lant, lender	land	lender
'ribbon'	band, bender	band	bender
'cattle'	rint, rinder	rind	rinder
'child'	kint, kinder	kind[12]	kinder
'forest'	walt, welde/welder	vald	velder
'field'	vëlt, vëlde(r?)	felt/feld	felder
'blind' (adj.)	blint, blinde	blind	blinde
'wild' (adj.)	wilt, wilde	vild	vilde

In some words, however, the voiceless [t] was generalized completely. In many cases, the change from /d/ to /t/ was probably already under way in MHG, for example, NEY *gelt* 'money' derives from MHG *gelt* ~ *geldes* ~ *geltes*.[13]

---

[12] Interestingly, some NEY dialects retain the singular form [kint] with plural [kindər], continuing to obey final devoicing; see Herzog (1965, 222) for the geographical distribution.

[13] This may have been part of a more general [t]/[d] confusion (cf. MHG *tâht* 'wick' ⇒ NHG *Docht*, MHG *dûsent* 'thousand' ⇒ NHG *tausend*, and so on), but the effect was especially strong for [nd] and [ld]. See Paul, Wiehl, and Grosse (1989, §104) for discussion.

In other cases, such as NEY *hunt* 'dog', MHG always shows a [d] in suffixed forms.

(9.23)   Generalization of [t] from MHG [t] ~ [d]

	MHG unsuff., suff.	Yiddish sg	Yiddish pl	Compare
'money'	gelt, geldes/geltes	gelt	geltər/ geltən (??)	
'attire'	gewant, gewandes (/gewantes)	gevant	gevantən	
'healthy'	gesunt, gesuntes/gesundes	gezunt	gezuntə	
'dog'	hunt, hunde	hunt	hint	hintəl 'doggie'
'hand'	hant, hende	hant	hent	hantik 'handy'
'wall'	want, wende	vant	vent	ventəl (dimin.)
'region'	gegent, gegende	gegnt	gegntən	gegntik 'regional'
'screw thread'	(NHG Gewinde)	gevint		

In a few words, devoicing is optional or variable within the inflectional paradigm, with traces of voicing sometimes remaining outside the paradigm:

(9.24)   Variability in [t] ~ [d]

	MHG sg, pl	Yiddish sg	Yiddish pl	Compare
'base'	grunt, gründe	grunt/grund[14]	grundən (/gruntən?)	
'friend'	vriunt, vriunt/ vriunde	fraynd/fraynt[15]	fraynd/ fraynt	
'force'	gewalt, gewelde/ gewelte	gvalt/gvald	—	gvaldik 'forceful'

[14] These may be variant pronunciations of the same word, though King (1980) and Weinreich list *grunt* and *grund* as separate words, the first meaning 'soil, ground, foundation, basis' and the second meaning 'ground, reason, basis'. If it is true that the meaning 'soil, ground (as in the earth)' can appear only with [t] (*grunt*), this is unsurprising, since this meaning would for all practical purposes lack a plural form to restore voicing.

[15] YIVO orthography prescribes *fraynd* for this word, and King (1980, 384) lists it as an unproblematic [d] word. It is my impression that there is considerable variation in the pronunciation of this word, however, and Sapir (1915, 259) lists it as a problematic [t] word. The same holds for *faynt* 'enemy' and *gevalt* 'force', both written consistently with <d> but often pronounced [t].

At one time, all of these words had [t] in the singular, and [d] in the plural and related forms–so why are there different outcomes in Modern NEY? Two facts seem to be relevant here. The first, noted by King (1980, 409), is that [d] tended to be preserved in nouns when the plural ending was [-ər], but [t] was generalized when the plural was [-ə] or null. The devoicing among [-ə] plurals is suggestive, since [-ə] subsequently underwent apocope (*hendə > hend*), putting the *d* in final position. This alone could not explain the difference, however, since apocopated words did not usually get devoiced (cf. *ta:gə > tɔg*); in fact, apocope is generally thought to be the source of final voiced obstruents that led to the loss of final devoicing. Therefore, some additional factor must be contributing to devoicing in these cases.

The second relevant fact is that during the same period, late MHG/early NHG was gradually eliminating nasal+voiced stop sequences. For *mb*, this was solved by deletion: earlier *lember* > modern *Lä*[m]*er* 'lambs'. For *nd*, however, the solution was often, for some reason, devoicing: *hinder* > *hinter* 'behind', *munder* > *munter* 'lively'. This process was not exceptionless, however, (*ander* remains *ander* 'other'), and, most relevant to the current discussion, it never affected plurals in *-er*: (*lender* > *Länder, kinder* > *Kinder*, etc. (See also Sadock 1973 on devoicing of *-nd*.)

Putting these two facts together, we arrive at the following scenario: at around the same time as apocope, expected [-ə] plurals like *hend* and *vind* often devoiced to *hent, vint*, due not to final devoicing but rather to a special **nd* ban (Hyman 2001).[16] (Since devoicing of [nd] > [nt] occurred both intervocalically and word-finally, the exact timing relative to apocope is not crucial.) Owing to the sporadic nature of [nd] > [nt], some exceptions remained, at least optionally (*grund, fraynd*). Because plurals in *-er* were never affected by [nd] > [nt], they consistently maintained [nd]. Modern Yiddish retains whatever form of the noun was found in the plural (usually [nt] in the former case, always [nd] in the latter). It is beyond the scope of this chapter to provide a full formal account of the word-by-word and context-by-context differences seen here; it is sufficient to observe that the outcome of /nd/ in Yiddish is related to the context that the /nd/ occurs in in the plural. If it is word-final it is often devoiced, whereas if it is intervocalic, devoicing also occurs but in a more sporadic and context-dependent fashion.

---

[16] I leave open the proper formulation of this constraint. Hyman (2001) simply states it as **ND*, though Zsiga, Gouskova, and Tlale (2006) argue that such a constraint is not only theoretically unappealing but also fails to capture the facts of at least one relevant language (Setswana). Without knowing more about the phonetics of earlier stages of Yiddish, it is difficult to resolve this issue.

9.2.8 *Further evidence for leveling from the plural in nouns*

There is one last source of evidence that the restoration of voicing was due to paradigmatic pressure from the plural, and not merely a blanket markedness demotion: in addition to final voicing, vowel length was also imported from plural to singular.

In late MHG, a sound change lengthened vowels in open syllables, creating paradigmatic alternations (Paul, Wiehl, and Grosse 1989, §45; Russ 1982, 139–40, and refs. therein):[17]

(9.25) MHG lengthening

a. "Classical" MHG

	Sg	Pl
Nom	tak	tagə
Acc	tak	tagə
Gen	tagəs	tagə
Dat	tagə	tagən

b. Late MHG:

	Sg	Pl
Nom	tak	taːgə
Acc	tak	taːgə
Gen	taːgəs	taːgə
Dat	taːgə	taːgən

In the development from MHG to NEY, short [a] remained [a] (seen in *makhən* 'make', *haltən* 'hold', *vartən* 'wait'), while long [aː] became [ɔ] (*fɔrən* 'travel', *tsɔlən* 'count', *shlɔgən* 'strike', all corresponding to [aː] in NHG). If MHG [tak] had survived into NEY with only the voicing restored, we would expect [tag]; in fact, the NEY form is [tɔg], with the reflex of a long [aː]. Similar facts can also be seen for words with original short [o], which lengthened and diphthongized to [ɔɪ]: MHG *lop* ~ *loːbə* 'praise-Sg/Pl' > *lop* ~ *loyb(ə)* ⇒ *loyb* ~ *loyb*. As Sapir (1915, 238) points out, the most plausible source for length in such words is by leveling from the plural, either before or after diphthongization.[18]

---

[17] This is not the only possible formulation of length alternations in MHG; see Reis (1974) for an overview and critique of Paul's original analysis.

[18] Jacobs (1990; 2005) has argued extensively that leveling of length must have occurred prior to the earliest stages of Yiddish, primarily for the reason that Hebrew component words retain length alternations: *sod* ~ *soydes* 'mystery' with [o] ~ [ɔɪ] in closed vs. open syllables. It is also possible, however, that the lack of leveling in Hebrew words could be due to Hebrew singular and plural forms not acting as a paradigm in the same sense that German component nouns do–an idea already

Thus, we see that final obstruent voicing was not the only feature to be imported from the plural to the singular. If we attribute the loss of final devoicing to a voicing-specific markedness demotion, we have no account for the leveling of vowel length.

9.2.9 *Summary of loss of final devoicing*

We have seen so far that the shape of nouns and adjectives in Modern NEY depends on the properties of their historical plural form. When there was a plural with a root-final voiced obstruent, this was "restored" to the singular (final devoicing *underapplied*), e.g., *veg* 'way' instead of expected *vek*. In the relatively rare event that the plural devoiced, either because of a Ø suffix or the tendency to devoice [nd] > [nt], then voicing was eliminated throughout the paradigm (final devoicing *overapplied*). When the plural had a long vowel, that too was imported to the singular. When there was no paradigmatic pressure, the normal effects of obstruent devoicing can still be seen in various ways, including through the ban on voiced codas obstruents outside roots and the reluctance to create voiceless codas within roots.

This provides strong support for the traditional view that the Yiddish change was, at its core, motivated by paradigm leveling. The result, however, was overall more marked paradigms, precisely of the type that OP predicts should never be favored:[19]

(9.26)   Leveling to a more marked paradigm:

/bund/, /bund-ə/	OP-Ident(voi)	FinDevoi	IO-Ident(voi)
a. [bunt], [bundə]	* (t~d)		*
☠ b. [bund], [bundə]		*	
☞ c. [bunt], [buntə]			**

This is certainly not the only example in the literature in which paradigms have apparently leveled to a particular slot in the paradigm, regardless of markedness; see, for example, Kraska-Szlenk (1995) on over- and underapplication of *jer* deletion in Polish diminutives, Sturgeon (2003) on over- and underapplication of depalatalization in Czech nouns, and Albright (2002b)

proposed for different reasons by Perlmutter (1988) and Lowenstamm (2005). Furthermore, even among Hebrew words, length alternations between [a] and [ɔ] are not observed: *tag* ~ *tagən* 'serif', *tɔgən*; orthography may play an additional role in suppressing or allowing alternations in Hebrew words.

[19] It is worth noting that the word *bund* itself does exist in Yiddish, and is one of the "variable outcome" *-nd* nouns discussed in section 9.2.7; Weinreich glosses *bund* as 'tie, bond, alliance, league', and *bunt* as both 'rebellion' and 'bundle'.

on leveling of vowel alternations in Yiddish verb paradigms. These cases pose a challenge to the idea that leveling is driven by the effects of markedness and majority rules, and argue in favor of privileged bases within inflectional paradigms.

9.3 Analysis of the change using inflectional bases

The reason why the OP approach has difficulty capturing the change in Yiddish nouns is that the singular and plural get equal say in determining the outcome of the paradigm. This would be easily solved if, instead of an OP constraint, we used faithfulness to a pre-selected plural base form (either by transderivational correspondence (Benua 1997) or Base Identity (Kenstowicz 1996)), or a more direct form-to-form mapping as proposed by Bochner (1993), Barr (1994), Albright (2002b), and many others. For concreteness, an analysis using Base Identity to the plural is shown in (9.27).

(9.27)   Plural form has no devoicing:

/bund-ə/ (pl)		Base ID$_{pl}$	FinDevoi	IO-ID(voi)
☞ a.	[bundə]			
b.	[bunte]			*!

Singular form constrained to match plural:

/bund/ (sg)		Base ID$_{pl}$	FinDevoi	IO-ID(voi)
☞ a.	[bund]		*	
b.	[bunt]	*!		*

In actuality, the change was somewhat more complex than this because of the opaque interaction of final devoicing and apocope. I have argued elsewhere that such levelings are not necessarily the result of OO constraints at all, but rather the result of how learners learn to project alternations and how they assess the productivity of alternating and non-alternating patterns (Albright 2005). For present purposes, the exact mechanism of leveling is not critical; all that matters is that it must refer to the plural as a privileged base form.

The analysis for nouns rests, then, on the assumption that the plural may serve as the base of the paradigm. Such an assumption seems unappealing, since in this case the plural is suffixed and can in no way be seen as the "base of affixation" for the singular. This raises numerous questions: can any form in the paradigm be designated as the base? If so, is there any rhyme or reason to which form serves as the base? In this section, I show briefly how the use of the plural as a base form in Yiddish represents a principled choice and is correctly predicted by the base selection algorithm proposed in Albright (2002b).

9.3.1 *Selecting the plural as a base form in Yiddish noun paradigms*

The use of the plural as a base form in Yiddish may be unusual but it does not seem arbitrary. As Vennemann (1972, 189) notes: "... no contrasts are lost in the process ...: *k/k* : *g/g* is a better resolution of *k/k* : *k/g* than *k/k* : *k/k* would have been. This seems to be true in general: sound change neutralizes contrasts, analogy emphasizes contrasts by generalizing them." Vennemann refers to this as the "predictability principle". The intuition is that in this case, the plural is the form that most clearly exhibits lexical contrasts and extending the plural variant does the least violence to recoverability. This idea is formalized and developed in detail in Albright (2002b), in which it is proposed that bases are selected by language learners as part of a strategy that enables them to learn paradigms on the basis of incomplete information. The premise of this proposal is that learners must ideally be able to understand and produce whole paradigms of inflected forms and, in order to do this, they need to learn the morphological and phonological properties of each word. Not every part of the paradigm is equally informative, however, and learners do not have complete paradigms available to them. The hypothesis, then, is that learners identify the part of the paradigm with the most information and focus on that form to learn the properties of words.[20] (See Albright 2002b for details and algorithmic implementation.)

As applied to a stage of Yiddish prior to leveling, we can see that the plural most clearly displayed lexical contrasts. Consider the task of a language learner, faced with paradigms like those found in MHG:

(9.28)   A few of the many types of MHG noun paradigms

	Singular				Plural			
	Nom	Gen	Dat	Acc	Nom	Gen	Dat	Acc
'day'	tac	tages	tage	tac	tage	tage	tagen	tage
'sack'	sac	sackes	sacke	sac	secke	secke	secken	secke
'gift'	gëbe	gëbe	gëbe	gëbe	gëbe	gëben	gëben	gëbe
'word'	wort	wortes	worte	wort	wort	worte	worten	wort
'land'	lant	landes	lande	lant	lender	lender	lendern	lender
'guest'	gast	gastes	gaste	gast	geste	geste	gesten	geste
'tongue'	zunge	zungen	zungen	zungen	zungen	zungen	zungen	zungen

[20] This idea bears a relation to recent work on paradigmatic contrast (Kenstowicz 2005) and predictiveness (Blevins 2004; Ackerman and Blevins 2006), as well as to the "No Blur Principle" (Carstairs-McCarthy 1994), in which the information content of a cell in the paradigm is conceived of as the ability to uniquely recover the remaining suffixes of the paradigm. The main differences of the current approach are that not only affixal but also stem neutralizations are considered (both phonological and morphophonological). In addition, no absolute requirement is imposed on the degree of neutralization that may occur in any particular part of the paradigm. The focus here is not so much to make typological predictions as to understand how learners respond to cases in which there is at least some ambiguity or neutralization.

The learner must learn phonological properties of words, such as the underlying voicing value of stem-final consonants (obscured in the nominative/
accusative singular by final devoicing), as well as the identity of the root vowel
(which is sometimes altered in the plural). In addition, there are unpredictable
morphological properties to contend with, such as how the noun pluralizes
(*-e, -en, -er,* Ø; with or without umlaut) and other subtleties of morphological
class. Even without going into all the details of MHG noun classes, it is
clear that some forms would be better than others for purposes of inferring
these properties. The nominative/accusative singular neutralize most morphological classes (Ø suffix), and also undergo final devoicing (thereby losing
contrastive voicing information).[21] The genitive singular and dative plural
reveal stem-final voicing but also neutralize most morphological classes. The
nominative plural neutralizes some morphological classes but reveals more
distinctions than any other part of the paradigm; in addition, it has the virtue
of preserving stem-final voicing. Thus, the nominative plural is the maximally
informative part of the noun paradigm.

Early Yiddish had a smaller range of possible paradigm members to choose
from: essentially just the nominative and possessive, in the singular and plural.
Among these, the singular forms would have suffered from devoicing of the
stem-final consonant, and would also have been uninformative regarding the
plural suffix that the noun should take. The nominative plural, on the other
hand, would have continued to reveal both stem-final voicing and morphological class. Hence, the nominative plural was maximally informative: even
if it did not unambiguously reveal every property of every word, it would
have done better than any other form in the paradigm. Although a complete
computational simulation confirming this result is beyond the scope of this
chapter, it is clear that the principles laid out in Albright (2002b) would favor
the plural as the base form in early Yiddish. Furthermore, once this form is
selected as the base form, paradigm leveling is predicted to extend whatever
properties are found there, regardless of their markedness. This correctly predicts not only the loss of final devoicing by extending the voiced value found
in the plural but also the leveling of vowel length described in section 9.2.8.

It is important to keep in mind that nouns were not the only part of speech
affected by the loss of final devoicing in Yiddish. If the current theory of

---

[21] We will never know whether final devoicing in early Yiddish was completely neutralizing, or
whether the contrast was partly preserved through secondary cues, as has been argued for languages
like Modern German (Fourakis 1984; Port and O'Dell 1986) or Catalan (Dinnsen and Charles-Luce
1984)). In MHG and early Yiddish, devoicing was represented orthographically, raising the possibility
that these languages were more like Modern Turkish, in which the neutralization is argued to be
complete (Kopkalli 1993). No matter whether the neutralization was complete or partial, however, it is
undeniable that the singular afforded less evidence about stem final voicing than the plural did.

inflectional bases is correct, then it should be possible to identify inflectional bases that preserved voicing for all other affected parts of speech, as well. In the next few sections, I turn briefly to other parts of speech that showed "loss of devoicing" in Yiddish.

9.3.2 *Loss of devoicing in verb paradigms*

In verbs, final devoicing applied in MHG in the imperative of strong verbs, which lacked an overt suffix in MHG: *gip* 'give-2sg.IMP'. I have argued elsewhere (Albright 2002a) that the base of Yiddish verb paradigms is the 1sg present, and that historically a number of other properties have been extended from the 1sg to the rest of the present paradigm. The question, then, is whether the 1sg maintained stem-final voicing, so that it could have served as a source of final voicing in the imperative.

As it turns out, this is not a trivial question. In MHG, the 1sg had a vocalic suffix and maintained stem-final voicing (*gibə* 'give-1sg'). In late MHG or early Yiddish, however, the suffix was lost through a process of apocope, putting the stem-final stop in a potentially devoicing context: did apocope of *gibə* yield *gib* or *gip*? The available evidence suggests that, as with the noun paradigms discussed in (9.6)–(9.7), verb-final obstruents remained voiced after apocope, that is, apocope applied opaquely, counterfeeding final devoicing (for textual examples, see King 1980, 401).

One possible account of this effect is that schwa-ful (non-apocopated) forms persisted for some time as careful-speech variants and that the casual apocopated forms remained faithful to the voicing of these careful variants (Kawahara 2002). As we will see below, this idea appears to be useful not just for verbs but for other parts of speech as well. But regardless of the mechanism, the 1sg did indeed appear to maintain voicing opaquely even after apocope, and thus could have served as the basis of restoration of voicing in the singular imperatives of verbs. In other words, the analysis of restoration of voicing in the singular imperatives of strong verbs is fully parallel to the analysis of nouns: it involves extending a property found in the base form of the paradigm, which in the case of verbs is the 1sg.

9.3.3 *Loss of devoicing in adjective paradigms*

Adjectives also underwent final devoicing in MHG but here, too, voiced obstruents are allowed in Yiddish: MHG *blint* ∼ *blindes* ⇒ NEY *blind*. One might expect, given the leveling from plural to singular in noun paradigms, that a similar plural → singular explanation might hold for adjectives. There are reasons to think that the plural was not the source of voicing in adjectives, however. First, if the plural had been the base in adjectival paradigms, we would expect voicing to be restored in the adjectival suffix *-ik* (sg) ~ *-ige* (pl) ⇒ *-ig*; but, as we saw in section 9.2.3 above, this is incorrect, and the suffix remained voiceless (*-ik*). Furthermore, other segmental alternations also show leveling from the singular to the plural: [x] ~ [h] alternations seen, for example, in MHG *hôch* [hoːx] ~ *hôhe* [hoːhə] 'high-sg/pl' (Paul, Wiehl, and Grosse 1989, §140) have uniform [x] in Yiddish: *hoykh* ~ *hoykhə*. Similarly, the Ø ~ [w] alternation seen in MHG *gël* ~ *gëlwe* 'yellow-sg/pl' is uniform Ø in Yiddish: *gel* ~ *gelə*. These changes all diagnose a paradigm structure for adjectives in which the singular, not the plural, served as a base form.

There is also theoretical reason to believe that the singular should have acted as the base of adjective paradigms. Unlike nouns, MHG adjectives belonged to just a small number of inflectional classes, distinguished primarily by whether or not they possess a terminal schwa when no further ending follows: MHG *blint* ~ *blinde* 'blind-masc/fem sg' vs. *linde* ~ *linde* 'gentle-masc/fem sg' (Paul, Wiehl, and Grosse 1989, §§196–9). thus, unsuffixed and suffixed forms had different virtues in maintaining contrasts: the unsuffixed form revealed whether or not the adjective ended in a terminal schwa, while for adjectives that did not end in schwa, only the suffixed forms revealed the voicing of final obstruents. The neutralization of consonant- vs. schwa-final adjectives in suffixed forms would have been by far the more serious neutralization, since it affected all adjectives (as opposed to just obstruent-final adjectives like *blint*). The changes described in the preceding paragraph are exactly what we would expect, given the advantage in predictiveness of the unsuffixed form of adjectives.

This leaves us with a paradox with respect to voicing, however: how could Yiddish adjectives have had their final voiced obstruents restored, if the base form of adjective paradigms was the unsuffixed singular form? We should note first that many final voiced obstruents in Yiddish adjectives are the result of apocope of final schwas, just as in noun plurals and 1sg verb forms: MHG *müede*, *bœse* > NEY *mid*, *beyz*.[22] As with nouns and verbs, voicing may at first have been maintained through faithfulness to the more careful variants *midə*, *beyzə*. For other adjectives, MHG had variable terminal schwa: 'wild' is attested as both *wilde* and *wilt*, 'half' as *halbe* and *halp*, and so on. These lost the final schwa in both Yiddish and Modern German but preserved voicing in Yiddish: *vild*, *halb*. Voicing in these adjectives can easily be explained as restoration from the careful schwa-ful variant—or even from the apocopated

---

[22] Likewise MHG *gerade* 'even', *taube* 'deaf', *linde* 'gentle', *vremede* 'foreign' > Yiddish *grɔd*, *toyb*, *lind*, *fremd*.

variant, if it, too, was pronounced with a final voiced obstruent. As it turns out, all but a small number of NEY adjectives ending in voiced obstruents can be accounted for in this way.

There do remain, however, a few adjectives that seem not to have had attested variants with schwa, yet nonetheless had final voicing restored: *blind* 'blind' (MHG *blint*), *blond* 'light-haired' (MHG *blunt*), *grob* 'coarse' (MHG *grop*). For these, I can offer no more than a conjecture: at any early stage of Yiddish, as apocope became more and more frequent, it would have been quite difficult to know which adjectives actually had careful speech -ǝ variants (*lint* ∼ *linde*) and which did not (*blint*, but no **blinde*). It seems reasonable to suppose that at some point speakers could no longer distinguish these classes, and simply felt that all monosyllabic adjectives could have stem-final -ǝ in very careful speech (*blindǝ, grɔbǝ*), providing a basis for restoring final voicing from the unsuffixed form. (A similar phenomenon has occurred in NHG, in which the rarely pronounced imperative suffix -ǝ, originally reserved just for weak verbs, has been extended as a literary pronunciation also to most strong verbs.) Although such a stage is purely hypothetical, it has the potential to explain why voicing was restored in most monosyllabic stems, while polysyllabic stems, which as a class tended not to take final schwa etymologically, generally lost voicing in Yiddish: MHG *ellent* ∼ *ellende/ellente* ⇒ Yiddish *elǝnt*, as well as all -*ik* suffixed adjectives. It also reconciles the restoration of voicing in adjectives, which appears to require a suffixed form, with other leveling of other segmental alternations, which appear to require an unsuffixed form.

9.3.4 *Loss of devoicing in adverbs and prepositions*

Finally, there are a few words that lack paradigmatically related forms but nonetheless retain final voiced obstruents in Yiddish. These include *oyb* 'if, whether', *bald* 'soon', *bloyz* 'merely', *genug* 'enough', *biz* 'until', and *azh* 'as much as'. In the case of *oyb, bald, bloyz,* and *genug*, voicing may have been retained on the basis of existing variants with final ǝ: MHG *op* ∼ *obe, balt* ∼ *balde, blôȝ* ∼ *blôȝe, genuoc* ∼ *genuoge*. Just as with the adjectives, such variants would have provided a clear basis for restoring final voicing even without any other paradigmatically related forms.[23] In the case of *biz* and *azh*, voicing is the result of a separate process of voicing stem-final stridents in proclitic position (seen

---

[23] Plank (2000) also discusses the possible influence of a verb like *genügen* in preserving underlying voicing in *genug* in German. Modern Yiddish, likewise, has forms related to *genug* (e.g., an adjective *genugik*) that could have caused a similar effect, but this is clearly a less attractive account for the Yiddish data since it requires distinguishing between cases in which non-paradigmatically-related forms do exert an influence vs. those in which they do not.

also in etymological [s] words like *iz* 'is' and *muz* 'must', and variably in *doz* 'the-Neut Sg', *voz* 'what', etc.).

9.3.5 *Local summary*

To summarize, the Yiddish loss of final devoicing follows straightforwardly from a theory in which inflectional paradigms have privileged base forms, just like derivational paradigms. Crucially, however, the base must be allowed to vary from language to language and part of speech to part of speech. For early Yiddish, it is hypothesized that the base forms for almost all parts of speech preserved final voicing: the nominative plural for verbs, the 1sg present for verbs, and the unsuffixed form of adjectives (which preserved voicing in schwa-ful careful speech variants, at least for monosyllabic adjective stems). Moreover, the fact that all base forms preserved voicing is not an accident, under a theory in which base forms are selected precisely for their ability to recover contrasts that are neutralized elsewhere. I have shown here that the base selection procedure described in Albright (2002b) makes predictions that point in the right direction for changes to both voicing and other alternations within paradigms, and rests on principles that constitute a sensible learning strategy.

9.4 An OP + positional faithfulness account?

Throughout this discussion, I have assumed an analysis of obstruent devoicing that is based on positional markedness, using the cover constraint FINDEVOI to ban voiced obstruents in coda position ($\approx$ when not before a sonorant). As numerous authors have pointed out, however, it is also possible to analyze final devoicing using positional faithfulness constraints: IDENT$_{\text{PreSon}}$(voi) $\gg$ *VOICEDOBSTRUENT $\gg$ IDENT(voi) (see especially Lombardi 1999; Baković 1999; Padgett, to appear). As can be seen from the full ranking in Figure 9.3, positional faithfulness already plays an important role in the current analysis by forcing voicing assimilation to be regressive in order to preserve onset voicing. In fact, the entire analysis could be recast almost unmodified in terms of positional faithfulness, simply by replacing the FINDEVOI constraint with a simple *VOICEDOBSTRUENT constraint and using positional faithfulness constraints to distinguish among contexts that allow devoicing and those that do not. (See also Féry 1999 and Wagner 2002 for related discussion regarding the overlap and differences between these approaches.)

   The choice of positional markedness vs. faithfulness does have significant consequences for the predictions of the Optimal Paradigms approach, however.[24] In particular, if we restate final devoicing in terms of positional faithfulness, the prediction of attraction to the unmarked, shown in (9.3) above, no longer holds:

(9.29)   A language with final devoicing:

a.   No OP effect

/bund/, /bund-ə/	IO-Id$_{PreSon}$	*VoiObst	IO-Id(voi)	OP-Id(voi)
☞ a. [bunt], [bundə]		***	*	* (t~d)
b. [bunt], [buntə]	*!	**	**	
c. [bund], [bundə]		****!		

b.   OP effect

/bund/, /bund-ə/	OP-Id(voi)	IO-Id$_{PreSon}$	*VoiObst	IO-Id(voi)
a. [bunt], [bundə]	*! (t~d)		***	*
b. [bunt], [buntə]		*!	**	**
☞ c. [bund], [bundə]			****	

In the tableau in (9.29), we see that under a positional faithfulness account, promoting OP-IDENT actually selects the more faithful paradigm (attraction to the faithful). The reason is that under a positional faithfulness account, what it means for a language to "have a process" is reversed. Rather than an alternation being forced in some contexts via $\mathcal{M} \gg \mathcal{F}$ (harmonic = markedness-obeying), it is caused by faithfulness reining in a markedness constraint in a certain context (harmonic = contextually faithful). OP predicts "attraction to the more harmonic", which in a markedness-on-top account is the unmarked, but in a faithfulness-on-top account is the more faithful paradigm. This means that if we adopt a positional faithfulness analysis, the "attraction to the unmarked" prediction is lost. As a result, we actually predict the correct winner for the Yiddish change.

The sensitivity of OP predictions to positional faithfulness vs. markedness raises an interesting possibility: could the directionality of leveling be used as a litmus test for whether a particular type of alternation is due to positional markedness ($\Rightarrow$ attraction to the unmarked) or positional faithfulness ($\Rightarrow$ attraction to the faithful)? I leave this as a matter for future inquiry but point out in passing some reasons to doubt that it is on the right track. The first concerns the difference between roots and affixes. In section 9.2.3, we saw that within the very same language, we get leveling to the faithful within roots and leveling to the unmarked within affixes. At the very least, this suggests that it is not possible to predict the direction of leveling based on the type of

---

[24] Thanks to Michael Becker for bringing this issue to my attention.

alternation involved. Furthermore, this account makes no predictions about cases where satisfying OP-IDENT requires choosing between two conflicting markedness constraints, both of which are always satisfied in the original language. For example, the leveling to long vowels discussed in section 9.2.8 incurs new violations of $*V:C]_\sigma$ (the constraint driving closed syllable shortening)–but there is no obvious reason why this is better than leveling to short vowels and incurring $*V]_\sigma$ (= open syllable lengthening) violations.

In sum, then, even if positional faithfulness constraints allow OP to make the correct prediction for the leveling of final voicing, it is not clear that they would be able to solve the larger problem of distinguishing between cases that exhibit attraction to the unmarked vs. attraction to the faithful. This problem is avoided in a theory that attributes the direction of leveling not to the markedness of the segments involved but, rather, to where in the paradigm they occur. What the Yiddish changes of leveling to voiced obstruents and leveling to long vowels have in common is that they both extend the alternant that is seen in the suffixed base form.

9.5 Conclusion

The goal of this chapter has been to provide evidence that inflectional paradigms have bases, just like derivational paradigms. To this end, I have presented several new arguments that the change known as the "loss of final devoicing" in early Yiddish was paradigmatically motivated, as traditional accounts have assumed. This change constitutes a counterexample to some key predictions of the Optimal Paradigms approach–namely, that leveling should always favor overapplication and extension of less marked allomorphs. This is not a negative result, however. Such cases show that inflectional paradigms have more complex structure than is often supposed and, in particular, that they have privileged base forms, just like derivational paradigms. Furthermore, I have argued that the base form can be identified in non-circular fashion by independent principles, using implementable procedures. Thus, the proposed model actually represents a simplification, not a complication, in how relations between surface forms are computed in phonology.

References

Ackerman, F., and J. P. Blevins (2006) 'Paradigms and predictability', paper presented at the 2006 meeting of the Linguistic Society of America, Albuquerque, NM, 5–8 Jan.

Albright, A. (2002a) 'Base selection in analogical change: A German/Yiddish comparison', talk presented at the 28th Annual Meeting of the Berkeley Linguistics Society, 15–18 Feb.

—— (2002b) The identification of bases in morphological paradigms. Ph.D. thesis, UCLA.

—— (2005) 'The morphological basis of paradigm leveling', in L. J. Downing, T. A. Hall, and R. Raffelsiefen (eds.), *Paradigms in Phonological Theory*. Oxford: Oxford University Press, pp. 17–43.

Alderete, J. D. (2001) *Morphologically Governed Accent in Optimality Theory*. New York: Routledge.

—— (2003) 'Structural disparities in Navajo word domains: A case for LEXCAT-FAITHFULNESS'. *The Linguistic Review* 20: 111–57.

Baković, E. (1999) 'Assimilation to the unmarked', in J. Alexander, N.-R. Han, and M. M. Fox (eds.), *University of Pennsylvania Working Papers in Linguistics* 6.1, 1–16.

Barr, R. (1994) A lexical model of morphological change. Ph.D. thesis, Harvard.

Beckman, J. (1998) Positional faithfulness. Ph.D. thesis, University of Massachusetts.

Benua, L. (1997) Transderivational identity: Phonological relations between words. Ph.D. thesis, University of Massachusetts, Amherst.

Blevins, J. P. (2004) 'Inflection classes and economy', in G. Müller, L. Gunkel, and G. Zifonun (eds.), *Explorations in Nominal Inflection*, Berlin: Mouton de Gruyter, pp. 51–96.

Bochner, H. (1993) *Simplicity in Generative Morphology*. Berlin: Mouton de Gruyter.

Boersma, P. (1997) 'How we learn variation, optionality, and probability'. *Proceedings of the Institute of Phonetic Sciences of the University of Amsterdam* 21, 43–58. http://fon.hum.uva.nl/paul/.

—— and B. Hayes (2001) 'Empirical tests of the Gradual Learning Algorithm', *Linguistic Inquiry* 32(1): 45–86.

Borowsky, T. (2000) 'Word-faithfulness and the direction of assimilation'. *Linguistic Review* 17: 1–28.

Burzio, L. (1996) 'Surface constraints versus underlying representation', in J. Durand and B. Laks (eds.), *Current Trends in Phonology: Models and Methods*, CNRS, Paris and Salford: University of Salford Publications, pp. 97–122.

Carstairs-McCarthy, A. (1994) 'Inflection classes, gender, and the principle of contrast'. *Language* 70: 737–88.

Casali, R. F. (1997) 'Vowel elision in hiatus contexts: Which vowel goes?' *Language* 73: 493–533.

Dinnsen, D., and J. Charles-Luce (1984) 'Phonological neutralization, phonetic implementation and individual differences'. *Journal of Phonetics* 12(1): 49–60.

Ernestus, M. (2000) Voice assimilation and segment reduction in casual Dutch. Ph.D. thesis, Free University of Amsterdam/Holland Institute of Generative Linguistics.

Féry, C. (1999) 'Final devoicing and the stratification of the lexicon in German', in *Proceedings of HILP 4*, Leiden.

Fourakis, M. (1984) 'Should neutralization be redefined?' *Journal of Phonetics* 12(4): 291–96.

Hayes, B. (2004) 'Phonological acquisition in Optimality Theory: The early stages', in R. Kager, J. Pater, and W. Zonneveld (eds.), *Fixing Priorities: Constraints in Phonological Acquisition*. Cambridge: Cambridge University Press.

—— B. Tesar, and K. Zuraw (2003) OTSoft 2.1 software package. http://www.linguistics.ucla.edu/people/hayes/otsoft/.

Herzog, M. I. (1965) *The Yiddish Language in Northern Poland: Its Geography and History*. Bloomington, IN: Indiana University.

Hsu, C.-S. (1997) 'Voicing underspecification in Taiwanese word-final consonants', in M. K. Gordon (ed.), *UCLA Working Papers in Linguistics, Number 2: Papers in Phonology 3*, pp. 1–24.

Hyman, L. (2001) 'The limits of phonetic determinism in phonology: *NC revisited', in E. Hume, K. Johnson, E. Hume, and K. Johnson (eds.), *The Role of Speech Perception in Phonology*. San Diego: Academic Press.

Ito, J., and A. Mester (1997) 'Sympathy theory and German truncations', in V. Miglio and B. Morén (eds.), *University of Maryland Working Papers in Linguistics 5, Selected Phonology Papers from Hopkins Optimality Theory Workshop 1997/University of Maryland Mayfest 1997*, pp. 117–39.

—— —— (2002) 'The phonological lexicon', in N. Tsujimura (ed.), *A Handbook of Japanese Linguistics*. Oxford: Blackwell.

—— —— (2003) 'On the sources of opacity in OT: Coda processes in German', in C. Féry and R. van de Vijver (eds.), *The Syllable in Optimality Theory*, Cambridge: Cambridge University Press, pp. 271–303.

Jacobs, N. G. (1990) *Economy in Yiddish Vocalism: A Study in the Interplay of Hebrew and Non-Hebrew Components*. Mediterranean Language and Culture Monograph Series. Otto Harrassowitz.

—— (2005) *Yiddish: A Linguistic Introduction*. Cambridge: Cambridge University Press.

Jansen, W. (2004) Laryneal constrast and phonetic voicing: A laboratory phonology approach to English, Hungarian, and Dutch. Ph.D. thesis, Rijksuniversiteit Groningen.

Katz, D. (1987) *Grammar of the Yiddish Language*. London: Duckworth.

Kawahara, S. (2002) 'Faithfulness among variants'. *On-in-kenkyuu [Phonological Studies]* 5: 47–54. http://www-unix.oit.umass.edu/~kawahara/OVFaith_in_Oninkenkyuu.pdf.

Kenstowicz, M. (1996) 'Base identity and uniform exponence: Alternatives to cyclicity', in J. Durand and B. Laks (eds.), *Current Trends in Phonology: Models and Methods*, Salford: University of Salford, pp. 363–94. Available for download from the Rutgers Optimality Archive, http://ruccs.rutgers.edu/roa.html.

—— (2005) 'Paradigmatic uniformity and contrast', in L. J. Downing, T. A. Hall, and R. Raffelsiefen (eds.), *Paradigms in Phonological Theory*. Oxford: Oxford University Press, pp. 145–69.

Kenstowicz, M., M. Abu-Mansour, and M. Törkenczy (2003) 'Two notes on laryngeal licensing', in S. Ploch and G. Williams (eds.), *Living on the Edge: 28 Papers in Honour of Jonathan Kaye*. Mouton de Gruyter.

King, R. D. (1969) *Historical Linguistics and Generative Grammar*. Englewood Cliffs, NJ: Prentice-Hall.

——(1980) 'The history of final devoicing in Yiddish', in M. I. Herzog, B. Kirshenblatt-Gimblett, D. Miron, and R. Wisse (eds.), *The Field of Yiddish: Studies in Language, Folklore, and Literature, Fourth Collection*. Philadelphia: Institute for the Study of Human Issues, pp. 371–430.

Kiparsky, P. (1968) 'Linguistic universals and linguistic change', in E. Bach and R. T. Harms (eds.), *Universals in Linguistic Theory*. New York: Holt, Rinehart, and Winston.

——(1982) 'Lexical morphology and phonology', in T. L. S. of Korea (ed.), *Linguistics in the Morning Calm: Selected Papers from SICOL-1981*. Seoul: Hanshin Publishing Company.

Kopkalli, H. (1993) A phonetic and phonological analysis of final devoicing in Turkish. Ph.D. thesis, University of Michigan.

Kraska-Szlenk, I. (1995) The phonology of stress in Polish. Ph.D. thesis, University of Illinois at Urbana-Champaign.

Lieber, R. (1981) 'Morphological conversion within a restrictive theory of the lexicon', in M. Moortgat, H. van der Hulst, and T. Hoekstra (eds.), *The Scope of Lexical Rules*. Dordrecht: Foris.

Lombardi, L. (1999) 'Positional faithfulness and voicing assimilation in Optimality Theory'. *Natural Language and Linguistic Theory* 17: 267–302.

Lowenstamm, J. (2005) 'The loud noise of n', talk presented at the Sounds of Silence Conference, Tilburg University, October 2005.

Łubowicz, A. (2002) 'Derived environment effects in Optimality Theory'. *Lingua* 112: 243–80.

McCarthy, J. (2003) 'Comparative markedness'. *Theoretical Linguistics* 29: 1–51.

——(2005) 'Optimal paradigms', in L. J. Downing, T. A. Hall, and R. Raffelsiefen (eds.), *Paradigms in Phonological Theory*. Oxford: Oxford University Press, pp. 170–210. Available from the Rutgers Optimality Archive, ROA-485.

Padgett, J. (to appear) 'Russian voicing assimilation, final devoicing, and the problem of [v]'. *Natural Language and Linguistic Theory*.

Paul, H., P. Wiehl, and S. Grosse (1989) *Mittelhochdeutsche Grammatik* (23rd ed.). Tübingen: Max Niemeyer Verlag.

Perlmutter, D. (1988) 'The split morphology hypothesis: Evidence from Yiddish', in M. Hammond and M. Noonan (eds.), *Theoretical Morphological: Approaches in Modern Linguistics*. San Diego: Academic Press, pp. 79–100.

Plank, F. (2000) 'Morphological re-activation and phonological alternations: Evidence for voiceless restructuring in German', in A. Lahiri (ed.), *Analogy, Levelling, Markedness: Principles of Change in Phonology and Morphology*. Mouton de Gruyter, pp. 171–91.

Port, R., and M. O'Dell (1986) 'Neutralization of syllable-final voicing in German'. *Journal of Phonetics* 13: 455–71.

Prince, A., and P. Smolensky (2004) *Optimality Theory: Constraint Interaction in Generative Grammar*. Blackwell Publishing.

Reis, M. (1974) *Lauttheorie und Lautgeschichte; Untersuchungen am Beispiel der Dehnungs- und Kürzungsvorgänge im Deutschen*. Munich: W. Fink.

Russ, C. V. J. (1982) *Studies in Historical German Phonology: A Phonological Comparison of MHG and NHG with Reference to Modern Dialects*, vol. 616 of *European University Studies, Series I: German Language and Literature*. Bern: Peter Lang.

Sadock, J. M. (1973) 'Word-final devoicing in the development of Yiddish', in B. B. Kachru, R. B. Lees, Y. Malkiel, A. Pietrangeli, and S. Saporta (eds.), *Issues in Linguistics: Papers in Honor of Henry and Renée Kahane*. Urbana, IL: University of Illinois Press, pp. 790–97.

Sapir, E. (1915) 'Notes on Judeo-German phonology'. *The Jewish Quarterly Review* 6: 231–66.

Smolensky, P. (1996) 'The initial state and "Richness of the Base" in Optimality Theory'. Technical report, Johns Hopkins University.

Stampe, D. (1969) 'The acquisition of phonetic representation'. *Papers from the Fifth Regional Meeting of the Chicago Linguistic Society*, pp. 443–54.

Steriade, D. (1997) 'Phonetics in phonology: The case of laryngeal neutralization'. UCLA Ms.

——— (2000) 'Paradigm uniformity and the phonetics/phonology boundary', in J. Pierrehumbert and M. Broe (eds.), *Papers in Laboratory Phonology*, vol. 6. Cambridge: Cambridge University Press.

Sturgeon, A. (2003) 'Paradigm uniformity: Evidence for inflectional bases', in G. Garding and M. Tsujimura (eds.), *WCCFL 22 Proceedings*. Somerville, MA: Cascadilla Press, pp. 464–76.

Tesar, B., and A. Prince (2004) 'Using phonotactics to learn phonological alternations', in *Proceedings of CLS 39, vol. II: The Panels*. Chicago Linguistics Society. http://ruccs. rutgers.edu/~tesar/papers/cls39.pdf.

Tessier, A.-M. (2006) 'Learning stringency relations and the contexts of faithfulness', paper presented at the 2006 meeting of the Linguistic Society of America, Albuquerque, NM, 5–8 Jan.

Vennemann, T. (1972) 'Phonetic analogy and conceptual analogy', in T. Vennemann and T. H. Wilbur (eds.), *Schuchhardt, the Neogrammarians, and the Transformational Theory of Phonological Change: Four Essays by Hugo Schuchhardt*, Number 26 in Linguistische Forschungen. Frankfurt am Main: Athenäum, pp. 183–204.

Veynger, M. (1913) 'Hebreyishe klangn in der yidisher shprakh', in Shmuel Niger (ed.), *Der Pinkes*. Vilna.

Wagner, M. (2002) 'The role of prosody in laryngeal neutralization', in A. Csirmaz, Z. Li, A. Nevins, O. Vaysman, and M. Wagner (eds.), *MIT Working Papers in Linguistics #42: Phonological Answers (and their Corresponding Questions)*, pp. 373–92.

Weinreich, M. (1973) *Geshikhte fun der yidisher shprakh: Bagrifn, faktn, metodn [History of the Yiddish Language: Concepts, Facts, Methods]*, vol. 2. New York: Yidisher Visnshaftlikher Institut (YIVO).

Weinreich, U. (1990) *Modern English-Yiddish, Yiddish-English Dictionary*. New York: YIVO Institute for Jewish Research.

Wright, J. (1950) *A Middle High German Primer* (4th ed. revised by M. O. C. Walshe). Oxford: Clarendon Press.

Zsiga, E., M. Gouskova, and O. Tlale (2006) 'On the status of voiced obstruents in Tswana: Against *ND', in C. Davis, A. Deal, and Y. Zabbal (eds.), *Proceedings of NELS 36*. Amherst, MA: GLSA.

Zuraw, K. (2000) 'Patterned exceptions in phonology'. Ph.D. thesis, UCLA.

10

A pseudo-cyclic effect in Romanian morphophonology

DONCA STERIADE*

Abstract

Romanian phonology is shown to be subject to inflection dependence, a systematic restriction on phonological alternations. Inflection dependence means that segmental alternations are permitted in the derivatives of a lexeme only if certain inflected forms of that lexeme, its inflectional bases (Albright 2002), independently display the alternation. The study documents this pervasive constraint on alternations and proposes an analysis for it, based on a modified variant of Lexical Conservatism (Steriade 1999b).

The broader significance of inflection dependence is the need to allow access in phonological computations to a broader class of lexically-related, derived lexical items relative to what the phonological cycle (Chomsky et al. 1956) and its descendants permit. I discuss the difference between inflection dependence and the phonological cycle and propose a mechanism that reduces the formal differences between them to rankings of correspondence and phonotactics.

10.1 Introduction

10.1.1 *The phenomenon*

This is a study of the interaction between lexical structure, paradigm structure, correspondence, and phonotactics. I document a new type of alternation

* The chapter has benefited from Rebrus and Törkenczy (2005), a revealing analysis of the interaction of paradigm structure and phonotactics in Hungarian, and from discussions with Adam Albright, Karlos Arregi, Luigi Burzio, Dani Byrd, Anna Cardinaletti, Edward Flemming, Bruce Hayes, Giorgio Magri, and with audiences at UCLA, LSRL 28 (Rutgers University), the LSA Winter 2007 meeting (Anaheim, CA), and in 24.965 (MIT). Finally, I am grateful to the editors of this volume, Asaf Bachrach and Andrew Nevins, for their very helpful comments, their patience, and for insisting that I get everything right.

avoidance whose preliminary formulation appears below:

(10.1)   A phonological modification of the stem is avoided when triggered by a derivational affix, unless the modification is independently found in the inflectional paradigm of the stem.

A simplified scenario loosely based on Romanian illustrates in (10.2) the basic phenomenon. The words /bak/ and /pak/ represent two inflectional classes, Class 1 and 2. These classes take different inflectional suffixes, /i/ and /u/. As a result, the verbs in each class undergo different alternations: inflected /bak + i/ undergoes palatalization (k → tʃ/_i) and becomes [batʃi], while in /pak + u/ the rule cannot apply and the stem remains intact. Had /pak/ inflected as /pak-i/, it too would have become [patʃi]. This difference in the range of predictable root alternants found in inflection has consequences for the derivational behaviors of /bak/ and /pak/: a derivational suffix /ik/ attaches to both classes and triggers, in principle, the same rules as the inflectional /i/, so /ik/ should cause /k/ to palatalize to [tʃ] when added to both stems. The suffix /ik/ does indeed cause Class 1 /bak-ik/ to become [batʃik], just like inflectional /i/ did. But /ik/ has no effect on Class 2 items like /pak/, which fail to generate [tʃ] alternants throughout the system.

(10.2)   A schematic illustration of inflection dependence

Lexicon	root /bak/, Class 1	Inflection	Class 1: suffix /i/, /bak-i/
	root /pak/, Class 2		Class 2: suffix /u/, /pak-u/
Phonology	velar → palatoalveolar/ __ front vowel		
IO Mappings	/bak-i/ → [batʃi]		/pak-u/ → [paku]
Derivation	/bak/ +/-ik/: /bak-ik/		/pak/ + /ik/: /pak-ik/
IO Mappings	/bak-ik/ → [batʃik], not *[bakik]		/pak-ik/ → [pakik], not *[patʃik]

10.1.2 *An outline of the ingredients*

Intuitively, this pattern of inflection dependence suggests an analysis in which the phonology of derived forms takes into account the set of stem variants that are known by the speaker to "exist independently", that is, in this case, the stem variants that arise independently of derivation, in inflection. If a stem variant in [-tʃ] "exists independently", in this sense, it can be deployed in a phonotactically appropriate context, e.g., before an [i]-initial derivational suffix. In that case, the constraint triggering palatalization can be satisfied. If no such variant exists, the palatalization constraint cannot be satisfied: that is why we get [pakik].

What exactly does it mean for a form to "exist independently"? Does it mean "to be listed in the lexicon"? If so, are all members of inflectional paradigms lexically listed? Why they and not other morphologically complex forms? The chapter proposes answers to these questions based on a combination of analytic ingredients originating in the theory of Lexical Phonology (Kiparsky 1982), Correspondence Theory (McCarthy and Prince 1995), and modifications of the latter (Steriade 1999a,b). We will need for our analysis a distinction between a core lexicon of basic atomic entries (roots and affixes) and a derived lexicon containing morphologically complex words, organized in successive layers. We will also need a grammar with extensive access to members of the derived lexicon. Access of the grammar to the list of derived lexical items is regulated in most conceptions of phonology by the phonological cycle (Chomsky, Halle, and Lukoff 1956). The findings in this study suggest that the cyclic dependence of one form upon another (e.g., the dependence of *originálity* upon *original*) represents just a limiting case of a broader form of potential dependence between lexically-related forms.

Directly below, section 10.2 presents the outlines of the Romanian phenomenon of inflection dependence. Section 10.3 provides its analysis and section 10.4 extends the basic pattern studied earlier to related processes. The concluding section 10.5 discusses the structure of the derived Romanian lexicon based on the evidence of inflection dependence.

10.2 Inflection dependence in Romanian

10.2.1 *Segment inventory*

The segmental contrasts of Romanian are outlined below, with corresponding orthographic symbols added in angle brackets, for the non-obvious cases. More descriptive detail and an analysis of Romanian nuclear alternations appear in Steriade 2006.

(10.3)   a.   Vowels   b.   Tautosyllabic vocoid sequences

i	ɨ <î, â>	u
e	ʌ <ă>	o
	a	

i̯e, i̯u, iu̯	ɨi̯, ɨu̯	ui̯,
e̯a, e̯o, eu̯, ei̯	ʌi̯, ʌu̯	o̯a, oi̯, ou̯
	ai̯, au̯	

c.   Consonants

p	t	ts \<ţ\>	tʃ \<ce, ci\>	c \<che, chi\>	k \<c\>
b	d		dʒ \<ge, gi\>	ɟ \<ghe, ghi\> g	
f		s	ʃ \<ş\>		
v		z	ʒ \<j\>		
m	n				h \<h\>
	l, r				

The Romanian material presented here appears in IPA transcription, as the Romanian spelling does not distinguish glides from vowels.

10.2.2 *Declension basics*

Romanian declension makes two overt binary distinctions for number and case. The four forms are distinct in pronouns, below, and in definite forms of nouns and adjectives.

(10.4)   Pronominal declension pattern

	Singular		Plural	
	masculine	feminine	masculine	feminine
NOM-ACC	X-u	X-ʌ	X-i	X-e
GEN-DAT	X-u-i	X-e-i	X-or	

In indefinite forms, these distinctions are systematically compressed. Each noun and adjective has no more than two–and typically exactly two–overtly distinct forms: a nominative singular and one other. The form and function of the other form depends on gender and declension type. Typical masculines have a distinct singular and plural form, with no case distinctions within each number in the indefinite declension; typical feminines have an undifferentiated plural form, and a singular in which the NOM-ACC is distinct from the GEN-DAT, the latter being identical to the plural. The distinct structure of masculine and feminine paradigms is illustrated below:

(10.5)   Gender-based distribution of endings: masculine and feminine e/i adjectives

	NOM-ACC sg	GEN-DAT sg	Plural	gloss
masculine	vérd-e		/verd-i/ [vérz-i̯]	green
feminine	vérd-e		/verd-i/ [vérz-i̯]	

The same effect is observed with nouns: [peréte] 'wall' and [petʃéte] 'seal' belong to the same declension but have different genders and thus distribute the same case forms differently.

(10.6) Gender-based distribution of endings: masculine and feminine -e/-i declensions

	NOM-ACC sg	GEN-DAT sg	Plural	gloss
masculine	perét-e		/peret-i/ [perétsi̯]	wall
feminine	petʃét-e	/petʃét-i/ [petʃétsi̯]		seal

A classification of the declension classes of the language is provided in (10.7). The classes are generated by freely combining any of the three NOM-ACC singular markers with any of three plural markers.[1] All combinations are attested.

(10.7) Declension classes as combinations of singular/plural markers[2]

Singular \ Plural	-e	-i ([i]/[i̯])	-uri ([uri̯]/[uri])
-u ([u]/[u̯]/∅)	lémn-u, lémn-e 'wood'	lúp-u, lup-i 'wolf'	trúp-u, trup-uri 'body'
-ʌ	áp-ʌ, áp-e 'water'	árip-ʌ, arip-i 'wing'	líps-ʌ, lips-uri 'lack'
-e	núm-e, núm-e 'name'	lúm-e, lum-i 'world'	vrém-e, vrem-uri 'time'

The nine declension classes are denoted here by listing the defining combination of endings; thus, [lemn] 'wood' belongs to the u/e class.

The neuter nouns, left out of the picture until now, represent a subset of the declension types definable on the set of endings in (10.7)–the u/e, u/uri, e/e classes. These induce agreement as masculines in the singular and as feminines in the plural, a pattern that raises interesting issues (cf. Bateman and Polinsky 2006) that are unrelated to the point of this chapter. They are left unaddressed here. I summarize next the distribution of declension types by gender; this is the minimum that will be immediately relevant in this chapter.

---

[1] The classification of declension types in (10.7) is non-standard. Traditional classifications do not factor in the predictable effects of gender and phonology (see GLR 1966, Lombard and Gâdei 1981, Hristea and Moroianu 2005).

[2] Variants in parenthesis arise as a function of the noun's position in the clitic group: group-final high vowels become glides and post-consonantal w is deleted. (For analysis, see Steriade 1984, Chitoran 2002, Popescu 2000).

(10.8)   Gender distribution across declension classes

Singular \ Plural	-e	-i	-uri
-u	N	M	N
-ʌ	F	F	F
-e	N	M or F	F

10.2.3 *Inflection dependence*

The descriptive focus in this study is a generalization about the effect of a word's inflectional class on the phonology of its derivatives. The generalization is that stem alternants generated in inflection determine the range of possible stem modifications the word can undergo in derivation. The generalization encompasses all consonantal alternations active in Romanian and possibly some vocalic alternations as well. The robustness and generality of the effect suggest that it arises from a central mechanism in the grammar of the language. The discussion here will use one alternation to illustrate the phenomenon in some detail, with a sketch of the full picture deferred to section 10.4.

10.2.3.1 *K-Palatalization*   This section documents the effect of inflection dependence on one process, K-Palatalization. This process turns [k] to [tʃ] and [g] to [dʒ] before front vowels and glides:

(10.9)   K-Palatalization

The process	Noun alternatizons	gloss	Verb alternations	gloss
k → tʃ/_[−back]	núk-ʌ nútʃ-i̯	'nut(s)'	fák fátʃ-i̯	'do': indic. 1sg/2sg
	fíik-ʌ fiitʃ-e	'daughter(s)'	fák-ʌ fátʃ-e	'do': subj/indic. 3sg
g → dʒ/_[−back]	mág mádʒ-i̯	'mage(s)'	súg súdʒ-i̯	'suck': indic. 1sg/2sg
	álg-ʌ áldʒ-e	'seaweed(s)'	súg-ʌ súdʒ-e	'suck': subj/indic. 3sg

K-Palatalization is automatic before plural suffixes. It applies in the plurals of all recent loans (e.g., [pfeniŋg], pl [pfenindʒ-j], cf. German *Pfenning* 'coin'; [demiurg], pl [demiurdʒ-j] cf. Greek *demi-ourgos* 'artisan, creator') and in wug words. The process is limited to derived environments:

(10.10)   Non-derived environment blockage

    a.   kilográm 'kilogram'; kʲestije[3] 'issue, thing'; oki̯[4] 'eye'

    b.   ginion 'bad luck'; gʲém 'pool of thread'; triuŋgi̯ 'triangle'

---

[3] The surfacing [ke], [ge] sequences are realized with fronted velars and a palatal on-glide: [kʲe], [gʲe]; so are, probably, [ki], [gi] but the lack of a [ji]–[i] contrast makes it hard to detect their on-glide.

[4] UR is /oki̯-u/, /triungi̯-u/, with word final /u/ regularly deleting; the /u/ resurfaces in the definite forms [oki̯-u-l], [triungi̯-u-l]. The restriction of K-Palatalization to derived environments explains the

A minimal constraint-based analysis appears below. As we are concerned here not with the nature of the phonotactics triggering palatalization but with the correspondence constraints competing with them, the phonotactic constraint is only sketched. (See Flemming 2002 and Wilson 2006 for an analysis of the factors leading to velar palatalization.) To formalize derived environment restrictions, I rely on Comparative Markedness (McCarthy 2002). The active phonotactic penalizes only violations not found in the lexical entry of the base morpheme. In the case at hand the phonotactic $*_N$KE is violated only by the introduction of velar+[−back] sequences absent from the lexical entries of component morphemes.[5]

(10.11) K-Palatalization

    a. $*_N$KE: Sequences of non-strident [−anterior] C's before front vocoids that are new relative to the base morpheme are prohibited.

    b. $*_N$KE ≫ Ident F

nuk-i̧	$*_N$KE	Ident F
a. [nuki̧]	*!	
☞ b. [nut͡ʃi̧]		*

10.2.3.2 *Derived verbs*   We now consider the effect of K-Palatalization in derivation. The analysis is based on a broader survey of derivational morphology but space limits the discussion to derived verbs in [i̧], [á], [uí, and to nominal suffix [íst]. This section provides background information on these derivatives. All suffixes are attached to stems stripped of their nominal declension markers:

(10.12) Deriving a verb from a noun or adjective with [í], [á], [uí]

    a. pʌdúr-e 'forest' : im-pʌdur-í 'to cover with forests'

    b. kléʃt-e 'pliers': des-kleʃt-á 'to force open, to pull apart'

    c. píld-ʌ 'example': pild-uí 'to make/give an example'

---

fact that the velars of such forms are never palatalized, including before suffixes that invariably trigger the process. The plural of [oki] is [oki], not *[ot͡ʃi], from /oki-i/. There are interesting and unresolved issues here regarding the interpretation of what is new and what is old in these plural [ki] sequences but the most plausible explanation for the lack of K-Palatalization in the plural is that the [ki] is non-derived because an identical sequence occurs internal to the root.

[5] Here I deviate from the technical details of McCarthy's proposal in ways that are not germane to the main points.

There is no observable syntactic or semantic difference among the three verbalizing suffixes. Data like (10.13) suggest that, in native stems, the choice of suffix is variable or lexically arbitrary.

(10.13)   Variation between [í], [á], [uí]

    a.   pʌjánʒen-(u) 'spider': im-pʌjenʒen-á ~ im-pʌjenʒen-í 'become covered in spider webs'

    b.   drépt-(u) 'right, straight': in-drept-á 'to make straight'; in-drept-uí 'to justify a right'

    c.   gríʒ-ʌ 'care, worry': in-griʒ-á 'to cause/feel worry'; in-griʒ-í 'to take care'

We observe next that the variation in suffix choice is modulated by consonantal phonotactics. The suffix [í] requires K-Palatalization. For this reason, its selection is severely restricted after stems that lack palatalized allomorphs generated in inflection. This is one aspect of inflection dependence. The other is the differential application of K-Palatalization in derivatives marked by [i]-initial suffixes, depending on the structure of the inflectional paradigm of their base.

10.2.3.3 *Inflection dependence of K-Palatalization*   In the declension classes u/i, ʌ/i, u/e, and ʌ/e, K-Palatalization generates alternations between k/tʃ, g/dʒ. In the declension class u/uri these alternations are not expected and do not occur.

(10.14)   K-Palatalization and declension classes

		Singular	Plural	Gloss
Alternations: k/tʃ, g/dʒ	Class u/i	sʌrák-(u)	sʌrátʃ-i	'poor' (masc.)
	Class u/e	katárg-(u)	katárdʒ-e	'mast'
	Class ʌ/i	núk-ʌ	nutʃ-i	'nut'
	Class ʌ/e	sʌrák-ʌ	sʌrátʃ-e	'poor' (fem.)
No alternations: k/k, g/g	Class u/uri	lók-(u)	lók-uri	'place'

Turning now to derived verbs, we expect K-Palatalization to be triggered by [í], but not by [á], [uí]. An effect of inflection dependence will emerge if K-Palatalization is blocked or otherwise avoided in derivatives of words lacking a palatalized allomorph generated in inflection. This can be detected by comparing the derivatives of the classes in which alternations arise (u/i, u/e, ʌ/i, ʌ/e) with those of the non-alternating u/uri class. One expects one of two effects: either invariant nouns like [fok, fok-urɨ] will avoid the verbal [í] suffix, while alternating stems like [sʌrák, sʌrátʃɨ] permit it; or [í] will attach freely to nouns of all classes but verbs derived from the invariant u/urɨ class will block K-Palatalization, while bases from other classes undergo it.

(10.15)   Possible manifestations of inflection dependence

(a) affix avoidance	Inflected forms	Choice of verbalizing suffix
Alternating classes: u/ɨ, u/e, ʌ/ɨ, ʌ/e	sʌrák, sʌratʃ-ɨ	-í ok
Non-alternating class: u/urɨ	fók, fók-urɨ	-í avoided
(b) phonotactic violated	Inflected forms	K-Palatalization
Alternating classes: u/ɨ, u/e, ʌ/ɨ, ʌ/e	sʌrák, sʌratʃ-ɨ	/...k-í/ → [...tʃí]
Non-alternating class: u/urɨ	fók, fók-urɨ	Blocked: /...k-í/ → [...kí]

Both effects are encountered but only the former arises with derived verbs. What we find is that the choice of verbal suffix is adjusted, and invariant stems (henceforth referred to as K/K stems) avoid [í]. (10.16) compares variable stems (referred to as K/Tʃ) and invariant ones (K/K) with respect to their selection of verbalizing suffixes.

(10.16)   Derivatives of alternating K/Tʃ and invariant K/K bases: choice of [-í] vs. [-á], [-uí]

		Base		Derived verb
		Singular	Plural	
a	Class u/urɨ	fok 'fire'	fók-urɨ	-a: in-fok-á, *-fotʃ-í 'to fire up'
	Class u/ɨ	kolák 'bagel'	kolátʃ-ɨ	-i: iŋ-kolʌtʃ-í, *-kolʌkí 'to roll up'
b	Class u/urɨ	tɨrg 'market'	tɨrg-urɨ	-ui: tɨrg-uí, *tɨrdʒí 'to go shopping'
	Class u/ɨ	pribɘág 'wanderer'	pribédʒ-ɨ	-i: pribedʒ-í *pribegí 'to wander'

Note that in this case there is a default preference for the verbalizer [í]: K/Tʃ stems like [kolák]/[kolátʃ-ɨ] tend to select it. This preference is overridden after

K/K stems, whose inability to undergo K-Palatalization forces the selection of the alternative verbalizing [á], [uí] suffixes. More detail on these points appears below.

When the suffix offers a single [i]-initial form, the derivatives of invariant stems violate K-Palatalization. This is typical of currently productive suffixes, like [ist], whose effect on K/K and K/Tʃ bases is seen below:

(10.17)   -ist derivatives of K/Tʃ and K/K bases

	Base		-ist noun
	Singular	Plural	
K/K	fók 'fire'	fók-uri̯	fok-íst, *fotʃíst 'locomotive engineer'
K/Tʃ	stíŋg-ʌ 'left (hand)'	stíndʒ-i̯	stindʒ-íst, *stiŋgíst 'leftist'
K/K	[fránk-o] (<Franco>, the generalissimo)		frank-íst *frantʃist 'Franco supporter'
	[góg-a] (<Goga>, Romanian politician)		gog-íst, *godʒ-ist
K/Tʃ	faláŋg-ʌ 'falanx'	falándʒ-e	falandʒ-íst, *falaŋgíst 'falangist'
	lódʒik-ʌ 'logic'	lódʒitʃ-i̯	lodʒitʃ-íst

All masculine proper names (e.g., Franco) behave as invariant K/K stems. That is because their only chance to undergo palatalization would have been the plural, which they lack. (Feminine singularia tantum behave identically but this requires more analysis, deferred to section 10.5). The effect holds more generally for all singularia tantum and thus includes mass nouns as well, e.g., [vlág-ʌ] 'life force, energy' lacks a plural, hence cannot palatalize in inflection. For this reason it cannot palatalize in derivation either. It cannot select the common -i verbalizing suffix, yielding instead [vlʌg-uí] 'to deprive of force'; *[vlʌdʒ-í] cannot be a derivative of [vlág-ʌ].

10.2.3.4 *Effects of *$_N$KE *in derivation* We verify now that what was referred to earlier as "the application of Palatalization in derivation" is indeed a phono-tactically driven effect rather than an unrelated fact of allomorph selection. The point is made by the observation that palatalized stem allomorphs of K/Tʃ bases appear only before front-vocalic derivational suffixes. Two examples illustrate this below; more detailed lexical counts establish this in the next section.

(10.18)   The Phonotactic *$_N$KE distributes dʒ/tʃ-final allomorphs before –{e,i,j}

    a. Inflection: [stíng-ʌ] 'left (hand)'; [stíndʒ-j] 'left-pl'

    b. Front-vocalic derivational suffix: [stindʒ-íst] 'leftist', *[sting-íst]

    c. Back-vocalic derivational suffix: [sting-átʃ] 'lefty', *[stindʒ-átʃ]

  d. Inflection: [kovrig] 'pretzel'; [kovridʒ-j] 'pretzels'

  e. Front-vocalic derivational suffix: [ɨn-kovridʒ-i] 'fold like a pretzel', *[-kovrig-í]

  f. Back-vocalic derivational suffix: [ɨn-kovrig-á] 'fold like a pretzel', *[-kovridʒ-á]

In the derivatives of K/tʃ nouns like [stíng-ʌ]/[stɨndʒ-j], the palatalized allomorph occurs only before front suffixal vowels–forms like [stɨndʒ-átʃj] are impossible. This is consistent only with the idea that a phonotactic constraint identical or related to the one triggering the alternation in inflection distributes the stem allomorphs in derivation.

10.2.3.5 *Lexical counts* We now verify on a larger scale the existence of the suffix selection effect seen in the preceding sections. A set of 157 derived verbs from k/g-final stems was assembled from the dictionaries DEX (2002) and *Dictionar Invers* (1957). The aim was to have an exhaustive list. Whether the result is exhaustive in a lexicographic sense, it very likely exceeds the limits of any Romanian speaker's active vocabulary. Many of the items found in the *Dictionar Invers* were previously unknown to the author and could not be Googled. They were counted in all cases where a velar-final base for the verb could be identified and where the verb sounded like a possibly usable one.

This survey sought to establish several points: the dispreference for [-í] suffixation in K/K bases compared to K/Tʃ bases; the blockage of K-Palatalization in derivatives from the same K/K bases; and use of palatalized Tʃ-allomorphs only before front suffixal vowels. All points were informally suggested by examples above; all will be predictions of the analysis given below.

We establish first the baseline relative frequency among the three verbalizing suffixes, [-í], [-á], [-uí]. This could be inferred from the frequency of [-í], [-á], [-uí] verbs from bases that end in consonants unaffected by alternations: [r, n, m, ts, ʃ], and the labials [p, b, f, v, m]. (Bases ending in [t/d] and [s/z] are subject to further alternations and are discussed in section 10.4.) A list of 388 derived verbs whose bases end in these consonants was assembled. The list excludes clear loans from French (e.g., [remark-á] 'remark', French *remarquer*) whose assignment to the [-á] conjugation is based on their French inflectional class rather than a preference for [-á]. The relative frequencies of [-í], [-á], [-uí] in this set appear below.

(10.19)   Frequencies of [-í], [-á], [-uí] in native derived verbs from bases ending in non-alternating C's (n=388).

[-í]-verbs	57%
[-a]-verbs	40%
[-uí]-verbs	3%

These figures indicate a preference for [-í] and a strong dispreference for [-uí]. We can encode this by a ranking of affixal preference: Use [-í] ≫ Use [-á] ≫ Use [-uí]. There is nothing in the rankings that predicts the exact numerical pattern of preference. The ratios in (10.19) may be arbitrary, or shaped by other constraints, and the complete analysis will require additional technology, such as the use of stochastic or weighted ranking (Boersma and Hayes 2000).

Against this background, I give next the frequencies [-í], [-á], [-uí] in the 157 verbs surveyed that are susceptible to K-Palatalization of the stem-final C. I divide the verbs into those derived from bases that possess a palatalized allomorph in inflection (K/Tʃ) and those that lack it (K/K).

(10.20)   Distribution of [-í], [-á], [-uí] suffixes as a function of K/Tʃ alternations in the base

	K/Tʃ bases, n=108	K/K bases, n=49	K/Tʃ bases have palatalized allomorphs,
í-verbs	77%	6%	e.g., [kolák]/[kolátʃi̱]
á-verbs	19%	38%	K/K bases lack palatalized allomorphs,
uí-verbs	4%	45%	e.g., [lók]/[lókuri̱]

The distribution of [í], [á], [uí] among the verbs derived from velar-final bases shows a pattern that approaches complementarity: [í] is markedly overrepresented among alternating K/Tʃ bases and substantially underrepresented as a suffix to non-alternating K/K bases. The analysis will predict the underrepresentation effect; the overrepresentation of [í] on K/Tʃ is not incompatible with the analysis but will remain unexplained. It may indicate that in calculating the baseline frequency of verbalizing suffixes we have underestimated the preference for [í].

There are 3 [í] verbs on K/K bases. All three undergo palatalization, e.g., [nimík] 'nothing', [nimík-uri̱] but [nimitʃ-í] 'destroy'. These are lexical exceptions in two senses. First, the use of [í] is normally blocked on K/K nouns and novel derived verbs follow this pattern without exception (e.g., [dig]/[dig-uri̱] 'dike', [in-dig-uí] 'to surround by a dike'). Second, we have seen that in the derivatives of K/K bases the option of blocking palatalization is standard, e.g., [fokist], [frankist]. Verbs like [nimitʃi] are archaisms dating back to stages of the language where the relevant nouns inflected differently: [nimik], in particular, comes from an earlier feminine form, still in occasional use, [nimikʌ] 'small thing, nothing'. As a feminine, [nimikʌ] could have pluralized only as [nimítʃ-i̯] or [nimítʃ-e]. Either form will explain the shape of [nimítʃ-í] 'destroy'. Synchronically, [nimítʃ-í] has become idiosyncratic when [nimíkʌ] dropped out of common use; only its relative frequency allows the verb to survive now in its old form. The discussion of this case simply underscores that even the exceptions to the pattern of inflection dependence have some explanation, in this case a historical one. The phenomenon is, in other words, robust.

Finally, of the 108 K/Tʃ bases in the corpus, none displays the Tʃ allomorph in derivation before anything other than a front vowel. This does not reflect a restriction on the distribution of [tʃ] and [dʒ], which need not be followed by {e, i, j}; cf. [aritʃ] 'hedgehog', [dʒuvaer] 'jewel'. Rather, this is a restriction on the Tʃ-allomorphs of alternating K/Tʃ nouns. It shows that when *ₙKE, the constraint triggering palatalization, is moot, the stem chosen is the velar-final one: [stiŋg-atʃ] (10.18c.), [in-kovrig-a] (10.18f.). This choice can be a markedness effect (e.g. *affricate) or a faithfulness effect, or both. The point of interest is that there is some default dispreference for the use of Tʃ-allomorphs, a dispreference overcome before front-vocalic suffixes, where *ₙKE triggers their selection.

10.3 The analysis

How can we understand inflection dependence? We can approach the question by considering the structure of lexical entries and the way in which the grammar makes use of information they contain.

10.3.1 *Derived lexicon*

We have seen that the grammar remembers which stem allomorphs have been generated in inflection and that it references these, that is, it checks to see if they exist, in derivation. So, in deciding whether to generate the derivative *[stiŋg-ist] or [stindʒ-ist] 'leftist', the grammar checks the inflected forms of [stiŋg-ʌ] 'left' and finds [stindʒ-i̯]. It is normally the function of the lexicon to remember things, so the following proposal emerges: the inflectional morphology assembles and the phonology generates inflected forms for each lexeme. These are then stored in a derived lexicon and made available as reference terms in the generation of other complex forms. Here is a first version of the analysis of palatalization in -ist derivatives which makes concrete the process by which [stɨndʒ-ist] and [fok-ist] are selected: relevant items of the derived lexicon appear in the upper left cell of each tableau.

(10.21) Ident$_{lex}$ [F] ≫ *$_N$KE

•fok-u •fók-urɨ	Ident$_{lex}$[F]	*$_N$KE	•sting-ʌ •stɨndʒ-ɨ	Ident$_{lex}$[F]	*$_N$KE
☞a. [fok-íst]	*!		☞a. stɨndʒ-íst		
b. [fotʃ-íst]		*	b. stɨŋg-íst		*!

For the moment, the constraint Ident$_{lex}$ [F] can be taken to be identical to any Ident F constraint (cf. McCarthy and Prince 1995) and the $_{lex}$-subscript can be ignored.

10.3.2 *Deriving palatalization in the plural*

Plural forms like [stɨndʒɨ] cannot be underlying lexical items: their phonology is predictable. We cannot list the effects of palatalization because we know that the process applies to any novel item as well as to wug words. Thus a Romanian speaker might not know what a [fislag-ʌ] is[6] but he does know that its plural must be [fisladʒ-e] or [fislʌdʒ-ɨ]. The analysis cannot proceed on the assumption that such forms are listed in the core lexicon but it must derive them instead. It must do so in a pass through the phonology that is antecedent to the one represented in (10.21). This earlier pass provides the reference terms used in (10.21). However, deriving the palatalized plurals is impossible with the ranking in (10.21):

(10.22) Deriving palatalization in plurals?

• sting- -ɨ	Ident$_{lex}$ [F]	*$_N$KE
a. stɨndʒ-ɨ	*!	
!☞b. stɨŋg-ɨ		*

The solution will be to split *$_N$KE into a general version, which continues to be outranked by Ident$_{lex}$ [F], and a morpheme-specific one,[7] *$_N$KE$_{pl}$, which penalizes KE sequences specifically assembled by concatenating a stem and a plural suffix. The morpheme-specific version of the phontactic outranks faithfulness:

[6] It is a wug word.   [7] Cf. Pater 2006

(10.23) Deriving palatalization in plurals: a morphemically indexed constraint

• sting–i̯	$^*_N KE_{pl}$	Ident$_{lex}$[F]
☞a. stind͡ʒ-i̯		*
b. stiŋg-i̯	*!	

Evidence that confirms the analysis is the behavior of palatalization in verbs. Productive verbs of the first conjugation – the heirs to the Latin first conjugation – block palatalization. The suffix -ez-/ęaz- that characterizes all singular forms is expected to trigger it but systematically does not:

(10.24) No palatalization in productive verbs

mark-a 'to mark'	Indicative singular	Subjunctive singular
First person	mark-éz	sʌ mark-éz
Second person	mark-éz-i̯	sʌ mark-éz-i̯
Third person	mark-ęáz-ʌ	sʌ mark-éz-e

In unproductive verb classes, including in the first conjugation, palatal alternations occur everywhere one might expect them. Here is a sample paradigm:

(10.25) Palatalization in unproductive verbs

sek-á 'to dry' (trans.)	Indicative singular	Subjunctive singular
First person	sék	sʌ sék
Second person	sét͡ʃ-i̯	sʌ sét͡ʃ-i̯
Third person	sęák-ʌ	sʌ sét͡ʃ-e

Phonologically, forms like [sʌ sét͡ʃ-e] 'that he dry' and [sʌ mark-éz-e] 'that he mark' look like minimal pairs: one undergoes palatalization, the other does not. In fact, the application of palatalization is predictable from the suffix containing the front vocoid: -ez/ęaz never triggers palatalization, while -e and -i̯ always do. This is support for the notion that the application of palatalization in inflection is triggered by morphemically-indexed constraints like $^*_N KE_{pl}$ and, thus, indirectly, it is support for the analysis in (10.23).

The evidence that the palatalized plurals are generated by a morpheme-specific version of $^*_N KE$ should not obscure the continuing role of the general constraint in the system. We will still need the general version $^*_N KE$ to explain the lawful distribution of t͡ʃ/d͡ʒ stem allomorphs before front vocalic derivational suffixes.

10.3.3 *The lexical entries of the derived lexicon*

What is the internal structure of a derived lexical entry? How are the complex items [sting-ʌ] and [stɨndʒ-i̥] recorded in the derived lexicon? What will matter for our analysis is, for the moment, just the possibility of recognizing whether such derived forms are lexically related or not. Lexical relatedness reduces, in sparse models of the lexicon, to pure morphemic identity:[8] [stɨng-ʌ] and [stɨndʒ-i̥] are related in such models if and only if they reduce to one root, when all effects of phonology and morphology have been factored out. But in analyzing inflection dependence we need more than access to the sparse core lexicon; we need, for instance, to know that the complex surface form [stɨndʒ-i̥] exists – not potentially but actually[9] – and that it is related, not accidentally similar, to the root of [sting-ʌ]. Only if they are related does palatalization in one license palatalization in derivatives of the other.

Here is an example that makes the point concrete. The term for 'century, extended time interval' is [vęak], plural [vęák-uri̥]. A plural [vétʃ-i̥] appears in the phrase [pe vétʃ-i̥] 'forever' (lit- "for ages") and relates to the abstract [vetʃ-íe] 'eternity'. Although all phonological differences between [vétʃ-i̥] and [vęák] are due to fully productive processes, speaker intuition and the derivational behavior of [vęák] suggest that [vétʃ-i̥]/[vetʃ-íe] are lexically unrelated to it. The derivatives of [vęák] are those of a K/K noun and do not palatalize, e.g., the derived verb is [vek-uí] 'to live out one's life', not *[vetʃ-í].

Exactly why the noun in [pe vétʃ-i̥] does not count for Romanian speakers as an alternate plural of [vęák] is unclear. The point of the example is simply to illustrate that the analysis of inflection dependence must rely on a very specific understanding of lexical relatedness: the regular, all-purpose plural of one noun is related to its singular; the masculine of one form is related to its regular feminine. Less clearly characterized relations, like that of the contextually restricted plural [vétʃ-i̥] to [vęák], do not appear to qualify and do not license the processes we discuss.

Beyond this, one can envision the structure of the derived lexicon in two ways: one macro-entry could house the entire pool of phonological variants, e.g., the derived stems [stɨŋg-] and [stɨndʒ-], along with syntactic, lexical semantic, and inflectional class information. The other possibility is to assume that the derived lexicon is related or identical to the notion of the access

---

[8] See Stockall and Marantz 2005 for recent discussion.

[9] All productive feminine nouns ending in velars have the *potential* of a palatalized allomorph because all productive feminine plural endings cause palatalization. The singularia tantum like [vlag-ʌ] do not *actually* have such allomorphs because they lack a plural. It is only this fact about actual presence or absence that matters to the phonology of their derivatives.

lexicon (Marslen-Wilson et al. 1994): a modality specific, redundantly specified access set of forms linked to a single, modality neutral, sparsely specified central entry. In our example, the items [stiŋg-] and [stind3-] would be located in the auditory access lexicon, and linked to the central entry /sting/. Whether lexical relatedness is encoded via the concept of macro-entry or by positing links between the related items will not matter here. What will matter though is exactly which forms are accessible in the computation of which other forms.

10.3.4 *Access to the derived lexicon and the cycle*

Thus far we have proposed that morphologically complex items are generated in several passes through the grammar. First, inflected forms are assembled and their phonology is computed, with the results being stored in the derived lexicon. Then, derived forms are assembled, with their phonology computed by reference to the derived lexical items stored on the first pass. Now we consider what type of access to derived information the grammar needs in order to model the inflection dependence effect.

The distinction between a basic and a derived lexicon and the notion that the latter is built in successive passes through the grammar come from Lexical Phonology and Morphology (LPM, Kiparsky 1982). The model motivated by inflection dependence must incorporate these elements.

But LPM, in its rule- and constraint-based versions, also contains a hypothesis about the limited access the grammar has to the derived lexicon. This is the hypothesis of cyclic application initiated by Chomsky, Halle, and Lukoff (1956) and which, for our purposes, can be formulated as follows: when the grammar derives an expression E, it can access as its input only the cyclic outputs of the morphosyntactic subconstituents of E.[10]

In our case, the hypothesis of cyclic application is an obstacle to the analysis: [stind3-i̯] 'left-pl' is not a syntactic subconstituent of [stind3-íst] 'leftist', but the derivation of the latter must be based on knowledge of the former. If, in some way, [stind3-i̯] is declared a syntactic subconstituent of a derivational form like [stind3-íst], then it should also be one for similar derivatives, like [stiŋg-átʃ] 'left-handed', but a cyclic derivation based on first cycle [stind3i̯] predicts overapplication, *[stind3-átʃ].

What we need here is access to multiple derived, lexically-related forms rather than to just the one subconstituent of the larger form under evaluation. This is not a new finding. The need to compute the phonology of complex

---

[10] The Strict Cycle Condition (Mascaró 1976) makes the additional requirement that only the cyclic outputs of the immediate subconstituents of E be consulted.

forms from inflected words that are related to but not nested within them was demonstrated by Kraska-Szlenk (1995) among others:[11] Kraska-Szlenk (1995: 108ff) shows that the stem vocalism of Polish inflected diminutives is determined by the vocalism of the NOM singular form, even though this form is not syntactically or phonologically contained within any of the case forms dependent on it. The data fragment below illustrates how raising of [ɔ] to [u] (normally triggered by underlyingly voiced codas) applies in diminutives if and only if it has lawfully applied in their NOM singular.

(10.26)   Polish stem vocalism in diminutive nouns (Kraska-Szlenk 1995)

	NOM sg	GEN sg	GEN pl
'cow': /krɔv/	kruf-k-a	kruf-k-i	kruv-ek
'ditch': /dɔw/	dɔw-ek	dɔw-k-a	dɔw-k-uf

Raising applies as expected in the NOM sg of 'cow'–before the underlying /v/ of /kruv-ka/–but not in the NOM sg of 'ditch', where the voiced /w/ is not a coda. Raising is not expected to apply in the GEN pl of 'cow', but it applies anyway; it is also expected to apply in the GEN forms of "ditch" but it does not. That is because application or non-application is determined entirely by the NOM sg form, which acts here as an inner cycle. The point is that if this is an inner cycle, it is one without the benefit of syntactic subconstituency. That is also what happens in Romanian [stĭndʒ-ist], which can consult the plural [stĭndʒ-i̯] without containing it.

What is fundamentally new about the Romanian case is that it shows the need to allow grammatical computations freer access to derived lexical items, not only for the purpose of generating uniform paradigms – as in Polish – but also for the purpose of satisfying phonotactic constraints. Romanian also shows the widespread need for such access to the derived lexicon throughout the entire system, rather than limited to a small subparadigm. The entire derivational system works by consulting the phonology of the derived inflected items, as suggested for Palatalization in section 10.2 and below, in section 10.4, for other processes.

If the architecture of the cycle is generally insufficient to model the phonological dependence of derived lexical items on each other, we still need additional mechanisms that bring back the cycle in the cases where a liberalized access to the derived lexicon overgenerates. These will be discussed in 10.3.6.

---

[11] See also Burzio (1996); Steriade (1999a, b); Albright (2002); Pertsova (2004) for cases with a similar character.

10.3.5 *How the grammar uses lexical resources: LexP constraints*

The grammar we assume uses correspondence constraints (McCarthy and Prince 1995) to verify that the properties of the candidates evaluated find correspondents in the properties of lexically-related listed forms. Correspondence constraints were formulated, however, on the assumption that for each candidate there is exactly one relevant, underlying or derived, input form.

Here we have seen the reason why this cannot be maintained in the general case. Thus, when [stɨndʒ-íst] is computed, its [dʒ] is sanctioned by the [dʒ] found in the plural [stɨndʒ-i̯]. However, the grammar was not specifically looking for the plural in computing [stɨndʒ-íst] – there would be no syntactic or semantic reason to look for a plural–rather, it was looking for any listed form that might contain a [dʒ], and just found that one. The kind of correspondence constraints we need check candidate properties not against one specific item but against a pool of lexically-related items and are satisfied if at least one form in the pool provides the correspondent. I call these constraints LexP constraints (Steriade 1999a, b) and identify them here by the subscript $_{lex}$. These differ from standard correspondence constraints in just this respect that they are satisfied if any one in a larger list of inputs provides the correspondent property. Ident$_{lex}$ [±F] is defined below; to understand how it operates, we re-examine one of the tableaux in (10.21).

(10.27)   Ident$_{lex}$ [αF]: For any segment s in a subconstituent C of an expression under evaluation, if s is [αF] then s has an [αF] correspondent in a listed[12] allomorph of C.

• {sting-; stɨndʒ} • {-ist}	Ident$_{lex}$[F]	*$_N$KE
☞a. stɨndʒ-íst		
b. stiŋg-íst		*!

Candidate (a.) in (10.27) satisfies Ident$_{lex}$ F in the following way. It contains two subconstituents, a stem and an affix. Every segment in the stem subconstituent of [stɨndʒ-íst] has a featurally identical correspondent in the [stɨndʒ] allomorph of the stem, and every segment in the suffix has a featurally identical correspondent in the one allomorph of the suffix. Candidate (b.) satisfies (10.27) in the same way but by reference to the [stiŋg] allomorph.

Nothing prevents, in principle, different elements in an expression from finding their listed correspondents in different listed allomorphs. This case is encountered in English, e.g., *buréaucrat-ism* takes its stem stress from that of

---

[12] *Listed* means listed in the core or the derived lexicon and is consistent with predictable properties.

bureáucracy but its t-final from *búreaucràt*. Relevant cases are also encountered in French liaison (Steriade 1999a, b). The phenomenon has been dubbed "the split-base effect": the elements of one surface stem originate in two distinct listed allomorphs, or bases, of it. Romanian does not offer comparable phenomena in the cases discussed here but the analysis of agent nouns like [vʌz-ʌ-tór] 'one who sees' requires reference to several distinct verbal forms: the present participle [vʌz-í-nd] supplies the stem consonantism while the infinitive [ved-ɛá] supplies the height of the theme vowel (Steriade 2003). The split-base effect is the predicted consequence of the use of LexP constraints, so its verified existence confirms the general lines of the analysis. Militating against the combination of elements from distinct listed allomorphs, there are also constraints promoting strict identity of the surface stem to just one listed form. These are discussed in greater detail in Steriade (1999b) on the basis of French data.

Other correspondence constraints are defined analogously to Ident$_{lex}$ [aF]. DEP$_{lex}$ appears in (10.28):

(10.28)   DEP$_{lex}$: For any segment s in some subconstituent C of a candidate expression, s has a correspondent in a listed allomorph of C.

The status of MAX in this system is less straightforward. If a surface candidate has potentially more than one lexically-listed correspondent then the question is what circumstances will satisfy MAX. Suppose MAX$_{lex}$ is formulated as below:

(10.29)   MAX$_{lex}$: Given a subconstituent C of a candidate expression, if C has a set S of listed allomorphs {A1, A2, ... An}, then every segment in each member of S has a correspondent in C.

This condition is violated unless every segment in each listed allomorph shows up in the unique surface candidate of the subconstituent C. To see how this might work, consider the hypothetical evaluation of MAX$_{lex}$ in *brotherly*, making the assumption that *brother* and *brethren* are the listed allomorphs of the stem. Neither *brotherly* nor **brethrenly* satisfy MAX$_{lex}$ on the definition in (10.29) because either form misses a segment or more from the other one of the two listed stems. The danger associated with (10.29) is that it will promote candidates like **brotherenly*, whose stem combines the segments of both stems. No comparable cases exist, to my knowledge, and this suggests that (10.29) is never active, so the wrong constraint. The alternative is a version of MAX that requires at least one listed allomorph to be such that each of its segments find a surface correspondent in the candidate.

(10.30) MAX_{lex}: Given a subconstituent C of a candidate expression, if C has a set S of listed allomorphs {A1, A2, ... An}, then at least one member of S is such that every segment in it has a correspondent in C.

The constraint in (10.30) will have to be tested against systems in which stem variants involving segment deletion arise routinely. Leaving aside this case, the purpose of this section has been to indicate that it is feasible to reformulate correspondence constraints on the assumption that candidates are compared to a set of potential input correspondents rather than to only one.

10.3.6 *The cycle again*

Until now, the case was made here for allowing grammar greater access to the derived lexicon in computing new forms. I consider now the class of well-known cases that seem to argue to the contrary, that is, that the only accessible phonological information in computing some form is found in the cyclic outputs of its subconstituents. Such cases represent the empirical evidence for the cyclic claim outlined earlier, namely that, in deriving an expression E, the grammar can access only the cyclic outputs of E's subconstituents. The purpose of this section is to make this type of evidence compatible with the proposals motivated here by inflection dependence.

Consider Levantine Arabic *fihím-na* 'he understood us'. A large body of literature (Brame 1974; Kenstowicz and Abdul Karim 1982; Kager 1999; Kiparsky 2000) has discussed the fact that, in forms like this, reference to cyclic subconstituents explains the otherwise unexpected failure of syncope on the first syllable: stressless non-final [i] should have deleted, given syncope's general mode of application, yielding **fhím-na*. The cycle, in an OT grammar equipped with correspondence, explains the blockage of syncope in *fihím-na* by comparing this form with its immediate stem subconstituent *fíhim* 'he understood'. Syncope does not apply in *fíhim* because one [i] is stressed and the other is in a closed syllable. Faithfulness to *fíhim* blocks syncope in *fihím-na*.

The question for us is what causes *fihím-na* to choose to be faithful to just the one stem allomorph *fíhim* when other stem variants are also available: these other forms arise from the application of syncope to other verbal forms, where one or the other of the two [i]'s are unprotected by stress or closed syllables. We will consider just one of these allomorphs, that of *fhím-t* 'I understood'. Here stress falls on the extra-heavy final syllable, leaving the initial unstressed [i] ready to syncopate: /fihim-t/ → [fhímt]. Now, in any constraint-based account of these data, syncope is promoted by a constraint that's satisfied in *fhím-t* and violated in *fihím-na*. It is violated in the latter under the compulsion of a higher-ranked faithfulness condition which requires the stressed vowel of the base *fíhim* to have a correspondent in its derivative *fihím-na*.[13] The situation is depicted in (10.31), making the assumption that *fíhim* 'he understood' is the only input in computing *fihím-na*.

(10.31)   Selecting *fihím-na*: evaluation based on a single accessible stem allomorph

fíhim	MAX stressed V	Syncope trigger
☞ fihím-na		*
fhím-na	*!	

Consider now what happens when we make available to the grammar of Levantine multiple-stem allomorphs: the attested *fihím-na* seems no longer able to win. That is because the alternative *fhím-na* – based on the stem of *fhím-t* – satisfies both MAX stressed V (under the only conceivable lex-version of this constraint, in (10.33)) and the phonotactic triggering syncope.

(10.32)   Selecting *fihím-na*: evaluation based on all stem allomorphs attested in inflected verb forms

{fíhim, fhím-}	MAX$_{lex}$ stressed V	Syncope trigger
fihím-na		*!
!☞ fhím-na		

(10.33)   MAX$_{lex}$ stressed V: Given a subconstituent C of a candidate expression, if C has a set S of listed allomorphs {A1, A2, ... An}, then at least one member of S is such that its stressed vowel has a correspondent in C.

What prevents then 'he understood us' from being realized as *fhím-na*? The question is generally one about the compatibility between the Romanian system, where phonotactics are satisfied by redistributing stem allomorphs without regard to cyclic restrictions, and the Levantine system, where the same process of stem swapping is blocked. It is not clear that some independent factor differentiates Romanian from Levantine; so it is not clear why the two systems must differ as they do. We will assume then that the difference between them stems from constraint ranking. The mechanism we need, similar to the LexP/M conditions in Steriade 1999b, is tentatively introduced here. It requires both a better understanding of syntactic structure and a comparison between

[13]   *Fhím-t* lacks such a base. Its stem *fhím* is an uninflected verb form lacking stress properties.

pairs of systems that are more similar than Romanian and Levantine, but a proposal is spelled out here in the interest of having a concrete possibility before us.

The general idea is that of a constraint that promotes phonological identity between morphosyntactically identical expressions. So, in the case of *fihím-na* 'he understood us' the stem *fihím-* is syntactically identical to the isolation *fihím* 'he understood': both represent the exponents of the third person singular perfect. Syncope in *fihím-na* is inhibited in order to signal through phonological identity the syntactic identity of the inner stem to the third singular verb *fihím*. Had syncope applied, the result **fhim-na* would contain a stem that is phonologically identical not to the third singular but to the stem of the first singular verb. What we need then is a system of conditions penalizing the phonological divergence between syntactically identical expressions.

To formulate our constraint, we need to make precise the notion of morphosyntactic identity that conditions phonological identity. We will assume that syntactic properties like person, number, aspect, and case are represented as syntactic feature values. The stem of a plural noun will thus be referred to as being [+plural], that of a first singular verb will be marked as [+participant, +speaker] (Halle 1997). Candidates being evaluated and listed stems will differ potentially in their feature specifications. We will assume that the candidate stem is specified strictly for syntactic properties of the stem constituent, ignoring information contributed by the larger syntactic context in which the stem occurs. So the verb stem *fihím-* of *fihím-na*, when viewed as a candidate, is assumed to be marked as $[-\text{participant}_{subj}, -\text{speaker}_{subj}, +\text{singular}_{subj}]$ (that is, as having a third person singular subject) and it will bear no specification corresponding to the person and number of any object argument. Information about the object argument is outside the domain of the stem. When considered, however, as an item of the derived lexicon, as a potential reference term, the stem will be assumed to carry syntactic information provided by the immediate context, whenever this information is not incompatible with stem-internal information. Thus, the stem *fhim-* of *fhim-t* will be specified as first person singular based on information provided by the first person singular suffix -t and given the absence of incompatible person/number information present on the stem itself. Similarly, the stem [stind͡ʒ] of the Romanian plural [stind͡ʒ-i̯] will be specified as plural, based on information provided by the plural suffix and given the absence of incompatible information inherent in the stem.

Granted these assumptions about syntactic feature specifications in the stem, the general proposal is that a candidate stem must stand in correspondence to any lexically-related listed expression possessing the same set of syntactic specifications. The condition promotes global correspondence between the two expressions, based on their syntactic identity. Once correspondence is established, the detailed aspects of phonological identity – segment-to-segment correspondence, featural, and prosodic identity – are handled by standard one-to-one correspondence constraints like MAX, DEP, Ident, etc. Our condition establishing global correspondence between syntactically identical expressions appears below:

(10.34) Given a subconstituent C of a candidate expression characterized by a set of syntactic specifications $\{[\alpha F], [\beta G]..., [\gamma H]\}$, C stands in correspondence to that one of its listed allomorphs that is characterized by the same set of syntactic feature values.

In the Levantine case, the correct result is obtained by letting (10.34) and the standard correspondence constraint MAX stressed V (as distinct from the MAX$_{lex}$ constraint in (10.33)) outrank the syncope trigger constraint. (10.34) selects *fihim* as the derived lexical item standing in correspondence with the stem of 'he understood us'. (10.34) excludes as a correspondent the stem *fhim-* of first person *fhim-t*: This stem has been marked as first person singular and is thus syntactically non-identical to the stem of 'he understood us'. Having established correspondence between *fihim* and the stem of 'he understood us', the ranking of MAX stressed V over the syncope trigger blocks the deletion of the initial [i] and selects *fihim-* as the stem of *fihim-na*. (Stress is determined entirely by the phonotactics and will not concern us here.) Below stems are given subscript indices to mark correspondence relations:

(10.35) Effect of (10.34) in selecting *fihim-na* over *fhim-na*

• fihim$_i$- [−participant$_{subj}$, −speaker$_{subj}$] • fhim$_j$- [+participant$_{subj}$, +speaker$_{subj}$]	(10.34)	MAX stressed V	Syncope trigger
☞ fihím$_i$ - na			*
fhím$_i$ - na		*!	
fhím$_j$ - na	*!		

In Romanian, the effect of (10.34) is to establish correspondence between the stem of [stǐndʒ-ist] and the listed allomorph [stiŋg] of [stǐng-ʌ] 'left' on the grounds that both are non-plural. Then if (10.34) and Ident strident outrank the phonotactic *$_N$KE, we would predict *[stiŋg-ǐst], a sort of cyclic identity effect. The actual outcome [stǐndʒ-ist] can be modeled by ranking *$_N$KE above Ident strident or above (10.34). Of the two available rankings that select [stǐndʒ-ist], we choose the former. The limited extent of linguistic variation we have observed does not require that (10.34) be anything but undominated. Ident$_{lex}$ strident dominates $^*_N$KE, as argued earlier, and thus continues to play a key role in prohibiting forms like [foʧ-íst], on non-alternating [fók], [fók-urȷ].

(10.36) $^*_N$KE $\gg$ Ident strident selects [stɨndʒ-ist] over [stɨng-ist]

•sting$_i$- [−plural] • stɨndʒ$_j$- [+plural]	(10.34)	Ident$_{lex}$ strident	$^*_N$KE	Ident strident
sting$_i$-íst			*!	
stɨndʒ$_j$-íst	*!			
stɨndʒ$_i$-íst				*

The discussion of cyclicity can now be summarized. I have proposed a mechanism that establishes correspondence under syntactic identity between expressions listed in the (derived or underlying) lexicon and subconstituents of expressions being evaluated. As is standard under the theory of Correspondence, correspondent elements need not be identical. They are non-identical under rankings in which a constraint like (10.34), which establishes global correspondence, and some competing phonotactic outrank individual correspondence constraints like MAX or Ident. Consistent with this, the analysis of [stɨndʒ-íst] in (10.36) establishes correspondence between the stem of this noun and the singular stem of 'left' [sting-]: lack of identity between the correspondent stems is generated by the ranking $^*_N$KE $\gg$ Ident strident. Cyclic identity arises only when an individual correspondence constraint like Ident outranks the competing phonotactic.

The proposal sketched here succeeds in finding the common ground between standard cases of cyclicity and the newly found phenomenon of inflection dependence. It upholds the claim made earlier that the grammar has broader access to the derived lexicon than previously assumed in the analysis of cyclicity. The appearance of restricted access – for example, the appearance that *fihím-na* is computed by a grammar that can consult *fihím* but not *fhím-t* – emerges under just one of several possible rankings between correspondence and phonotactics. If the ranking of the Syncope trigger and MAX stressed V in (10.35) is reversed, the grammar generates *fhím-na*; and if constraint (10.33), MAX$_{lex}$ stressed V, becomes active in a Levantine-type system, then syncope in hypothetical *fhím-na* becomes possible just for roots in which a subject-inflected form of the verb, e.g., *fhím-t*, has undergone syncope of the initial vowel. Thus, only a couple of rankings differentiate systems that appear as radically different as Romanian and Levantine.

10.4 Inflection-dependence and related beyond K-Palatalization

In addition to Palatalization, several other phonological processes operate at various levels of productivity in Romanian phonology. This section
presents evidence that some of them are inflection-dependent in ways that
are substantially identical to those documented for Palatalization. The purpose is not to provide an exhaustive analysis of the system but to hint
at the generality of the phenomenon described here. The fact that we are
in the presence of a general phenomenon here is also suggested by the
existence of something like inflection dependence in Italian (Burzio 1996),
where the irregular application of Palatalization in inflection (e.g., *comico,
comi[tʃ]-i* 'comical'; vs. *antico, anti[k]-i* 'old, antique') mirrors the possibilities for Palatalization in derivation (e.g., *comi[tʃ]-ità* 'comicalness'; *anti[k]-ità*
'antiquity').

10.4.1 *Segmental alternations: Assibilation and S-Palatalization*

Alveolar stops become stridents–voiceless [ts] and voiced [z]–before [i] in
derived environments; the fricatives [s], [z] becomes palatoalveolar [ʃ], [ʒ]
in the same context. The examples below come from declension; comparable
alternations arise in verbal inflection:

(10.37)   Assibilation and S-Palatalization

Assibilation	t → ts/_[−back, +high]	frát-e fráts-i̯	'brother'	'-pl'
	d → z/_[−back, +high]	vérd-e vérz-i̯	'green, masc'	'-pl, masc'
S-Palatalization	s → ʃ/_[−back, +high]	supús supúʃ-i̯	'subject, masc'	'-pl, masc'
	z → ʒ/_ [−back, +high]	viteáz vitéʒ-i̯	'brave, masc'	'-pl, masc'

Nouns and adjectives that form their plurals by suffixing [-e] or [-uri] will
have no occasion to assibilate or S-Palatalize. Forms that lack a plural because
they do not inflect (e.g., they are adverbs) will also be non-alternating.
The inflection-dependent status of the processes in (10.37) is established
by comparing the derivatives of nouns/adjectives with [i]-plurals, which
undergo Assibilation and S-Palatalization, with those of otherwise similar
non-alternating items. Here we focus on the derived verbs in -í, -á, -uí. I will
refer to non-alternating nouns and adjectives as T/T and s/s bases, respectively,
and to the alternating ones as T/Ts and s/ʃ bases. We observe below that
the derivatives of T/T and s/s bases do not undergo either Assibilation or
S-Palatalization, in the same way that derivatives of K/K bases do not undergo
K-Palatalization.

(10.38) Derived verbs on T/T bases compared with those of alternating T/Ts
bases

		Base		Verb in -í
a	T/T: Adverb	gáta 'ready'		pre-gʌt-í, *pregʌtsí 'to make ready'
	T/Ts: u/i Adj.	lat-(u) 'wide'	lats-i̯ 'pl'	lʌts-í *lʌtí 'to make wide'
b	T/T: Adverb	amínte 'in mind'		amint-í, *amintsí 'to bring to mind'
	T/Ts: e/i Adj.	kumínte 'wise'	kumínts-i̯ 'pl'	kumints-í *kumintí 'to make wise'

(10.39) Derived verbs on s/s bases compared to those of alternating s/ʃ bases

		Base		Verb in -í
a	s/s: u/uri N	popas 'rest'	popás-uri	popos-í, *popoʃí 'to stop and rest'
	s/ʃ: u/i N	pás 'step'	páʃ-i	pʌʃ-í, *pʌsí 'to step'
b	s/s: numeral		ʃás-e 'six'	in-ʃes-í, *inʃeʃí 'multiply by six'
	s/ʃ: u/i Adj.	sʌnʌtós 'healthy'	sʌnʌtóʃ-i̯	in-sʌnʌtoʃ-í, *insʌnʌtosí 'recover'

Lexical counts support the idea that the contrasts above reflect systematic
restrictions. For reasons of space, we will consider just the applicability of
Assibilation in T/Ts bases like [kumínte]/[kumínts-i̯] compared to T/T bases
like [amínte]. Of the 90 [-í] derived verbs based on T/Ts bases, fully 85%
undergo Assibilation in derived verbs, so 85% of these verbs behave phonologically like [a kumints-í] 'to make wise'. By contrast, only 5% of the [-í] verbs
derived from the T/T bases (n=65) undergo Assibilation: the vast majority of
the non-alternating verbs block Assibilation. Second, we observe that the [í]
verbal suffix is underrepresented in derivatives of T/T bases, which tend to
prefer non-assibilating suffixes like [á] and [uí]; by contrast, [í] is somewhat
overrepresented in derivatives of T/Ts bases. So, of the 243 derived verbs surveyed that are susceptible to Assibilation of the stem-final C, 79% of the verbs
derived from T/Ts bases (n = 101) use the assibilating suffix [í]. As we have
seen, the majority do assibilate. Only 46% of the verbs derived from T/T bases
use [í], and, as indicated above, most of these do not assibilate. So inflection
dependence works, in the case of Assibilation, both to limit assibilation to the
derivatives of alternating T/Ts verbs and to limit assibilating suffixes to those
same bases.

The deviations from a categorical 100%-0% distribution of Assibilation
across the two classes of [-í] verbs are lexical exceptions: thus, [dovád-ʌ],
[dovéz-i̯] 'proof' is exceptional in having as derived verb [doved-í] 'to prove'
as against expected *[dovez-í]. Conversely, the verb [in-suflets-í] 'to breathe
life into' shows Assibilation despite the fact that its u/e base [súflet], [súflet-e]
'breath, soul' lacks it. These cases are relatively rare and many have diachronic
explanations. The current analysis cannot encode them without appeal to
some form of exception feature, which I leave unspecified. The clear prediction

of our analysis is that novel [-í] verbs follow the general trend and assibilate only if their inflected base already has. Although this is not yet verified on a larger scale, I can report anecdotally that a nonce verb like [rinz-í] is uninterpretable as based on the T/T form [rind], [rind-uri̯] 'row': its only conceivable [d]-base is a non-existent noun like [rind], [rinz-i̯].

10.4.2 *Overview of inflection dependence*

In the previous section, I have shown that two more processes display the symptoms of inflection dependence found initially for K-Palatalization. To put this information in broader perspective, one can add that Assibilation, K- and S-Palatalization are the most productive consonantal alternations operating in inflection and, in principle, applicable in derivational contexts as well. This finding suggests then that, at least for consonants, inflection dependence is a central mechanism operating in Romanian grammar. It is characterized, in its general form, by the ranking in (10.40a.) below, where F(C) refers to any consonantal feature and *F(C)/K to any phonotactic constraint targeting a consonantal feature in some context K.[14] The ranking in (a.) states that the Ident$_{lex}$ constraint for any feature F(C) outranks the phonotactic. This describes the inflection dependence effect, the impossibility of C-alternations generated in derivation for nouns that fail to alternate in the same way in inflection. For the subset of C-phonotactics studied here, we have established also the class of rankings summarized in (b.). This describes the absence of cyclicity effects, that is, the potential phonotactically-driven dissimilarity between correspondent stems (as defined by (10.34)) with respect to values for consonantal features F(C).

(10.40)   a.   Ident$_{lex}$ F(C) ≫ *F(C)/K

b.   *F(C)/K ≫ Ident F(C)

Under the opposite ranking to (10.40b.)–Ident F(C) ≫ *F(C)/K–correspondent stems must have identical values for the features of their C's. This would describe a system in which, say, [sting-ʌ, stindʒ-i̯] has only derivatives like *[sting-íst], with the [g] of the non-plural inflectional stem kept identical to the [g] of its derivational correspondent. Cases of this sort probably do occur in Romanian, for alternations that we have not considered; their analysis requires considerably more space than we have available here and is left to future discussion.

---

[14] The notion that a phonotactic constraint targets a specific feature is adopted from Wilson (2001) and left here unformalized: K-Palatalization targets the C-features [dorsal] and [strident] and not the V-feature [−back] because it has the effect of modifying the former and not the latter.

For vocalic alternations, inflection dependence is harder to document, in part because the processes triggering vocalic alternations in inflection and derivation are distinct. In at least two cases, it is very likely that vocalic processes are not inflection-dependent: the raising of [a] to [ʌ] (illustrated by (10.41a.)) and the compression of the diphthongs [ɛa], [ǫa] to [e], [o] (in (10.41b.)) happen productively regardless of whether the base noun displays these alternations in inflection.

(10.41) Vocalic alternations are not inflection-dependent:

		Base		-í verb
		Singular	Plural	
a	Class u/urį	ʒáf 'robbery'	ʒáf-urį	ʒʌf-uí, *ʒaf-uí 'to rob'
	Class ʌ/urį	blán-ʌ 'fur'	blʌn-urį	ìm-blʌn-í, *ìm-blan-í 'line with fur'
b	Class ʌ/e	glǫát-ʌ 'crowd'	glǫát-e	in-glot-í, *ingloatí 'to crowd'
	Class ʌ/į	grǫap-ʌ 'grave'	gróp-į	ìn-grop-á, *ìngrǫapá, 'to bury'

The vowel [a] raises before high vowels in the plural of feminine nouns (e.g., blán-ʌ/blʌn-urį]) and in stressless syllables ([ìm-blʌn-í], on [blán-ʌ]). Raising of [a] happens not only in the derivatives of alternating nouns like [blán-ʌ] but also to nouns like [ʒáf], which have no occasion to alternate in inflection; [ʒáf] is neuter and thus not subject to the [a]-[ʌ] raising found in plural feminines but it does raise to [ʒʌf-] when stressless, in derivatives like [ʒʌf-uí]. The same pattern is found with diphthongal alternations: [o] is expanded to [ǫa] under stress, before a non-high vowel, and this yields alternations like [gróp-į] (no expansion) vs. [grǫáp-ʌ] ([o] expands to [ǫá] before non-high [ʌ]). In feminine nouns of the ʌ/e declension (e.g., [glǫát-ʌ, glǫát-e]) both the singular and the plural are eligible for expansion and the vocalism is then invariant in inflection. Both alternating [o]/[ǫá] and non-alternating [ǫá]/[ǫá] nouns are able to alternate in their derivatives, so the expansion process is not inflection-dependent.

Both the details and the rationale of this difference between consonantal and vocalic processes are yet to be explored. For a native speaker, the intuition is that the vocalic alternations in (10.41) generate only minimal dissimilarity between stem variants compared to the C-alternations discussed in the rest of this study, so it seems intuitively possible to recover [ʒaf] from the stem [ʒʌf]- of a verb like [ʒʌf-uí] but not [fok] from a stem variant [fotʃ] of hypothetical *[fotʃ-ist]. This conjecture that the basis for inflection dependence relates to mechanisms of similarity computation awaits further elaboration.

10.4.3 *Use of plural stems in other contexts*

The avoidance of hiatus and the preference for polysyllabic stems leads to another use of plural stems in non-plural contexts. This section outlines the evidence.

(10.42) illustrates feminine stems in [l], related to [l-e] plurals, occurring before vowel-initial derivational suffixes.

(10.42)   The plural stem in _C before vowel-initial derivational suffixes:

Singular	Plural	Derivative with V-initial suffix	gloss
stẹá[15]	sté-l-e	stel-úts-ʌ, *ste-úts-ʌ	'star, little star'
likẹá	liké-l-e	likel-ízm, *like-ízm	'scoundrel, scoundrelism'
zi	zí-l-e	zil-iʃǫár-ʌ	'day, little day'

The roots in (10.42) do not end in /l/ and [l]-insertion is not a general solution to hiatus but a lexically specific one. Only nouns that have [l] before plural vowel-initial suffixes use it before derivational suffixes.

(10.43)   Nouns lacking plural stems in _C

Singular	Plural	Derivative with V-initial suffix	gloss
Manike-w	(Manike-j)	manike-ízm, *manikel-izm	'Manichee, Manichaeism'
ví-e	ví-i̯ /vi-i/	vi-iʃǫár-ʌ, *vil-iʃǫarʌ	'vineyard, little vineyard'
í-e	í-i̯ /i-i/	i-iʃǫár-ʌ, *il-iʃǫar-ʌ	'shirt, little shirt'

A sketch of the analysis of this case appears below, using the constraint $DEP_{lex}s$ (10.28).

(10.44)

$[zil-e]_{pl}$, $[zi]_{sg}$	$DEP_{lex}s$	*HIATUS	$[vi-i̯]_{pl}$, $[vi-e]_{sg}$	$DEP_{lex}s$	*HIATUS
☞a. $[zil]_{sg}$ iʃǫarʌ			☞ a. $[vi]_{sg}$ iʃǫarʌ		*
b. $[zi]_{sg}$ iʃǫarʌ		*!	b. $[vil]_{sg}$ iʃǫarʌ	*!	

A different consideration that calls for the frequent use of the plural stem in derivatives is the rhythmic preference for stems having at least two syllables before the tonic. This is illustrated by alternations between the suffix allomorphs [-i.ǫárʌ]/[-i.ór] ('Diminutive fem/masc', after one syllable) vs. [-i̯ǫárʌ]/[-i̯ór] ('Diminutive fem/masc', after stems with two or more syllables):

---

[15] The underlying structure is /st-e/, with regular lengthening and diphthongization of final [e] → [ea] under stress. What is phonologically unpredictable is the presence of [l] as hiatus breaker in the plural.

(10.45) Satisfying stem minimality:
Glide/vowel alternations in [ior]~[i̯or]/ [i̯oarʌ]~[i̯oarʌ]

Monosyllabic stems	Disyllabic stems	Trisyllabic stems
sur-i.o̯árʌ 'sister-DIM'	ini.m-io̯á.rʌ 'heart-DIM'	prepeli.tʃ-io̯á.rʌ 'quail-DIM'
frʌts-i.ór 'brother-DIM'	dulʌ.p-i̯ór 'cupboard-DIM'	nʌzdrʌvʌ.n-i̯ór 'smart-DIM'

This preference is pervasive in Romanian morphology and triggers a wide range of otherwise inexplicable allomorphic choices (Steriade 2003). The derivatives of monosyllabic nouns of the u/uri declension like [vint(u)]/[vint-ur-i̯] 'wind' satisfy it by selecting as their stem the plural stem in -ur-, which extends the pre-tonic string by one syllable (10.46).

(10.46) The plural stem extension -ur- used to satisfy stem minimality

Singular	Plural	Derivatives	glosses
vint(u)	vint-ur-i̯	vint-ur-á, *vint-á, vint-ur-él, *vint-él	'wind, shake in the wind,' 'wind-DIM'
val	val-ur-i̯	vʌl-ur-él, *vʌl-él	'wave, wave-DIM'
frig	frig-ur-i̯	in-frig-ur-á,- *frig-a, frig-ur-él, *frig-él	'cold, make cold,' 'cold-DIM'

The diminutive suffix observed in (10.46) is [-el], not [-ur-el]. The 1957 edition of *The Romanian Academy's Reverse Dictionary* ("*Dictionar Invers*") lists 36 diminutive forms ending in [-ur-el]. All but one come from monosyllabic stems that form their plurals with the [-ur] extension. This means that only words with [-ur-i̯] plurals have the option of suffixation to the [-ur]-stem:

(10.47) The plural stem extension [-ur] is not used if the base lacks an [-ur] plural

Singular	Plural	Derivatives	gloss
alb	alb-i̯	alb-í, alb-él, *alb-ur-í, *alb-ur-él	'white, whiten, white-DIM'
lung	lundʒ-i̯	lundʒ-í, lundʒ-él, *lung-ur-í *lung-ur-él	'long, lengthen, long-DIM'
albástr-u	albáʃtr-i̯	albʌstr-él, , *albʌstr-ur-él	'blue, blue-DIM'
gálben	gálben-i̯	gʌlben-él, *gʌlben-ur-él	'black, black-DIM'

Polysyllabic roots with [-ur] plurals also fail to use the [-ur] extension in derivation:

(10.48)   The plural stem extension -ur- is not used
if the root is disyllabic or longer

Singular	Plural	Derivatives	gloss
virtéʒ	virtéʒ-ur-i̧	virteʒ-él, *virteʒ-ur-él	'maelstrom, maelstrom-DIM'
postáv	postáv-ur-i̧	postʌv-él, postʌv-jór *postʌv-ur-él	'woolcloth, woolcloth-DIM'

The analysis of these cases follows the pattern illustrated earlier in (10.44). The phonotactic here is the effect of EDGEMOST L (Prince and Smolensky 1993) dominated by *CLASH: together, these require a stress on the initial, provided that no clash ensues with the main stress.[16] The use of the [-ur] extension provides this buffer syllable between the initial and the main stress. I assume the ranking *CLASH, DEP$_{Lex}$ s ≫ EDGE L, although the only critical part of the analysis is that DEP$_{Lex}$ s outrank at least one of the two rhythmic constraints.[17]

(10.49)   Analysis of the contrast between [vʌl-ur-él] and *[alb-ur-él]

Listed: • [val-ur-i̧]$_{pl}$, [val]$_{sg}$ • [él]$_{dim}$	*CLASH	DEP$_{lex}$s	EDGE L
☞ a. [vʌl-ur]$_{sg}$-[él]$_{dim}$			
b. [vʌl]$_{sg}$-[él]$_{dim}$			*!
c. [vʌl]$_{sg}$-[él]$_{dim}$	*!		
Listed: • [alb-i̧]$_{pl}$, [alb]$_{sg}$ • -[él]$_{dim}$	*CLASH	DEP$_{lex}$s	EDGE L
☞ a. [alb]$_{sg}$-[él]$_{dim}$			*
b. [àlb-ur]$_{sg}$-[él]$_{dim}$		*!* (ur)	

A complete analysis must explain the distribution of various diminutive suffixes. In particular, we need to know why longer diminutive suffixes like [-itʃél], [-iʃór] (e.g., [alb-itʃél], [alb-iʃór] 'white-DIM') are not regularly used with monosyllabic stems. I assume that the short diminutive suffix [-él] is the object of a variable preference[18] relative to longer suffixes like [-iʃór]. It is this preference that forces the use of the [ur] extension.

Both *HIATUS and the rhythmic constraints invoked above have widespread, albeit subtle, effects on Romanian phonology. In this section we have observed that these constraints motivate the use of syntactically inappropriate plural extensions in forms where a stem unmarked for number would

---

[16] Secondary stress in Romanian is discussed by Chitoran (2002).

[17] Unlike Chitoran (2002), I find the difference between 0 stress and 2 stress hard to detect. I am not sure if the winner in (10.25b.) is [alb-él] (violating EDGE L) or [àlb-él] (violating *CLASH). I assume, arbitrarily, the former.

[18] Diminutives are productively formed on line. The variable preference for [-él] is seen in the possibility of generating forms like [vinturél] and [albél], as against [vintiʃór], [albiʃór]. The latter are also possible.

normally be expected. This use illustrates the same general point as the phenomena we documented at the beginning of this study: plural stems are made available by the system in order to optimize phonotactic satisfaction.

10.5 The layered lexicon

10.5.1 *Outline of the argument*

The evidence thus far indicates that stems of plural nouns and adjectives are consulted in generating derivatives for these lexemes. The investigation is now extended to other inflected forms and it reveals a difference between the status of plurals and that of other inflections. We use this difference to address a question left unformulated until now: why should the plurals determine the shape of a lexeme's derivatives? The suggested answer will be that plurals are inflectionally diagnostic forms in Romanian–they are invariably more informative than other items in identifying a noun's inflectional type. This section shows that it is the inflectionally diagnostic forms (Albright's 2002 "inflectional bases") that are assembled and phonologically processed first; and it is these derived lexical items that are then consulted in the generation of other derivatives and that of other, less informative, inflectional forms. We will suggest then that the derived lexicon is layered, with information found in the early layers (the plurals) available to be consulted in later layers (derivatives; and non-plural inflected forms) but not the other way around. The layers look superficially similar to the lexical strata of Lexical Phonology and Morphology but differ from the latter in that they do not necessarily correspond to layers of affixation or to layers of syntactic information. Rather derivational priority–which forms are generated "early" and which ones "late"–is a function of morphological informativeness: more informative forms are generated first and consulted by less informative ones.

10.5.2 *Plurals and obliques in feminine paradigms*

In this section I demonstrate a phonological dependence between two inflected nominal forms: the plural and the oblique (GEN-DAT) singular. The dependence involves the applicability of phonological processes (Assibilation, K- and S-Palatalization) in the oblique; only if these processes are observed in the plural is it possible to apply them in the oblique.

10.5.2.1 *Feminine paradigm structure*   In Romanian feminine declensions, the oblique singular forms are generally identical to the plural forms. The identity holds across declension types for regular or suppletive nouns.[19]

---

[19] Feminines forming their plural in [-uri], e.g., [mʌtas-e]/[mʌtʌs-uri] 'silk', deviate from this rule.

(10.50) Identity between singular oblique forms and plurals in feminine nouns and adjectives

	NOM-ACC sg	GEN-DAT sg	Plural	gloss
ʌ/e	run-ʌ		run-e	'rune'
ʌ/i	lun-ʌ		luni-ị	'moon'
e/i	pʌʃun-e		pʌʃun-ị	'pasture'
suppletive	sor-ʌ		suror-ị	'sister'

Masculine nouns and adjectives have a single singular indefinite form and a single, typically distinct, plural, as seen in earlier in (10.5–10.6). They will not be of further interest here.

There are three distinct facets of the formal identity between the feminine plural and the feminine singular oblique. One is the identity of the suffix (e.g., the fact that [ị] appears as both the plural and the GEN-DAT sg suffix in [lun-ị] 'moon'). Another is the identity of the stem (e.g., the fact that [suror]- is the stem allomorph of the plural and GEN-DAT sg). The third is the identity of "rule application" in the two cases, which the following examples illustrate:

(10.51) Stem-allomorph identity between singular oblique and plural in feminine N's and Adjs.

	NOM-ACC sg	GEN-DAT sg	Plural	gloss
ʌ/i	nuk-ʌ		nutʃ-ị	'nut'
ʌ/i	plas-ʌ		plʌʃ-ị	'district'
e/i	kart-e		kʌrts-ị	'book'
ʌ/e	broask-ʌ		broʂt-e	'frog'

Table (10.51) shows that the processes undergone by the GEN-DAT sg form— the K-[20] and S-Palatalization, Assibilation, the raising of [a] to [ʌ]–are identical to those undergone by the plural. This looks like a trivial consequence of the fact that the stem and the suffix forming the oblique singular are identical to those used in the plural; the same segmental ingredients should yield the same alternations. However, it is not trivial. The consonantal alternations do not independently apply in the plural and the oblique; rather they apply in the oblique only if there is a plural form in which they have also applied. This is shown next.

10.5.2.2 *Feminine singularia tantum*   This section focuses on the phonological realization of oblique (GEN-DAT sg) feminine singularia tantum nouns. Proper names and mass nouns are singularia tantum: they lack plural forms

---

[20] [broʂt-e] illustrates the fact that [sk] and [ʃk] become [ʃt] in the contexts of K-Palatalization. This process has not been not discussed here as it almost never applies in derivational morphology.

but not necessarily oblique singulars. In the absence of the plural, we can observe how the processes expected to apply in the oblique operate. The generalization we document is that the obliques of feminine singularia tantum cannot undergo K-Palatalization, Assibilation or S-Palatalization, that is, the consonantal processes we have shown to be inflection-dependent in earlier sections.

10.5.2.2.1 Feminine mass nouns

The behavior of mass nouns is illustrated below by comparing these to formally parallel count nouns. The only difference between the two classes of nouns is that one has a plural form and the other does not. What is constant across the mass nouns seen below is that none undergo Assibilation, K- and S-Palatalization.

(10.52)   Declension of feminine mass nouns (e/i, ʌ/i types) compared to count nouns[21]

	Mass nouns		Count nouns	
	Indefinite	Definite	Indefinite	Definite
NOM/ACC	línt-e 'lentils'	línt-e-a	mínt-e 'mind'	mínt-e-a
GEN/DAT	(*línts-i̯)	línt-e-i̯ (*línts-i-i̯)	mínts-i̯	mínts-i-i̯
NOM/ACC	sét-e 'thirst'	sét-e-a	tʃetát-e 'fortress'	tʃetát-e-a
GEN/DAT	(*séts-i̯)	sét-e-i̯ (*séts-i-i̯)	tʃetʌ́ts-i̯	tʃetʌ́ts-i-i̯
NOM/ACC	vlág-ʌ 'force'	vlág-a	plág-ʌ 'wound'	plág-a
GEN/DAT	(*vlʌ́dʒ-i̯)	vlág-ʌ-i̯ (*vlʌ́dʒ-i-i̯)	plʌ́dʒ-i̯	plʌ́dʒ-i-i̯
NOM/ACC	tus-e 'thirst'	tus-e-a	plás-ʌ 'district'	plás-a
GEN/DAT	(*tuʃ-i̯)	tus-e-i̯ (*tuʃ-i-i̯)	plʌ́ʃ-i̯	plʌ́ʃ-i-i̯

Some of the oblique forms of mass nouns avoid violating the phonotactics triggering Assibilation, K- and S-Palatalization by adjusting the quality of the suffixal vowel: in the definite forms, an expected [i] in the obliques (e.g., [mínts-i-i̯] 'of the mind') is replaced by [e] in mass nouns like [línt-e-i̯] 'of the lentils'. This affixal adjustment occurs only after the alveolars [t], [d], [s]; its purpose is to avoid triggering Assibilation or S-Palatalization, both of which are expected before [i]. After mass nouns ending in a velar, the affixal vowel of the oblique is changed from [e] or [i] to [ʌ]; the latter will not trigger

---

[21]   The morphological structure of (in)definite forms is indicated below: the two morphemes [i] (a clitic marking the definite sg oblique and the plural/oblique suffix) regularly alternate, with [i̯] word-finally and [i] elsewhere.

Root	Case-number suffix	Definite marker	gloss
mint	e		'mind'
mint	e	a	'the mind'
mints	i		'of/to mind', 'minds' (indef.)
mints	i	i̯	'of/to the mind'
mints	i	le	'the minds'

K-Palatalization, nor cause a *KE violation. Indefinite oblique forms of mass nouns seem to lack any acceptable realization but I am not sure if this is a phonological or a syntactic phenomenon. What is constant for all mass nouns like (10.52) is that none displays any consonantal modification relative to the NOM-ACC sg.

10.5.2.2.2 Analysis

The analysis of (10.52) makes the assumption that the plural serves as a reference term in the computation of the GEN-DAT sg, as it does in the computation of derivational forms. The absence of a plural form does not prevent a GEN-DAT sg from being assembled but it does deprive a noun of a palatalized or assibilated listed stem allomorph that could satisfy Ident$_{lex}$F. To offer this explanation for the data in (10.52) we must, however, assume that not all inflected forms are computed at the same time or in the same way. The plural is computed before the oblique form; the plural consonantism is generated by morpheme specific phonotactics *$_N$KE$_{pl}$, *$_N$Ti$_{pl}$ (triggering Assibilation), and *$_N$Si$_{pl}$ (triggering S-Palatalization), while the oblique is generated by the general, and lower-ranked, phonotactics *$_N$KE, *$_N$Ti, and *$_N$Si. Here is the analysis of three relevant cases: a new constraint employed is Affix$_{OBL}$, a cover term for penalties assessed on an inappropriate choice of an oblique affix.

(10.53)   K-Palatalization in the oblique form of [plág-ʌ] (count noun) and [vlág-ʌ] (mass noun)

(a) generating the plural

plag-; -i̭	$_N$KE$_{pl}$	Ident $_{lex}$ F
plʌg-i̭	*!	
☞plʌdʒ-i̭		*

(b) generating the oblique

plag-; plʌdʒ-; -i, -i̭	Ident $_{lex}$	$_N$KE	Affix$_{OBL}$	vlag-; -i, -i̭	Ident $_{lex}$	$_N$KE	Affix$_{OBL}$
☞plʌdʒ-i-i̭				vlʌdʒ-i-i̭	*!		
plʌg-i-i̭		*!		vlʌg-i-i̭		*!	
plág-ʌ-i̭			*!	☞vlág-ʌ-i̭			*

(10.54)   Assibilation in the oblique form of [mínt-e] (count noun) and [línt-e] (mass noun)

(a) generating the plural

mint-; -i̭	$_N$Ti$_{pl}$	Ident $_{lex}$ F
mínt-i̭	*!	
☞mínts-i̭		*

(b) generating the oblique

mint-; mints-; -i, -i̯	Ident lex F	N Ti	Affix OBL	lint-; -i, -i̯	Ident lex F	N Ti	Affix OBL
☞ mínts-i-i̯				línts-i-i̯	*!		
mínt-i-i̯		*!		línt-i-i̯		*!	
mínt-e-i̯			*!	☞ línt-e-i̯			*

(10.55) S-Palatalization in the oblique form of [plás-ʌ] (count noun) and [tús-e] (mass noun)

(a) generating the plural

plas-; -i̯	N Si pl	Ident lex F
plás-i̯	*!	
☞ pláʃ-i̯		*

(b) generating the oblique

plas-; pláʃ-; -i, -i̯	Ident lex F	N Ti	Affix OBL	tus-; -i, -i̯	Ident lex F	N Ti	Affix OBL
☞ pláʃ-i-i̯				túʃ-i-i̯	*!		
plás-i-i̯		*!		tús-i-i̯		*!	
plás-e-i̯			*!	☞ tús-e-i̯			*

10.5.2.2.3 Verifying the analysis

We verify next that the affixal adjustment observed in the preceding section – e.g., the substitution of [línt-e-i̯] for expected [línt(s)-i-i̯] – is strictly due to the threat of phonotactic violation posed by [i]. This is shown by feminine mass nouns ending in non-alternating consonants, and which can display in the oblique form the expected [i] suffix. Note the identity of affix structure between the definite oblique forms of mass and count nouns in the table below.

(10.56) Declension of feminine mass nouns ending in non-alternating C's

	Mass nouns		Count nouns	
	Indefinite	Definite	Indefinite	Definite
NOM/ACC	mi̯ér-e 'honey'	mi̯er-e̯-a	kʌrár-e 'path'	kʌrár-e̯-a
GEN/DAT	(?mi̯er-i)	mi̯er-i-i̯	kʌrár-i	kʌrár-i-i̯
NOM/ACC	lén-e 'sloth'	lén-e̯-a	pʌʃún-e 'pasture'	pʌʃún-e̯-a
GEN/DAT	(?lén-i)	len-i-i̯	pʌʃún-i	pʌʃún-i-i̯
NOM/ACC	fasól-e 'beans'	fasól-e̯-a		
GEN/DAT	(?fasól-i)	fasól-i-i̯		
NOM/ACC	alám-ʌ 'bronze'	alám-a	kírtʃium-ʌ 'pub'	kírtʃium-a
GEN/DAT	alʌm-i	alʌm-i-i̯	kírtʃium-i	kírtʃium-i-i̯

It is not impossible to find forms like [mi̯er-e-i̯], [lén-e-i̯], [alám-e-i̯] alongside [mi̯er-i-i̯], etc. However, there is no ban on the morphologically expected forms in these phonotactically neutral cases. This verifies the central role of the markedness constraints ($*_N$KE, $*_N$Ti, $*_N$Si) and of faithfulness in the analysis of (10.53)–(10.55).

10.5.2.2.4 Plurals as inflectional bases

The evidence presented above of an asymmetric dependence of oblique singulars on plurals argues in favor of an interpretation of inflectional paradigm structure akin to Albright's (2002). I sketch this here in partial answer to a question raised earlier: why do the derivatives of a lexeme consult its plural form? Why do the oblique forms (of feminine nouns) consult the plural?

A possible answer is that across the entire nominal system of Romanian, for all genders and declensions, the NOM-ACC singular (the citation form) and the plural provide indispensable information about the noun's declensional type. If these two forms are known, all other forms of the noun are predictable. The oblique forms of singular masculine nouns are identical to the citation form; the oblique forms of the feminine are identical to the plural; the definite forms can be predicted from the corresponding indefinites, singular or plural, citation or oblique. However, the plural is not predictable from the citation form, nor the other way around. The suggestion then is that the forms assembled and computed first are the informative items of a nominal paradigm, rather than all inflected forms at once.

10.5.2.2.5 Proper names

10.5.2.2.5.1 K-Palatalization in proper names Romanian grammars (e.g., GLR 1966: 89) record an unexplained difference between proper names from the feminine declensions and common nouns. Common nouns palatalize [k], [g] before the oblique endings [-e], [-i̯], as before the plural [-e], [-i̯], but proper names (of persons or places) block palatalization in the oblique. Normally, the feminine plural is identical to the oblique but in proper names these forms diverge; pluralized names exist but, unlike singular obliques, they always undergo palatalization. Relevant data appear below. Romanian proper names follow the definite declension, as in other languages,[22] so to facilitate the comparison I show them side by side with the definite forms of similar common nouns.

(10.57)   K-Palatalization in feminine proper names vs. common nouns

	NOM/ACC sg	GEN-DAT sg	Plural	gloss
a	púi̯k-a	púi̯tʃ-i-i̯ (*púi̯k-ʌ- i̯)	púi̯tʃ-i-le	'little hen'
	Púi̯k-a	Púi̯k-ʌ-i̯, Púi̯k-i-i̯ (*pui̯tʃ-i-i̯)	Púi̯tʃ-i-le	'(woman's name)'

---

[22]   Cf. Elbourne 2005: 172

b	álg-a	áldʒ-e-i̯ (*álg-ʌ- i̯)	áldʒ-e-le	'sea grass'
	Vólg-a	Vólg-ʌ-i̯ (*Vóldʒ-i-i̯)	Vóldʒ-i-le	'(place name, Volga)'
c	doi̯k-a	doi̯tʃ-i-i̯ (*doi̯k-ʌ- i̯)	doi̯tʃ-i-le	'nurse'
	Doi̯k-a	Doi̯k-ʌ-i̯, Doi̯k-i-i̯ (*Doi̯tʃ-i-i̯)	Doi̯tʃ-i-le	'(woman's name)'

Further examples of velar-final proper names are found in (10.58), including masculines in [-a/ʌ]; all of these have obliques in [-ʌi̯] or [-ii̯]. As a rule, they do not palatalize:[23]

(10.58)   Velar-final proper names

    a. Persons' names: [Vói̯ka, Rodíka, Veroníka, Ralúka, Anka, Ilínka, Katínka, Mʌriúka, Kóka, Olga, Rebéka, Frantʃíska]; masculine [-a] nouns: [Lúka, Dúka]. Their obliques: [Vói̯kʌi̯] or [Vói̯kii̯] etc.; [Dúkʌi̯] etc.

    b. Place names: [Méka, Kalúga, Vólga]. Their obliques: [Mékʌi̯] etc.

Two facts must be explained: the lack of palatalization in the singular oblique forms and the fact that the plurals of these names are subject to palatalization.

The analysis starts from the idea that proper names are systematically *singularia tantum*, in the sense that a semantic property of these expressions, perhaps their status as rigid designators,[24] makes it impossible for them to possess a referentially-related plural form. If this is right, the impossibility of K-Palatalization in proper nouns like [Vólg-a] follows and is parallel to that of mass feminines like [vlág-a]. The ranking Ident$_{lex}$F $\gg$ *$_N$KE blocks K-Palatalization in both oblique forms, as neither could have acquired a palatalized allomorph, a plural. The definite oblique of [vlág-a] is, if anything, [[vlág-ʌ]-i̯], and likewise the oblique of [Vólg-a] is [[Vólg-ʌ]-i̯]. In both cases, the inner constituent would normally be expected to contain a palatalizing oblique suffix, [e] or [i], and in both cases that suffix is replaced with the unmarked singular feminine suffix [ʌ] to avoid a violation of *$_N$KE. Using Affix$_{OBL}$ again as a cover term for the constraint that requires an oblique inner suffix in

---

[23] Continent names in -ika—e.g., [Amérika], [Afrika]—deviate from the general rule; their obliques are [Améritʃii] etc., perhaps because they are analyzed as containing the derivational suffix-ik. All new proper names block K-Palatalization, cf. *Toska, Malka, Helga, Vega*.

[24] Kripke 1970.

GEN-DAT forms, we outline the analysis of [[Vólg-ʌ]-i̯] vs. [[áldʒ-e]-i̯] below:

(10.59)   K-Palatalization in oblique singulars:
          Common nouns and proper names

•[alg-ʌ], [aldʒ-e], •-e (oblique marker for feminine nouns) •-i̯ (NP-level clitic marking oblique case)	Ident$_{lex}$ [±F]	*$_N$KE	Affix$_{OBL}$
☞a. [[áldʒ-e]-i̯]			
b. [[álg-e]-i̯]		*!	
c.. [[álg-ʌ]-i̯]			*!

•[Volg-a] •-e (oblique marker for feminine nouns) •-i̯ (NP-level clitic marking oblique case)	Ident$_{lex}$ [±F]	*KE^N	Affix$_{OBL}$
a. [[Vóldʒ-e]-i̯]	*!		
b. [[Vólg-e]-i̯]		*!	
☞c. [[Vólg-ʌ]-i̯]			*

A few names of women have alternate obliques in [i-i̯]: [[Vói̯k-i]-i̯], [[Púi̯k-i]-i̯]. I assume that these are cases where Ident$_{lex}$ [+strid] and Affix$_{OBL}$ outrank *$_N$KE. The constraint Affix$_{OBL}$ is satisfied at the expense of *$_N$KE in these cases. These variants confirm the undominated status of Ident$_{lex}$ [+strid]; despite the variation, proper nouns are constant in shunning K-Palatalization.

10.5.2.5.5.2 *Proper names and their pluralized counterparts* K-Palatalization does apply to pluralized proper names: *two Volgas* are [dóɥʌ vóldʒ-i̯]. Despite this, the palatalized plurals have no effect on the oblique forms of the basic proper name. I show now that this observation is consistent with the analysis developed thus far and that it provides evidence for a derived lexicon with some internal structure, over and above what has appeared to be necessary until now.

Any proper name can give rise to a pluralized form, if only for the purpose of asserting that an individual with some specified property is, or is not, unique: "There are(n't) two X's." I claim that the process of pluralization involves a step of turning the proper name into a common noun, which can then be standardly pluralized. Then the plural [Vóldʒile] 'the Volgas' is the plural not of the name Volga but of a common noun [o Vólgʌ] 'a Volga', whose meaning is 'a thing that shares with Volga some property P {being a large Russian river, having Cossacks sing on its banks, bearing the name [Vólga],...}'. The descriptive predicates in curly brackets will vary with the discourse context, so the statement [Nu egzístʌ dóʉʌ Vóldʒ-i̜] 'there aren't two Volgas' will mean that one of these things, whichever one is determined by context, is unique. Because the singular form of such derived common names as 'a Volga', is rare, one's immediate impression may be that the proper name [Vólga] is the singular of the plural [Vóldʒile] 'the Volgas'. I suggest that the relation is indirect; the proper name is converted into a common noun, by a zero derivation process that alters its referential properties and makes it available for pluralization. The paradigm of the item thus derived is identical to that of any basic common noun. This scenario predicts that, for any proper name, there will be not only a corresponding plural but also a singular common noun. In the context of Romanian phonology, we predict that this common noun should undergo K-Palatalization, as it can have a plural and thus the chance to acquire a palatalized allomorph in inflection. This is verified: 'of a Volga' is [únei̜ Vóldʒi̜], 'of *that* Volga' is [Vóldʒ-i-i̜ ʌlei̜a].

(10.60)   A scenario for pluralizing proper names (PN) via turning them into common nouns (CN) (a description of the referent of each noun appears in slashes):

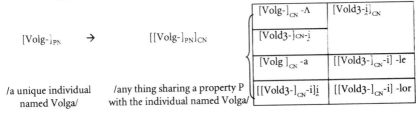

Based on the scenario in (10.60) I propose a property of the grammar that prevents it from palatalizing the oblique forms of proper names like [Vólga]. This property involves the flow of information in the computation of derived lexical items: information about the existence of the plural common noun [Vóldʒ-i̜] is available when the oblique singular form of this plural is computed but is not when the oblique singular form of the original proper name was. The path we must assume through the derived lexicon is outlined below using the example of [alg-a] and [Volg-a], in its proper name and common noun versions. Arrows connecting lexical layers indicate the extent to which information generated in one layer is made available in later ones.

(10.61)   Accessibility of information in the derived lexicon

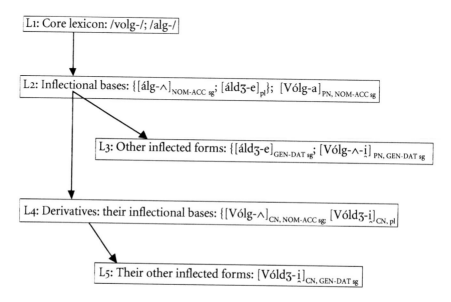

The hypothesis depicted in (10.61) is that the derivatives of a lexeme can consult its inflectional bases–so derivatives of [alg-ʌ] may consult its plural, just like [stɨndʒ-ist] consults [stɨndʒ-i]–but that no information is returned from the lexical layer generating a derivative to any "upstream" layers. Information about the pluralized common noun [vóldʒ-i̥], generated in L4, is not available to L3, where the oblique form of the proper name is computed. Making this assumption, the current analysis can generate both the non-palatalized oblique form of the proper name and the palatalized oblique of the common noun derived from it. Critical to the analysis are the assumption about limited information flow–which makes the pluralized common noun [Vóldʒ-i̥] unavailable to the formation of the proper name's oblique–and the assumption that the plural palatalization constraint $*_N KE_{pl}$ outranks the competing $Ident_{lex}$ constraint.

(10.62) K-Palatalization in oblique singulars: Proper names and common nouns derived from them

a. L3: The oblique of the proper name Volga

• [Vólg-a]PN • -i (oblique marker for feminine nouns) • -i̯ (NP-level clitic marking oblique case)	Ident$_{lex}$ [±F]	*KE^N	Affix$_{OBL}$
a. [[Vóldʒ-e]-i̯]	*!		
b. [[Vólg-e]-i̯]		*!	
☞c. [[Vólg-ʌ]-i̯]			*

b. L4: The plural of the derived common noun Volga

• [Vólg-a] • -i (plural marker for feminine nouns)	*$_N$KE$_{pl}$	Ident$_{lex}$ [±F]	*$_N$KE
☞a. [[Vóldʒ]-i̯]		*	
b. [[Vólg]-i̯]	*!		*

c. L5: The definite oblique singular of the derived common noun Volga 'a Volga'

• [Vólg-a], [Vóldʒ-i] • -i (oblique marker for feminine nouns) • -i̯ (NP-level clitic marking oblique case)	Ident$_{lex}$ [±F]	*$_N$KE	Affix$_{OBL}$
☞a. [[Vóldʒ-i]-i̯]			
b. [[Vólg-i]-i̯]		*!	
c. [[Vólg-ʌ]-i̯]			*!

The analysis sketched above is one among several conceivable ones and is given here in the interest of presenting a complete and completely analyzed paradigm.

10.6 Conclusion

This study has documented in Romanian an inflection-dependence effect. A cohesive class of phonological processes have been shown to apply in morphologically complex forms containing a lexeme L only if the same processes have applied to an inflectional base of L.

I have shown that it is actual application rather than potential applicability that matters: K-Palatalization is potentially applicable to any velar-final noun. But it is not actually applied to plural-less mass nouns like [vlág-ʌ] or to proper names like [Vólg-a]. It is the actual difference between application and non-application that matters, suggesting that the source of the phenomenon of inflection dependence is to be found in the structure of the derived lexicon and in the grammar's mode of accessing it.

The layered lexicon proposed in the last section follows the basic intuitions behind Lexical Phonology and Morphology (LPM), in its classical or OT incarnations. However a substantial departure was motivated here from the model of cyclic application/evaluation which LPM inherits from earlier versions of generative phonology; the phonology needs to reference the shape of inflectional bases that are not necessarily subconstituents (e.g., [stɨndʒ-j], in [stɨndʒ-íst]). This is inconsistent with the cycle as a general model of the phonological dependence between lexically-related expressions. I have proposed a slight modification of Correspondence Theory under which both types of phonological dependence – cyclicity and inflection dependence – can be characterized. The differences between the two types of systems can be seen to arise from minimally different rankings of correspondence and phonotactics.

Finally, on the need to extend access to the derived lexicon, over and above what the cycle allows, a substantial body of work has established this point independently by demonstrating the need to let constraints on paradigmatic contrast (Crosswhite 2001; Kenstowicz 2002; Ichimura 2002; Rebrus and Törkenczy 2004; Hsieh 2005; Ito and Mester 2005; Urbanczyk 2005) carry out a global comparison of inflected forms not contained within each other. Putting together the conclusions of our study with the results of these works should be the next step.

References

Albright, Adam (2002) The identification of bases in morphological paradigms. UCLA Ph.D. thesis, available at http://web.mit.edu/albright/www/.

Bateman, N., and M. Polinsky (2006) 'Romanian as a two-gender language', UCSD ms.

Boersma, Paul, and Bruce Hayes (2000) 'Empirical tests of the gradual learning algorithm'. *Linguistic Inquiry* 32: 45–86.

Brame, Michael (1974) 'The cycle in phonology: Stress in Palestinian, Maltese, and Spanish'. *Linguistic Inquiry* 5, 39–60.

Burzio, Luigi (1996) 'Surface constraints vs. underlying representation', in J. Durand and B. Laks (eds.), *Current Trends in Phonology*. Manchester: European Studies Institute, pp. 123–41.

——— (1998) 'Multiple correspondence'. *Lingua* 104: 79–109.

Chitoran, Ioana (2002) *The Phonology of Romanian*. Mouton de Gruyter

Chomsky, Noam, Morris Halle, and Fred Lukoff (1956) 'On accent and juncture in English', in *For Roman Jakobson*. The Hague: Mouton, pp. 65–80.

Crosswhite, K. (1999) 'Inter-paradigmatic homophony avoidance in two dialects of Slavic', in M. Gordon (ed.), *UCLA Working Papers in Linguistics 1*, pp. 48–67.

Cutler, Anne, N. Sebastián-Gallés, O. and B. Van Ooijen Soler-Vilageliu (2000) 'Constraint of vowels and consonants on lexical selection: Cross-linguistic comparisons'. *Memory and Cognition* 28: 746–55.

Dictionarul explicativ al limbii române (DEX) (2002) Academia RSR (Institutul de lingvistica din Bucuresti), Editura Academiei RSR, Bucuresti.

Dictionar Invers (1957). Institutul de Lingvistica din Bucuresti, Editura Academiei Republicii Populare Romîne.

Elbourne, Paul (2005) *Situations and Individuals*. MIT Press, p. 172.

Flemming, Edward (2002) *Auditory Representations in Phonology*. New York and London: Routledge.

Gordon, Matthew (2002) 'A factorial typology of quantity-insensitive stress'. *Natural Language and Linguistic Theory* 20: 491–552.

Grammatica Limbii române (1963), Editura Academiei R.P.R., Bucuresti.

Halle, Morris (1997) 'Distributed Morphology: Impoverishment and fission', in Benjamin Bruening, Yoonjung Kang, and Martha McGinnis (eds.), *MITWPL 30: Papers at the Interface* Cambridge, MA: MITWPL, pp. 425–49.

Hristea, Theodor, and Cristian Moroianu (2003) 'Generarea formelor flexionare substantivale si adjectivale în limba româna', in Florentina Hristea and Marius Popescu (eds.), *Building Awareness in Language Technology. Papers of the Romanian Regional Information Centre for Human Language Technology*. Editura Universitatii din Bucuresti, pp. 185–202.

Hsieh, Feng-Fan (2005) (forthcoming) 'Winners take all: Missing paradigms in Jinghpo', to appear in the *Proceedings of Western Conference on Linguistics 2006*, California State University, Fresno.

Ichimura, Larry (2006) Anti-homophony blocking and its productivity in transparadigmatic relations, BU Ph.D. thesis.

Ito, Junko, and Armin Mester (2004) 'Morphological contrast and merger: *ranuki* in Japanese'. *Journal of Japanese Linguistics* 20: 1–18.

Kager, René (1999) 'Surface opacity of metrical structure in Optimality Theory', in B. Hermans and M. van Oostendorp (eds.), *The Derivational Residue in Phonological Optimality Theory*. Amsterdam: John Benjamins, pp. 207–45.

Kenstowicz, Michael (2005) 'Paradigmatic uniformity and contrast', in L. Downing, T. Hall, and R. Raffelsiefen (eds.), *Paradigms in Optimality Theory*. Oxford: Oxford University Press, pp. 145–69.

Kenstowicz, Michael and Kamal Abdul-Karim (1980) 'Cyclic stress in Levantine Arabic'. *Studies in the Linguistic Sciences* 10.2: 55–76.

Kihm, Alain (2004) 'The case for one case/one gender in Romanian: A tentative account of Romanian "declension"', Ms., Université Paris 8.

Kiparsky, Paul (1982) 'From cyclic phonology to lexical phonology', in Harry van der Hulst and Noval Smith (eds.), *The Structure of Phonological Representations*, part I. Dordrect: Foris, pp. 131–75.

——— (2000) 'Opacity and cyclicity'. *The Linguistic Review* 17: 351–65.

Kraska-Szlenk, Iwona (1995) The phonology of stress in Polish. Ph.D. thesis, University of Illinois at Urbana-Champaign.

Lombard, Alf, and Constantin Gâdei (1981) *Dictionnaire morphologique de la langue roumaine*. Ed. Acad. Rep. Soc. Romania, Skrifter utgivna av Vetenskaps-Societeten i Lund, 76, Bucuresti.

Marslen-Wilson, W. D., L. K. Tyler, R. Waksler, and L. Older (1994) 'Morphology and meaning in the English mental lexicon'. *Psychological Review* 101: 1, 3–33.

McCarthy, John (2002) 'Comparative markedness'. *Theoretical Linguistics* 29: 1–51.

——— (2005) 'Optimal Paradigm', in L. Downing, T. Hall, and R. Raffelsiefen (eds.), *Paradigms in Optimality Theory*. Oxford: Oxford University Press, pp. 170–210.

——— and Alan Prince (1995), 'Faithfulness and reduplicative identity', in Jill N. Beckmann, Laura Walsh Dickey, and Suzanne Urbanczyk (eds.), *Papers in Optimality Theory*. UMOP 18, 607–36.

Mascaró, Joan (1976) Catalan phonology and the phonological cycle. MIT Ph.D. thesis.

Pascu, G. (1916) *Sufixele Românesti*, Bucuresti: Editiunea Academiei Române.

Pater, Joe (forthcoming) 'The locus of exceptionality: Morpheme-specific phonology as constraint indexation', to appear in S. Parker (ed.), *Phonological Argumentation*. London: Equinox Publications.

Pertsova, Katya (2005) 'How lexical conservatism can lead to paradigm gaps', in Jeff Heinz, Andy Martin, and Katya Pertsova (eds.), *UCLA Working Papers in Linguistics, no 11, Papers in Phonology 6*.

Popescu, Alexandra (2000) Morphophonologische Phänomene des Rumänischen. Ph.D. Dissertation, Heinrich-Heine-Universität, Düsseldorf.

Prince, Alan, and Paul Smolensky (1993) 'Optimality Theory: Constraint interaction in generative grammar', RuCCS-TR-2; CU-CS-696-93.

Rebrus, Peter, and Miklos Törkenczy (2005) 'Uniformity and contrast in Hungarian verbal paradigms', in L. Downing, T. Hall, and R. Raffelsiefen (eds.), *Paradigms in Optimality Theory*. Oxford: Oxford University Press, pp. 263–95.

Steriade, Donca (1984) 'Glides and vowels in Romanian'. *BLS* 10: 47–64.

——— (1999a) 'Lexical conservatism'. *Linguistics in the Morning Calm 4*, Linguistic Society of Korea, Hanshin, Seoul, pp. 157–81.

——— (1999b) 'Lexical conservatism in French adjectival liaison', in B. Bullock, M. Authier, and L. Reed (eds.), *Proceedings of LSRL 25*. Benjamins, pp. 243–71.

——— (2003) 'Chained correspondence and Romanian agent expressions', LSRL talk, University of Utah.

—— (2006) 'Nuclear contrasts and alternations in Romanian', Ms. MIT.

Stockall, Linnea, and Alec Marantz (2004) 'A single route, full decomposition model of morphological complexity: MEG evidence'. *The Mental Lexicon* 1:1.

Wilson, Colin (2001) 'Consonant cluster neutralization and targeted constraints'. *Phonology* 18: 147–97.

—— (2006) 'Learning phonology with substantive bias: An experimental and computational study of velar palatalization'. *Cognitive Science* 30 (5): 945–80.

Urbanczyk, Suzanne (2005) 'Enhancing contrast in reduplication', in B. Hurch (ed.), *Studies on Reduplication*. Mouton de Gruyter, pp. 431–54.

Language Index

Topic Index

OXFORD STUDIES IN THEORETICAL LINGUISTICS